'The first article of an Englishman's political creed must be that he believeth in the sea.'

Charles Montagu, 1st Earl of Halifax, 1694

BRITANNIA'S GLORY A MARITIME STORY

GREAT BRITAIN'S SEAFARING HISTORY TOLD IN VERSE

MAGGIE BALLINGER

UNIFORM

Published by Uniform
An imprint of Unicorn Publishing Group
5 Newburgh Street
London W1F 7RG

www.unicornpublishing.org

A catalogue record for this book is available from
the British Library

5 4 3 2 1

ISBN 978-1-912690-16-9

Cover design Unicorn Publishing Group
Typeset by Vivian@Bookscribe

Printed and bound in Turkey

CONTENTS

FOREWORD

'Planet Earth' is a misnomer. Of all the planets in our solar system our planet is unique. It is, no doubt, a very rare exception among those in the vastness of the Universe beyond as well. It is not Planet Earth but Planet Ocean. Life on Earth was born in the sea and its existence depends on the waters which clothe 70 per cent of our living planet. If you use a well-known search engine to survey the planet from over the Pacific, you can see virtually nothing but water. Water is essential for life and 97 per cent of the planet's water is in the oceans. Most people live within a hundred miles or so of the coast and between 80 and 90 per cent of the world's trade, by volume, travels by sea. For the United Kingdom and Ireland, surrounded by sea, that is more than 90 per cent. And, if 30 per cent of the planet is land above water – and remember that sea levels are expected to rise – then there is 70 per cent of the earth's crust below that ocean, which has an average depth of six kilometres. That 70 per cent of the earth's crust contains the same proportion of the world's mineral and energy resources. And, since it is obviously thinner than the higher parts which are land, they are closer to the seabed.

The British Isles – the 'North-East Atlantic archipelago' – and their history are the epitome of this truth and the progeny of the sea. Yet few people today understand our utter dependence on the seas and oceans and how every aspect of our lives depends on the enveloping watery womb. In April 2010, the Icelandic volcano Eyjafjallajökull erupted through a covering of ice, producing volcanic ash which was finer and climbed higher than usual. Fearing that aircraft flying through the ash cloud would fall from the skies, the UK authorities closed UK airspace for five and a half days. The Government was deluged with messages asking when petrol and food would run out. Of course, they did not. There were no queues in petrol stations or gaps on supermarket shelves. Apart from a very small volume of high-value goods, everything – or 90 per cent of everything – comes by sea. There could be no clearer indication of the 'sea-blindness' that, paradoxically and counter-intuitively, afflicts our maritime nation.

Maggie Ballinger and her friends, colleagues and collaborators have retold this story in penetrating and memorable form. In verse. We are so used to conducting all serious and intellectual debate in prose that some might find this unusual. But why? The very first – and much of the greatest – literature and history created and told by the mind of man was in narrative verse. Among those immortal lines the sea features prominently from the very beginning. Homer's *Odyssey* is a story of the sea. The 'wine-dark sea', a description that had intrigued and mystified commentators in our language. Was it because the Ancient Greeks had no word for blue, because their wine was that colour, or because of an outbreak of reddish marine algae? We can discount blue wine, and can note that three of the uses of the poetic meme 'wine-dark sea' precede events at nightfall, when the sea often reflects a red sky. But most scholars agree the words refer to richness of hue, rather than a specific colour. Whatever the explanation, the sea is the subject of poetry throughout human history. What more appropriate way to tell the story of nations that rose from the sea and spread out over it to permeate the world with their language of Government and their institutions, including another Greek idea – democracy.

The nations of the United Kingdom and Ireland have been populated by waves of immigrants since prehistoric times. Celts, Romans, Saxons, Vikings, Normans, Flemings, those fleeing persecution anywhere, Huguenots, peoples from South and South-East Asia, Africa, the Caribbean, the Middle East and eastern Europe – all have come and been absorbed into and enriched our society. Until very recently – until the 1960s, really – they came by sea. Witness the story of the *Emperor Windrush*.

The mirror side of the tale is how people from these islands went forth to woo, win and sometimes whip the world. This book also tells the story of Britain's maritime expansion. That expansion was driven, it must be said, not by any Imperial grand design – or any design – but mainly by trade, and sometimes by the sheer desperation of hard-up adventurers. It is rather more than 400 years since the perspicacious first Elizabethans identified the oceans as a route to gain commodities, resources and riches. In so doing, though probably not consciously, they were able to offset the status of the most populous British kingdom – England – as a 'rogue state' – the nemesis of Catholic Spain. The oceans were a road to riches which eventually balanced and then outweighed the empires and indigenous agricultural wealth of our continental rivals. By the end of the sixteenth century the unique nature of the seas – their 'oneness', their vastness, their insusceptibility to state control – was seen as a vehicle to be exploited. As Queen Elizabeth I's sharp intellect summarised in a letter: *'The use of sea and air is common to all; neither can a title to the ocean belong to any people or private persons, forasmuch as neither nature nor public use and custom permit any possession therof'.* This was shortly before the Dutch jurist Hugo Grotius formulated the concept of freedom of the seas and freedom of navigation. Our own Francis Bacon observed that *'the wealth of both Indies seems in great part but an accessory to the command of the seas'* in 1595, and soon afterwards, in 1600, the East India Company was formed, which played the pivotal role in forming the (accidental) British Empire. Trade did not 'follow the flag'. Trade preceded the flag. Administration and control followed.

The story of Britain and the sea is inevitably also a story of war and conflict. It was Bacon, again, who encapsulated the 'British way in warfare'. *'He that commands the sea'*, wrote Bacon, *'is at great liberty, and may take as much and as little of the war as he will.'* That idea manifested itself time and time again – in the Seven Years' War (1756–63), the Revolutionary and Napoleonic wars, in the First and Second World Wars. In all cases British grand strategy involved use of the flexible medium of the sea (and, in the last only, the air) to woo Allies, who usually took a larger share of the land fighting, to defeat powers and coalitions which were stronger by land. Over the last four centuries, it has worked.

The story is far from over. The North Sea provided offshore energy, and now we are seeking to create renewable energy from solar and wind power. But the United Kingdom has probably the greatest potential of any comparably sized state for tidal power, as the tidal range off our coasts is extremely great. The ebb and flow of the tides is utterly reliable – more so than sun or wind – and will continue until the moon falls from the sky. There is huge potential here, as yet hardly tapped.

This book tells the most important single story in the origins, evolution, development and formation of our country. The story of its indissoluble engagement with the sea. British history is infused into the maritime dimension like salt in seawater. Simple. And, crucially, the book tells it in a lively and uniquely accessible way. It is far easier to memorise a verse than a passage of prose. As we plunge further into the twenty-first century – a century which several commentators have labelled 'the maritime century' – an understanding of the maritime dimension, which has been and will remain crucial to globalisation – is essential. So please read on. It is not always a tale for the faint hearted. But that, in turn, means it is a story of uncertainty, suspense, adventure and romance as well. So, dare I say – enjoy!

Professor Chris Bellamy
Professor of Maritime Security,
University of Greenwich
Spring equinox, 2015

ACKNOWLEDGEMENTS

Firstly, credit must be given to the Shipwrecked Mariners' Society. This very worthwhile charity provides support to those who bravely earned their livings at sea, should they or their families find themselves in need of financial and/or practical assistance. Had I not entered the Society's inaugural limerick competition in February 2012, the idea of a maritime history in verse would not have been triggered, and none of this would ever have happened.

Huge thanks are due to Professor Chris Bellamy of the (then) Greenwich Maritime Institute, for writing the foreword, for his enthusiasm for the project from its early stages, and for offering access to the expertise of his colleagues. In particular, Dr Martin Wilcox (now at the University of Hull), has been a sustaining source of support, encouragement and practical advice. Without his always ready willingness to find time for us, we would certainly have erred — and may well have flagged.

Gratitude is also due to others for sundry, and sometimes obscure, contributions. These are Professor N.A.M. Rodger (thoughts on early impressment), Dr David Jenkins (the development of steam power), Dr Cathryn Pearce (smuggling and wrecking), Dr Chris Ware (Tudor pilotage), Dr Matt Kerr (literary references), Lorna Hunter and Neil Jones of the Northern Lighthouse Board and Trinity House respectively (light ships and fog horns), Nikki Miller, The Worshipful Company of Shipwrights (steam boxes), Gill Wilson, International Boatbuilding Training College, Portsmouth (timber), and Glenn Goodman, Maritime Statistics, Department of Transport, (port figures).

I am grateful to many friends, whom I have probably bored for England on matters maritime, but who have nevertheless always proved keen to put forward ideas. Most surprised themselves by how much they already knew about Great Britain's seafaring past, and their keenness to find out more has greatly helped us to maintain belief in the emerging book.

A big thank you goes to Unicorn Publishing Group for having faith in a slightly unconventional submission.

The project would most certainly not have been completed without the unwavering support and tireless input of my husband Stephen. He researched and produced the graph, plus all the original drawings and maps, demonstrated an uncanny ability to spot inaccuracies, (my apologies for any that still lurk), and sustained a relentless quest for perfection throughout. The frustration of my being made to re-write some of the verses (because they contained over-long lines) was a small price to pay.

Finally, to all those from the past who played a part in Great Britain's epic and fascinating maritime story, thank you for helping to demonstrate how very different our islands' history looks when viewed from the sea.

Maggie Ballinger
2019

PICTURE CREDITS

1 Pre-history to 1066

1

Pre-history to 1066

How it all started

Since human life began
The temptation's been for man,
When confronted with a river, sea or lake,
To use whatever floats,
And turn it into boats:
Now the safety of dry land he can forsake.

To satisfy their needs,
People lashed up bundled reeds,
Or used air-filled skins, or logs such as bamboo.
Well-constructed rafts aren't leaky,
(If in doubt, just think *Kon-Tiki*).
And a dug out tree trunk makes a good canoe.

With pointed ends it glides,
Then: 'Our platforms need some sides!
By adding these, capacity we'd swell.'
Now the coracle we're crafting –
Much better than plain rafting –
The shape akin to half a walnut shell.

(It was mainly used to fish:
Two men – one man per 'dish' –
With a net between would catch their daily feast.
The hapless fish, once trapped,
Would on board be quickly zapped
With a block of wood – the 'knocker' or the 'priest'.)

Though lightweight and compact,
Stability it lacked,
So a hull with ribs and planks we'd next devise.
Boats developed in this way,
To the shape we know today,
Which is capable of being any size.

One such boat appears,
Dating back three thousand years,
To the time known as the Bronze Age, long ago.
Six feet wide its deck,
It's a reconstructed wreck.
In Dover now this treasure is on show.

Thor Heyerdahl crossed the Pacific on a raft called *Kon-Tiki* in 1947.

The earliest known British log boat dates back to between 4000 and 3000 BC. Traditionally made of willow rod, coracles were, (and still are), popular on rivers in Wales, the South West and parts of Scotland.

There is a limit on how large boats constructed of wood can be (see verse 1082). The first boats were probably covered by animal skins. With the advent of metal working, wooden planks were used from around 2000 BC (see verses 72–73).

One early English boat, discovered in 1992, and dating from around 1550 BC, has been reassembled from excavated parts and is in Dover Museum. Some of it remains under the carriageway of the A20. A total of seven Bronze Age boats have been found in England.

The world's largest ever ship was the Japanese-built oil tanker *Seawise Giant*, with an overall length of 1,504 feet (321m).

Raft made of logs   **Tree trunk canoe**

Raft made of skins   **Coracle framework**

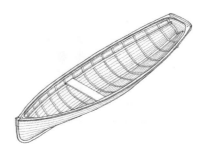

Basic boat

Was sea-going in mind?
This is not the only find:
Such discoveries our knowledge have enriched.
Preserved by mud or silt,
It is known how they were built:
Caulked with moss; their oaken planks were firmly stitched.

Early Britain

In the so-called Age of Ice,
Conditions here weren't nice,
And sustenance was difficult to find.
In the dry and chilly air,
People wandered here and there:
They could walk to Europe, if they had a mind.

They could make a basic spear,
They killed mammoth, they killed deer,
They ate plants, and they ate water-dwelling creatures.
But as yet there is no sign,
That they used a hook with line:
From digs, this item isn't one that features.

(Hunter gatherers were they,
But in time will come the day
When, with what they farm, their diets are supported.
They'd grow barley, they'd grow wheat,
They'd keep animals to eat –
And the wherewithal from France would be imported!)

When things warmed up a bit,
This land of ours was hit
By a wave which cut that one remaining link.
It was not that long ago –
Perhaps eight thousand years or so –
More recently than many folk might think.

(Other views propose
That water levels rose,
Causing where we're joined more slowly to submerge.
Either way, we'd disconnect:
Melting ice had its effect
Whether gradual, or via one massive surge.)

By water now surrounded,
Our identity is founded,
Though 'The Continent' is really not that far,
We've become somewhat unique:
It can make us strong or weak,
But, for good or ill, it makes us what we are.

Three boats, discovered in mud by Ted Wright in North Ferriby on the River Humber, date back to between 2030 BC and 1780 BC. An even older fragment was found at Kilnsea. The Dover and Ferriby boats appear to have been designed for the purpose of going to sea, but most other early boats were probably confined to sailing in estuaries and close to the coast. Bronze Age society has been re-evaluated as a result of such discoveries. These early boats were sewn together with yew withies, and wooden wedges were also used. Ribs were added later, and the Dover boat is unusual in that it was also caulked with animal fat and beeswax.

There have been several Ice (or, more accurately, Glacial) Ages, the last major one ending around 10,000 years ago.

There is a suggestion that shellfish formed part of primitive diets, for those who lived near water, rather than other less easily caught fish. However, primitive paintings around the world show people with fishing lines. Any hooks would have been made from plant thorns, shells or bone until the advent of metal working.

In the period 4200–3000 BC, the so-called Neolithic Revolution took place in Britain, and the import of farming practices from Armorica (an area of western France around the Brittany peninsula) was probably accompanied by some immigration from the continent. For a while, fish became a less important source of protein, and eating it may even have become taboo.

Instead of a gradual rise in sea level, there is an alternative theory that a huge tsunami, caused by the bursting of a large inland sea in Norway, gouged out a waterway between the south of the North Sea and the English Channel, thus severing the land link with continental Europe. Britain also sits on the Continental Shelf, which means its surrounding waters are relatively shallow. This, in turn, allows plankton and therefore other marine life to flourish.

The land link between Britain and Ireland disappeared about 10,000 years ago. Both islands had larger landmasses in what is now the Irish Sea, and the link was in the south between what is now Land's End and the southern Irish coast.

Map showing Britain with links to Ireland and Continental Europe

Of the heroes we hold dear,
You will find some featured here –
'Great Britons' who gave reason to be famed.
From a 'Beeb' poll's top fifteen
Where important folk convene,
Eleven in what follows will be named.

From the Neolithic age,
Before we'd reached the stage
Of fashioning such things from types of metal,
In a place on Suffolk's shore,
They found flint tools and much more,
Making Lowestoft an early place to settle.

Great Britain, as a nation,
Is a strange configuration,
Of six thousand (and the rest) assorted isles.
People live on quite a few,
But even though that's true,
A lot are not much more than rocky piles.

If you ask the average Brit,
He will readily admit,
That the climate here is rarely a delight.
And, when weather fronts conflict,
It's not easy to predict:
Thus the forecasters don't always get it right.

So the seas around our coast
Are more hazardous than most,
And though lighthouses are there to act as guides,
Through fog, or howling gale,
It is difficult to sail,
And to take account of currents, and of tides.

There are shoals and many rocks...
Shifting sands which serve to fox...
Such obstacles are purely geographic.
And, as if these don't suffice,
There's the energy device,
The lobster pot, plus other coastal traffic.

Tricky waters also beckon,
With the Race of Corryvreckan;
There's another to be found off Portland Bill.
As they struggle to hold steady
In a rip, or swirling eddy,
Those in boats could do without that sort of thrill.

In 2002, the BBC conducted a television poll to find out whom the British public considered to be the greatest Britons of all time. This book includes the following:
Sir Winston Churchill (1st), Isambard Kingdom Brunel (2), Charles Darwin (4), Sir Isaac Newton (6), Elizabeth I (7), Horatio Nelson (9), Oliver Cromwell (10), Sir Ernest Shackleton (11), Captain James Cook (12), Alfred the Great (14), the Duke of Wellington (15).

The Stone Age was from c.10000 BC, the Bronze Age c.2500–800 BC, and the Iron Age c.800 BC–AD 100.

Britain's most easterly point is the fishing port of Lowestoft, one of our country's earliest known sites for human habitation.

Nowhere in Britain is further than 70 miles from the sea, though there are different ways of calculating exactly where this is (eg does distance relate to the coast or to tidal water?). Only about 130 of Britain's islands are inhabited, and most of these (97) are off the coast of Scotland.

Britain has 7,723 miles of coastline. Its first lighthouse was built by the Romans in AD 90 and still stands at Dover Castle (see verses 1047–1079 **Lighthouses**).

The Great Race of Corryvrekan, with associated whirlpools, occurs due to water forcing its way through a narrow channel. The Race of Portland is created by a combination of factors, including shallow water over Portland Ledge. A 'rip' is a rip current, sometimes inaccurately referred to as a rip tide. Man-made structures around the coast and in the seas of Britain include wind farms, barrages and tidal devices.

To be surrounded by water makes a State infinitely more vulnerable to invasion than to be surrounded by land, since all history shows that it is far easier to transport an invading force by sea, and to deliver a hostile blow at a nation's vulnerable point, than it is to do so by land.

From The Spectator (8 September 1906)

'Britain enjoys one immense natural advantage. She is completely surrounded by a gigantic anti-tank ditch.'

Adolf Hitler

The sea is our approach and bulwark, it has been the scene of our greatest triumphs and dangers, and we are accustomed in lyrical strains to claim it as our own... We should consider ourselves unworthy of our descent if we did not share the arrogance of our progenitors, and please ourselves with the pretension that the sea is English.

Robert Louis Stevenson

The Bizzies and the Bellows,
Might catch out unwary fellows,
And perilous the Swellies (Menai Strait)...
Or the Overfalls of Lizard...
Add some mist, a storm or blizzard,
For a concept of the dangers that await.

There are hazards: even so
Going back to long ago,
Our Atlantic seaways saw a lot of traffic.
The science of today,
Using tests on DNA,
Can shed light on certain factors demographic.

Where linguistic clues were leading
Re: our links and inter-breeding,
Genetic studies further can explain.
Though what's argued some might question,
There has been a strong suggestion
That many early Britons came from Spain!

Tides

The sea comes in... goes out...
But what's this all about?
And why can there be so much variation?
The shift's made operational
By forces gravitational:
The moon, the sun and planet earth's rotation.

The highest tides appear
At the start of every year:
When we're closest to the sun that surge we'll find.
There are also spring tide peaks,
Which happen each two weeks,
When the moon and sun are more or less aligned.

If the moon is new or full,
It exerts its greatest pull,
And its weakest when a shiny half is shown.
In a semi-moonlight gleam,
Ebbs and flows are less extreme:
As 'neap tides' these phenomena are known.

A huge catastrophe,
In 1953,
Caused much loss of life and massive devastation.
Flood defences had been breached,
As the North Sea inland reached,
With a storm surge and a spring tide combination.

The Bizzies and the Bellows are rocky patches off Dodman Point on the south coast of Cornwall.

The commonality of certain burial practices, along with versions of the Celtic language, suggest connections stretching from the Tagus Valley in Iberia right up to the Orkney Islands. There is much archaeological evidence to support the extent of such pre-history journeys. In addition, Professor Stephen Oppenheimer argued (in 2006) that peoples in Ireland and in parts of western Britain originated in the Basque region of Spain. He also propounds that the Scandinavian input into the British make-up has been underestimated.

In most places, the biggest influence of these rotations, is the principal lunar semi-diurnal, which has a period of about 12 hours 25 minutes, meaning the tide comes in and goes out roughly twice a day.

Planet earth is closest to the sun in early January (the date varies). The highest tides and, conversely, the lowest tides, appear at this time. The term 'spring tide peaks' has nothing to do with seasons.

The flooding that affected the east coast of Britain overnight 31 January/ 1 February 1953 has been described as 'the worst national peacetime disaster to hit the UK'. An estimated 307 people in Britain died as a result and 30,000 more were evacuated. However flooding was worse in the Netherlands, where 1,835 people perished, a further 70,000 had to be evacuated and some 30,000 animals died.

Winter storms in December 2013/January 2014 also caused extensive flooding, when storm surges and high spring tides affected, in turn, the North Sea coasts, and then the south and west.

There had been a lack of warning,
That fateful night and morning.
Now, with satellites, it's all sophistication.
Though the seas can't be diverted,
Those at risk can be alerted,
So at least folk have some time for relocation.

Archaeologists have found
(Though it now flows underground),
What was perhaps a mill on London's River Fleet.
Did this run on tidal power?
Did it turn grain into flour?
Was it yet another clever Roman feat?

It's certainly most clear
That the tide mill did appear,
In Anglo-Saxon times around our coast.
The sea's in/out polarity,
Occurs with regularity:
Free energy, of which some made the most.

Currents and winds

In 1992
A container vessel strew
Its consignment – many thousand bathtub toys.
In the course of being shipped,
On the ocean these were tipped.
There they bobbed around like strange un-tethered buoys.

Halfway round the world they floated.
Brightly coloured, they got noted,
On the surface of the seas went with the flux.
Their routes from the Pacific
Have helped studies scientific –
These proved useful plastic turtles, frogs and ducks.

Just why do currents flow?
They are caused by winds that blow,
And variance in ocean water density.
Winds are the creation
Of planet Earth's rotation,
Which determines their direction and intensity.

To propel across the seas,
Sails require a swelling breeze,
Without which crews might well become alarmed.
There's a lack of this inflator.
Very close to the equator:
In The Doldrums, ships for days can be becalmed.

The 'Storm Tides Warning Service' was set up as a result of the East Coast floods. This became the Flood Forecasting Centre, run jointly by the Environment Agency and the Met Office (see verse 898). The Met Office claims that its 'high resolution atmospheric forecast models', coupled with ocean models, can predict a storm surge up to 5 days in advance, and provide accurate guidance on the height of the surge and wave overtopping up to two days ahead. However, this proved over optimistic with the massive storm surge that hit the east coast in December 2013.

A large building project carried out between 1988 and 1992 enabled archaeologists to explore the lower Fleet estuary, and a possible tide mill was discovered on a previously unknown island.

A 6th century mill was located in Southern Ireland, and several in England were mentioned in the Domesday Book (1088). The potential for using tidal energy is being examined in modern times (see verses 1719–1729 **Tidal Energy**).

An estimated 28–29,000 plastic toys were spilled from a ship, as they were being transported from China to the USA. The turtles, frogs and ducks were so-called 'Friendly Floaters', and some washed up on British beaches.

Winds are the principal cause of surface currents. Variances in water density are caused by variations in temperature (heat flows from hot to cold) or salinity. Underwater events such as earthquakes can also give rise to currents. The 'Coriolis Effect' causes trade winds, to the north (west to east) and south (east to west) of the equator, where an absence of wind is called The Doldrums.

A few superstitions

Sailors are no strangers
To the oceans and their dangers:
The elements are fickle, full of traps...
Even for the wary
It must sometimes be quite scary,
Which explains why they are superstitious chaps.

On ships, (or on the quay
When one's setting out to sea),
A redhead means that rotten luck is due.
But this can be reversed,
By speaking to him first,
Before he has a chance to talk to you.

Peril is assured
If a woman is on board,
And there seems to be no antidote for that!
Don't cut your hair or nails;
To whistle raises gales;
For good fortune, keep a well-contented cat.

Those who fished were not immune:
They were superstition strewn,
And certain words weren't spoken whilst afloat.
'Pig', 'fox', 'hare' were banned,
As were mentions of the land.
To part with salt, ill-fortune will denote.

Eat your fish from head to tail,
And in eggshells witches sail,
So crush these into tiny little pieces.
Don't count the fish you've caught,
Until safely back in port,
And a lucky extra net a catch increases.

Back at home, these seamen's wives
Have restrictions in their lives,
For washing clothes will 'wash him' overboard.
Don't wave goodbye, they say,
Lest your man be swept away.
Calling after him brings something untoward.

The only antidote for a woman on board would be to ask her to undress: a naked woman is good luck for sailors!

Sailors' wives also avoided whistling. 'A whistling woman and a crowing hen, Bring the Devil out of his den.'

Mentions of cats, salmon, rabbits and the church were also avoided. The clergy, known to fishermen as 'sky-pilots', were generally not welcomed onto boats, though there were exceptions. Passing the salt pot from one crew member to another signified 'passed sorrow'. Starting to eat a fish at the tail will warn shoals away from the shore back into deep water.

Setting an odd number of nets was believed to be lucky.

To call after a husband once he has set foot outside the front door is unlucky, as too is going to see him off at the fish dock.

'I never knew a woman brought to sea in a ship that some mischief did not befall the vessel.'

Admiral Cuthbert Collingwood

Bronze Age and Iron Age

Perhaps we should begin
With an element called tin:
In Cornwall and in Devon this was mined.
But pretty much elsewhere,
The substance was quite rare,
And supplies of it were difficult to find.

Of bronze it's an ingredient.
To seek it was expedient:
And from Europe many set forth on this quest.
With these foreigners arriving
And the metal business thriving,
There were links beyond these islands' far south west.

There is evidence we traded:
Long before we were invaded;
Archaeologists deduce this from their digs.
We sent, across the waves,
Grain and minerals and slaves,
And imported swords and olives, wine and figs.

Others came here, without question,
But there's very scant suggestion
The initiative was anything but theirs.
We may have gone to Gaul,
If we crossed the sea at all,
But we didn't travel far to tout our wares.

Forever we'd remain
An insular domain,
If we weren't prepared to venture from these shores.
Before engines were invented,
We had to be contented,
With propulsion by the wind, or sometimes oars.

At first, the oar prevails,
In preference to sails,
Though, in time, the power of wind its place would earn.
Strong gusts or gentle breeze
Would propel ships through the seas,
Once we'd learnt to fix a rudder to the stern.

This poem cannot hope,
To describe each spar and rope.
In terms of rigging, think lateen or square.
The latter from yards drape,
And the name describes their shape.
The former's a triangular affair.

Tin was being mined from before 2000 BC. By the early Bronze Age, copper too was being mined in south-west England, Wales and Southern Ireland. Elsewhere in Europe, it was found only in Brittany, Iberia and Sardinia. Copper with a varying (5–23 per cent) tin content is the traditional composition of bronze. The addition of tin produces an alloy which is harder and more durable than copper alone.

Mount Batten (Devon) was possibly one of England's first overseas trading centres (Bronze Age). Hengistbury Head (Dorset) was another similarly early international centre, visited by traders from afar. Early Britons certainly traded with Gaul (France), northern Europe and Greece. In 1974, divers found Middle Bronze Age (c.1100 BC) artefacts, almost certainly of French origin, in Langdon Bay, Kent. The condition of these tools, weapons and ornaments has led to the supposition that there was a cross-Channel scrap metal trade. Though no vessel remains were discovered, this designated wreck site is the oldest in northern Europe.

If the Britons of pre-history did venture forth and sail to France, they may also have gone further afield, but this would have involved overland journeys.

In 2010, it was announced that the cargo (copper and tin ingots) of a vessel dating back to 900 BC had been discovered off the coast near Salcombe, Devon.

There is evidence of immigration by European 'Beaker culture' people around 2700 BC.

Hunting dogs were another sought-after English export. Goods and people would have been exchanged, rather than bought and sold (coins were not introduced until 700–600 BC).

Square rigging involves one or more vertical masts, with a horizontal beam or beams at right angles to the length of the deck. These beams are called yards, and at their ends are the yardarms. Lateen sails can be hung from upright or angled spars, and can be swivelled to catch the wind and assist with steering.

Simplest form of square rig　　**Lateen rig**

Square is what you need
For travelling at speed,
But on the weather all your hopes are pinned.
The advantage of lateen,
As will readily be seen,
Is it helps a sailor tack into the wind.

To find your way, few tools;
Just a few quite simple rules
Such as, 'Always keep the coastline in your sight.
And try not to forget
Every headland's silhouette.
Heed this, then there's a chance you'll get it right.'

From experience, they'd know
The way the wind would blow:
Its direction might be something they could use.
They submerged the sounding weight
As a means to calculate
The water's depth, which gave them helpful clues.

And, in case the weather's dire,
You might just as well acquire,
Some knowledge of safe havens for a stay.
Open sea's a hostile place,
When storms and gales you face,
So it's best you find a creek or sheltered bay.

In full anger, or just querulous,
The sea can be quite perilous:
The elements aren't easily endured.
The problems will compound,
If pirates are around,
For our coastal waters cannot be secured.

Invaded

The Romans

If you start a long way back,
We were subject to attack:
The Romans have to be among the first.
Next, the natives had their tangles
With the Saxons, Jutes and Angles,
Then the Norsemen came to do their very worst.

The ships that came from Rome,
Had for many weeks been home
To the livestock and the passengers on board.
These vessels, double-decked,
Must have quickly earned respect:
The place they called 'Britannia' the reward.

In terms of shape, 'square' is used here loosely. Four-sided sails can be in the form of trapeziums or trapezoids. Square also means at right angles to the length of the boat. Fore- and aft- rigging is when the sails run along the length of the boat (see also verse 868). Tacking results in zig-zag progress.

The Vikings used a lodestone stuck to a piece of wood, as a primitive compass. When floated in water, it would point to the magnetic north.

Pilotage is the term for navigating by means of visual reference to landmarks.

The study of the ocean floor is called bathymetry.

The sounding weight prevailed until the 1930s, when sonar was first used to measure water depth (see verse 1266).

Cloud formations on land, and the direction taken by roosting birds at dusk also helped orientation.

Pirates were an almost constant threat, in varying degrees, throughout the centuries.

The Roman occupation of Britain lasted from AD 43 to AD 410. 40,000 troops invaded, probably landing at Richborough (Rutupiae) in east Kent, which once had a large natural harbour (but is now inland).

Triremes (three rows of oars) have been mentioned in contemporary accounts, but not as frequently as liburnians. These were originally uniremes (one row of oars) to which the Romans added a second tier.

First invasion by Northern Europeans circa AD 360.

> **ON AGRICOLA (GOVERNOR OF BRITANNIA AD 77–83)**
> **AND HIS CONQUEST OF SCOTLAND**
>
> Agricola 'used his fleet to reconnoitre harbours'... The coast of the remotest sea was first rounded at this time by a Roman fleet which first established that Britain was an island. At the same time it discovered and subdued the Orkney Islands, hitherto unknown.
>
> **Tactitus, circa AD 98**

Beyond their empire's flanks
Were the Saxons and the Franks –
Germanic tribes who weren't averse to war.
For our land to be protected,
Forts were very soon erected,
At strategic points along the Saxon Shore.

Romans also were acquainted
With a people who were painted:
For their bodily adornments, 'Picts' were named.
Much bother they'd evoke,
For aggressive were these folk:
'Albion', by Rome was never tamed.

And, though later 'barricaded',
Our west coast too was raided:
Two Irish peoples troubled us this way.
One was called the Scotti,
And the other Attacotti.
In parts of Wales and Cornwall some would stay.

The Romans kept a fleet,
Primarily to meet
The need to ferry troops, and their supplies.
Cargo vessels carried grain,
Wine – and olive oil (from Spain) –
And must have been considerable in size.

The Northern Europeans

The Saxons weren't so knowing:
Came with twenty strong men rowing
In open boats, to settle here their bid.
Though they lacked sophistication,
They overwhelmed our nation,
And a lot of what we'd learnt from Rome undid.

History records,
That Scots and Irish lords
Were constantly at one another's throats.
Their battles – hand to hand –
Were often on dry land,
But one, at least, involved a clash of boats.

Anglo-Saxon Trade

We know of one embargo
That was placed on Frankish cargo,
By a ruler who's now famous for his dyke.
Revenge was Offa's game:
Charlemagne, had done same,
Offended by a plan he didn't like.

Five watchtowers were also constructed on the north-east coast, primarily to look out for seaborne Picts. The Roman name 'pictae' means painted people. They, along with 'Saxon' pirates, made the North Sea a dangerous place. For a schematic map of the fortifications, see Plate A, page 61.

Albion was the name by which Scotland was known. The Romans did fight their way into Scotland, but decided not to stay there. In AD 122, Hadrian began constructing a wall (also known as the Picts' Wall) across northern England, which defined the limits of the Roman Empire.

Fortresses were constructed in Cumbria, Lancashire, on Anglesey, and at Caernafon and Cardiff. The Irish raiders were in action from the third to the early seventh century. By 396 AD, the situation was so bad that Rome sent a force to deal with maritime attacks from the Irish, Picts and Saxons.

It was after the Irish Scotti tribe that Scotland was ultimately named.

The Roman Fleet was the *Classis Britannica*, which patrolled the south coast. Troops were transported across the Channel from Boulogne. The main English port was either Lympne (near Hythe) or Dover. Richborough was also an important Kent port, and all three had roads direct to Canterbury. The carrying capacity of the largest Roman cargo ships was not surpassed until the 19th century.

An Anglo-Saxon ship dating back to circa 700 was found at Sutton Hoo. This was probably a functional ship used for burial. Archaeologists are now questioning the extent to which Northern Europeans invaded Britain, and argue that there may have been fewer, and more prosperous, settlers than has long been believed.

Dalriada, a Gaelic kingdom encompassing western Scotland and north-eastern Ulster in Ireland, appears to have had a ship levy system, whereby groups of households had to provide and man a ship. The fighting at Sailtire off Kintyre, in the Dál Riata area, took place in 637 and is the first recorded battle to take place in British waters. There were probably others.

Charlemagne or 'Charles the Great' (c.747–814) ruled over the vast Carolingian Empire. Offa was king of the less extensive Mercia from 757–796. The two men corresponded with each other.

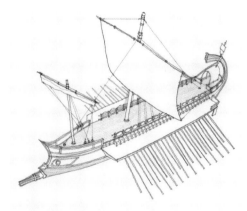

An example of a Roman ship

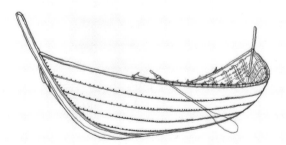

Anglo-Saxon open boat

His own empire's a vast sprawl,
Whereas Mercia is small.
How dare Offa think his son should wed Charles' daughter?
Offa too got in a funk,
When Frankish millstones shrunk!
The counter-claim was 'English cloaks are shorter.'

We can also get a fix
On trading ports (called wics),
Which were organized, though seemingly chaotic.
We imported lots of stuff:
And there's evidence enough
To suggest that some of this was quite exotic.

Of silk we can be sure,
From what perhaps were haute couture –
Saint Cuthbert's vestments give a major clue.
And amethyst's been found,
With souls buried in the ground;
Plus a Coptic bowl turned up at Sutton Hoo.

Royal coffers were enlarged,
Once tolls on ships were charged:
On their share of wealth all rulers were intent.
A proportion each receives,
Via officials known as reeves,
(The first employed by Hlothere, King of Kent).

Into English kingdoms flowed
A blue dye known as woad
Which, like garlic and like onions, was tax-free.
We imported coats of mail,
We bought linen by the bale,
And wine and furs would reach our shores by sea.

And how does England pay
For whatever comes our way?
It might be goods, though coins are used instead.
As may even be surmised,
Cornish tin's still highly prized,
As are people, leather, wool (and salt and lead?).

What came in/went out by sea
Up in Scotland was low key:
The details are not fully understood.
Soapstone from the Scots
Could be fashioned into pots,
And from Norway may have come supplies of wood.

The response to Offa's proposal that their children wed, was to declare that no one from the island of Britain, or the people of the Angles, was to set foot in Gaul for the purposes of trade (789). Commercial pressure led to the ending of Charlemagne's embargo, after Offa had retaliated with a similar ban on traders from 'Francia'. The subsequent agreement protected traders.

The Old English (OE) verb wician can refer to a sailor landing and spending a night on shore. Foreign traders could be permitted to stay for up to forty days. A wic-reeve would have served as a collector of the king's tolls and customs, and as a controller of foreign traders and hostels in royal ports and markets.

The suffix -wic is/was reflected in places names such as Ipswich (Gippeswick), Sandwich, Southampton (Hamwick), Swanage (Swanwic) and Harwich. Hull was originally called Wyke (or Wic), and even London was Lundenwick.

St Cuthbert's vestments were woven between 909 and 916.

Various Anglo-Saxon burial sites have yielded amethyst and amber beads. The material for the former probably came from India or Ceylon, and the amber was almost certainly a Baltic import.

The Coptic bowl is of eastern Mediterranean origin and dates back to the 6th or 7th century.

Hlothere reigned 673–685. He appointed the first known royal official.

We also cultivated our own woad, (in East Anglia and Somerset). The Picts (see verse 56) almost certainly didn't import it. During the 16th century, substantially more was home grown when foreign supplies became erratic and expensive.

There was a form of import duty on most goods, probably 10% (the decima). Chainmail came from Mainz. Millstones and whetstones also came from Germany. Cloth and linen arrived from Constantinople. Imported, too, were Rhenish textiles, wine from the Mediterranean and France, and furs from Regensburg. Fine pottery dating from the fifth to seventh centuries was reaching Britain. Fragments of this, from places like Carthage, Alexandria and Palestine, have been found. Decorative amber probably originated in the Baltic states. Foodstuffs included European spices, citrus fruits and dates.

However, trade with the Mediterranean had ceased by the 7th century, possibly due to the rise of Islam, and did not restart until 600 years later. This trade had brought various goods (some luxuries) from as far away as Turkey, North Africa and Egypt to (principally) south-west England.

People were exported as slaves. The north European slave trade may have continued until as late as the 12th century.

Soapstone is found in the Shetland Islands. Possibly iron, as well as wood, may have come from Scandinavia – both were used for shipbuilding.

ON BRITANNIA

... nowhere has the sea a wider dominion, that it has many currents running in every direction, that it does not merely flow and ebb within the limits of the shore, but penetrates and winds far inland, and finds a home among hills and mountains as though in its own domain.

Tactitus, *Agricola* 10

See Matthew Paris's 13th century map of Britain (Plate A, page 61), demonstrating the perceived dominance of rivers.

Pilgrims went abroad,
Their Christian God to laud.
Two English kings to Rome both did a bunk.
To rule not their vocation,
They would opt for abdication –
One even saw his time out as a monk.

Enter the Northmen (or Vikings)

By the time these folk were raiding,
We'd become quite good at trading,
With countries only reached by means of water,
Yet when hostile tribes arrive,
It's a struggle to survive,
And like little lambs we're driven to the slaughter.

The attacks we must endure,
For no place was secure:
Being distant from the coast was no immunity.
The Vikings' type of craft
Had a very shallow draught.
They could navigate our rivers with impunity.

Despite the monks they slew,
One thing the Vikings knew,
(And this is maybe worthy of our thanks);
Their boat-building – a marvel –
Their system not the 'carvel'
But the 'clinker', which used overlapping planks.

This method still holds good,
For vessels made of wood,
And although the carvel method looks much sleeker,
The long ships' clever strakes,
Could leave others in their wakes,
(Plus the carvel needs more resin, so is weaker.)

Alfred the Great, King of Wessex (*r.*871–899)

King Alfred (known as 'Great'),
Would now throw in his weight
And set about an organized defence.
He built a lot of forts,
Especially near ports,
And he figured building ships would make good sense.

Pope Gregory the Great (tenure 590–604) sent missionaries to England. Monks, nuns and lay people travelled to Rome at this time. In one letter, Charlemagne criticised Offa for sending traders disguised as pilgrims to the Mediterranean. The abdicating kings were Ine of Wessex (688–726), and Coenred of Mercia (675–709), who became a monk. After the Norman Conquest, pilgrims also travelled to Lucca, Compostela and Jerusalem.

Vikings from Denmark attacked the south and east of Britain. Those from Norway attacked the north and Scotland, sweeping round to the Irish Sea as far as Wales, which they raided but which they could not successfully invade, due to its geography. However, the first recorded landing party at Portland (Dorset) in 789 involved three shiploads of Norwegians.

The draught is the distance from the waterline to the keel. Viking longboats could sail in water as shallow as three feet. They were also double-ended, which meant they could easily reverse, and were lightweight, so could be carried over obstacles (portage).

Vikings raided Lindisfarne (Holy Island) in 793. St Columba's Abbey (on Iona) was later sacked, when the Vikings travelled round to the west coast of Scotland.

The Mediterranean countries used the carvel construction. The Romans also built lightweight coastal vessels covered with hides rather than planks of wood. Planks are also referred to as 'strakes'. The wreck of a Roman cargo ship was discovered in the River Thames in 1962. Known as *Blackfriars 1*, and built around AD 150, it is the oldest confirmed seagoing vessel ever discovered.

Alfred the Great's fortified settlements were known as burhs.

ON THE RAID ON LINDISFARNE

Never before has such terror appeared in Britain as we have now suffered from a pagan race, nor was it thought that such an inroad from the sea could be made. Behold the church of St Cuthbert splattered with the blood of the priests of God, despoiled of all its ornaments; a place more venerable than all in Britain is given as prey to pagan people.

Alcuin of York, Scholar, from a letter to King Æthelred of Northumbria

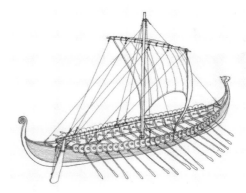

Viking longship

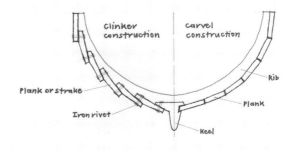

The differences between clinker and carvel constructions

In those days of long ago,
One didn't face the foe,
In battles that took place in open sea.
The thing to understand,
Was 'make sure they cannot land',
So the estuaries of rivers were the key.

Alf exercised his mind,
And eventually designed,
A type of ship to challenge an assault.
The vessels he made ready,
Were pretty sound and steady
But, for purpose, had a fundamental fault.

Too big his ships were proving
When it came to nippy moving:
They were difficult to twist and turn around,
And it isn't hard to guess,
(Though they met with some success),
That, in shallow waters, quickly ran aground.

If they didn't always float,
It is worth our while to note
What is represented, by the king's creation:
Our land's first standing fleet,
With proper crews complete,
All funded by a system of taxation.

(Certain kingdoms – once distinct –
Will as one land soon be linked.
England's now the word that these describe.
The source of this new name,
From northern Europe came:
The 'Angles' were a Jutland-dwelling tribe.)

King Edgar (r.959–975)

Alf's great-grandson (little known)
Made this nation quite his own.
'The Peaceful' Edgar brought it into line.
To patrol the coast, what's more
(Sometimes split up into four),
Was a navy which was far from in decline.

He acquired the needed blokes,
Through a system of ship-sokes,
(Localised enlistment's fancy name).
He was clever, well-intentioned,
But he's very rarely mentioned;
As a fan of ships, he should have found more fame.

The first seaborne engagement was in 882 against four Danish ships. It took place in the Stour estuary. Further Danish attacks were repelled off Essex and in the Thames estuary (896–7). Essentially, however, resistance was only possible against small raiding parties. There were minor home victories at sea in 882 and 884, and a more decisive one involving nine of the king's warships in 896.

A standing fleet is a permanent (and permanently manned) force that is not disbanded during peacetime.

Named after the Angle tribe from northern Europe, England did not become England until its various kingdoms merged in the 10th century during the reign of Æthelstan (924–27).

Six other kings attended Edgar's coronation, and pledged that they would be his liege-men on sea and land. The illustration shows an optimistic eight kings! In a show of force, Edgar periodically deployed his navy around the coast.

ON KING EDGAR

His Sommer progresses, and yerely chiefe pastimes were, the sailing round about this whole isle of Albion, garded with his grand navie of 4000 saile at the least, parted into four equall parts of petite Navies.

Richard Hackluyt (c.1552–1618), Geographer and Writer

King Edgar's coronation barge

The Seafarer was written,
By an Anglo-Saxon Briton,
Who sailed the chilly waves so lonely-souled.
His feet were bound by frost...
When, near cliffs, the prow was tossed.
Then his heart was hot with cares – despite the cold.

Tribute Money

Once Edgar isn't there,
Things fall into disrepair;
Three years on, the Vikings once again are raiding.
Our monarch says, 'I'll pay,
To make you go away,'
And this is how he stops them from invading.

This is much too good a thing:
A soft touch English king!
There's a chance here that the 'sea thieves' can't ignore.
So, in time, this Danish foe
Come and have another go,
Of their 'Tribute Money' wanting more and more.

'The Unready' sees some sense.
Too late, thinks about defence:
So nationwide, the navy's resurrected.
There's a problem for his royalty –
A commander's lack of loyalty,
Leads to discontent, and sailors who've defected.

The Vikings' tough campaigns,
Meant an England ruled by Danes:
(King Canute and co – they didn't stay here long).
The navy was stood down,
By Ed, who wore the crown,
A decision he soon realised was wrong.

So the fleet of our domain
Had been built up once again
By the time old Edward made his last confession.
Harold took the throne,
Which he thought should be his own,
But a foreigner disputed the succession...

The only copy of *The Seafarer* is in the Exeter Book, an anthology of Anglo-Saxon poetry donated to the library of Exeter Cathedral in 1072 by Bishop Leofric.

Edgar was succeeded by his son, Edward the Martyr (*r.*975–78), who was followed by Æthelred II (*r.*978–1013 and 1014–16), known as 'the Unready'. Unræd is Old English for 'bad counsel'. The term 'sea thieves' was used in an Old English poem about the Battle of Maldon (991), after which the 'tributes', known as Danegeld, began. Having been paid in 991, the Danes returned in 997, and in several succeeding years. The final payment was in 1012. The Danes had occupied most of England by 1016.

In 1008, a contribution of ships, boats and even coats of mail to protect English sea warriors was demanded from each 'hundred' (an administrative unit).

One of the new navy's commanders took to piracy.

During Æthelred's reign, Icelander, Leif Ericson, having first established a settlement in Greenland, reached Newfoundland (circa 1000).

King Canute (or Cnut) (*r.*1016–1035).

Edward the Confessor (*r.*1042–1066). Edward mustered naval forces in 1045, 1046 and 1047 to resist a Norwegian attack that never materialized. Another force was stationed at the key port of Sandwich in 1049, but his fourteen ships were paid off in 1050–1.

Harold Godwinson was Edward the Confessor's brother-in-law.

William, Duke of Normandy, was Edward's cousin and claimed the king had promised him the throne of England.

EXTRACT FROM *THE SEAFARER*

I can make a true song about me myself,
Tell my travel, how I often endured
Days of struggle, troublesome times,
(how I) have suffered grim sorrow at heart,
Have known in the ship many worries (abodes of care),
The terrible tossing of the waves, where the anxious night watch
Often took me at the ship's prow,
When it tossed near the cliffs.
Fettered by cold were my feet,
Bound by frost in cold clasps,
Where then cares seethed
Hot about my heart
A hunger tears from within the sea-weary soul.
This the man does not know for whom on land
It turns out most favourably,
How I, wretched and sorrowful,
On the ice-cold sea dwelt for a winter
In the paths of exile, bereft of friendly kinsmen,
Hung about with icicles,
Hail flew in showers.
There I heard nothing but the roaring of the sea,
The ice-cold wave.
At times the swan's song I took to myself as pleasure,
The gannet's noise and the voice of the curlew
Instead of the laughter of men,
The singing gull instead of the drinking of mead,
Storms there beat the stony cliff,
Where the tern spoke, icy-feathered;
Always the eagle cried at it, dewy-feathered;
No cheerful kinsmen
Can comfort the poor soul... Amen.

Anonymous (written before 975)

2 Post-conquest and a world beyond

2

Post-conquest and a world beyond

Norman Britain

Norman ships from the Bayeux Tapestry – Tapestries 38–39

1066 the year
When the Normans would appear:
An English navy waited, fully manned.
But supplies were soon diminished,
And its vigil thus had finished,
By the time the hostile army chose to land.

William One sired William Two.
The line continued through.
But after Henry, things would disconnect.
His heir – a teenage son –
With some mates is having fun
Aboard a ship. They're drunk. The 'White Ship's' wrecked.

The youngster sadly drowned.
Now confusion would abound:
A daughter is, by rights, the next in line.
The events of that November,
Were a lesson to remember:
Ensure the crew has not quaffed too much wine.

William's invasion attempt was delayed by bad weather and, meanwhile, Harold's army had had to dash off to Yorkshire to fend off a Viking attack. Harold was defeated by William (William I *r.*1066–1087) at the Battle of Hastings.

William the Conqueror's son was known as William Rufus, (William II *r.*1087–1100) due to his ruddy complexion. Henry I (*r.*1100–1135) was also a son of William I.

The White Ship was a nef, a sea-going carrack favoured by the Normans. William Adelin was Henry I's only legitimate male heir. Just two of the 300 or so on board survived the disaster (1120).

Matilda, Henry's oldest daughter, was usurped by her cousin Stephen. The ensuing period of upheaval was known as 'The Anarchy'.

The White Ship sinking

For five hundred years or so,
The navy's 'ebb and flow'
Was a pattern that would often be repeated –
There would be some sea-bound mission...
A fleet put in position...
Then disbanded when the task had been completed.

Up in Scotland, a campaign
Was briefly fought in vain.
Those aboard a fleet freed Lisbon from the Moors.
Holy ventures – there were others –
By Christian bands of brothers,
And against the French, the never-ending wars.

By providing Lisbon aid,
The foundations would be laid
For the longest-lasting treaty still in force.
We and Portugal allied,
And would take each other's side,
As the twists and turns of history took their course.

Henry II (*r.1154–1189*)

Our surrounding seas have calmed,
Now we shouldn't feel alarmed:
From elsewhere, the threats no longer are alive.
The Vikings are the past,
Henry's empire is quite vast,
And this all means our ports can grow and thrive.

With new warehouses and quays,
Ships unloaded now with ease.
(Soon we'd introduce the useful wooden crane).
But our ships are not capacious:
We want something much more spacious.
That the answer was the cog is very plain.

This vessel would evolve,
And another problem solve:
A war-time need could crop up, who knew when?
It 'grew' castles – fore and aft.
Slits to take the arrow shaft:
And what carries goods, can also carry men.

Richard I (*r.1189–1199*)

Father's empire's under threat!
But it might be reclaimed yet.
Richard's target was the River Seine's whole valley.
From Portsmouth as his base,
And requiring ships with pace,
He thus preferred the merits of the galley.

There was no professional navy as such. Any force was essentially a collection of whatever ships could be mustered. It did not invariably remain the case that merchant vessels were suitable for war (see verse 327).

In 1072, William I attempted, unsuccessfully, to invade Scotland.

The crusades were a number of missions to free the Holy Land from Islamic expansionism. England was largely uninvolved in the First Crusade (1095–99). During the Second Crusade (1147–49), when predominantly French and German armies crossed Europe on foot, up to 200 ships in a multi-national fleet set off from Dartmouth. En route to the Holy Land, the crusaders became involved in a successful bid to recapture Lisbon from Moorish occupation.

The Anglo-Portuguese Treaty was signed in 1373. It was briefly disrupted between 1580 and 1640 when the crowns of Portugal and Spain united, but has otherwise remained strong. It resulted in Portugal's assistance to Britain during the First World War, and her neutrality during the Second World War. It explains Britain's involvement in the Peninsula War (see verses 702–706) and has been cited as recently as 1982. (See section/verses 1648–1664 **The Falklands War, 1982**).

Henry II's empire included about half of medieval France and, after the invasion which he launched from Pembroke in 1171, parts of Ireland too. The Viking threat disappeared because the Scandinavians were dealing with internal problems.

Early cranes would be dwarfed by the five 433 feet (132m) high MegaMex cranes recently delivered to the new Liverpool 2 container terminal.

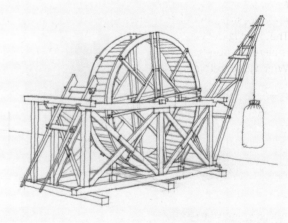

Wooden crane

Richard's penetrating ventures in France were reminiscent of the riverine Viking raids. The Third Crusade to Palestine, Syria and Mesopotamia (1189–92) is known as 'The Kings' Crusade', because Richard I and Philip II of France patched up their differences to lead it.

Galleys had a shallower draught than cogs. The term is also used generically for galley-type vessels.

Our king – 'the Lionheart'–
Also played another part,
Doing something that had not been tried before:
A set of rules that cites,
Captains' duties and their rights –
For seafaring, an early piece of law.

King John (*r.*1199–1216)

France got into a jam,
With our fearless raid at Damme.
(Her king had set his mind upon invasion.)
An English armed force swooped
On a fleet all nicely grouped.
It proved a very lucrative occasion.

Fishing traps

With entitlements enshrined,
Magna Carta next was signed,
And this document leads some to hold the view
That fishing out at sea,
Is all restriction-free,
Which is something that is only partly true.

Fishing methods in the past
Were nets (pulled, dipped or cast)…
The rod and line… the spear… the bow and arrow…
The simple human hand…
Or the weirs that rivers spanned.
(These funnelled fish to where the weir was narrow.)

'The Laws of Oléron' (1190), the earliest example of maritime law in England, had been promulgated by Eleanor of Aquitaine, mother of Richard I, who acted as his regent. They covered onboard conditions, and matters such as punishment. Later taken up by Henry VIII, they made an important contribution to the *Black Book of the Admiralty*.

The Battle of Damme took place in 1213. The English captured 300 ships, and burned more than a hundred. The remainder of the 1,700 ships in France's fleet were scuttled.

King John was forced to sign the *Magna Carta* in 1215. It established the right to be tried for alleged crimes within a legal system, and gave access to common resources, including saltwater fishing. Though sea angling and digging bait from the fore-shore remain largely unrestricted, subsequent legislation has placed certain necessary bans and limits relating to conservation zones, protected species and catch sizes. Shellfish (see verses 1677–1691) eg mussels and oysters, are still hand-harvested. Fishing weirs (or fish garths) are a way of trapping fish (or of re-directing them to traps). They were widely used on rivers and in tidal waters. Because they could cause flooding and hinder the passage of boats, the *Magna Carta* required the removal of these weirs 'from the Thames, the Medway and throughout the whole of England, except on the sea coast'.

Combat de deux nefs médiévales

There were traps, too, on the coast;
Massive structures that played host
To lots of fish that came in with the tide.
These had nowhere else to go
When ebb succeeded flow,
As nets or screens would keep them all inside.

Unpopular was John,
And his 'greedy' tag lives on.
Against him, barons took French Louis' side.
'I'm England's king,' said he,
So John was forced to flee,
But the rebels switched again, once John had died.

Louis had to be expelled,
But the South East he now held.
His reinforcements sailed across to Dover.
With 'they must not land' in mind,
We approached them from behind,
And ship by ship, we took the French fleet over.

Edward I (r.1272–1307)

Of our home fleet 'by and large',
The king had been in charge,
But as admiral, de Leybourne gets this title.
Often noted as a 'first'
As a soldier he's well versed.
So let's hope the 'navy's' role would not be vital.

For campaigns north of the border,
Ships were certainly in order,
To carry troops and all that soldiers need.
To defeat one 'Rob the Bruce',
They had no other use,
In helping Edward's armies to succeed.

Edward II (r.1307–1327)

His father had done lots
Of 'hammering of Scots',
But Edward Two was not a clever man.
An attempt would soon be made
To create the first blockade,
But this wasn't such a practicable plan.

It was at this king's behest,
That seamen were impressed,
And forced to serve. They probably weren't pleased.
Later centuries eclipse,
This manning of five ships,
For which mariners – three hundred plus – were seized.

Traps were especially common along the coasts of northern Somerset and Wales, but were also found off the coast of Cumbria. Weirs were made of various materials (stone walls into which wooden stakes were set, and screens fashioned from woven branches and twigs). The walls averaged about 150 metres in length, but could be considerably longer.

King John managed to lose most of France. Prince Louis of France was later King Louis VIII of France. After John's death in 1216, the barons, who had forced him to sign the *Magna Carta*, now decided to support John's son, who became Henry III.

The English Fleet was assembled by Hubert de Burgh, Constable of Dover. The French Fleet was commanded by Eustace the Monk (a notorious pirate), who had defected from support of the English. English victory at the Battle of Sandwich (1217) persuaded Louis to abandon thoughts of conquering England.

'By and large' is a nautical expression, meaning 'in general', from the Age of Sail. A 'large' is a strong wind blowing in the right direction enabling square sails to be filled. 'By' signifies less favourable conditions, necessitating the skilful use of triangular sails such as those found on tea clippers (see verses 955–958). For nautical sayings, see verses 666–669.

William de Leybourne (Laybourne), appointed in 1297 by Edward I as 'Admiral of the Sea of the King of England', is often regarded as England's first admiral. However, in 1224, Henry III had appointed Richard de Lucy, and he had been followed by Sir Thomas Moulton (Molêton) in the mid 13th century, (appointed 'Captain and Guardian of the Seas').

At the time, the seas were split into three areas – north (which covered the east), south and west.

In 1390/91, Edward, Earl of Rutland and Cork, was appointed the first Lord High Admiral, (though the title appears to be of much earlier origin). The holder of this post is, to this day, one of the nine Great Officers of State.

Edward I was also known as 'Longshanks' because he was tall, and as 'the Hammer of the Scots' because he waged war against that country. In so doing, he used English merchant ships, along with others mustered from Ireland, and from those Scottish isles that took England's side during this conflict. Edward I also made Wales part of his kingdom, initially by sending a fleet from Winchelsea to help capture Anglesey.

Faced with Robert the Bruce's successful campaigns to regain land taken by Edward I, Edward II planned to surround Scotland with a fleet. Unsurprisingly, the scheme did not work.

On 26 July 1313, the king commanded that 60 seamen be impressed to serve on *la Michele*. The same number was required for both *la Isabelle* and *le Petre*. A further 100 and 50 were needed for 'la cogge' *Sainte Marie* and *la Katelyn* respectively.

In earlier reigns, ships had been impressed, as had men for military duties under Edward I. Sailors, by various means, would certainly have also been forced to serve. The first Act of Parliament allowing impressment was in 1563, and the Vagrancy Act of 1597 allowed certain men to be forced to serve on ships. The notorious press gangs were a feature of 18th century naval recruitment (see verses 467–471).

> July 26. Writ of aid, until Christmas, directed to all bailiffs, for John Syberswelde,
> Westminster. master of the king's ship called *la Michele* of Westminster, whom the
> king has commanded to impress 60 mariners to man the ship at his wages,
> in the parts where it shall seem best to him to do so.
> By K., on the information of R. de Northburgh.
> The like for the undermentioned masters when impressing seamen,
> viz.:—
> John Griffoun, master of the king's ship called *la Isabelle* of West-
> minster, for 60 mariners.
> Richard Golde, master of the ship called *le Petre*, for 60 mariners.
> The like for Peter Bard, master of the king's ship called *la cogge*
> *Sancte Marie* of Westminster, for 100 mariners.
> John le Taillour, master of the ship called *la Katelyn*, for
> 50 mariners.

From parliamentary records (1313)

Medieval Trade

The Hanseatic League

We were not unique disliking
The interfering Viking:
Northern Europe suffered piracy fatigue.
To thwart the would-be rival
And ensure their own survival,
Some cities formed the Hanseatic League.

In the Baltic and North Sea,
They wanted to be free,
To go about their business without fear.
This strong confederation's
Linked to towns from other nations:
We had some of their kontors over here.

With no need to be coerced,
Our capital was first,
The rest included Bristol and King's Lynn,
Now restored, the warehouse there's
Known to many a fine pair,
Who choose to take their wedding vows within.

Baltic Trade

The Hanse (and Dutch) are mates
With the range of Baltic states,
Which trade timber, potash, metal bars and grain...
Leather, minerals and flax...
Hemp and skins and fur and wax...
In return, cloth, spice and wine they thus obtain.

On us, not much impinges:
We (and France) are on the fringes,
But certain of these goods traverse the seas.
Of their few things we import,
Pitch and iron are now bought.
Though we've Sussex oak, we still buy Swedish trees.

The Hanseatic folk
Used cog ships made of oak,
The bottom in the middle was quite flat.
Although long ago designed,
They'd been steadily refined:
One mast, one sail and room to swing a cat.

The Hanseatic League, also referred to as 'the Hansa', was more a confederation of trading guilds rather than of cities. A major impetus in its formation was to protect trade along the Kiel 'Salt Road'. Salt was needed to preserve the herring caught out of places such as Lübeck in north Germany.

Kontors (or Counters) were warehouses, which also acted as trading posts. The London kontor was established in 1320, on the site of what is now Cannon Street Station. In 1157, Cologne Hansa merchants persuaded Henry II to free them from all tolls in London, and allow them access to all of England's trade fairs.

King's Lynn was, at the time, Bishop's Lynn. The medieval Hansa warehouse is now the town's registry office. There were others at Norwich, Ipswich, Boston, Bristol and possibly Hull.

The kontors of the Hanseatic League

Oak was, and still is, plentiful in the Baltic region, where it is fast growing. The timber is therefore lighter, straighter, knot-free and easier to cut into planks. Excavations (1994) of a medieval friary at Hull unearthed coffins made of this. English oak, although not depleted in medieval times, is slow growing.

Cogs were used extensively throughout northern Europe, including Britain, as cargo boats (see verse 95). The first recorded cog (948) was in Muiden, near Amsterdam. A cog, dated 1380, was found near Bremen in 1962 and reconstructed. It was carvel-built. The cog was superseded by the hulk or 'holk' (14th century) – not to be confused with hulk, which is a hull incapable of going to sea.

The expression 'room to swing a cat' is thought to originate from swinging the 'Cat o' nine tails' (a whip used in the navy from around 1695). Sailors would not, of course, have done anything to harm their lucky ship's cat! (see verse 37).

Cog

Progress was soon made
To protect the herring trade,
In which barrels as containers are essential.
And activities are halted
If the catch cannot be salted;
Monopolies were proving influential.

Trade with Eastern countries, and wine imports

The exploits of crusaders,
Had benefitted traders,
By reopening the access to the East.
But you'll have to understand,
The main routes were overland:
Traversed by man and ever-faithful beast.

The Levant was reached in ships,
But the balance of these trips
To where they would do business was a chore.
A means – there had to be –
To go all the way by sea;
Something future generations would explore.

In the quest for silks and spices
For now, the trek suffices:
One Marco Polo went through Asia Minor.
Though it isn't known for sure,
He may have done much more:
His writings claim he got as far as China.

A number played it cute,
And they found a Red Sea route,
Which minimised the overland bit's distance.
From this trade we are excluded,
Every direct link eluded,
Though pursued by some with obdurate persistence.

Venice held the key –
A 'middleman' was she! –
Her monopoly provided massive wealth.
She even rode the fate
That, in 1348,
Proved to be injurious to health.

In the ships that she is sending,
To Europe, there is wending
The Black Death, that would cause such devastation.
With the spice that was unloaded,
Was a virus that eroded
About a third of England's population.

Wooden barrels have been around for about two millennia, and the method of making them has changed very little. In Europe, they were probably developed by the Celts. Barrels were, (and in some cases still are), important for transporting (and keeping) wine, spirits and beer, for preserving perishable foodstuffs such as fish, and as containers for gunpowder etc. Oak is the wood of choice. One major Baltic export was klapholz, widely used for barrel making.

For fish preservation see verse 133.

The all-powerful city of Lübeck had a monopoly on the export of the highly prized Lüneburg salt. In terms of value, this accounted for almost one third of the port's exports in 1368/9.

The so-called 'Silk Road' was actually several routes from the eastern Mediterranean to India and beyond.

Historically, the Levant was a geographical term to describe the eastern Mediterranean from Greece to the east coast of Libya.

The prized spices included cinnamon, turmeric, ginger and pepper. The Far Eastern trade also involved opium, drugs, herbs and incense.

The Venetian, Marco Polo (1254–1324) wrote *Il Milione*, (*The Million*), an account of his travels.

Centuries later, the Suez Canal (see verses 1193–1195) would be built, making possible the passage of ships to the Red Sea.

Bristol merchants, in particular, tried and failed to establish a direct spice trade link.

Other Italian cities, such as Genoa, also enjoyed the benefits of a role similar to Venice's.

The Black Death, a bubonic plague pandemic, reached England in June 1348. The first known case was a seaman, who arrived in Weymouth from Gascony. By the summer of 1349, it had spread throughout England. Recent research suggests that as many as half the population died. This led to a shortage of workers, which is the main reason England turned from agriculture (labour intensive) to sheep.

The Black Death affected Venice again in 1630 and, this time, did contribute to the city's ultimate decline.

The Englishman adores
Stuff from closer to our shores,
Most especially the wine he likes to sup.
Our need was quite prodigious:
Reasons social and religious.
This explains why parts of France we won't give up.

Fishing in the Middle Ages

Boats sail out. Some fish get caught.
Men bring these back to port.
Folk buy. The system ticks along quite merrily.
On fresh herring, newly dead,
A community gets fed.
Quite that simple? It would seem not necessarily.

In harbours that are small,
This (almost) says it all:
There'll be tax to pay – not too sophisticated.
But where coastal towns are bigger
Other parties also figure,
So the situation's much more complicated.

A fisherman's concern
Is that money he will earn,
Not what happens to the netfuls that he lands.
They might fetch a bit more but
Others need to have their cut:
Enter middlemen, who'll take them off his hands.

Some, whose patch was fairly local,
Were reputed to be vocal,
As around the streets with baskets they would go.
Were those fishwives really squawking
As their goods they went a-hawking?
Popular belief would have it so.

Were their horses in a lather?
For the rippiers went farther
And, for those days, covered distances quite fast.
The packhorse was the mode,
On the coast to inland road;
If kept damp, then fresh fish could be made to last.

And where best to sell your wares?
There were many trading fairs,
And in eastern England none of them was bigger
Than Yarmouth's huge event,
(Which gave rise to discontent
When monopolies were introduced with vigour).

Although only the richer classes could afford wine for domestic consumption, it was needed for the celebration of mass, which is why so many religious orders were involved in wine production. Our main source of wine was Gascony, an area which was once part of Henry II's French empire (see verse 94).

Most small fishing communities had little more than a jetty. There were tolls in every town and port. Tithes (tenths) were also payable to the church, and manorial lords had rights to claim a payment, which might include a proportion of the catch.

Fish were sometimes sold direct from the quay, or from a section of the local market place, but catches were often passed on to various types of merchants, who may or may not have been specialised fishmongers. Fishwives were also known as hukksterres.

Rippiers were specialised retail-transporters who bought at sea ports for sale inland. They used baskets called dossers. Fish were wrapped in wet canvas or seaweed.

The Yarmouth fair was held annually from 29 September–11 November.

Great numbers of the fishermen of France, Flanders and of Holland, Zealand and all the lowe countries yerelle, from the feaste of Sainte Michaell the Archangell, untylle the feaste of Sainte Martine, about the takinge, sellinge and buyenge of herrings.

Thomas Damet, 16th century historian from Great Yarmouth

Once available to all,
The locals had the gall
To try to keep the profits for their own.
To prevent this situation,
Was a piece of legislation.
As the 'Statute of the Herring' it is known.

One guild with lengthy history –
Once referred to as a 'mistery' –
Is the fishmongers'. All London it controlled.
A major part it played:
It monopolized the trade.
By no one else could any fish be sold.

Preserving fish

Some fish will have to wait,
On their trip from sea to plate.
If they've rotted, then as food they're not alluring.
Disintegration's halted,
If they're smoked or dried or salted.
These processes are different forms of curing.

Stockfish they'd prepare,
Dried out in the open air,
(Once cut in half) and then it would be stored.
To fund the right facility,
There were some with the ability,
Like an abbot or the local feudal lord.

Basic salting always pays,
But for just a few short days:
Fish thus treated reaches customers inland.
Shelf-life is improved
If the guts are first removed,
Which is something that the Swedish understand.

'It's the method that we need,'
Our authorities agreed.
They certainly were right with what they reckoned.
There were further destinations,
Than the local populations –
For the European export market beckoned.

Certain tales are documented,
Of how kippers were invented,
But their origins are certainly much older.
Since the dim and distant past,
Smoke's been used to make fish last.
(They're hung up above a fire that's left to smoulder).

The Statute of Herring (1357), to give it its correct title, was passed to ensure open competition.

Formed long before its first charter was granted by Edward I in 1272, the Mistery of Fishmongers had exclusive rights, enjoyed until the 15th century, to sell fish.

Fish could either be dry salted or pickled in brine (or, less commonly, in vinegar). A sprinkling of dry salt would preserve fish for two or three days. Barrelling fish in a strong brine solution had a longer-lasting effect.

Disposal of the unwanted parts of the fish was prescribed by regulation.

Members of the cod family were often prepared as stockfish.

Monasteries and lords often built store houses and curing houses for their own use. Substantial quantities of fish were also exported.

Kippers are split cold-smoked whole herring. Many tales relate to the accidental discovery of the process of creating them, the most notable and enduring version's being that of John Woodger of Seahouses in 1843, who reputedly left herring in a room with a smoking stove. Kippering was doubtless discovered well before this date.

A smokehouse was often attached to fishermen's cottages.

Medieval fish barrel

By medieval measures,
Meeting foreign fishy pleasures
Was big business – that the merchants would embrace.
In this booming situation,
There was lots of regulation,
Which prescribed the proper manner, time and place.

By appointees who inspected,
Cheating ploys could be detected,
Like displaying better specimens on top.
And re-watering's not truthful,
To make ageing stock look youthful,
Thus deceiving those who've come along to shop.

The religious institution,
Had made its contribution,
To what the wider populace could eat.
Up to Christmas and in Lent,
People had to be content,
With a diet that lacked foodstuffs such as meat.

Shellfish oft sufficed
For the poor – and 'poor in Christ'.
Abstinence, a gesture in the cloisters,
Also saved a bit of dosh –
Cheap and plentiful such nosh –
So monks dined on mussels, cockles, whelks or oysters.

And, too, these men of God
Liked their herring and their cod
For the protein that is needed to keep healthy.
With a very hefty tab,
Were the lobster and the crab:
Crustacea were the province of the wealthy.

Fishing Methods

Largish creatures were harpooned,
And then on deck marooned.
With the good old rod and line, fish could be captured.
This today is not just sport:
It's how some types best are caught.
But for leisure, it has many folk enraptured.

Since the not so recent past,
Different types of net were cast,
Most kept vertical by using weights and floats.
Some drifted with the tide,
And the fish were trapped inside.
The dragnet types were pulled along by boats.

It was common to restrict the selling of fish to daylight hours ie between dawn and sunset.

For religious reasons, meat was forbidden on certain days of the week, and during Advent and during Lent. Inconveniently, these were not the best times of the year for fishing.

The saying 'not worth an oyster' reflects just how cheap shellfish were. For shellfish see verses 1677–1691.

For longline fishing see verse 1699.

The first reference to fishing as a recreational sport was the 1496 publication *Treatyse* on *Fysshynge with an Angle* by Dame Juliana Berners.

Medieval fishing boats

These ways were tried and tested,
But some thought had been invested,
To find a way of maximising hauls.
Men, around this time deduced
Bigger catches were produced
By using special nets, now known as 'trawls'.

Shoals of fish, fast swimming scared,
In these new trawls were ensnared:
(And much else too, till relatively recently.)
Now we've quotas and restrictions,
(And associated frictions),
For the eco-system must be treated decently.

In the third King Edward's reign,
Men were driven to complain
Of this practice, which progressively had flourished.
They were anxious to avoid
What these 'wondyrechauns' destroyed:
All the smaller stuff on which the 'great fish' nourished.

Now of sustenance deprived,
'Plenteous' fish no longer thrived,
And this is why a ban was being sought.
It was surely well intentioned –
Even 'close meshed' nets were mentioned,
In which all that therein entered would be caught.

They set up a Commission
To look into the position.
The process took a very lengthy time.
Regulation came about,
Which two men sought to flout:
They were executed for their blatant crime.

In those distant days of yore,
Men did not sail far from shore,
As their fragile boats were easily capsized.
Fish that near the surface dwelt –
Herring, mackerel and smelt –
Were plentiful, and very highly prized.

They would go out for the day,
For some hours would be away.
Yet others did a night or maybe two.
To Norway some ships strayed:
Soon intended trips were made –
Which then meant a longer absence for the crew.

Some sources say trawling originated as early as the 12th century.

More accurately than snared, fish were surrounded by nets. Nets designed to entangle fish are called gill nets.

A bycatch comprises fish or other marine creatures, which are caught whilst targeting another species. The term also includes under-sized fish (juveniles). The bycatch may be retained and sold, but is often discarded (see verses 1693–1694).

Edward III (r.1327–1377). A Commons petition against trawling-type fishing methods was made in 1376, the first example of complaints about over-fishing. There was no specific reference to cetaceans (whales, dolphins, porpoises etc), which became of concern in more recent times.

Wondyrechauns were beam trawls 'made in the manner of an oyster dredge' (see verse 1686), but longer and with an attached net. Most fishing boats operated close to land, and trawling was predominantly conducted in river estuaries. Restrictions were put into place in various places in Europe eg there was a ban on trawling for shrimp in Dutch estuaries (1583) and a French ruling in 1584 that made trawling a capital offence.

The English fishermen were executed for using metal chains on beam trawls – standard practice today!

Pelagic fish live in the upper areas of the sea. Demersal fish live on or near the sea bed, and include flat fish (eg plaice) and species such as cod, which was not caught commercially until the 19th century. Those British ships that travelled to more distant waters were mainly fishing for cod. Those who fished more locally rarely ventured out for more than two days.

Wondyrechaun

(For babies to be born
The adults first must spawn,
In the place where they themselves were once begotten.
They return when they've a mind,
And boats aren't far behind,
To catch abundant fish that now are 'shotten'.)

We'll return to this at length,
But now what of naval strength?
All too often, borrowed vessels were deployed.
If big enough and sailable,
It must be made available...
In time, the merchant owners got annoyed.

Early duties on goods

Oriental treasures
Had become the West's great pleasures:
Exotic cargoes traders' ships contained.
Very limited our range
Of things offered in exchange;
And the benefits weren't easily sustained.

Cities such as Venice
Could spurn the pirate menace:
With warships, they could prosper and grow great.
But our merchants oft fall prey
To attack, whilst underway.
In sea power terms, this country was third rate.

The French controlled the seas,
Sometimes helped by Genoese,
(Though this could prove a rather frail alliance).
Add to this the pirate's greed
And it's clear we're much in need
Of more than worthless gestures of defiance.

Pirates are no joke,
Though the word will oft invoke
A Caribbean composite lampoon.
But these seaborne thieves did roam,
In the waters close to home:
In our lawless seas, no vessel was immune.

English ships were full
Of our major product: wool.
It was processed into cloth in other lands.
But our seas were uncontrolled,
So the bags of soft 'white gold',
Would fall often into ruthless grasping hands.

Herring spawn off south-west Norway in spring and, in autumn, off south-west Sweden at the entrance to the Baltic Sea. These areas were all known to English fishermen by the 1300s.

Edward III notably continually impressed merchant ships and didn't pay for them, resulting in the ruin of many traders, and a cessation of shipbuilding.

In the early Middle Ages, raw wool was England's main and, along with hides, almost only export. Processing wool into cloth was principally done in the Low Countries. Cloth produced in England was of poor quality, and only the wealthy could afford imported fabric. In the mid 14th century, Edward III encouraged the immigration of skilled weavers, and by the end of that century, cloth for export was being manufactured here – by which time the export of fish (see previous section) was also taking place. Fleeces could only legitimately be traded with foreigners at staple towns. There were ten such towns in England, four in Ireland and one in Wales, plus Calais (then an English possession).

Goods could only be imported legally by using one of thirteen official ports. There were difficulties keeping watch on long stretches of coast, and a fairly lackadaisical approach to collecting revenue prevailed, at least until the 15th century.

Venice had a monopoly of the spice trade, and other European cities failed to secure access to this valued and lucrative commodity. Bristol merchants in particular were keen to deal direct with the eastern Mediterranean ports that handled spices (see verse 120).

The consent of the House of Commons, (Parliament was well established by Edward III's reign), was needed to sanction the levy (a domestic tax), but this did not necessarily apply to customs duties (until the supposed loophole was rectified by the 1353 Ordinance of the Staple).

For pirates in general see verses 479–480, and for local piracy see verses 333–334.

Even worse, like feudal lords
Forever crossing swords,
Sailors weren't above such private strife.
There'd be little wars of sorts,
Affecting rival ports –
An undisciplined, unruly kind of life.

(Very soon the day would dawn
When we used wool as a pawn
In a complicated plot to force support.
The payback could be handsome
If the fleece was held to ransom,
But the scheme did not quite play out as it ought.

Unhappy those who weave
If their wool they don't receive:
As a tactic Edward held back their supplies.
Thus there was a shortage but,
A dearth and then a glut
Doesn't always mean the 'price' is bound to rise.)

A pirate named John Crabbe,
Many trading boats would nab,
Which caused a lot of trouble for exporters.
Then this chap whom all had feared –
Of his crimes completely cleared –
Was put in charge of making safe our waters.

(King John had had the thought
That, at every major port,
The levying of duties was required.
To assess, collect, account
For the full and correct amount
Half a dozen men at each were duly hired.)

The first king Edward chose,
A duty to impose.
This marked the start of something known as smuggling.
Import/export duties soar
When the country goes to war
And, for fighting funds, the crown is really struggling.

It wasn't now just wool,
That would keep the coffers full:
Other goods were hit, and these included wine.
But the collection of the tax
Was really very lax,
And the system would take decades to refine.

Edward III, in a bid to acquire allies in his quest for the French throne, attempted without much success to use trade tactically.

In common with their third namesake, both Edward I and Edward II had claimed sovereignty over the sea, but were unable to police it.

King John (r.1199–1216) had developed a royal fleet of galleys, and tried to establish a naval administration, but neither he, nor his successor (Henry III r.1216–1272), succeeded in producing a solid administration. A formal lay administration did emerge during Edward III's reign headed by a Clerk of the King's Ships. Aside from waging war with France, the need for a naval force was prompted by piracy.

John Crabbe (1305 or earlier –1352) was a Flemish merchant, pirate and soldier. In a classic case of poacher turned gamekeeper, Edward (impressed by Crabbe's abilities) had the bright idea of hiring him to improve security for English shipping. Crabbe proved to be of considerable use to the king. It was at his suggestion that a large enough fleet was mustered to enable the English victory at Sluys (1340) (see verse 172).

In 1202, King John had imposed the first tax on trade, a custom duty on all imports and exports levied at one fifteenth their value. This seems to have been discontinued by 1206.

The first lasting export duties on wool were imposed by Edward I in 1275.

The 1303 *Carta Mercatoria* granted freedom of trade to foreign merchants, and guaranteed them no increase in duty payable. In 1334, the rights of such merchants were embodied in a charter granted to the Hanseatic League (see verses 109–111), in exchange for financial assistance.

To fund his war with France, Edward III imposed a tax called tunnage on wine, (and duties on further goods including wool cloth), at 5 per cent of their value. In addition to tunnage, if an English ship brought in more than 20 tuns, the king claimed his 'prise' of two tuns (barrels), whereas foreign vessels paid butlerage (2 shillings a barrel) on the excess.

For smuggling see verses 419–426 & 749–787.

Lex Mercatoria

Whatever the activity,
There's always a proclivity,
For practices and rules to be evolved.
From the time of its inception,
Doing trade was no exception,
And disagreements had to be resolved.

In the case of a dispute,
One side could bring a suit;
On the merits of the case a court decides.
Everyone's agreed
That of essence here is speed:
A decision must be made within three tides.

The Cinque Ports

Exempt from tax and toll,
As they had a special role,
Was a group of ports in Sussex and in Kent.
For the privilege they earn,
Every year and in return,
Fifty seven ships for fifteen days are lent.

The king can thus rely
On a regular supply
Of vessels, should he ever have the need.
Then the likes of Hythe and Dover
Said, 'We'll have to think this over,
For it's proving very difficult indeed.

We need to get support,'
Which from nearby towns was sought.
Other places now helped out with ships and crews,
The reward for such communities
Was sharing the immunities,
Which smugglers very quickly would abuse.

The Cinque Ports' role diminished,
Once the need for them had finished,
And an English fleet at last was here to stay.
Some in any case were wilting,
Due to raids or floods or silting:
Only Dover is a major port today.

Many years ago
The Lord Warden ran the show,
(He was also known as something most baronial).
The post's still held today,
But there's no real role to play:
It's an honour, and is solely ceremonial.

Lex Mercatoria, or 'the Law Merchant', refers to the body of rules and principles devised, and largely administered, by merchants to regulate their dealings. First described in the late 13th century by an anonymous author, it was used throughout Europe. It could be enforced through public courts but, because of the need to resolve disputes quickly (and as inexpensively as possible), judgements were usually made informally, taking into account fair price, good commerce and equity. Decisions were sometimes made within the hour.

The five 'head' Cinque Ports were Dover, Hastings, Hythe, New Romney and Sandwich. Originally at the mouth of the River Rother, which changed course, New Romney is now a mile and a half inland. Sandwich is almost two miles from the sea. Hythe's natural harbour has now silted up. Hastings, which lacks a natural harbour, was almost washed away by the sea in the 12th century, was raided and burnt (twice) in the 13th century, and went into decline.

The ports came together informally in the 11th century, during the reign of Edward the Confessor (r.1042–1066), to mobilise merchant ships against attacks by pirates and England's enemies – and possibly to regulate the annual Yarmouth Herring Fair (see verse 128). (This right was abandoned in 1663.)

They first formed a distinct group in 1155, when Henry II granted charters to at least three of the head ports, possibly in order to raise ships for a trip to Normandy, and/or for his planned invasion of Ireland (see verse 94).

A charter giving rights in common to the Cinque (pronounced 'sink') Ports was granted by Henry III in 1260.

The provision of ships and crews was known as ship service. Manned ships (a crew of twenty-one and a boy) were needed not just for warfare, but also to transport the king and his entourage.

The other towns involved, (eg Lydd, Folkestone, Margate and Ramsgate), were known as 'limbs'. There were also two 'ancient towns': Winchelsea and Rye. When New Romney silted up, the latter took its place as one of the main five.

The Confederation today has fourteen member towns.

Lord Wardens were also called Barons of the Cinque Ports. These days an honour bestowed by the sovereign, the post has been held by former Prime Ministers (eg Sir Winston Churchill), and by members of the royal family.

For the establishment of a permanent navy see verse 343.

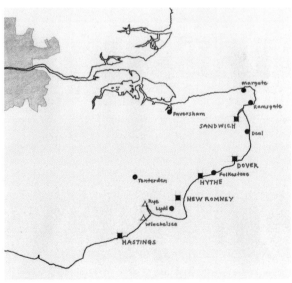

■ **CINQUE PORTS** ● **Limbs** △ **Ancient Towns**

The Hundred Years' War, 1337–1453

Edward III (*r.1327–1377*)

Though it seems a bit unfair,
A woman can't be heir
And wear the crown: her claim would be discounted.
When the king of France expired,
And no boy child had been sired,
Our king had claims, and now his challenge mounted.

This sparked a lengthy war
Of a century and more;
For the first time, we despatch an English fleet.
At Sluys, we engaged,
Won the bloody fight that raged:
But our mastery as yet is incomplete.

(Galley tactics were the mode:
Combat vessels by men rowed,
Whilst others on the decks all gamely tried,
To shoot and bring down those
They were seeking to oppose,
And with whom they'd shortly, hand to hand, collide.)

France rallied. Things got messy,
Till our victory at Crécy.
Calais fell to us at last, and that was great.
A crucial acquisition,
It strengthened our position:
On both sides, we command the Dover Strait.

But the merchants were not paid.
With no ships, they couldn't trade.
And vessels were continually impressed.
Demand was unabated,
Building new ones thus stagnated,
As England's king pursued his 'rightful' quest.

Henry V (*r.1413–1422*)

There's no navy, by and large,
Except a single barge,
And a fleet with just one boat's a real no-hoper.
To improve things now the task:
Henry knew just whom to ask –
A merchant from Southampton, William Soper.

Charles IV ('the Fair') of France died in 1328, leaving only a daughter.

The first naval engagement of this war was the Battle of Arnemuiden (1338), whereby a huge French fleet captured 5 English cogs that were carrying wool, massacring their crews. It is regarded as the first European naval battle in which artillery was used – the English nef, the *Christopher*, had three cannon and a hand gun. The Battle of Sluys (1340) was essentially a land battle at sea, with opposing ships lashed together. The French captured two English ships. Their own navy was decimated, though it was ultimately revived. English archers, using longbows, could shoot five or six arrows to every opposing one shot by crossbow.

During the successful siege of Calais (1347), bomb vessels (aka bomb ketches) were deployed for a seaborne attack on a land target – the first ever recorded use in such an assault. These ships carried bombards (a type of cannon used throughout the Middle Ages) and other artillery.

The English also fought (and won) a battle at Winchelsea in 1350, when an aggressive Castilian fleet, which had been exporting Spanish wool to Flanders, was engaged on its return journey. Edward III, accompanied by his son (the Black Prince), personally led the interception. The battle took place close to shore, and was witnessed by many cliff top spectators. Historians have suggested that this was one of many hard-fought, but unrecorded encounters. Spain got her revenge in 1372 off La Rochelle, where an entire English convoy of thirty-two to forty ships, plus barges, was captured, and England lost the use of an important port.

Throughout the Hundred Years' War, ships were needed to carry troops to France for land battles, notably Crécy (1346), where the English used cannons fired by gunpowder – another notable first.

Battle of Sluys, from Jean Froissart's *Chronicles* (14th century)

At the turn of the 15th century, the navy comprised a mere five or six vessels. Like his predecessors, Henry V did not compensate merchants for the use of requisitioned vessels, which often had to be adapted (for example to accommodate horses below decks).

William Soper (*c.*1390s–1459).

With her pals, the Genoese,
France is vying for the seas.
After Agincourt, we move on to Harfleur.
We beat a joint blockade,
But the point has been well made:
Only bigger ships can properly deter.

In the wake of this deduction,
Soper supervised construction
Of the *Grace Dieu*, a new flagship quite immense.
She spoke of England's might,
With her huge imposing height.
Her existence was enough of a defence.

Other vessels, too, were built,
But the navy soon would wilt:
All but four ships sold to pay a massive debt.
This last quartet was moored.
Then to all intents ignored,
And over time no longer posed a threat.

Henry V won a famous victory at Agincourt (1415).

In 1416, a French and Genoese fleet surrounded the harbour at Harfleur, and an English fleet was raised to secure its relief – achieved after a gruelling seven-hour sea battle (the Battle of the Seine).

Clinker-built at Southampton (1416–7), *Grace Dieu* towered 52 feet (15.8m) above the waterline at a time when height mattered. She needed a large crew, and reputedly rarely put to sea. She can probably be regarded as an early example of gunboat diplomacy (see verses 1182–1188). Prior to *Grace Dieu* (1,400 tons), Henry V had built *Jesus*, the first ship over 1,000 tons.

Henry V died in 1422 aged thirty-five or thirty-six (his exact birth date is not known), leaving the throne to an infant son, Henry VI (r.1422–1461 and 1470–1). Henry, who married Margaret of Anjou, suffered periods of insanity in later life.

The Wars of the Roses, 1455–1485

Henry would have been the bastion,
That kept the crown Lancastrian
But, sadly, he is prematurely dead.
With the next king in the link,
Rival Yorkists spot a chink
In a peaceful man, who's troubled in his head.

But his motivated wife,
Fights his cause in all this strife:
She wants to keep the crown safe for their son.
With the contest twixt two factions
We have plentiful distractions,
Which continue till the Roses' Wars are done.

A short-lived Scottish navy

Whilst two dynasties segment,
A Stewart king's intent
On establishing a Scottish force at sea.
To his nation he'll bequeath,
A dockyard based at Leith,
Which would function until 1983.

Things decline again up north,
Then his namesake James the Fourth
Decides that building lots of ships appealed.
His country's fleet grew strong,
But it didn't last too long,
Once the king was shot and killed at Flodden Field.

James I of Scotland (r.1406–1437).

The Leith dockyard, which ultimately produced tug boats, operated for 660 years.

The Royal Scottish Navy of James IV (r.1488–1513) totalled thirty-eight ships, and included the *Great Michael* (1511), the largest in Europe at the time. This was built at the new royal dockyard at Newhaven near Leith. After the defeat of the Scots at Flodden (1513), James's ships were sold off.

The start of the Age of Exploration

We now have reached the time,
When the subject of this rhyme,
Returns to those whose yearning was to travel.
Marco Polo had inspired,
And imaginations fired...
The mysteries of this world would soon unravel.

The intrepid Portuguese,
Well placed to sail the seas,
Would now produce a champion most royal.
As 'The Navigator' known,
Prince Henry stood alone:
Over every matter nautical he'd toil.

The waves upon an ocean,
And their upwards-downwards motion,
Mean that heavy seas a small craft can consume.
For his ventures to enable
Henry needed something stable –
And something that provided lots of room.

The carrack now would score
With its masts – three, maybe four –
And its 'castles', and its bowsprit at the stern.
It would later be refined,
But was cleverly designed,
To withstand the water's tendency to churn.

By now, much use was made
Of the compass, as an aid
To finding ways to ever-distant shores.
But one of Henry's missions,
(Better ways to plot positions),
Meant his men could find Madeira... the Azores...

Cabo Verde was espied,
Not long 'ere Henry died:
In all, a lot of progress by these chaps.
As charts had been required,
Cartographers were hired,
With consequent improvements made to maps.

Well before the whole wide world
Had gradually unfurled,
At making 'mappa mundi' men were fond.
They were talented, for sure
But there was a major flaw:
Most 'world maps' covered Europe – not beyond.

Christopher Columbus in particular is known to have been impressed by Polo's accounts (see verse 118).

Prince Henry of Portugal (1394–1460).

The carrack (or 'nau') was a three or four masted ocean-going ship. It was developed from the cog, and was the forerunner of the great ships of 'The Age of Sail'.

The single-sailed caravel, more suited to coastal waters, was also used, notably to explore the West African coast.

The magnetic compass was known to the Italians by the 12th century, but not used extensively until the 14th. The inherent magnetism of a ship can cause deviation. Matthew Flinders (see verses 591–593) developed a soft iron bar to counteract this. William Thomson (1824–1907) worked to perfect an adjustable compass.

Madeira was formally discovered in 1418, and the Azores circa 1427, but the existence of these islands was known before these dates. The Portuguese (and Genoese) were the first Europeans to land in the Cape Verde Islands (circa 1456).

See Plate A on page 61 for the Anglo-Saxon Mappa Mundi, the oldest surviving map of Britain.

**Henry the Navigator (holding a quadrant)
(Museu de Marinha, Lisbon)**

Columbus' ships (G.A. Closs, 1892). The *Niña* shown as a caravel on the left, and the *Santa María* and *Pinta* (carracks)

(Though a man, Ceuta born,
Once cleverly had drawn
A map, upon which quite a lot appears.
Based on travels most extensive,
It was *the* most comprehensive,
And remained so for the next three hundred years.)

Improvements in navigation

Since ancient times, all tars
Had been guided by the stars,
And bodies in the heavens they could track.
The North Star's height was taken
And the home port then forsaken,
In the knowledge they'd be able to get back.

Although measuring in fingers
In Europe sadly lingers,
The next few years improvements were to bring.
The Arabs' trusty pal,
Known to them as a kamal,
Was a gadget with a length of knotted string.

Then, with string not so impressed,
They put new tools to the test
And the quadrant was developed in its place.
The Arabs also scored,
Putting astrolabes on board –
Two moves Prince Henry quickly would embrace.

Polaris didn't cater
For seas south of the equator:
Beyond this point, that star would disappear.
So how could sailors hope
Navigation-wise to cope?
Something else was needed – that was very clear.

Unless obscured and shrouded
By a sky unduly clouded,
The sun's location proved to be the key.
Where it should be, day by day,
The astronomers could say...
Now the sailors had to work it out, at sea.

The Cross-staff

We may as well now mention,
A significant invention,
The cross-staff with its transoms on a pole.
It could calculate an angle,
With adjustment and a wangle,
But this proved a dodgy business on the whole.

Muhammad al-Idrisi (1099–1165/6) produced the Tabula Rogeriana (1154), (shown in Plate A). His own travels were confined to Europe, but he also drew on traders' accounts of the Far East.

Polaris (commonly known as the North Star or Pole Star) is on the horizon at the equator (zero degrees) and rises to 90° at the North Pole, thus enabling latitude to be plotted from its position.

The kamal was used to measure the height of heavenly bodies.

Sometimes called a 'ring', a marine or sea astrolabe is an instrument which measures the elevation of an object with respect to gravity.

Kamal

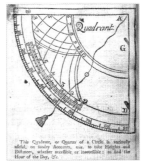

Quadrant

Using a quadrant

Astrolabes (Museu Nacional de Arqueológico, Lisbon)

It is held against the face
In precise and proper place,
And its user sights two objects for surveying.
Both at once he must affix,
Not the easiest of tricks,
Especially as boats are prone to swaying.

It wasn't that much fun,
All this squinting in the sun.
To minimize the glare, they used smoked glass.
Though a doddle it was not,
This tool was used a lot
Till eventually the sextant came to pass.

All of this relies,
On having nice clear skies,
So sailing was a seasonal pursuit.
If you had no way of knowing,
Where on earth you may be going,
Putting out to sea was not astute.

Not sure how all this fits
With a history of Brits?
Five hundred years ago, the world was small,
So any innovation,
Developed by a nation,
In time would prove of relevance to all.

More about exploration

The Portuguese move on.
Their monarch is King John.
To discover more of Africa he craved.
Much investment's now repaid,
By a rather nasty trade,
Whereby native men are captured and enslaved.

Columbus, so we hear,
Was the next great pioneer.
His direction would be following the sun.
Thus, in 1492,
When he 'sailed the ocean blue',
Exploration, with a vengeance, had begun.

This intrepid European
Was to reach the Caribbean:
His sailing feats immortalized the man.
But he went on to surmise,
That Asia was his prize:
Was convinced that the Bahamas were Japan.

The cross-staff was officially proposed for use by Johannes Werner in 1514, but earlier versions may have been around. The user of a cross-staff places it on his cheekbone, and attempts to assess the height of the relevant heavenly body, relative to the horizon.

For the sextant see verses 505–506.

Even in the Mediterranean, (until the end of the 13th century), sailing was curtailed between November and March. The more extensive use of the compass then made it possible to extend the sailing season, and the activity was only avoided in December and January.

It would appear that the cross-staff was not used in England until the 1550s, when it was introduced at the suggestion of John Dee, who advised on navigational matters.

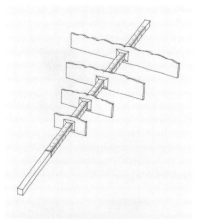

Cross-staff with removable transoms

Using a cross-staff

John II of Portugal (1455–1495) was the great-nephew of Henry the Navigator. He pushed further south along the known Atlantic coast of Africa with the main objective of discovering a route to India.

The Portuguese slave trade was later to accelerate to provide labour for plantations in Brazil (see verses 271–273, 410–414 & 734–741).

The Italian, Christopher Columbus (1451–1506) sailed under the patronage of the Catholic Kings of Spain. He cleverly used the circular trade winds both to sail west, and to return eastwards. In addition to thinking he'd discovered Japan, he also thought Cuba was China.

The German, Martin Behaim, produced the first extant globe in 1492.

Vespucci would, 'ere long,
Prove his countryman quite wrong:
This 'New World' and the Far East weren't the same.
He asserted, for a start,
They were half a world apart.
'America' was soon to take his name.

The world had had to wait
Until 1498,
To finally reach India by ship.
Da Gama was astute:
Round Africa his route.
Two years later, he would make a second trip.

Our own king, too, commissions
An Italian's expeditions:
From England, Zuan Chabotto sailed away.
His first trip a false start
But, in time, he reached a part
Of the country that is Canada today.

This 'Newfoundland' proves alluring,
It has cod for the procuring:
Plentiful the shoals in this location.
Too important to ignore,
We're soon fishing there inshore:
This is seasonal, dependent on migration.

Though stocks of fish abound,
A method must be found
Of preserving what's so easily been caught.
Fish perish very fast,
And must be made to last:
It will take some time to reach an English port.

Light salting, washing, drying
Is the system we are trying.
This is done on land, once fishing boats are moored.
This met with the objective,
For the process was effective:
Cod are edible for years, once they've been cured.

These trips were later versions,
Of earlier excursions:
The regular Icelandic expedition.
It's a very well-stocked zone,
So in time we're not alone,
For the Hansa, and the French, are competition.

Amerigo Vespucci (1454–1512), an Italian sailing for Portugal, discovered Brazil in 1501. There is an alternative claim that America was named after a Bristol businessman, Richard Amerike.

In 1488, Bartolomeu Dias (c.1451–1500) had established the possibility of the sea route to the east. He rounded the Cape of Good Hope but did not continue into the Indian Ocean.

Vasco da Gama (c.1460s–1524).

Zuan Chabotto (John Cabot c.1450–c.1499) reached the north-west coast of North America in 1497. He had turned back without landing on the first of his three voyages. He worked out that, by following more northerly latitudes, he would reduce the distance to be travelled. He was sponsored by Henry VII.

There is a possibility that some Bristol merchants had successfully undertaken a similar trip shortly before this date.

The French, Spanish and Portuguese also fished off Newfoundland but preferred offshore areas. This pattern of where different nationalities preferred to fish would be echoed with whaling (see verse 395).

Fishing by the English was done in small boats using nets, or fishing baskets. Settlements were established, the biggest of these being St John's (now the capital of Newfoundland and Labrador).

The British continued to fish off Newfoundland until 1904, when the activity was turned over to the inhabitants of that province. It reached its height in the 18th century. It was conducted mainly from West Country ports.

For early methods of preserving fish see verses 131–133.

English fishermen were the first foreigners to travel to the coast of Iceland, starting in 1409. Large fleets from the north-east coast went there each year, and the English were so influential, the 1400s are sometimes referred to as 'The English Century' in Icelandic histories.

Competition led to armed conflicts, and the Hanseatic League (see verses 109–111) (with the support of the Danish king) eventually gained the upper hand. However, English fisheries in the area persisted for many centuries, culminating in the so-called 'Cod Wars' (see verses 1569–1575).

ON THE NEWFOUNDLAND FISHERIES

A brave desseigne it is, as Royall as Reall: as honourable as profitable. It promiseth renowne to the king, revenue to the Crowne, treasure to the kingdom, a purchase for the land, a prize for the sea, ships for navigation, navigation for ships, mariners for both, entertainment of the rich, employment for the poore, advantage for adventurers, and encrease of trade to all the subjects.

English merchant Edward Misselden, *The Circle of Commerce* (1623)

**Christopher Columbus
(Sebastiano del Piombo, 1519)**

**John Cabot
(Giustino Menescardi, 1762)**

All the shoals that can be found,
In a North Sea fishing ground,
Mean the herring buss is steadily encroaching.
We don't like this very much:
That sea's ours. It isn't Dutch!
And, in effect, these foreigners are poaching.

Onboard processing's arrived.
By a Zealander contrived.
Some innards and the gills are first removed.
These produce a bitter taste,
But the liver's not yet waste:
Its retention means the flavour is improved.

This method, known as gibbing,
Is something we'd be cribbing.
Fish are salted… barrelled… then they're left to cure.
And that Dutch boat called the buss,
Was of relevance to us:
This versatile design would long endure.

A bit more about maps

Men began to understand,
That a great big chunk of land,
Existed where none thought it had before.
They also formed the notion
Of another massive ocean:
All this Waldseemüller set about to draw.

'America' is shown
As a landmass on its own:
Though, in contrast to the known world's detailed sprawl,
Whilst the south part's clearly in,
It is looking rather thin,
And the northern bit is hardly there at all.

As the century progresses,
There are maps that feature guesses:
The cartographers invented things to fit.
But the English weren't faint-hearted
And left out what was uncharted,
Their map accurate – but missing quite a bit.

Australasia, don't forget,
Wasn't due to feature yet.
The Americas had put on loads of weight.
Our much better understanding,
Is the reason they're expanding,
For it can't have been the Big Macs that they ate.

North Sea herring were caught by means of drifting gill nets.

For protection, the Dutch fishing fleets (typically comprising 400–500 boats) were usually escorted by naval vessels.

Willem Beukelszoon devised gibbing in the 14th century.

The enzymes produced by a fish's liver (and pancreas) are essential for flavour.

There was one part salt to twenty fish in a barrel.

Busses were still being constructed in the early 19th century. Off season, they were used as merchant vessels. Their design was widely adapted.

A project was conducted at St Dié (near Strasbourg) to document, and update, new geographic knowledge.

Waldseemüller's map was produced in 1507. He called the 'New World' America: the first ever mention of the name in print.

Edward Wright (1561–1615) was an English mathematician and cartographer. Emery Molyneux (d.1598) made mathematical instruments, and also celestial and terrestrial globes. Based on one of Molyneux's terrestrial globes, Wright produced his 'A Chart of the World on Mercator's Projection' in around 1599 (see Plate A on page 61).

Macdonald's didn't introduce the Big Mac until 1967.

Waldseemüller's world map (1507)

Ships' bells

The first ship's metal bell,
As far as we can tell,
Was from China, and dates back to Bronze Age times.
Our records little yield,
'til the year of Bosworth Field,
When an English bell, aboard the *Grace Dieu*, chimes.

As a 'wache bell' it's referred,
And its clanging would be heard
For the purposes of keeping men from harm.
In emergencies, they knew
That they must alert the crew,
And the bell was used for sounding the alarm.

These bells are also working,
Lest another boat be lurking,
In conditions such as very murky fog.
Another of their beauties
Is to sound the times of duties,
From the first watch to the last one, called 'the dog'.

At Lloyd's, the Lutine Bell,
Bad tidings might foretell:
Struck once, it meant a ship was overdue.
If she hadn't come to grief,
Two dongs would bring relief:
Doubtless followed by a loud and collective 'Phew'!

The original *Grace Dieu*, (see verse 178), one of the largest wooden ships ever constructed, was destroyed by lightning in 1439.

The first recorded mention of a ship's bell was around 1485. Ten years later, an inventory of the *Regent* indicates that this English vessel carried two wache bells.

Some sources suggest that the soul of a ship was vested in its bell. Others say that a ship's soul resided in the figurehead.

Watches were timed using an hour glass. The system described is used in the Royal Navy. Merchant ships use a slightly different one, and there are other variations.

The end of the last watch is sounded by eight bells.

HMS *Lutine* (a captured French frigate) was wrecked off the Dutch coast in 1799 with a cargo of gold, silver and possibly also the Dutch crown jewels. Lloyd's paid out around £1 million within two weeks. The ship's bell was recovered in 1857, and has since hung in four successive Lloyd's underwriting rooms. Its use today is largely confined to ceremonial occasions.

For Lloyd's see verses 942–943.

The Lutine Bell housed in the Lloyd's building, City of London (1986)

3 The Tudors

3

The Tudors

Henry VII (*r.*1485–1509)

The dynastic wars have ended,
And two royal houses blended
When a new king, for his bride, a Yorkist chose.
This selection for a wife
Signalled 'no more civil strife':
The symbol is the famous Tudor rose.

Wars with France had left us weak,
But Henry now would seek
Prosperity. He carefully took stock.
He protected English trade,
And with ships a start was made
At Portsmouth, where he built our first dry dock...

... An important introduction,
That's required for ship construction.
(And very soon, yet more will be unveiled.)
First a log bed must be laid,
On which the keel is made,
Then a frame, to which the wooden planks are nailed.

Timber mustn't split or shrink,
When it's floating in the drink:
In a mast pond, lengths of wood would be immersed.
Once the sturdy English oak
Had enjoyed a nice long soak,
It was ready to withstand the ocean's worst.

Tools were not sophisticated...
Something sharpened and serrated
For cutting wood to suit its varied roles...
Axes... knives... red chalk...
Things for jamming in the caulk...
Adzes... and an auger to drill holes.

For pieces that were curved,
Rough cutting tools first served:
Lots of effort was required to hack and scrape.
But dampened wood will bend,
So a steam box meets this end:
Lengths can readily be fashioned into shape.

'The Wars of the Roses' (1455–1485) were fought between two rival branches of the House of Plantagenet – the houses of Lancaster and York. Henry of Lancaster, whose claim to the throne was tenuous, defeated Richard III at Bosworth Field in 1485.

Henry VII introduced strict navigation laws, including a provision that trade between England and the south of France could only be conducted in English ships, with English crews. The result was that English waters were safer than before – an effect that was undermined when Henry VIII started sanctioning privateers in the later years of his reign.

Work began on the dry dock, (now home to Nelson's flagship HMS *Victory*,) in 1495.

Wooden blocks, on which the keel was built, were placed on the smoothed and planked log bed. Initially, the beds were closed by earthen barriers, which took 20 men a month to remove. A sluice gate was introduced at Deptford by John Hawkins (1570s), which simplified matters. Dry docks are also needed for repair and maintenance.

Lengths of wood of up to 35 metres would be seasoned in ponds.

Typically a two-man saw would be used, but up to the Middle Ages, wood was cut with axes. Early cutting methods produced a great deal of waste wood.

The chalk, for marking timber, was oker, a reddish orange coloured mineral. Preparatory to caulking, a tool called a beetle was used to drive wedges into seams to force them open. Application required a caulking (or horsing) iron and mallet. Adzes shaped the timber, and wooden pins (nogs or treenails) were used to connect the parts.

It is uncertain when steam boxes were introduced, but they were around by the 17th century. They allowed wood to be bent following the grain, and were mainly used for smaller vessels. For ships, the branches of English oak were often trained, while the tree was still growing, into the required shape for knees etc.

For a ship to sail (and fight),
It must be watertight.
A leaky vessel very often sank.
To avoid this fatal glitch,
Boats were covered in hot pitch,
After oakum had been stuffed between each plank.

There were buildings round about:
Every ship needs fitting out.
All this involved a lot of varied tasks.
Craftsmen... unskilled troupers...
Riggers... caulkers... coopers,
(Most supplies aboard a ship were stored in casks).

Henry VIII (*r.*1509–1547)

The first Tudor's life is done.
He's succeeded by his son.
The eighth King Henry's ruling now instead.
The quest for power and glory,
Forms a large part of his story,
Along with all the ladies he would wed.

His father left him rich.
Frugal ways he sought to ditch,
Extravagance the watchword at his court.
The careful life he spurned;
For new Agincourts he yearned;
But was also fond of women, food and sport.

When past sea battles raged,
And two vessels were engaged,
Any shooting wasn't aimed at causing wrecks:
Guns were used as a distraction
From the imminence of action,
Which was fighting hand-to-hand upon the decks.

At the outset Henry chose,
To build the *Mary Rose*,
Equipped with guns no forerunner possessed.
From the vessels he'd inherited,
He thought that England merited
A navy, with which all would be impressed.

Another vessel, too –
The *Henry Grace à Dieu* –
Was more than just a flashy pleasure barge.
With gold it was bedecked,
And designed to earn respect:
Its firepower writ this message very large.

One of the many trades involved in shipbuilding was that of pitch-melter, who used a ladle. Oakum was made from mixing fibre (eg flax) with oil (eg pine oil). When ships were broken up, oakum was often recycled, (using a jerry iron) – a job which often fell to the inhabitants of prisons or workhouses.

Fitting out took place in wet docks.

Henry V's victory against the French at Agincourt was in 1415 (see verse 177).

Constructed between 1509 and 1511 at Portsmouth, the *Mary Rose* was named after Henry's younger sister.

England had had larger fleets in the past (eg around 700 ships in Edward III's reign), but these were not fighting ships. The navy numbered fifty-eight ships at the time of Henry VIII's death. The half dozen or so ships built under Henry VII *were* carracks and *were* fighting ships, but Henry VIII increased cannon power.

The *Henry Grace à Dieu* was also known as the *Great Harry*. Built in 1514, it was the largest warship in the world.

For hand-to-hand fighting (galley tactics) see verses 173 & 1235.

Mary Rose (from the 1st Anthony Roll)

Henry Grace à Dieu (from the 1st Anthony Roll)

On these ships, a new delight:
Gunports (hinged and watertight),
Meant the cannons could be set much lower down.
On gun decks they resided,
And ballast there provided.
It's no wonder that the fleet gained such renown.

Plus those ships with guns that fired,
Certain others were required:
His pinnaces had different roles to play,
They were light and small in size,
They could carry ships' supplies,
And messages between the fleet convey.

There is now an innovation,
To assist with navigation
In the waters by which England is surrounded,
To give 'pilotage' advice,
For where hazards might entice,
A fraternity of mariners is founded.

This very special guild,
Over time will help to build,
A system showing sailors where to go.
This arrangement now deploys,
Lots of lighthouses and buoys,
All of which the safest route will show.

William Gonson's stint is done.
The navy he has run
To all intents alone and single-handed.
For twenty years or so,
It has been a one-man show.
With no infrastructure, Henry's somewhat stranded.

Two years on, the problem's solved
For the Navy Board's evolved:
It has seven posts, supported by bureaucracy.
But its remit does exclude
The supply of arms and food;
In command of ships, it's still the aristocracy.

An Ordnance Office clerk
In his own way made his mark,
With a gesture that was really rather sweet,
To the monarch was donated
The 'roll' he'd illustrated:
It depicted every vessel in the fleet.

Master shipwright James Baker designed the means of mounting cannon at lower level, though Henry took the credit. The guns could fire broadside ie simultaneously. The term 'broadside' can also mean the side of a ship, or the battery of cannon on one side.

Ballast improves stability.

In addition to the carracks and galleys, more than a dozen galleasses (eg the *Antelope*) were constructed. In 1549, their oars were removed and they were re-classed as 'ships'.

The pinnace was a ship's boat, carried aboard larger vessels. Propelled by both oar and sail, these vessels could also scout for anchor points and carry armed men or passengers. The Dutch used them for raids, and the Spanish for smuggling activities.

In 1514, a Royal Charter was granted to the 'Guild of the Holy Trinity' 'so that they might regulate the pilotage (see verse 49) of the ships in the king's stream'. In 1604, James I conferred rights relating to the compulsory pilotage of shipping.

Henry also formalised 'flag signalling' methods. The first documented use was in 1530. The system was unwieldy. See verses 645–653 **Signalling**.

Shipping lanes were marked out using wooden floats (probably barrels coated in tar). (See verses 1054–1059 on **The Corporation of Trinity House**).

Gonson committed suicide in 1544. In his role of 'Keeper of the Storehouses at Erith and Deptford' he exercised control over almost every aspect of the king's navy.

Established in 1546, the Navy Board's members were known as the 'Principal Officers' of the navy. By 1548, there were 4 shipwrights and an anchor-smith on the payroll, as well as the likes of shipkeepers, clerks, storemen, guards, purveyors and chaplains.

An independent body, the Board of Ordnance was responsible for the armament of ships, and others were landed with the task of victualling. The first was Bishop Gardiner, who was known as 'Stephen Stockfish'.

The clerk's name was Anthony Anthony. The Anthony Roll was actually three rolls of vellum on which the ships, complete with flags, were shown. They were given to Henry in 1546. Two rolls were passed on to Samuel Pepys by Charles II in 1680, and are now at Magdalene College Cambridge. The third is in the British Museum.

Phenyx – a pinnace (from the 3rd Anthony Roll)

Embarkation of Henry VIII for the Field of the Cloth of Gold, 1520 (James Basire, 1775)

A diversion along London's river

Two dockyards Hal created,
Which in London were located,
At Deptford, and at Woolwich on the Thames.
For the former a hiatus
'Twixt obscurity and status:
A host of magic moments thereby stems.

It's here that Drake we'll find,
Aboard the *Golden Hinde*,
Being knighted by his queen for derring-do.
And another well-known bloke
Will be laying down his cloak,
On a puddle, lest she spoil her pretty shoe.

From a much much later year,
All Cook's ships had refits here.
The first of these was HM *Bark Endeavour*.
And Marlowe death would meet
In a pub along a street,
(His demise was neither maritime nor clever.)

On the Thames, another place
Was favoured by His Grace:
At Greenwich he could hunt and play... and more.
His lovely palace there,
Would fall into disrepair,
When the English with the English were at war.

But the borough fame has found,
And today is well renowned:
Its Old Naval College really can't be missed.
It retains a lovely park,
Displays the *Cutty Sark*,
And a Maritime Museum's on the list.

And WHEN would people be,
If it weren't for GMT?
And the north/south line by which the world's divided?
Some folk weren't that sure
Until 1884,
When the matter would be finally decided.

Woolwich was already home to the Royal Arsenal, which dates from 1471. The need to equip ships with guns was one of the reasons why Henry chose these locations. Another was that he liked to watch his ships being built, and proximity to his palace at Greenwich was an advantage. The dockyards eventually silted up, but remained important for repair work until their closure in 1869.

The story of Sir Walter Raleigh's gallant gesture is probably fictional but, if it happened at all, it happened in Deptford.

HM *Bark Endeavour* was originally an east coast collier named the *Earl of Pembroke*, which was refitted in 1768. All three of Captain Cook's ships (see verses 577–590) underwent Deptford refits. So did HMS *Bounty* (see verses 613–626) and many others.

The dramatist Christopher Marlowe was stabbed and killed in 1593, after a pub brawl over an unpaid bill.

The Greenwich 'Palace of Placentia' was built in 1447. Henry was born there in 1491, and it was also where he married two of his wives. The original Tudor palace, having served as a biscuit factory, and as a prisoner of war camp during the English Civil Wars (see verses 337–342), was then demolished.

Greenwich was declared a UNESCO World Heritage Site in 1997 and became a royal borough in 2012. The Old Naval College was formerly The Royal Hospital for Seamen established by Mary II after the Battle of La Hogue (1692) (see verse 438). It was designed by Sir Christopher Wren and was vacated by the Royal Navy in 1997.

The National Maritime Museum was opened by King George V in 1934. The Royal Observatory is part of this museum.

GMT stands for Greenwich Mean Time, alternatively referred to as 'Coordinated Universal Time' (UTC). The International Meridian Conference (1884) held in Washington DC voted for 0° longitude to be set at Greenwich. Until then, only 72 per cent of world commerce used sea charts based on this Prime Meridian. Standard time zones were gradually adopted thereafter.

Greenwich Palace or 'Palace of Placentia' (artist unknown)

The Old Royal Naval College with Queen Anne's House in the foreground

Back to the sixteenth century

For Spain, a five-strong fleet
Had a journey to complete –
The circumnavigation of the earth.
Just one ship and eighteen men,
Were to make it back again,
After sailing round the world's enormous girth.

Magellan and his team
Had embarked upon a dream.
For many, it would never be fulfilled.
Yes, it must have been terrific,
To get to the Pacific
But that is where a few of them were killed.

Unlike countries such as Spain,
In our King Henry's reign
At sending off explorers we weren't great,
Though to counter this low ebb,
A fellow known as Seb,
Looked for silver, somewhere near the River Plate.

There's a need for stimulation...
Some commercial inspiration...
For trade, we use the old familiar beat.
Wider markets, we're ignoring
Whilst some are off exploring,
And how, we'll wonder soon, can we compete?

William Hawkins (Henry's friend),
Was a man who bucked this trend.
To distant lands, he ventured forth to buy.
In Guinea he'd appear,
(Purchased ivory from here),
Next brazil wood (which contained a valued dye).

Henry should have been well placed
When an enemy he faced,
But wind's required before his navy sallies.
A breeze was sadly lacking,
When the French first came attacking:
And our static ships were faced with oar-powered galleys.

The encounter in the Solent
Left His Majesty quite dolent:
No triumph for his England would be notched.
Why it happened no one knows
But he lost the *Mary Rose*.
She sank, as poor old Henry stood and watched.

The expedition of Ferdinand Magellan (*c*.1480–1521) was from 1519–22. The *Victoria* was the only ship to return.

Three of Magellan's party, including Magellan himself, were killed at the Battle of Mactan in the Phillipines. The trip was completed by navigator Juan Sebastian Elcano.

Sebastian Cabot (son of John – see verse 211) planned to follow the course taken by Magellan (1525–28), but ended up in Rio de la Plata.

Following the first naval battle of the Second World War, the German pocket battleship, *Admiral Graf Spee*, was scuttled near here by her own captain (see verse 1448).

'The old familiar beat' refers to our trading principally with the Low Countries.

William Hawkins (*c*.1495–1554/5). Brazil wood was acquired (unsurprisingly) from Brazil, where Hawkins managed to circumvent the Portuguese embargo on foreign traders.

Henry VIII, who is known as 'the Father of the Royal Navy', called his fleet the 'Navy Royal'. The attacking French fleet was an invasion force, mustered in the Seine estuary.

The encounter in the Solent was in 1545. It is possible that the gun hatches on the *Mary Rose* hadn't been closed after the ship had attempted to ward off the French attack during this inconclusive battle. Henry might actually have been sitting as he watched from Southsea Castle.

Sebastian Cabot (S. Rawle after Hans Holbein, 1824)

The navy briefly on the wane again

Henry's son and elder daughter,
Lacked affinity with water.
Luckily, their reigns did not last long.
First a boy who'd soon expire...
Then a queen who played with fire...
The navy that they left was far from strong.

(Perhaps, in fairness to the kid,
There is something that he did:
Seb Cabot was recalled from lands afar.
His experience might aid
Certain sorties that were made,
To Guinea, and the court of Russia's Tsar.)

A company was started
To find places not yet charted:
The Northeast Passage lured the brave and bold.
Finding China might entice,
But one ship got trapped in ice,
And the men aboard all perished in the cold.

So our navy's now bereft –
Only twenty-six ships left,
Their condition poor, because they've been neglected.
There'd be more years of stagnation –
Such a sorry situation
Needed one day soon to quickly be corrected.

Enter now our 'Good Queen Bess'
Who found England in a mess;
There was lots to do, and much that needed sorting,
Religion for a start,
Was tearing things apart:
Which left little time for building ships – or courting.

The Elizabethan 'Sea Dogs'

The Pope (his guide divine)
On the map had drawn a line,
To demarcate a 'New World' who owns what.
Spain received all to the west,
And Portugal the rest.
Other nations do not feature in this plot.

Iberia was strong,
So with this we went along,
But from Rome, the English now are firmly split.
What the Pope says doesn't count,
And a challenge we'll soon mount:
Tordesillas we'll ignore as we see fit.

Edward VI reigned 1547–53. His uncle, Thomas Seymour, was in effectual charge of the navy as Edward's first Lord Admiral, and ran a gang of pirates from the Scilly Islands. This was not exactly compatible with controlling lawlessness at sea.

Mary I reigned 1553–58. Mary is notorious for her fanatical Catholicism, and for burning so-called heretics at the stake. Married to Phillip II of Spain, she was opposed to maintaining a fleet that could attack Spanish vessels.

Sebastian Cabot had been working for the Spanish and Portuguese Crowns, and mariners such as Thomas Wyndham and John Locke were seeking to engage in trade with Guinea.

Sir Hugh Willoughby, Richard Chancellor and Cabot formed the 'Mystery and Company of Merchant Adventurers for the discovery of Regions, Dominions, Islands and Places unknown' in 1551. This was the forerunner of the Muscovy Company, rechartered in 1555. (See illustration with verse 274.)

Willoughby and the crew aboard the *Bona Esperanza* all froze to death after sheltering in a bay on the Kola Peninsula, to the east of Murmansk.

Britain's navy consisted of only twenty-four vessels in 1575, but by then a new purpose-built dockyard had been established at Chatham.

Elizabeth I reigned 1558–1603.

Thomas Seymour in later life (Nicolas Denisot, *c.*1545–49)

The Treaty of Tordesillas was signed in 1494. This would have important implications, as it restricted Spanish activities in West Africa, the future source of slaves. They would therefore have to 'contract' for these labourers (see verse 457 on the 'Asiento').

Henry VIII had been excommunicated by Pope Clement over the issue of his divorce from Catherine of Aragon (1533) and the Church of England, headed by the monarch, had been established in 1534 by the Acts of Supremacy.

It takes no smart detective,
To guess they'd be protective,
And against the would-be interloper guard.
But until the first attacks,
Spain in fact had proved quite lax:
To seize those first few vessels wasn't hard.

We seek not now attrition...
Lack colonial ambition
(Which will follow for the European powers)...
But we're starting to prepare
To nab a healthy share:
The right to bag some loot was surely ours?

Of new countries (and their gold),
Spain by now had taken hold.
Argentina for its silver would be named.
Mexico, Peru,
And Paraguay too –
By degrees, some ancient empires had been tamed.

We couldn't fail to note
What was coming back by boat,
With all the tales of riches that we'd hear,
Some wanted 'in', and so,
The likes of Drake and co,
Set off westwards, in the role of privateer.

This status of theirs meant,
That they had the queen's consent,
To purloin whatever treasure could be seized.
With assistance of brigades
Of locals, there were raids
On the Spanish who, to say the least, weren't pleased.

In 1568
Things start to escalate,
When the Spanish contravene a local truce.
Their flota turned pursuer
Out of San Juan de Ulúa,
And subjected English sailors to abuse.

We'd been taken by surprise,
Hadn't loaded up supplies,
And headed off with insufficient food.
Men must thus be sent ashore,
(There faced treatment to deplore).
This, in England, fuelled the anti-Spanish mood.

Henry VIII, in the last years of his reign, had sanctioned attacking Spanish vessels and, in so doing, had opened the door to increased piracy around English shores.

The first reference to the name Argentina was in 1602. The ancient empires were notably those of the Aztecs in Mexico and the Incas in Peru. Sir Francis Drake (c.1540–1596).

A privateer is a private person (or ship) acting under a letter of marque from a government, allowing him to attack enemy ships during wartime. England did not, however, go to war against Spain until 1585 (and even then, not officially) (see verses 287–311).

A pirate does not operate under government licence, and will raid and plunder any ship. The term buccaneer generally applies to privateers, operating in the Caribbean and attacking only ships of other nations.

Although many Spanish ships were intercepted at sea, some treasure-snatching happened on land, where the natives' knowledge of the terrain was particularly helpful.

The Battle of San Juan de Ulúa (in modern day Veracruz, Mexico) was in 1568. A flota is a Spanish fleet. In this context, it was part of a convoy system which carried goods and passengers between Spain and its American empire.

John Hawkins and his cousin, Francis Drake, never forgave the Spanish for their betrayal. They had been in a party of six ships on a slave run from Guinea, and only one ship, the *Minion*, and about twenty crew managed to make it back to England.

Sir Francis Drake, *c.1590*   Sir Walter Raleigh, 1588

Sir Martin Frobisher, 1577   Sir Richard Grenville, 1571

Most especially with Raleigh,
The queen was very pally,
Though he wasn't quite as handsome as reputed.
The hoards each 'Sea Dog' offers,
Help to fill the royal coffers,
As Spanish treasure steadily gets looted.

And what, you may now wonder,
Did they do, as well as plunder?
Hawkins' exploits weren't especially glorious:
He traversed the ocean's waves,
In ships he filled with slaves,
So today he's not just famous – but notorious.

Triangular this trade,
Whereby three stops would be made:
First in Africa, where goods were swapped for men.
Who were taken – not in style –
To some Caribbean isle,
In the knowledge that they'd not see home again.

Next, produce from plantations,
Reached the European nations,
Which were keen to turn molasses into rum.
Then, with guns and cloth and more,
Back to Africa's west shore...
A profit-making enterprise for some.

Ventures – doomed to fail –
Sought all traders' 'holy grail':
To eastern lands a 'Northwest Passage' way.
But as lots of ice had formed,
(By climate change unwarmed),
They needed not a vessel but a sleigh.

Frobisher sailed forth,
Into the frozen north,
Where some before had perished in the cold.
Though his trip was no success,
He returned there nonetheless,
As some backers thought he'd found a source of gold.

Grenville sought a place,
For a military base:
On establishing a settlement intent.
North America the host,
On an island near the coast:
A group of would-be colonists was sent.

Sir Walter Raleigh (c.1554–1618) was a great favourite of the queen until she discovered he had secretly married one of her ladies-in-waiting. Despite the efforts of the 'Sea Dogs' a huge amount of treasure nevertheless did reach Spain. The Portuguese, who had steadily been strengthening their position in Brazil, were not immune from English attack.

Admiral Sir John Hawkins (1532–1595) was also a shipbuilder/designer, navigator, naval administrator and spy. From one of his voyages he brought back a shark, which was exhibited in London in 1569. He was the son of William Hawkins of Plymouth (see verse 253).

He should also be remembered for ship designs which resulted in improved manoeuvrability and, along with Drake, for the establishment of a charity (in 1590) for the relief of sick and elderly mariners, the work of which (with an extended remit) continues to this day.

Hawkins' first voyage with slaves (301 Africans from Sierra Leone, who had been captured from a hijacked Portuguese ship) was in 1555. This prompted Spain to ban English ships from trading in their West Indies colonies. Before the development of the triangular slave trade, captured men were exchanged for silver or gold.

Later (and alternative) triangular trade routes included a stop in 'New England' in North America, instead of in Europe. Each triangular trip took between five and twelve weeks to complete. See verses 410–414 & 734–741 on the Slave Trade.

Welsh explorer Captain Thomas James (1593–1635) embarked upon a two-year voyage to discover the Northwest Passage in 1631 aboard the *Henrietta Maria*, and is said to have been the inspiration for Coleridge's *Rime of the Ancient Mariner* (see verse 417).

The Northwest Passage is a sea route through the Arctic Ocean comprising a number of waterways. Roald Admundsen was the first to navigate it (between 1903–6).

Sir Martin Frobisher (c.1535–1594) returned with pyrite ('Fool's Gold'), but the fact that one assayer thought his black pebble might be gold bearing was enough to attract new investment.

Sir Richard Grenville (1542–1591) chose Roanoke Island off the coast of what is now North Carolina.

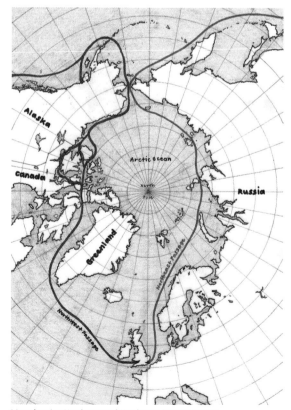

Map showing Northeast and Northwest Passage routes

New lives they couldn't hack,
So Drake would bring them back:
With a new bunch Grenville later was to try.
But what was really weird,
Is they all then disappeared,
The questions are to where, and how, and why?

With colonial ambition,
Another expedition
Was led by one whose life the trip would cost.
Humphrey Gilbert was his name...
To Newfoundland staked our claim...
Then his ship went down and every hand was lost.

Raleigh had been told
Of a city, rich with gold:
Venezuela and Guyana he explored.
His account, full of bravado,
Helped the myth of 'El Dorado',
Though he never found his precious metal hoard.

Tobacco was his 'friend':
He established quite a trend,
The habit one in which he oft delighted.
And whilst his pipe was smoking,
He sometimes got a soaking,
Drenched by those who thought he'd suddenly ignited.

Roanoke is known as 'The Lost Colony'. It was abandoned between August 1587 and August 1590. See Plate B on page 113 for map of Roanoke Island.

In 1583, Harbour Grace in Newfoundland had become a permanent settlement, making it the first in North America.

English fishermen had started visiting Newfoundland waters c.1512. They dried their catches ashore (see verse 214) and, by 1550, a permanent seasonal community existed.

Sir Humphrey Gilbert (c.1539–1583) spent many years in Ireland (which was being colonized by England), before heading for the North American continent. His ship, the *Squirrel*, sank and the event was witnessed by those aboard the *Golden Hinde*.

Like his half-brother Gilbert, Raleigh spent much of his early career in Ireland. It is likely that potatoes, sent from North America (probably by Hawkins in 1563 or 1565), reached Ireland before being introduced into England.

El Dorado ('The Golden One') was a tribal chief in Columbia but, over time, the term became an imaginary empire, and a second location (Venezuela) was inferred from rumours. There were, however, gold deposits in some of the places he visited.

Despite Raleigh's being credited with bringing tobacco to England, John Hawkins had introduced the substance from North America to England c.1565.

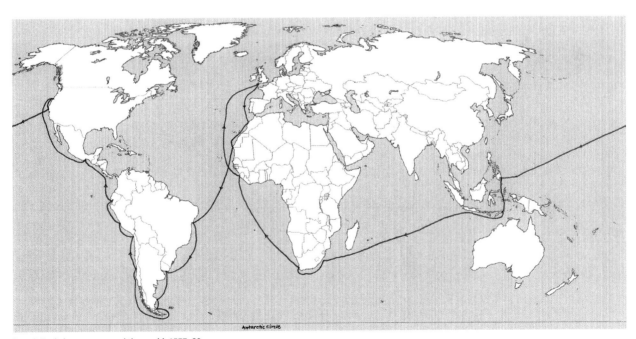

Francis Drake's voyage around the world, 1577–80

Francis Drake could boast,
That America's west coast
He had shadowed, on his well known round world trip.
The queen was so excited,
That the man was promptly knighted,
On his equally renowned and hardy ship.

He'd have used a traverse board,
A gadget to record
The direction and the speed a ship was going.
It had pegs and it had strings
And eight concentric rings.
(As for longitude, as yet no means of knowing.)

Emulating Drake,
Tom Cavendish would take
An ambitious route: his ship with loot was stuffed.
A whole year's Spanish hoard,
Was the prize he took on board,
So once again, the queen was rather chuffed.

On trip two, the final curtain:
Why he died remains uncertain.
His navigator back to England came.
What he found along the way,
Are still making news today:
To The Falklands, Argentina still lays claim.

The year Drake found Cape Horn,
A chap named William Bourne
Designed a craft, unlike the world had seen.
Though his plan remained a plan,
All credit to the man:
He'd designed what we now call a submarine.

Some forty odd years later,
The work of this creator
Was constructed and propelled by means of oar.
In the centuries ahead,
Subs provoked a sense of dread,
As deadly stealthy instruments of war.

Drake's voyage around the world was 1577–80 and he raided Spanish treasure ships on the way. He was knighted in 1581. The *Golden Hinde* was a galley built for speed at Aldeborough, Suffolk. Originally called *Pelican*, it was renamed after Drake had rounded Cape Horn.

The traverse board was used in dead reckoning navigation and showed thirty-two compass points. Each watch logged the necessary information, though there was considerable room for error with this system.

See verses 510–521 on **Determining Longitude**.

Thomas Cavendish (1560–1592) raided the Spanish ship *Santa Ana* in 1587 near the Baja California peninsula, north-west Mexico.

Cavendish's navigator was John Davis, who went on to develop the Davis Quadrant, a version of the back staff (see verse 503).

See verses 1648–1664 on **The Falklands War, 1982**. The islands were annexed by the Royal Navy in 1833.

Drake found Cape Horn in 1578.

Leonardo da Vinci had designed a craft for underwater use, which he called 'a ship to sink another ship'. It has been demonstrated that this was incapable of functioning. Later attempts were designed at first as exploratory boats, and their potential for use against an enemy was only later reconsidered (see verses 922–933 **Submarines**).

The creator of the oared submersible was Cornelis Drebbel, a Dutchman in the employ of James I. He built three versions between 1620 and 1624, the last two of which were successfully tested. The first had six pairs of oars.

Winston Churchill once said that, if Germany had not had U-boats, he would never have doubted that Britain would win the war.

Drebbel's submersible on the River Thames

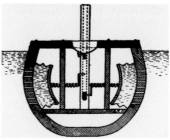

Cross-section of Bourne's submersible, 1578

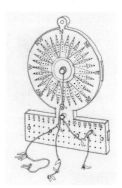

Traverse board

The Anglo-Spanish War, 1587–1604

Because of royal backing,
For the looting and attacking,
(And because we'd helped the Netherlands as well),
The King of Spain got tough –
He said, 'Enough's enough!
England is a nation I must quell.'

Though war was undeclared,
He had to be prepared,
(And making ready didn't take that long.)
His shipwrights worked with speed,
To provide what he would need,
And soon his fleet was sixty carracks strong.

A cunning plan we hatched,
And 'El Drago' was despatched,
To do something which might thwart, or cause delay.
No wonder he was feared,
For he 'singed King Phillip's beard',
By sinking lots of ships in Cádiz Bay.

Drake's tactical attack
Had set preparations back:
Destroying all those ships and their supplies.
Now Philip is to lose
His commander, Santa Cruz,
When this admiral unfortunately dies.

The Duke who takes his place,
(Must feel sorry for His Grace),
Is a soldier, whose experience is lacking
For a mission of this kind,
But Philip doesn't mind:
He's confident the Spanish have God's backing.

The Spanish Armada, 1588

By our antics merely flustered,
His resources he re-mustered,
One year later, the Armada would set sail.
Our country – with breath bated –
Gathered vessels and then waited…
In this contest, would we win or would we fail?

Spain's fleet was slow to start,
(For the weather played its part).
Two months later, all the hype was slowly sapping.
Then in Plymouth (for supplies),
We were taken by surprise:
The Armada very nearly caught us napping.

In 1585, Queen Elizabeth had stated that 'privateers were at liberty to attack Spanish shipping'.

Modern day Holland, Belgium and Luxembourg were part of the Spanish empire ('The Spanish Netherlands'). With help from England, the Dutch effectively gained independence and, in the 17th century, would become England's major rival in terms of trade and colonization.

War against Spain was never formally declared.

The Spanish referred to Drake as 'El Drago' (The Dragon). Queen Elizabeth rescinded her orders to Drake, but did not do so in time to stop him. The 'singeing of the beard of the King of Spain' resulted in the loss of twenty-two to thirty-three carracks (April 1587).

Álvaro de Bazán, 1st Marquis of Santa Cruz de Mudela, was a skilled admiral. He died in February 1588. His replacement was the Duke of Medina Sidonia, who carried out Philip's plans to the letter – often ignoring the advice of his very able second-in-command, whose approach was more opportunistic.

A series of beacons was created, the lighting of which would signal that the Armada had been sighted.

Drake's attack on Cádiz

Along the Channel chased,
Our speedy ships made haste.
There were inconclusive skirmishes en route.
Guns fired to no effect:
Abject failure to connect,
For no one's ships came near enough to shoot.

The *Rosario* was lost,
Which would prove to Spain's great cost.
With another Spanish ship, it had collided.
Not the blithest of collisions:
It was loaded with provisions.
'We'll go and loot it!' Francis Drake decided.

In doing so, he'd find
How such ships had been designed.
He knew their guns weren't easily reloaded.
(Very soon, in battle proper,
When Spain's fleet comes a cropper,
Its ammunition's mainly unexploded.)

For its era quite high tech,
An Elizabethan wreck
With cannons – all of standard sizes kitted –
Has been found. Now some allege
That our gunners had the edge,
As they didn't have to seek a ball that fitted.

The Armada we'd been dreading,
To the Isle of Wight is heading.
To settle in the Solent is the aim.
Safe, an army to await –
Invasion, England's fate! –
We do our best to spoil this little game.

Our sea dogs soon hold sway,
Drive the Spanish ships away.
In Calais, these hole up in strong formation.
This crescent shape holds steady,
But the troops are not yet ready,
Which causes quite a lot of consternation.

Our sailors, in the night,
Set some English ships alight,
(These aren't 'hellburners', but give the same illusion.)
The trick is all that matters.
Spain's defence now quickly scatters:
As those aboard cut anchors in confusion.

Designed by John Hawkins, the English navy included about twenty race-built galleons. Developed from the carrack, these had a lowered forecastle (which reduced wind resistance) and an elongated hull. They were exclusively wind-powered. A number were built by master shipwright Mathew Baker, (son of James Baker, see verse 236), who was the first to put on paper the practice of shipbuilding.

The Spanish out-gunned the English by 50 per cent, though the English had a five times faster rate of fire, and more ships (200:130).

Looting the *Rosario* was useful because, by now, the English were running low on supplies and explosives. Queen Elizabeth was unable and unwilling to send more. The fact that much of Spain's ammunition remained unused was later confirmed when a Spanish shipwreck was found off the coast of Ireland. The invention of the blast furnace had enabled easier production of armaments.

A pinnace with twelve cannons has recently been found off the Channel Islands. It sank in 1592 and may have seen action during the Armada. Its 'super guns' had an amazing one-mile range. Standardization on other English ships of the time cannot necessarily be deduced from this discovery, so they may still have carried the (then) usual bewildering array of cannons of all types and sizes.

Lord Howard of Effingham (1536–1624) was in overall command. Drake and John Hawkins were Vice Admiral and Rear Admiral respectively. The likes of Frobisher were also key players.

The Duke of Parma had been charged with assembling a 30,000 strong army in the Spanish Netherlands.

Ordinary ships were sacrificed to trick the Spanish off Calais.

'Hellburners' were specialised fire ships filled with gunpowder.

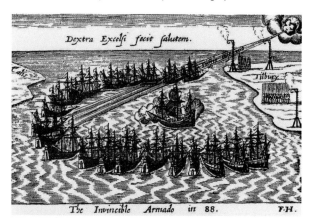

The Armada off Calais (artist unknown)

Sir John Hawkins (artist unknown, 1581)

Their ships are well dispersed,
The weather does its worst.
A southwesterly is blowing, right on cue.
Not the strongest type of storm,
But the Spanish can't re-form,
In spite of all their efforts so to do.

Thus, in fortune's fickle tide,
The fates seem on our side,
Near Gravelines the English ships close in.
In a bloody eight hour fight,
We get our tactics right,
And, in battle, just about achieve a win.

In large part thanks to Drake,
We'd known that it would take,
Much too long for all their guns to be re-packed.
The English do just fine:
Aim below the waterline –
Which weakens ships whenever they are whacked.

As each English shot connects,
Our foes are thinking 'decks'.
They plan to fight according to tradition.
It's a scheme that's badly flawed,
For they cannot get on board.
This in part explains the failure of their mission.

With success within our reach,
Our monarch makes a speech.
Great victory her navy soon will bring.
A brave queen's at the helm,
Telling all, 'Hands off my realm!'
That she has 'the heart and stomach of a king'.

A blow for Spain's been landed,
And the fleet is somewhat stranded.
Their sailors think, 'Whatever's to be done?'
In the choppy grey North Sea
Isn't where they'd planned to be:
They're far from home, pursued, and on the run.

They are chased much further north,
Up to the Firth of Forth.
They're using chains to hold ships' hulls together.
They struggle on and on.
Too far leeward they have gone.
And now they're at the mercy of the weather.

The English victory came just as ammunition had run out but, by then, five Spanish ships were lost, and many others were severely damaged.

A major lesson from the ill-fated Armada expedition was that hand-to-hand fighting on decks was not the way to engage the enemy.

Part of Queen Elizabeth's famous 'Tilbury Speech' has been slightly paraphrased!

The English pursuit of the Armada was a tactical measure.

'Leeward' means in the direction the wind is blowing, in this case northeastwards. ('Windward' is into the wind.)

For Spain, the crews all yearn;
But there'll be no quick return:
Round Scotland and round Ireland is their route.
Their vessels – worse for wear –
Need attention and repair,
And some anchors have been jettisoned to boot.

Strong and chilly gales,
Are filling Spanish sails.
Ships are wrecked. There is no water and no food.
King Philip is sent word,
Of all that has occurred,
Which puts him in a pretty awful mood.

Those who made it back still die,
(Disease the reason why).
There is no happy ending to this story.
It's tedious. It's war,
And though both sides try to score,
Neither wins the triumph, or the glory.

At odds, we would remain,
Throughout Queen Bess's reign;
That breakthrough in the struggle proved elusive.
Hostilities would cease,
When James the First made peace,
But, as things turned out, it wasn't that conclusive.

The century would end,
With an increased trading trend.
James Lancaster had visited Malaya.
Deals in India, what's more,
In 1594,
Mean that Portugal's not now the only player.

And James knew that lemon juice,
Had a most important use
Treating scurvy – and a cure was badly needed.
For on long trips overseas,
Many died of this disease.
The report he wrote would sadly go unheeded.

In addition to about 8,000 sailors, there were 18,000 soldiers aboard the Armada's 130 ships. Only sixty-seven ships, and about 10,000 men, made it back to Spain.

The missing anchors had been cut in Calais.

1588 was during the period known as 'The Little Ice Age'.

Phillip is quoted as saying, 'I sent the Armada against men, not God's winds and waves'.

English losses in battle were relatively light (an estimated fifty to one hundred men), but many died later of disease.

In 1589, a Drake-Norris expedition failed to incite a Portuguese revolt against the Spanish. In 1596 and 1597, two further Armadas sent by Spain fell victim to storms.

James I concluded the Treaty of London (1604) between the two countries, but England and Spain were at war again in 1625, despite James's best efforts to preserve peace.

In 1591, James Lancaster (c.1554–1618) undertook the first great voyage to the East Indies, including the Malay peninsula. His trading and diplomatic skills succeeded in breaking the Portuguese spice trade monopoly in India. In 1600, he was given command of the East India Company's first fleet.

He issued the men on his ship, *Red Dragon*, bottled lemon juice (1601), which contains vitamin C, the lack of which causes scurvy. The value of citrus fruit, to both prevent and treat the disease, was not to be fully recognised for a further 200 or so years (see verses 385–389).

ROUTES OF THE ARMADA
X Fights in the channel
Wrecks

Sir James Lancaster (artist unknown, 1596)

Saxon Shore, showing Roman fortifications (produced in 1436)

Matthew Paris's map of Britain (13th century)

Anglo-Saxon Mappa Mundi, showing Britain (on its side) in a European context (created in Canterbury, 1025–1050)

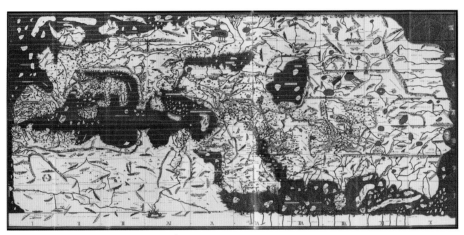

Tabula Rogeriana (Muhammad al-Idrisi, 1154)

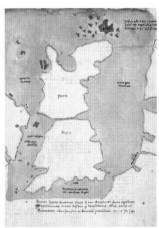

Ptolemy map of Britain (Emanuel Chrysoloras and Jacobus Angelus, first half of 15th century)

Typus Angliae map, showing Queen Elizabeth and her domains (Jodocus Hondilus, 1590)

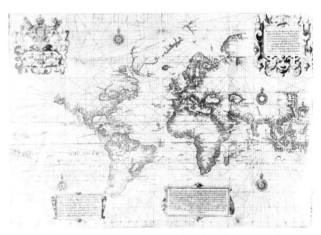

A Chart of the World on Mercator's Projection (Wright-Molyneux, c.1599)

4 The seventeenth century

4

The seventeenth century

James I: the beginnings of colonisation

The monarch who will rule
Has been dubbed the 'wisest fool':
The 'Union of Crowns' is now complete.
Though two navies still remain,
From the outset, it is plain
That they'll operate as though one single fleet.

There's a flag that is brand new
Crossed with red and white on blue
Which the king himself reputedly designed.
Thus Saint Andrew and Saint George,
In combination forge
An image as iconic as you'll find.

What we'd learned from the Armada
Was 'We really must try harder',
Though our sailors had proved skilful, shown such pluck.
Our way of life could vanish:
We might all be speaking Spanish,
If we hadn't had a massive dose of luck.

Would the message now be heeded
That a robust navy needed
Proper funding – both substantial and sustained?
That, when threats we must rebuff,
Ships alone were not enough:
Crews had to be experienced and trained...?

Plus, if this were England's goal,
Then there had to be a role
For an infrastructure, organizing things?
The answer (have you guessed?),
Was a, 'Not keen to invest'
From England's next disinterested kings.

King James (although in vain),
Tried to keep the peace with Spain,
But his reign would see colonial success.
Brits settled, and would stay,
In James Towne, USA,
A start from which we'd steadily progress.

James VI of Scotland became James I of England (1603–1625), (and also sat on the throne of Ireland.) He earned the epithet 'The wisest fool in Christendom'. The two nations would not become one entity until the 1707 Acts of Union (when Great Britain was formed), and Ireland joined what became the United Kingdom later still.

A jack is a small version of a national flag flown at the bow of a vessel in harbour to indicate its nationality. The claim that the Union Flag is only properly referred to as the Union Jack when in naval use, was disputed by The Flag Institute (London) in 2013. The present day design of the flag, including the diagonal red cross of St Patrick, dates from a Royal Proclamation following the union of Great Britain and Ireland in 1801.

The 1604 Treaty of London provided, *inter alia*, secure shipping lanes for Spanish treasure fleets.

In 1618, Sir Walter Raleigh was executed as an act of appeasement towards the Spanish.

The Virginia Company of London established a colony in 1607. It has been said that this is where the British Empire started. Jamestown (which no longer exists as a settlement) was given its name in 1619, and in the same year, the first Africans arrived on a Portuguese ship as 'indentured servants' (ie slaves). America was not at the time called the USA.

The Union Flag (1606–1707 for ships at sea and, from 1707–1801, in England and Scotland)

The Union Flag (adopted in 1801)

In Bermuda we arrived,
All were wet – but all survived.
There were sailors, would-be settlers, plus one dog.
Their ship was run aground,
And a new place thus was found.
It was full of pigs – the famed 'Bermuda hog'.

The *Mayflower* is the boat,
That we now move on to note.
Aboard, 'the Pilgrim Fathers' travelled west.
They'd tried Holland, but felt stranded,
A new Plymouth's where they landed;
Freedom of religion was their quest.

Next, a native 'king' permits
Us, to settle in St Kitts;
By the French, the population was soon swelled.
The locals planned a raid,
But their secret was betrayed:
Some were massacred and others were expelled.

Then the French, once invitees,
Decided they would seize
The English parts. From these we were ejected.
It didn't take that long,
To right this awful wrong.
By a treaty, this would shortly be corrected.

A pattern was emerging:
When armies were converging
In Europe, other places were affected.
Hostilities back home,
Would reach across the foam,
And enmities would thereby be reflected.

St Kitts was not immune.
Yet again it would be strewn
With evidence of Europe's conflagration.
(When the French next took up arms,
They destroyed the English farms.
The result was economic devastation.)

This tale's an illustration
Of a type of oscillation:
An island gained, then lost, then repossessed.
Even nicely managed change
Is resisted, as it's strange –
Leaving those who think they're settled quite distressed.

In 1609, Sir George Somers deliberately drove the *Sea Venture* onto the reefs off Bermuda in order to save those on board. One hundred and fifty people and their canine companion landed. The ship, on its way to Virginia, had become separated from the rest of the fleet in a storm. St George's, Bermuda, was founded in 1612. Bermuda is sometimes known as the Somers Islands.

England's first colonial ventures were in Ireland where, following the English Reformation, a policy of plantation had been pursued in the 16th century, with Protestant English and Scottish settlers ousting Catholic landowners.

To escape religious intolerance in England, the group of Puritans had first sought refuge in The Netherlands, but feared they would lose their identity there. They settled (1620) in what is now Plymouth, Massachusetts. Further English settlements followed in New Hampshire (1623), Maryland (1632), Conneticut (1633), Rhode Island (1636), North Carolina (1663), Delaware, New Jersey and New York (1664), South Carolina (1670), and Pennsylvania (1681).

Sea captain Sir Thomas Warner, welcomed by the leader of the Kalinago peoples, established an English colony on the island of St Kitts in 1624. He later took pity on stranded would-be French settlers, who occupied either end. St Kitts was both England's, and France's, first Caribbean settlement. When the island's native inhabitants turned against them, the settlers made a pre-emptive strike at what is now called Bloody Point (1626).

During the Thirty Years' War, a Spanish naval expedition was sent to St Kitts, and seized the island from the English and French (1629). This was in retaliation for the farcical Cádiz expedition, led by Sir Edward Cecil, against the Spanish. The English settlement was rebuilt following the peace treaty concluded a year later. The island became prosperous by growing tobacco, but later switched to sugar production. France took control during the second Anglo-Dutch War (1665–67). Under the Peace of Breda, English possessions were returned to their owners. During the War of the Grand Alliance (1689–97), the island changed hands twice. The status quo was restored by the Treaty of Rijswijk. The pattern of alternating control ended in 1783, with the island's affiliation to Great Britain.

After St Kitts, the English went on to establish settlements in Barbados (1627), Nevis (1628), Antigua and Montserrat (1632), and Eleuthra (the Bahamas) (1648).

The *Mayflower* in Plymouth Harbour (William Halsall, 1882)

Britain's navy in decline

Sundry quests for former glories,
Were naught but nightmare stories:
Our navy was shambolic and decayed.
Merchant ships weren't oft recruited
(Their design for war unsuited),
And our sailors were not fed, and were not paid.

The Dutch are to the fore,
Commercially secure,
From the Baltic to Iberia commanding.
Their Asian interests, too,
Significantly grew
And produced the spice that people were demanding.

From this, don't be assuming
That our businesses weren't blooming:
A lot of English merchants did just fine.
From America had come
Prosperity for some –
Despite the British navy's sad decline.

Charles I (*r.*1625–1649)

Of cash, King Charles was short:
He decided to resort
To an ancient tax – 'Ship Money' – which was collected
Initially with ease,
So he tried a further squeeze.
Unsurprisingly, his subjects soon objected.

They saw it as a ruse,
Which the crown sought to abuse:
(Parliament's consent was not obtained).
It was levied without cause:
(We weren't fighting any wars),
Thus, in part, the civil wars can be explained.

Some vessels were constructed
With the cash he had deducted,
And one of these could not have been much finer:
This 'first-rated' standards met,
Was the work of Peter Pett,
Son of Phineas, the talented designer.

Showy vessels such as this,
A major point would miss:
They could not assist where help was needed most.
Folk were being caught,
From the ship and from the port,
By the corsairs, who attacked our south-west coast.

The navy was so ineffectual in policing our seas that estimates suggest that, between 1622 and 1642, 300 ships and 7,000 plus people were captured by pirates. Barbary pirates had periodically been taking sailors from fishing vessels off Devon and Cornwall, and had also enslaved populations from coastal villages, an activity which intensified in the early 17th century.

Originally to be collected only from coastal areas, and only in the event of war, ship money was now demanded from inland areas.

The ship designed by Peter Pett (1610–?1672) was the *Sovereign of the Seas* (launched 1637). Possibly better known, was his father, shipwright Phineas Pett (1570–1647). The latter, and Mathew Baker (see verse 294), had been bitter rivals.

Ships' ratings, in relation to the number of guns carried, began in 1751. First-rated vessels had most (at least one hundred). Sixth-rated had fewer than thirty-two.

Sovereign of the Seas (J. Payne – contemporaneous engraving)

It will be a good few years,
'Ere this nuisance disappears,
But happily the threats in time did cease.
The Berbers were defeated,
And the task was then completed
With agreements that secured a lasting peace.

Ships' ratings once concerned
The pay their captains earned,
But guns aboard would later be the scheme.
Had they few? Or had they plenty?
(A sixth rate might have twenty).
With a hundred plus, the first rates reigned supreme.

Ships' features were quite classic;
The format would stay static –
For decades hence, essentially unchanged.
Three masts that pierced the air,
The sails were always square.
Through port holes all the cannons were arranged.

The English Civil Wars, 1642–46, 1648–9 and 1649–51

Charles had overstepped the mark,
So his country would embark
On a period of hard-fought civil war.
The 'Roundhead' would appear,
Versus Royalist 'Cavalier'
At Edgehill, Naseby, Worcester, Marston Moor.

For such battles to be fought,
Lots of arms must first be bought
And the source of these was largely continental.
Both factions need supplies,
So it's not hard to surmise
That control of English ports was fundamental.

Hull, where armaments were stashed,
Was the place two sides first clashed:
It was twice besieged – and Charles's troops twice failed.
Way down in the south west,
Was where the king fared best:
So in Dartmouth and in Bristol he prevailed.

But his country he had bled...
From his capital he'd fled...
Parliament of London was in charge.
And he really felt deflated
When the fleet that he'd created,
Defected from its monarch – by and large.

By the 1670s and 1680s, the Royal Navy was strong enough to inflict a series of defeats against the raiders (see also verses 742–748 **The Bombardment of Algiers, 1816**).

By the mid 17th century, the design of warships was well established, and there would be no major technological break-throughs until the beginning of the 19th century.

Charles I believed in 'The Divine Right of Kings', and refused to answer to parliament. Having dismissed parliament for the third time, he resorted to raising money by imposing illegal taxes (such as Ship Money), and to selling monopolies.

Arms came principally from France and Holland. Control of ports was also important because of the possibility that troops from others countries, in support of Charles, might be landed.

Armaments were held in Hull following a campaign against a Scottish invasion.

The Royalists also held the important coal port of Newcastle until 1644, when their defeat at Marston Moor led to a loss of control in the north east. The city was taken by Scottish anti-Royalist Covenanters.

Against the king's wishes, Parliament appointed Robert Rich, 2nd Earl of Warwick (1587–1658), as Lord High Admiral. His popularity helped ensure that the navy declared for Parliament (July 1642). The navy wasn't large but, for all its imperfections, it was the only professional and cohesive force in England until 'The New Model Army' was established.

Had the navy not been swayed,
Quite a role it might have played:
A blockade of London put into position.
All the wealth from stuff imported
Would thereby have been thwarted,
And the citizens perhaps starved into submission.

Charles relied on privateers
For half a dozen years,
But the fleet rebelled in 1648.
This advantage wasn't taken.
It might have saved Charles' bacon,
But a death upon the scaffold was his fate.

The First Anglo-Dutch War, 1652–54

Once our monarch's head has rolled,
And by Cromwell we're controlled,
Our land is free of civil strife and ructions.
We've a navy – hip hooray! –
It is one that's here to stay.
And moreover it is subject to instructions.

Thus our big ships, by design,
Are made to form a line
Broadside of an enemy – then shoot!
Though by many he's forgot,
Robert Blake devised this plot,
Unexpected and, in consequence, astute.

The Dutch, whom we'd once aided,
Now their dominance paraded,
Our interests and theirs were oft conflicting.
To counter this sad fact,
Was the Navigation Act
Which, on trade around our coast, was quite restricting.

This the Dutch does not impress,
And they quickly seek redress:
They don't recognize how well we are protected.
Faced by England's wooden walls,
Their fleet ultimately falls.
Back at home, on what had happened they reflected.

Though three battles they have lost,
(At huge economic cost),
Their predominance elsewhere is far from slipping.
In the Baltic and the Med,
They're a force our merchants dread,
As far and wide they harass English shipping.

London was key to Parliament's ultimate success. Not only was it the country's most valuable trading port: the Thames was also an important conduit to inland locations.

The navy's allegiance changed in favour of the king following the appointment of Colonel Rainsborough as Vice Admiral, which was resented, and which led to suspicions that New Model Army officers would be given naval commands.

King Charles I was executed in 1649. His head didn't roll: it was held up by the executioner.

Oliver Cromwell ruled 'the Commonwealth' 1651–60.

After the first Navigation Act (1651), there followed a series of acts designed to protect our interests in North America, by requiring all imported goods to be carried by English vessels. This cut out a lot of Dutch 'middleman' activity. The Acts were repealed in 1849.

The first Fighting Instructions (advocating an attack in linear formation) were issued in 1653 by the Commonwealth generals-at-sea. These were Robert Blake (1598–1657), Richard Deane and George Monck (1608–1670).

The post of 'General-at-Sea' combined the roles of Admiral and Commissioner of the Navy. Despite a lack of previous naval experience, Monck's leadership skills and artillery expertise enabled him to play a crucial role in the Battle of Portland (1653), when the English regained control of the Channel after some initial Dutch successes. There followed the Battle of the Gabbard (when the Dutch were driven back from the North Sea), and the Battle of Scheveningen.

**Oliver Cromwell
(Robert Walker, *c.*1649)**

**Robert Blake
(Henry Perronet Briggs, 1829)**

Battle of Scheveningen (Willem van de Velde I, 1657)

The Anglo-Spanish War, 1654–60

Do we warring now forsake?
Maybe have a little break?
No, for Cromwell's target now is acquisition.
His desire is that we own,
Somewhere sugar can be grown,
And he thus despatched a massive expedition.

In charge of it were men,
Surnamed Venables and Penn.
Hispaniola was the isle they sought to claim.
It was very well defended,
So the siege in failure ended.
On 'God's judgment' was where Cromwell put the blame.

Spain did not then place much worth
On Jamaica's fertile earth,
Which was captured by a weakened English force.
Occupation was begrudged
But, once there, we never budged,
Though the Spanish tried to get it back, of course.

Much to Cromwell's satisfaction,
In Europe, Blake saw action –
His blockade of Cádiz thorough and complete.
This stifled Spanish trade,
As his ships went there and stayed –
The first time we'd maintained a winter fleet.

Spain was dealt another blow
When – his brilliance on show –
A treasure fleet at Santa Cruz Blake fought.
But his triumph was eroded,
As its gold had been unloaded,
And was safely stored inside the Spanish port.

This war was unproductive
And mutually destructive:
Retaliation high on Spain's agenda.
It ended rather sadly,
With our shipping trade hit badly,
And economic blight for each contender.

Restoration of the Monarchy, 1660

Cromwell is now dead;
His son rules in his stead,
But he doesn't prove a charismatic sort.
In exile, Charles has waited,
As our king he's reinstated,
And a very 'Merry Monarch's' holding court.

Robert Venables was a soldier and, a noted angler, he also wrote a book on fishing. Admiral Sir William Penn (1621–1670), had been involved in many of the sea battles during the First Anglo-Dutch War. His son founded the Province of Pennsylvania. Cromwell imprisoned Venables and Penn in the Tower of London upon their return to England, despite their subsequent success.

Unlike Jamaica, most other Spanish possessions had recently had their defences strengthened. During the first 200 years of British rule, the island was one of the world's largest producers of sugar. Under the 1670 Treaty of Madrid, England took formal control of Jamaica and the Cayman Islands in return, *inter alia*, for agreeing to suppress piracy in the Caribbean. (See verses 375–379.)

The blockade of Cádiz was in 1656. Prior to this, the navy's activities were seasonal and confined to warmer months. The Battle of Santa Cruz (1657) resulted in the destruction of the Spanish plate fleet (its West Indies treasure fleet). Although the Mexican treasure had been unloaded, Spain was unable to use it due to the blockading tactics employed by Blake.

Battle of Santa Cruz (Charles Dixon, 1901)

Oliver Cromwell died in 1658. Richard Cromwell lacked support and abdicated in 1659.

Charles had escaped to Normandy and spent years wandering around Europe, eventually ending up in the Netherlands. He returned aboard the ship the *Royal Charles*, which was later destroyed during the Dutch raid on Chatham (see verse 366).

With Charles back on English soil,
What was once the 'navy royal'
Becomes 'the Royal Navy' of our nation.
On the seas, it will preside,
Our security, our pride,
And, whenever we are threatened, our salvation.

Once the Commonwealth's been axed,
English life is more relaxed:
We've said goodbye to Puritan propriety.
And our 'pretty witty king'
Does a very clever thing –
Grants a charter to a famous Royal Society.

This would help promote compliance
With the principles of science:
Its members were both curious and bright.
Many now were turning
To a quest for greater learning,
And exploratory ventures would incite.

Royal Marines

For the first time now is seen,
The future royal marine.
With an 'old gold' coat and musket he's equipped.
A distinctive kind of creature,
He will very often feature
In campaigns. To where he's needed, he'll be shipped.

His regiments, to start,
Of the army formed a part:
As required, these were recruited then disbanded.
Change, in due course, would occur.
To the navy they'd transfer:
Three permanent divisions, all rebranded.

In the war of seven years,
This professional appears:
Off the coast of France he's duly been assigned.
Though this isn't done with ease,
Belle Isle he helps to seize
And in doing so his future role's defined.

He amphibiously lands:
On so many foreign strands
From a little boat he'll readily alight.
Whatever the location,
He deserves his reputation –
For 'first ashore' means also 'first to fight'.

When Charles II came to the throne, he inherited a large fleet of 154 ships.

The Royal Navy was founded by statute in 1661 with the establishment of the Naval Discipline Act by Sir William Penn and Samuel Pepys. This also included the Articles of War, which governed the conduct of naval forces and which were originally issued as part of the 1653 fighting instructions. 'The Commonwealth' was the period from 1649 to 1660 (between the execution of Charles I and the restoration of his son Charles II) when England was ruled as a republic.

'Pretty witty king' are the words of court libertine John Wilmot, who added that Charles 'never said a foolish thing, and never did a wise one'. The Royal Society of London was founded in 1660 and was granted a royal charter in 1663. Its members' interests included seamanship, navigation, astronomy, geographical exploration and biology – all subjects which would prompt seafaring initiatives.

In 1664 the first English naval infantry (forerunner of Royal Marines) was established as the 'Duke of York and Albany's Maritime Regiment of Foot'. It comprised 1,200 infantrymen and soon became known as the 'Admiral's Regiment'. Initially, it was disbanded and re-formed as required. For example, 1,900 marines participated in the capture of Gibraltar (see verse 448), and six marine regiments would be raised in 1739 for the War of Jenkins' Ear (see verses 525–526). In 1755, His Majesty's Marine Forces were established. The three divisions were stationed at Chatham, Portsmouth and Plymouth Dock. For the Seven Years' War see verses 544–554.

Under the command of Admiral Augustus Keppel (1725–1786), Belle Île (off Brittany) was occupied in 1761 at the second attempt.

Marines have taken part in more battles on land and sea around the world than any other branch of the British armed forces. Their numerous battle honours are represented by a globe, and by the single honour 'Gibraltar'. Because hand to hand combat on ships' decks remained a feature of naval warfare, royal marines were equipped with boarding axes.

One of ten commemorative stamps issued by Royal Mail (2014) to celebrate 350 years of the Royal Marines (incorporating a painting by Victor Huen, 1664)

He'll be off to Bunker Hill,
Where a lot of blood will spill,
As America her independence claims.
Then Washington he burns,
(Until the weather turns,
And a hurricane extinguishes the flames).

In the centuries ahead,
As the scenes of conflict spread,
We'll discover that he features more and more.
Well trained, his nerve is steady
And he's always at the ready,
To help to keep this land of ours secure.

The Second and Third Anglo-Dutch Wars

The Dutch were quick to learn,
And soon victories would earn,
(These kinds of things are logical progressions),
But meanwhile we'd been bold,
Of some lands had taken hold:
They didn't like us taking their possessions.

New Amsterdam we claimed,
(As New York, it was renamed);
In West Africa, we also nabbed some land.
But it wasn't long before,
In this second round of war,
The enemy would gain the upper hand.

A sneaky trick was played,
On Chatham, a Dutch raid,
Which destroyed some heavy ships of England's fleet.
This earned the foreign raider
The so-called 'Peace of Breda',
A humiliating horrible defeat.

It comes as no surprise,
As you'd probably surmise,
That the English sought to even up the score.
But the French – our so-called friends –
Were pursuing their own ends,
As Louis sought advantage to secure.

This king had big ideas,
And he had, in recent years,
Been building up a navy that was huge.
We agreed to join his side,
So foolishly allied,
And unwittingly assumed the role of stooge.

The Battle of Bunker Hill (Massachusetts) took place in 1775 during the American Revolutionary War. Marines also fought at Lexington and Concord. Washington was burned in 1814, following a British invasion during the Anglo-American War (see verses 712–715). Marines participated in the Battle of Trafalgar (see verses 690–701). For more on amphibious landings see verses 863–864 & 1174–1175.

The title 'Royal' was bestowed in 1802 by George III.

Today, the Royal Marines are an elite force held at a very high state of readiness and trained for worldwide rapid response. Able to deal with a wide range of threats and security challenges, the main deployable force is 3 Commando Brigade RM with a Lead Commando Group held at five days' notice to deploy globally.

Second Anglo-Dutch War (1665–67). Instrumental in the Dutch victories was Cornelis Maartenszoon Tromp (1629–1691). He was a skilled commander, hailed by the Dutch as a naval hero, who saw action in the first three Anglo-Dutch wars.

New Amsterdam became New York in 1664.

The Dutch raided Chatham in 1667. The English flagship, His Majesty's Ship *Royal Charles*, was captured and later sold for scrap (1673). The abbreviation 'HMS' came into use in the 1790s, and was first used on HMS *Phoenix* in 1796.

The Treaty of Breda 1667. (See also verse 323.) *Inter alia*, the Dutch acquired a worldwide monopoly of the nutmeg trade.

Third Anglo-Dutch War (1672–74). Louis XIV and Charles II signed the secret Treaty of Dover in 1670, aimed at helping the French king to conquer the Dutch Republic (and secure Charles' conversion to Catholicism), in return for a large sum of money.

Raid on the Medway (Pieter Cornelisz van Soest, c.1667)

In this third sad bout of war
(Like the second one before),
The English failed to get their tactics right.
The Dutch were far too strong,
So it didn't take us long
To reason it was better not to fight.

Naval Reforms

Meanwhile, Samuel Pepys is putting
On a much much sounder footing
The ways the navy's organized and run.
Corruption had been mounting,
But new systems of accounting
Mean the days of dodgy dealings should be done.

The Victualling Board
Righted much which had been flawed,
And officers' exams now proved men's worth.
With skills put to the test,
Careers can't be progressed
On the basis of an accident of birth.

Control, when well applied,
Has a very useful side.
But an excess was just starting to appear.
They specified dimensions –
Too many interventions! –
And bureaucracy its ugly head would rear.

Ships' sizes must conform
To a pre-determined 'norm' –
The picking nits, and all that petty trifling
Meant the innovator's hope
Was afforded little scope.
The system was restrictive, and proved stifling.

There was no real incentive,
To prove oneself inventive.
Sizes... structures... layouts were defined.
Conservatism's way
Would sadly rule the day.
The French moved on, and Britain lagged behind.

The Caribbean lands
Quite frequently changed hands.
They were coveted as sources of vast riches.
No one could pretend
They were easy to defend,
Which accounts for why there were so many switches.

There would be a Fourth Anglo-Dutch War (1780–84).

Pepys (1633–1703), generally more famous as a diarist, played a significant part in naval affairs, despite a lack of first-hand knowledge. He ultimately became Secretary for the Admiralty from 1685–88, but resigned immediately after the ascension of William and Mary. See verse 431.

Established during the Anglo-Dutch Wars, the Victualling Board, (which essentially operated independently of the Navy Board), was charged with improving the standards of provisions for sailors and, after initial miscalculations and a dire shortage of beer, was largely successful. It was abolished as a separate entity in 1832.

The first set of dimensions was produced for the 'Thirty Ships' programme in 1677. 'The Establishment' of 1706 was asked to produce a set for second-rate vessels, but its remit also included third to fifth-rate ships. First rates were excluded. The dimensions also applied to rebuilds.

By now, in addition to the Spanish, the Dutch, French and English were all intent on acquiring colonies in the Caribbean. The English were relatively slow to appreciate the true value of their acquisitions, and had not built fortifications. For ownership switches see verses 322–326 (St Kitts).

> Englishmen, and more especially seamen, love their bellies above anything else, and therefore it must always be remembered in the management of the victualling of the navy that to make any abatement from them in the quantity of agreeableness of the victuals, is to discourage and provoke them in the tenderest point, and will soon render them disgusted with the king's service than any one other hardship that can be put upon them.

Samuel Pepys diary extract

Samuel Pepys (John Hayls, 1666)

With no handy naval crew,
What could a governor do?
The privateer might prove a useful soul.
He would plunder. He would raid.
He would interfere with trade.
But he wasn't always easy to control!

For example, heed the tales
Of a buccaneer from Wales.
Henry Morgan was a name that prompted dread.
When with Curaçao was tasked,
He didn't do as asked,
And sailed away to Providence instead.

Then to Cuba he was sent,
'Steal from Spaniards' the intent,
But the treasure that he nabbed there wasn't great,
So this brave and ruthless fellow,
Set off for Porto Bello,
Where the residents weren't mindful of their fate.

His men approached by stealth,
And took all the great port's wealth,
Once the final Spanish fort had been surrendered.
The pay-off, too, was handsome
When – the city held to ransom –
The money for its safe return was tendered.

Rum rations and scurvy

Captain Morgan's known to some
As a famous brand of rum.
A spirit which was issued every day
By the navy to its men,
Who'd drunk small beer up till then,
The nasty taste of water to allay.

Sailors took to, with a passion,
Their daily half-pint ration,
But not everyone to alcohol is suited.
This drink was the causation
Of extreme intoxication,
Which explains why it was later on diluted.

On this, Vernon took the lead,
But others soon agreed,
And 'grog' became the 'splice the main brace' toast.
His recipe in use,
Included lemon juice.
This is why his crews were healthier than most.

The term 'privateer' applied to either a person or a ship. It is used here to describe people rather than ships.

'Commerce raiding' is a form of naval warfare that disrupts by targeting merchant shipping. It was frequently used up to, and including, the Second World War.

Although Queen Elizabeth had 'encouraged the development of this supplementary navy,' neither James I nor Charles I permitted privateering.

Captain Henry Morgan (c.1635–1688). As second-in-command to veteran Dutch privateer Edward Mansveldt, the mission was to attack the Dutch settlement of Curaçao. The two men agreed this was not a lucrative enough project, and decided instead to attack the Spanish-controlled island of Providence. Thanks to a prisoner, who had escaped from Morgan's clutches, the Spanish had advance warning of the planned Cuban raid. Morgan and a fleet of buccaneers subsequently failed to take Cartagena de Indias (1741).

After daring raids on Maracaibo and Gibraltar (both in Venezuela), he sacked Panama, thereby violating the 1670 Treaty of Madrid. On trial for piracy in London, he proved he knew nothing of that treaty.

Subsequently knighted, he became Lieutenant Governor of Jamaica (1675–81).

SIR THOMAS MODYFORD (c.1620–1679)

In 1670, according to the commission to Henry Morgan to make war upon the Spanish, Modyford was 'Governor of His Majesty's Island of Jamaica, Commander-in-Chief of the said Island and in the islands adjacent [and] Vice Admiral to his Royal Highness the Duke of York in American seas.'

In 1671, Modyford was sent home under arrest on the charge of 'making war and committing depredations and acts of hostility upon the subjects and territories of the King of Spain in America, contrary to his Majesty's express order and command.'
This followed the 1670 Treaty of Madrid (see verse 350).

After England's conquest of Jamaica in 1655, some captains started issuing rum instead of ale or beer. The Royal Navy took over this practice in 1740. Drinking water, kept in barrels, quickly became contaminated by algae. The daily rum ration was abolished in 1970, and 31 July of that year was known as 'Black Tot Day'. The issue of two or three cans of beer, and improved recreational facilities, were substituted.

Edward Vernon (1684–1757) had served on the *Barfleur*, the flagship of Admiral Sir Cloudesley Shovell (1650–1707), in the Mediterranean during the War of the Spanish Succession (see verses 445–448), and spent some years in the Baltic. He was known as 'Old Grog' due to the grogram (a course silk fabric) coat he wore, hence the name of the drink.

Edward Vernon (Thomas Gainsborough, c.1753)

Meals on ships were no great treat:
They were mainly salted meat
And biscuits, which were hard and far from nice:
These were sometimes worm-infested
And not easily digested,
But, with no fresh produce, hardtack must suffice.

Such a diet was deficient,
And far from beneficent,
As the many deaths from scurvy long had shown.
But some, the more astute,
Figured vegetables and fruit,
Were important, (though for reasons not yet known).

Back in 1593
Richard Hawkins, whilst at sea,
Found that citrus helped the health of those on board.
The James Lancaster we've met
Reached the same conclusion – yet
What he'd noted, very sadly, was ignored.

The evidence was there:
The appalling naval fare
Lacked something, and made sailors go all flaccid.
Enter Scotsman, Doctor Lind.
On a trial his hopes are pinned,
To prove the cure for scurvy is an acid.

Twelve sick men were duly treated
With the 'extras' that he meted,
(Oil of vitriol may well have got two killed).
Two pairs' diets were augmented
By substances fermented.
Some got sea water, which first had been distilled.

A further added fix
Was a garlic/mustard mix.
The final duo swallowed something fruity.
The outcome for these last
Was they both recovered – fast –
And days later one returned to active duty.

The disease's early phase
Is a general malaise.
Spots, and spongy gums, in time will follow.
Then a 'healthy tars' campaign,
By physician Gilbert Blane,
Made lemon juice compulsory to swallow.

The meat was pork and beef.

The biscuits were variously known as 'hardtack', 'sea biscuit', 'worm castles' and 'molar breakers'. Diet on board might be supplemented with peas, cheese and oatmeal.

It is estimated that, between 1500 and 1800, at least two million sailors died of scurvy.

In 1593, Admiral Sir Richard (son of John) Hawkins advocated drinking orange and lemon juice, as did James Lancaster at around the same time (see verse 313).

In 1614, John Woodall (surgeon with the East India Company) recognised the problem of dietary deficiency. In 1740, lemon juice was added to grog.

James Lind (1716–94) became surgeon on HMS *Salisbury* of the Channel Fleet. Regarded as the first ever clinical trial, the experiment he conducted was whilst the ship was patrolling the Bay of Biscay. The dozen men were divided into six pairs.

Twenty-five drops of sulphuric acid in the form of oil of vitriol were administered to two unfortunates. This would not have been a fatal dose, although the acid is highly corrosive. Acetic acid (vinegar, or a daily quart of cider), was another supplement. Although the supply of oranges and lemons ran out after a few days, it proved sufficient to effect a cure. Lind published his *Essay on the most effectual means of preserving the health of Seamen* in 1762.

In 1794, Rear Admiral Alan Gardner issued lemon juice to his men on a trip to India, resulting in almost no incidence of scurvy.

Sir Gilbert Blane was Physician to the Fleet (1779–83). His advocacy led to the mandatory inclusion of lemon juice in sailors' diets from 1795. Limes were later substituted, which gave rise to the name 'limey' as a slang word for a British person.

The role of vitamin C (ascorbic acid) was not discovered until 1932.

James Lind (Sir George Chalmers, date unknown)

Whaling – seventeenth century

Hunting whales began,
With prehistoric man,
Who used little boats to drive his catch ashore.
It was smaller types of prey,
Which ended up this way:
The larger ones were harder to procure.

The method next in vogue,
Used something called a drogue:
A semi-floating object that was fired
With arrow or harpoon,
Into the whale – and soon,
The creature would be feeling very tired.

In northern Spain, the Basques
Were skilful in such tasks,
And they ventured in due course to English seas.
This didn't help relations
Between respective nations,
But we gained from them a lot of expertise.

To maximise our yield,
We too went far afield:
In Arctic bays were bowheads to be caught.
In targeting this zone,
We were clearly not alone.
So the situation often was quite fraught.

Finding spots to anchor,
Intensified the rancour:
There weren't that many places there to 'park'.
Things needed to be ready,
With the vessel holding steady,
Before men could, with safety, disembark.

Processing on shore,
Was relied on more and more,
Though this didn't prove to be a lasting trend.
To bays the English stuck,
But the Dutch soon tried their luck
In open seas. We'd get there in the end.

But for now, there was a lull,
Affecting ports like Hull,
As to buying from abroad we had resorted.
The government was saying,
That we ought not to be paying,
For the products of the whale to be imported.

Smaller species included belugas and porpoises.

Fishermen in the Bay of Biscay were the first European exponents of pelagic (open sea) whaling. Their seasonal trips to the English Channel had started by the 14th century. By the early 17th century, Biscayans were making trips to Canadian and Icelandic waters. Longer distance trips from the British Isles started in the last decade of the 16th century.

The bowhead was particularly valued for oil and baleen. Baleen, part of certain whales' filter-feeder systems, is not true bone but keratin.

True bone and whales' teeth (not all species have teeth) were used to make tools and, from the mid 18th century, scrimshaw (decorative engraved pieces) (see verse 816.)

The French, Dutch and Danes were competitors. There were many skirmishes, including some infighting amongst the English. King James I claimed sovereignty over Spitsbergen (Norway) with no real justification in 1613, after an unproductive expedition by the Muscovy Company in 1611.

Ships' anchors rely on weight and/or grip to secure the vessel to the seabed. The earliest were simply heavy rocks.

Emulating the Basques, whalers from other countries established onshore stations, but these were later abandoned in favour of processing on board ship, and in the home port.

Fig. 194.—Whale-Fishing.—Fac-simile of a Woodcut in the "Cosmographie Universelle" of Thevet, in folio: Paris, 1574.

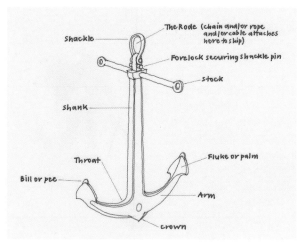

Parts of an anchor (Admiralty Pattern)

In addition to the cost,
Other benefits were lost:
The whaling trips developed 'hardy seamen',
Who were made of sterling stuff,
Who were skilled and strong and tough,
For everyone on board worked like a demon.

With activities suspended,
Many livelihoods were ended.
And not just on the ships that once were manned.
Suddenly now thwarted,
Were those who had supported,
In a range of jobs that took place on dry land.

Parliament passed acts,
Which imposed a heavy tax
On imports, and the English were exempted.
This should have proved a lure
But it never did procure
A revival: hardly anyone was tempted.

In centuries to come,
The scene for whales looked glum:
The industry surrounding them immense.
How the story would unfold
Is later to be told,
But explaining why now makes a lot of sense.

Whales were not pursued,
As just a source of food:
Their oil of course provided lubrication.
It was used to process rope…
To make products such as soap…
Or burned in lamps to give illumination.

The product called baleen,
Was often stitched unseen
In an undergarment, there to reinforce it.
To minimize her waist,
A woman would be laced
Into that dreadful thing – the 'whalebone' corset.

Flexible and tough,
Baleen was useful stuff,
It is shapeable, its range of use fantastic.
The Victorian employs
It for brolly struts and toys,
(In the absence of synthetics such as plastic).

Introduced in 1672 (and renewed for a further four years in 1690), the favourable terms of these acts failed to attract a single ship. The efforts of two English companies between 1697 and 1732 met with no, or only limited, success. The lack of English/British interest in whaling would continue until the 1749 government bounty was introduced (see verse 534). At its height, the revived whaling industry was carried out from thirty-five British ports.

Whale oil was obtained from blubber in a process called 'trying out'.

Flensing was the process by which blubber was stripped from the whale.

Baleen was also used for eyeglass frames, chimney sweeps' brushes and even early typewriter ribbon. It was often soaked in water first to facilitate shaping.

The development of trade

Holland's cargo ships were made
For one purpose, which was trade.
Unlike ours, they weren't equipped to carry guns.
Fluyts needed fewer crew,
They were more capacious too –
Ideal for those trans-oceanic runs.

Cheap to run and cheap to build,
(Competitors weren't thrilled),
Their tall masts helped them travel at great speeds.
Others soon sought to refine,
The basic Dutch design,
And adapt it to whatever were their needs.

Far off places were in range...
Growing stuff that once seemed strange.
Tea and coffee, by rich people, were adored.
Ships on certain distant routes,
Brought back exotic fruits:
Pineapples... bananas... were on board.

Large companies that bartered,
Were very often chartered.
The East India is probably best known.
Its powers were comprehensive,
And increasingly extensive:
The seeds of Britain's empire thus were sewn.

An empire which embraces,
So many far off places:
The one 'on which the sun would never set'.
Even now, we're holding sway,
In the future USA.
(As for the rest, we've not quite got there yet).

But we've colonies on most
Of America's east coast,
Plus Bermuda – so strategically placed.
Jamaica, much desired,
From the Spanish was acquired
And, in Canada, we're very firmly based.

Fluyts (fluits or flutes) had large cargo bays and relatively narrow upper decks. The boats were designed to maximise capacity, and to avoid heavy taxes imposed by the Danish (assessed on main deck area). Charles II once said, 'Don't fight the Dutch, imitate them'.

The English (later British) East India Company had received its royal charter from Queen Elizabeth I in 1600. It traded in many commodities, including silk and opium. The company established its first factory on the west coast of India in 1613.

Although popularly used in the 19th century, in reference to an empire that was so vast some of it would always be in daylight, the phrase 'on which the sun never sets' had first been used in the early 16th century to describe the extent of Spain's influence. 'El imperio en el que nunca se pone el sol.'

In America, there were British colonies from the 'New England' area in the north, down to South Carolina. Georgia would be added in 1731 making a total of thirteen colonies.

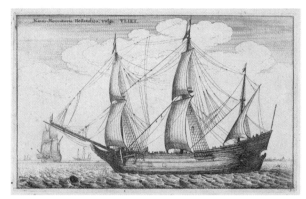

A Dutch fluyt (Wenceslaus Hollar, mid 17th century)

Growth of the Slave Trade

In 1672
A charter would renew
An outfit that from Africa supplied
What the sugar grower craves:
A steady stream of slaves,
Though en route a high proportion of them died.

The 'Royal African' (new name)
A monopoly could claim
On these human 'goods', regarded as expendable.
Slave labour – the foundation,
Of the prosperous plantation –
Was plentiful, and always very vendible.

When exclusive rights were ended,
This trade rapidly extended,
When others sought their profitable share.
As their enterprises boomed,
Lots more Africans were doomed
To servitude, harsh treatment and despair.

The 'cargo' on arrival,
(Those successful in survival),
Were washed and shaved, and made to look presentable.
From their families detached,
With new owners they were matched:
Calamitous, deplorable, lamentable.

There'd be measures that contrived,
To ensure more slaves survived;
The result was deaths in transit started falling.
But the men were still constrained
Cramped below, in leg irons chained.
Conditions were degrading and appalling.

Did Captain Cook discover Australia?

Though it's barely on the map,
To Australia a chap
Called Dampier has well and truly been.
He whiled away the hours,
Noting animals and flowers,
Which include the 'hopping' creatures he had seen.

A skilful navigator,
He also collected data,
On currents, tides and winds – such useful stuff.
And members of his crew,
Were the inspiration, too,
For written works familiar enough.

In 1660, a charter granted the 'Company of Royal Adventurers Trading to Africa' a monopoly over English trade with West Africa. It set up forts along the coast, most of which were subsequently lost to the Dutch. The main interest in Africa was initially gold, and the guinea coin was named after the area (now part of Ghana), from which most of this valuable metal came. In 1672, a restructured Royal Adventurers was given a new name and a new charter with extended rights, including a monopoly of trade in slaves.

Between 1672 and 1689, (when its monopoly was effectively lost), between 90,000 and 100,000 slaves were transported by the company.

In 1698, an act opened up the African trade to all English merchants, in return for a 10 per cent levy paid to the Royal African Company on all exports. Merchants from Liverpool, and more particularly from Bristol, began exporting slaves, who were either sold direct to plantation owners, or entered into auctions.

Families and friends were very often split up.

As well as sugar, plantation products included cotton and tobacco.

In 1750, an estimated 15–20 per cent of African captives died during their 'Middle Passage' Atlantic crossing, which could last two months or longer.

The 1788 Dolben's Act limited the number of people who could be carried on British slave ships, and required that a surgeon (often unqualified) be on board. He was paid head money based on the numbers kept alive. By 1800 death rates had fallen to <5 per cent (about one in eighteen).

See Plate B on page 113 for map of the Bight of Benin.

Beware, beware the Bight of Benin: One comes out, where fifty went in.

Said to be a slavery jingle about the dangers of malaria in the Bight

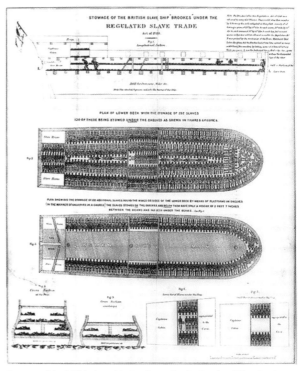

Stowage of the British slave ship *Brookes* under the Regulated Slave Trade Act 1788

A former pirate, the Englishman William Dampier (1651–1715), circumnavigated the globe three times. In north Australia he compiled notes on flora and fauna (1688).

The navigational data he collected were, years later, of help to both James Cook and Horatio Nelson.

An albatross was shot,
Which features in the plot
Of the famous 'rime' which Coleridge then penned.
And, alone for four long years,
A Scottish man appears,
As Crusoe (both were rescued in the end).

Here we may as well confess,
With considerable largesse,
(And because a fair account is the intention).
Certain Dutchmen of repute,
Found Oz first – there's no dispute –
So the likes of Nuyts and Tasman need a mention.

The start of big-time smuggling

An ancient system's creaking,
And revenue is leaking.
At ports, there is corruption in profusion.
Officials (poorly paid),
Creamed off the tax on trade,
And the 'half seal' safeguards couldn't stop collusion.

Thus there's duty being clawed
On the goods we send abroad,
But some shun making payment altogether.
Illicit goods embark,
On trips made in the dark,
And, better still, in truly awful weather.

When exporting wool was banned;
This a growth in smuggling fanned.
The activity of owling then emerged.
Those involved employed the ruse
Of a system of twit twoos.
Their illegal trade was something to be purged.

A law is passed and, hence,
It's a capital offence
To pursue this dodgy covert operation.
Moving English produce out,
This 'free trade' is all about,
And harsh penalties won't stop its emigration.

The controller and collector
Soon acquire a third inspector
To ensure that they are honest – the surveyor.
There are weighers. There are waiters.
There are searchers on the freighters,
As bureaucracy is added layer by layer.

Simon Hatley, a former crewmate of Dampier, is remembered for killing an albatross off Cape Horn in 1719. This incident features in Samuel Taylor Coleridge's *Rime of the Ancient Mariner*, published in 1798.

Alexander Selkirk asked to be left on an island in 1704 because he believed Dampier's ship to be unseaworthy. This castaway is thought to have inspired Daniel Defoe's book *Robinson Crusoe*. Dampier himself is specifically mentioned in Jonathan Swift's *Gulliver's Travels*, as the model for the seaman Lemuel Gulliver.

A Dutch East India Company ship, under Willem Janszoon, explored the western coast of Australia as early as 1605–6. The second recorded landfall there, under Captain Hartog, followed 10 years later. Peter Nuyts (1598–1655) mapped the southern coast of Australia during a 1626–7 expedition.

Abel Tasman (1603–59) mapped the northern coast in 1644. On the first of two Pacific voyages, he also reached Van Diemen's Land (now named Tasmania after him), and New Zealand. All four Dutchmen (and certain French explorers) reached Australia, then an unnamed land, well before James Cook's first sighting in 1770.

There is some evidence (unsubstantiated) to suggest that the Portuguese may have reached it as early as the 1520s.

For two 17th century world maps, not featuring Australia, see Plate B on page 113.

The Albatross (Engraving by Gustave Doré for an 1876 edition of the *Rime of the Ancient Mariner*)

The collector of customs was overseen by the controller of customs, and each had half of the full seal that was required to prove the correct tax had been levied.

Since the 13th century, when export duties were first imposed (see verse 162), there had been corruption, which increased when export duties (especially on wool and hides) were raised. Grain was also periodically smuggled out. The ban on exporting wool, introduced in 1614, remained in place until 1825. Kent was the centre of the illicit export activity, engagement in which was made a capital offence in 1661.

The new Board of Customs was set up under the 1671 Customs and Excise Act.

There are those whose major care
Is that ships don't dock elsewhere;
Eight officers on horseback are recruited;
Then the land guard there would be,
And a water guard at sea.
But activity continues undiluted.

In time, there's two-way traffic,
And our image – much more graphic –
Is of night time skies, and contraband brought in.
Whenever we were warring,
Taxation kept on soaring –
And so too, the price of coffee, rum and gin.

Many seize their opportunities;
Involved are whole communities,
Who depend upon an industry that's growing.
We'll leave this with the statement –
There won't be a quick abatement –
(As rhymes which feature later will be showing).

1688 – 'The Glorious Revolution'

We fight a civil war...
Then the monarchy restore...
But for James, our king, the future isn't bright.
His beliefs do not conform
To what's now the English norm:
He's pro-Catholic, pro-French – which can't be right.

Waiting in the wings,
Keeping careful track of things,
Is William, Prince of Orange, wed to Mary.
To England's crown he'd claims –
Very worrying for James –
Who, events will prove, had reason to be wary.

It doesn't suit Dutch ends,
To see France and England friends:
This alliance not at all one Will desires.
He is probably ambitious,
Which is also inauspicious.
To greater things he certainly aspires.

He's a mere prince – just not fair!
But his wife is England's heir.
She's his cousin, too, when all is said and done.
As a monarch absolute,
King James was not astute,
Then his queen, at last, produced the longed-for son.

The riding officers were recruited in 1690, at which point the first sea patrols were abandoned. The land guard was created in 1698. At the turn of the 18th century, 21 vessels were stationed all around the coast (see verse 790). These were backed up by the Royal Navy.

Tea was the major smuggled commodity in the 17th century. Silk and lace were also brought in, as well as the goods more familiarly associated with the 'industry'.

Local populations did not always cooperate or turn a blind eye willingly, and were sometimes terrorized into doing so (see verses 767–772 & 787).

King Charles II died in 1685 and was succeeded by his brother, James II, who had converted to Catholicism. Mary was James's older daughter and heir presumptive. Like her younger sister Anne (who became queen in 1702), she was Protestant. Mary's husband, William of Orange, was a grandson of Charles I, and both James's son-in-law and nephew.

There were increasing indications, during James' reign, that the king was seeking to reduce the influence of parliament. Consternation levels rose upon the birth of a son, whom it was planned to raise in the Catholic faith. The queen had not appeared to be pregnant and there were rumours that the new Prince of Wales, (also named James), was an imposter.

Would 'popery' return?
It's a very real concern,
Thus many pinned their hopes on James's daughters.
But, it's also fair to say,
Not all folk thought this way
And the monarch wasn't wanting for supporters.

With success not guaranteed,
Will prepared what he would need.
He had backing from the famed 'Immortal Seven'.
His flotilla was impressive,
And as things turned out excessive:
He landed unopposed at Torbay, Devon.

His invasion was complete,
But where was England's fleet?
The answer is 'in Portsmouth'— quite a distance.
Hampered by the wind,
Or by fog that had now thinned,
It could offer not a scrap of real resistance.

To Ireland James escaped,
And our future is reshaped.
Queen Mary and a foreigner now reign!
Dutch ways will now begin,
(We acquire their taste for gin),
And at least the new king's not from France or Spain.

The War of the Grand Alliance, 1688–97

We've lost one major foe,
But – well wouldn't you just know? –
Another now pops up to take its place.
It's France again what's more,
That declares a state of war.
Now 'the Sun King's' huge resources we must face.

He's seeking to expand
France's European land,
So we all gang up and form the 'Grand Alliance'.
Armies fight and armies spar,
Which gets no one very far,
And Louis has no option but compliance.

Others want to join the fray
In places far away.
In Canada, the fur trade's causing tensions.
In this tedious affair,
There are skirmishes elsewhere,
And the conflict thus has very wide dimensions.

Samuel Pepys, who was later forced to resign, was amongst those who supported James.

William recruited experienced soldiers from Europe and assembled a huge fleet. A group of seven eminent Whig supporters had invited William to claim the English throne. They included Edward Russell, later 1st Earl of Oxford, who was an Admiral in James's navy.

The so-called 'Protestant wind' hampered the Royal Navy, which had positioned itself off Kent and had twice passed William's fleet, (which ultimately turned and sailed into the English Channel).

The Irish still regarded James as king, until the Battle of the Boyne (1690), when the victorious William asserted his authority.

William III (r.1689–1702) and Mary (r.1689–94).

Many largely beneficial changes eg to banking systems, were introduced. Holland started to decline from this period.

The Glorious Revolution was followed by the 1689 Bill of Rights, limiting the powers of monarchs.

Louis XIV's army was progressively seeking to extend France's possessions in mainland Europe. Already William's enemy, Louis XIV reigned 1643–1715.

The 'War of the Grand Alliance' was also known as 'The Nine Years' War', because that's how long it lasted. In Britain, it is sometimes referred to as 'The War of the English Succession', because France was backing the deposed James II (and would continue to support the Stuart cause, when it suited, for many years to come).

England and France had long been at odds for control of the lucrative Canadian fur trade. The spin-off fighting over this is referred to as 'William's War'.

There was largely inconclusive fighting in the Caribbean and in Asia.

England by now had a lot of control in India.

At Beachy Head we'd faltered.
Though our ships remained unaltered,
This encounter some important lessons taught.
From what we'd realised,
The 'instructions' were revised,
Which improved the way our battles would be fought.

But in 1693,
A convoy set to sea.
Its cargo was the produce of a year,
Of goods to be exported,
To start, it was escorted,
In case the hostile French chose to appear.

Once it safely got past Brest:
There was nothing to suggest
That it wouldn't now sail onwards unmolested.
With no danger of attack,
Most protective ships turned back –
Unfortunate for those with much invested.

Mustered French ships pounced,
And our merchant fleet was trounced,
In a battle that took place near Lagos Bay.
We hadn't stood much chance,
So the winning side was France.
Insurers had enormous sums to pay.

In the wake of this disaster,
We were building ships much faster
And numerical advantage soon secured.
A battle's rarely won,
Via the tactic or the gun,
But on how long fights at sea could be endured.

From whence the funding came
Is a now familiar name:
All this helped the Bank of England to be founded.
Folk invested cash to earn
A guaranteed return,
And prosperity for many soon abounded.

If it weren't for Argentina,
And her bellicose demeanour,
This stanza maybe wouldn't have been written.
By Captain Strong commanded,
On the Falklands *Welfare* landed.
(Their importance Anson later saw to Britain)...

The Battle of Beachy Head took place on 30 June 1690. It was a decisive French naval victory over an inferior Anglo-Dutch fleet. John Benbow (1653–1702) was involved in this campaign. He was later to rise to the rank of Admiral. He achieved fame fighting Salé and Moor pirates, and notoriety for instigating the trial of a number of his unsupportive captains.

Improved Fighting Instructions led to early successes, and a French fleet, supporting deposed King James, was sunk off the coast of Normandy in the linked Battles of Barfleur and La Hogue (English commander Edward Russell).

Some 200+ English and Dutch vessels, carrying exports, were heading for Smyrna, a port on the Aegean in what is now Turkey, when they were ambushed near Lagos Bay (southern Portugal). Admiral George Rooke (see also verse 448) was in command of the reduced escort. His skilled defence did much to limit the damage. A similar disaster would take place in 1780, during the American War of Independence, when all but eight merchant ships in a British convoy of sixty-three ships were captured by the Spanish, causing a financial crisis among marine insurance underwriters throughout Europe.

By 1700, our fleet numbered about 270 vessels. English ship construction was outstripping the French 4:1. Although ship design had not progressed, we did introduce the steering wheel some fifteen years before the French.

The Bank of England, established in 1694, secured investment in ship construction with the promise of an 8 per cent return. The minimum amount payable was £25, and many small investors in relatively menial occupations were attracted. And thus began the National Debt!

In 1690, Captain John Strong was indisputably the first to be recorded as landing on the Falkland Islands, which are strategically placed. The only direct route between the Atlantic and the Pacific was via Cape Horn, and a nearby base would therefore prove useful. Argentina still disputes ownership. See section/verses 1648–1664 on **The Falklands War, 1982**.

Three Positions in the Downs (Francis Holman, 1779) showing the Indiaman *Royal George*

The Battle of Barfleur, 1692 (Richard Paton, 18th century)

5 The eighteenth century

5

The eighteenth century

The War of the Spanish Succession

We are soon at war again.
Spanish power is on the wane,
But its empire is still one beyond compare.
This enormous slice of cake,
Means there's very much at stake,
When Spain's feeble king expires without an heir.

Almost everyone's affected:
Ruling houses are connected,
So several royal people have a claim.
There's a chance, that's quite distinct,
France and Spain may thus be linked:
Preventing this must surely be our aim.

And we have another goal,
For we'd like to have control
Of an English base that's somewhere in the Med.
In this we do not falter,
Take Minorca and Gibraltar,
(By the latter much resentment's being fed).

That lump of rock we took,
(Under Admiral George Rooke,
Assisted by a group of 'royal' marines),
Is a most important place,
Still today a naval base,
Where the Med with the Atlantic's sprawl convenes.

The Acts of Union, 1706 and 1707

By the time this war is ending,
Britain's star is fast ascending –
(For 'Great Britain' is the country we've become).
Scots and English are united,
Though not everyone's delighted,
(And undoing this remains the aim of some.)

In addition to large parts of North, Central and South America, Spain's possessions included the Philippines, and parts of Italy, North Africa and the Caribbean.

Charles II of Spain died 1700.

The French candidate, Phillip, did eventually secure the Spanish crown, but only on condition that he relinquish his claim to the throne of France.

Minorca changed hands a few times, but remained a predominantly British possession throughout the 18th century, before being returned to Spain for a final time in 1802.

In 2012, the former Queen of Spain, Sofia, boycotted Queen Elizabeth II's Diamond Jubilee celebrations over the issue of Gibraltar, which remains a British possession. Spain has 'first refusal' should we ever decide to give it up.

The capture of Gibraltar in 1704 marked the first major impact of the (not yet royal) marines (see verses 362–363), and it remains their only battle honour.

Admiral Sir George Rooke (1650–1709) (see verse 441) had also secured an important victory at Vigo Bay (1702).

An upper zone of inflowing Atlantic water travels above a lower zone of outflowing saltier Mediterranean water through the Straits of Gibraltar. This was discovered by Thomas Henry Tizard, who was one of the officers aboard HMS *Challenger* (see verses 1256–1262 **The *Challenger* Expedition, 1872–76**).

Sea Battle of Vigo Bay (North Netherlands artist unknown)

Britain's most famous successes in the War of the Spanish Succession (1702–1713) were land battles under the command of the Duke of Marlborough.

The English took the view
We were better one than two:
A Scotland that was acting on its own
Might ally with whom it pleased,
Leaving England somewhat squeezed.
It might even choose another for its throne.

Back then, the Scots agreed,
As of funds they were in need:
A recent scheme had proved to be ill-fated.
Of this they'd made a hash,
And had wasted lots of cash,
So the countries now are well and truly mated.

(Ireland's unaffected,
Though by monarchy connected,
This 'sister land's' a separate domain.
With the Catholic dimension,
She's a place where there is tension
And, for now, outside the union she'll remain.)

Scottish merchants can grow stronger
Now they're 'foreigners' no longer...
By the Navigation Acts are not constrained.
They are canny, work with vigour...
Britain's empire's ever bigger...
And access to its markets they've now gained.

Tobacco made some rich,
Though there'd later be a glitch
When America no longer pledged its troth.
But the lords did not despair,
As 'the weed' was grown elsewhere,
And the wealth it brought assisted Scotland's growth.

At this time a chance appears.
After reigning many years,
The Mughal empire's leader has expired.
We can now act with impunity,
And take the opportunity:
A greater hold on India's acquired.

The Peace of Utrecht, 1713

Cometh now the hour
Of attempts to balance power:
When a single state's too strong, it may well seek
To use the upper hand,
And nab other countries' land,
If the target's seen as vulnerable and weak.

The risk of French and Jacobite infiltration was still a lurking concern for England. France's support for the Stuart cause would not end until the 1716 Anglo-French Treaty. There were also fears, following the death of Queen Anne (see verse 459 opposite), that Scotland might oppose the Hanoverian succession.

During the 17th century, there had been several unsuccessful attempts at union between England and Scotland.

The Darien Scheme (or 'Darien Disaster') was a plan in the 1690s for Scotland to colonise part of Panama. It was a complete failure. The Scots believed it had been sabotaged by William III.

England and Scotland were united following the 1706 and 1707 Acts of Union. Ireland remained outside the Union until 1800, when the United Kingdom of Great Britain and Ireland was formed (see verse 688).

A small number of merchants, known as tobacco lords, grew extremely wealthy as a result of capturing this trade. Money found its way into Scottish industry, banking and agriculture. Glasgow supplanted London as Britain's main port for the import of tobacco.

Having ruled over most of the Indian subcontinent for forty-nine years, Aurangzeb died in 1707. His successors were weak, allowing British traders to progressively extend control.

Achieving a 'balance of power' in Europe was a specific objective at the end of the War of the Spanish Succession.

Utrecht, actually a series of treaties concluded in 1713, generally served Great Britain well in terms of trading concessions.

As a consequence of the Treaty of Tordesillas (see verses 261–262), Spain was the only European nation without establishments on the west coast of Africa, and could not therefore obtain slaves direct. Instead, the required supply came via an asiento – a licence under which a third party received the monopoly on a trade route or product. Under the terms of the Treaty of Utrecht, the Asiento was, for a period of thirty years, awarded to Great Britain. It included 500 tons of goods, in addition to an unlimited number of slaves, and afforded traders (and smugglers) access to the valuable markets in Spanish America.

Fighting had proved expensive for Britain and, in 1711, the South Sea Company was formed to consolidate and reduce the cost of national debt. The Asiento was contracted to this company. After complicated twists in fortunes and dodgy dealings, overheated speculation led to the bursting of its bubble in 1720.

Words: James Thompson   Music: Thomas Arne

The Brits have earned respect.
With the Treaty of Utrecht,
(After which Britannia starts to rule the waves).
Spain confirms our new possessions,
In addition makes concessions:
A monopoly supplying it with slaves.

In the so-called 'Queen Anne's War,'
We have evened up the score,
Though the fur trade's very nearly had its day,
Newfoundland we now own,
Plus the Nova Scotia zone,
And we've regained what we'd lost in Hudson's Bay.

Post-Utrecht, 1713–1739

1714
Saw the death of Britain's Queen,
Whose many children sadly too had died.
There's a German on our throne,
Which the Jacobites bemoan:
They're in favour of the Catholic claimants' side.

Our new king, George the First,
(In English not well versed),
Was followed by his namesakes Two to Four.
But the Stuarts' cause would thrive,
Until 'The Forty-five',
And throughout these reigns, our country was at war.

'Utrecht' had aimed for peace,
But hostilities don't cease.
Barely five years on, we're battling once again.
For those times, so very rare,
In this bellicose affair,
We've allied with France. The enemy is Spain.

The 'Asiento's' rights,
Would lead to frequent fights,
Spain fearing that its terms were not respected.
This principally explained
Why relations were so strained,
Then Jenkins and his ear were disconnected.

The first version of the patriotic song *Rule Britannia* featured in a masque called Alfred, performed at Cliveden in 1740.

For the Navigation Acts see verse 345.

For the loss of the American colonies see verse 569.

'Queen Anne's War' was the name given to the struggles that were taking place in Canada and elsewhere in the Americas (between 1701–1713). Newfoundland and Nova Scotia were ceded by France to Britain under the Treaty of Utrecht.

In the naval 'Battle of Hudson's Bay' (1690), the largest ever in the American North Atlantic, the French had taken the key York factory in the bay. Under 'Utrecht', control of trade was returned to the Hudson's Bay Company, which had held an English royal charter since 1670.

Queen Anne (r.1702–1714) had 17 children but none survived to adulthood, so who should succeed her? The 1701 Act of Settlement prohibited Catholics from inheriting the throne. The closest Protestant claimant was the Elector of Hanover. There were at least 50 ineligible Stuarts who were more closely related.

Britain's enemies (notably France) used the exiled Stuarts' claim to cause trouble. The Jacobite rising of 1745 ended with the defeat of 'Bonnie Prince Charlie's' supporters at the Battle of Culloden (1746).

Great Britain would be at war for at least three quarters of the time during the reigns of her first three Hanoverian monarchs. George II was the last British king to personally lead his troops into battle (Dettingen, 1743).

In the War of the Quadruple Alliance (1718–20), there was a decisive British victory near Cape Passaro (Sicily) in 1718 under the command of Admiral Sir George Byng.

Relations with Spain, increasingly tense, led to Britain's attempted blockade of Panama (1726), and to Spain's equally unsuccessful bid to retake Gibraltar – not to be confused with the Great Siege of Gibraltar (see verses 572–573). The ensuing Anglo-Spanish War (1727–29), ended with the Treaty of Seville (1729), which gave Spanish warships the right to stop British traders to check compliance with the Asiento's terms.

The 'War of Jenkins' Ear' – a name coined by Thomas Carlyle in 1858 – would last from 1739 to 1748 (see verses 525–526).

The Golden Age of Piracy, and Impressment

There were fortunes to be made
From the Caribbean trade,
But honest ways by some had been forsaken.
Silver (and much more),
Was continuing to pour,
From the New World – either earned, or simply taken.

Some was processed into coin,
Which the pirates might purloin,
Each 'piece of eight' worth fifty modern pounds.
This currency is global;
Its production most ignoble:
At Potosi much brutality abounds.

A navy life was tough.
The pay was not enough,
For a constant round of physical exertion.
For the disaffected chancer,
Turning freelance was one answer,
Which explains the quite high levels of desertion.

Not all would volunteer
For this seafaring career,
Though the conduct money offered helped a bit.
Plus, advanced, was two months' pay,
Some expended straightaway,
As men had to buy their hammock and their kit.

Those who weren't persuaded,
Might be not so subtly 'aided'
By a gang whose role was swelling naval ranks.
The likely, they would wrest,
And chaps were thus impressed.
This was not a job that earned a lot of thanks.

When it comes to new recruits,
Experience best suits,
Which service on a merchantman provides.
It is not part of the plan
To grab just any man,
As along the street he innocently strides.

But, if seafaring's his way,
He's legitimately prey,
As conscription's rarely been our chosen course.
In its absence, there's no surety
Of national security,
Unless the needed manpower's seized by force.

The Spaniards first found silver in Mexico during the 1540s. Another source was discovered in Bolivia a few years later at Potosi, which became known as Silver Mountain. Here, the metal was turned into octagonal coins using the enforced labour of local American Indians (and later, African slaves). Pieces of eight, accepted beyond the Spanish Empire, were the first global currency, and continued to be used until 1857.

Pay in the navy had been fixed in 1658, and was reasonable for about a century thereafter, when inflation started to erode its value.

To discourage desertion, payment was at least six months, (and sometimes as much as two years), in arrears. Pay aboard merchant ships was greater, but these vessels were often undermanned, especially in wartime, so the work was harder.

Conduct money was paid to those who volunteered. A man seized by the press gang could choose to sign up as a volunteer and receive the benefits, or remain a pressed man and receive nothing.

A merchantman is any non-naval (including troop ships) vessel. Crews from inbound merchant ships were seized more usually by naval warships, rather than by 'the press'.

It did occasionally happen that men who had no seagoing experience were taken, but impressment mainly affected 'eligible men of seafaring habits between the ages of 18 and 45'. Under a 1703 Act, those aged under eighteen, who were not apprenticed, were also included. In 1740 the upper age limit was raised to fifty-five.

There were certain 'protections' against impressment, but no one was exempt in times of crisis, when the Admiralty issued a 'hot press'.

A piece of eight (Museo Arqueológico Nacional, Madrid)

1780 Caricature of a Press Gang

The press gang cannot trick
A fellow they would nick,
But it's said they'd con a likely-looking male.
If he took his monarch's shilling,
It was deemed that he was willing,
So they'd slip a coin in tankards filled with ale.

If you're male and you're a Brit,
If you look quite strong and fit,
It's still possible your future fate is sealed.
Here is just a word of warning,
As you're strolling out one morning:
The Impressment Acts have never been repealed!

Prize Money

Sailors were induced
Their salaries to boost,
By seizing an opponent nation's vessel.
Which they wouldn't try to sink
And condemn it to the drink:
As in days of old, upon the decks they'd wrestle.

Officially the state
Owned the captured ship and freight,
But a share to every crewman was assigned.
For decades, though informal,
This arrangement had been normal;
Now an act was passed in which it was enshrined.

The Prize Court did its best,
And the worth of ships assessed.
It decided how the booty would be shared.
If a warship had been caught,
By the crown it would be bought,
Provided it was fit to be repaired.

A frigate and a sloop
On *Hermione* did swoop –
A Spanish ship worth taking, it appears.
The money that this earned
Meant great wealth for all concerned:
Equivalent to pay for thirty years.

Captain Kidd

Outright piracy's a crime,
And it was so at the time.
Men got punished for the stealing that they did.
But a privateering 'hit'
Was more or less legit:
Some protection from the fate of Captain Kidd.

It is said that inn keepers introduced tankards with glass bottoms so a man could see whether, in accepting his drink, he was also accepting a sneaky 'king's shilling'.

Impressment simply lapsed as a means of recruitment. Conscription was used during and after the First World War (1916–20), when it was known as Military Service, and again during and after the Second World War (1939–1960), when it was called 'National Service'.

Remember that taking a foreign ship when Britain was at war with that nation was privateering, not an act of piracy (see verse 266).

Apart from defeating the object, it was also very difficult to sink an opponent's ship during action.

Throughout the 16th and 17th centuries, those involved in capturing an enemy ship benefitted. In 1708, the Cruisers and Convoys Act established the Admiralty Prize Court, which evaluated claims, and formalised the longstanding divvying up practice. A system of allocation by eighths was developed. Two eighths usually went to the captain of the ship which had captured the prize.

The crews of the *Active* and the *Favourite* captured the *Hermione* following an engagement off Cádiz in 1762. Captains Herbert Sawyer and Philemon Pownoll each received the equivalent of almost £9 million in today's money. Each crew member got between £482 and £485 for their part in taking what was arguably the most valuable prize ever.

Pirates still operate in parts of the world today.

'Corsair' is another word for 'pirate' or 'privateer', but usually refers to those who were operating in, or from, the Mediterranean.

In 1856, under the Declaration of Paris, letters of marque were banned by most maritime nations, which outlawed privateering.

This Scotsman, it is clear,
Had a colourful career,
(And one which later stories have embellished).
Of piracy accused,
Certain papers were not used
In defence. His end was not one to be relished.

There are some who now declare
That his treatment wasn't fair,
That the evidence of piracy was fudged.
That he wasn't cruel or feared,
That his name should perhaps be cleared,
That this would-be Robin Hood has been misjudged.

Fact or Fiction?

Fiction is awash
With the buckle and the swash.
And the clichéd 'pirates' found in certain books.
All those 'Yo ho ho-ing' cries...
And the patches on the eyes...
And the parrots... and the peg-legs... and the hooks...

The jagged facial scar...
The utterance of 'Arrrr!'...
And the victims who were made to 'walk the plank'...
The treasure maps they drew...
And their ships' unruly crew...
For much of this, we've Hollywood to thank.

Yes, their lives were sometimes grim.
They might lose a hand or limb,
And, in the dark, an eye-patch can help vision.
They might keep a pet on board,
Use the cutlass and the sword,
But otherwise, this image needs excision.

That plank-walk thing was rare,
An elaborate affair
With a blindfold and perhaps a prodding sword.
Let's get it in perspective,
For equally effective
Was to throw the hapless victim overboard.

Being hauled beneath the keel,
Many victims' fate would seal.
Dragged from bow to stern, or pulled from side to side.
By a rope securely bound,
And cut to shreds or drowned:
Either way, it's almost certain that they died.

There is no doubt that, at one time, William Kidd (c.1654–1701) operated as a privateer and pirate hunter. Whether he turned pirate is now questioned.

The events for which he stood accused, (including a charge of murdering a subordinate by hitting him with a bucket), took place in the Indian Ocean. Kidd's influential backers did not help to defend him, and he was hanged for five counts of piracy and one of murder. In the early 19th century, two French passes, which might have shown him to have been acting in the capacity of privateer, turned up amongst government papers in a London building. The passes had been misfiled.

Both Kidd and Blackbeard (see verse 489 opposite) were eclipsed by notorious Welsh pirate 'Black Barty' (Bartholomew Roberts), who captured more than 400 ships.

Hanging of William Kidd, from Charles Ellms'
***The Pirates Own Book* (1837)**

'Swash' may derive from an alliterative term for the sound made through the air by a side-sword and buckler (a small shield).

Long John Silver in Robert Louis Stevenson's *Treasure Island* forms one enduring impression of a pirate.

Pirates did sometimes bury treasure. Francis Drake is known to have done so, but he didn't make a very good job of creating the means to find it again: there is no evidence of maps showing the location of hidden riches. Kidd also hid treasure, and kept the location secret as a potential bargaining tool.

Eye patches can help a person to see in the dark, but at the expense of peripheral vision.

Pirates' equipment included the grappling hook (a special cannon round that fired a large hook attached to a line). This took hold of a crippled ship and allowed it to be reeled in. 'Stinkpots' were containers of foul-smelling chemicals that were hurled onto the decks of victims' ships causing panic. The grenado (an early type of hand grenade), boarding axes, muskets and knipple knots (pairs of small iron balls joined by a chain and thrown, rotating, through the air) were also used.

Of the very few recorded occurrences of walking the plank, one involved a captured Dutch ship in 1829.

Marooning was also popular. The stranded were sometimes given a gun with which to commit suicide, in preference to starvation. Victims of keel hauling also often had lead weights secured to their legs. Sharp barnacles would be adhering to the ship's keel and hull.

The captain, during fights,
Has his full controlling rights,
He's obeyed and can afford to be dogmatic.
Day to day, things are relaxed.
By a vote he can be axed,
So the system's really rather democratic.

Pre-determined and thus fair,
Of the spoils, all get a share...
The boatswain whose domain is up on deck...
The cabin boy... the cook...
Their allotted slice all took,
And they spent it fast. Why save it? What the heck!

'An absconding slave? That's great!'
They did not discriminate,
Re the colour of a would-be pirate's skin.
But this liberalist-type splendour,
Did not extend to gender –
Though a handful of the female sex got in.

More famous pirates

Most ferocious and renowned,
Two on Rackham's ship were found:
Anne Bonny joined it first and was his lover.
Mary Read's own cunning plan,
Was to dress up as a man,
So she earned her place, to start with, undercover.

The women soon were friends,
But their story sadly ends
With the capture of the crew, and then a trial.
The girls had a solution,
And got stays of execution,
Claiming pregnancy, which spared them for a while.

To intimidate and scare,
Teach lit fuses in his hair,
Which was thick and black, as also was his beard.
Though his captives were alarmed,
They weren't killed, or even harmed:
His appearance was enough to make him feared.

One who's famed in pirate lore
Made a single major score,
Which was shared between the others he'd recruited.
'Long Ben' Every's huge haul,
Was the biggest of them all.
It was taken from a treasure ship he looted.

Jack Rackham, known as 'Calico Jack', was captain of the pirate ship *Revenge*.

Anne Bonny was from Ireland. Mary Read, from England, had been passed off as a boy by her mother, in order to get financial support from her supposed grandmother. Mary periodically resumed her male disguise to serve as a British soldier, and as a commissioned privateer in the Caribbean. 'Calico Jack' was hanged in Jamaica. Mary, who was genuine in 'pleading her belly', died shortly after childbirth. Anne's fate is not certain, though her father may have secured her release.

Edward Teach (*c*.1680–1718), popularly known as 'Blackbeard', operated mainly off Virginia and South Carolina, aboard a captured French merchant vessel he'd renamed *Queen Anne's Revenge*. His one-time associates were Captain Benjamin Hornigold and Stede Bonnet. The amount Teach stole was considerably less in comparison with some.

Engraving of Anne Bonny (probably 18th century)

Print engraving of Stede Bonnet (*c*.1725) from Charles Johnson's *A General History of Pyrates*

He had lain in wait to meet
The Mughal's well-armed fleet,
(From a pilgrimage to Mecca homeward bound).
Things were looking rather chancy,
For the pirate ship the *Fancy*,
Till a lucky broadside shot the mainmast found.

There was fighting. There was slaughter,
And a captured royal daughter.
There was torture, and of women, violation.
Some ladies, it is said,
Thought it better to be dead,
And chose suicide instead of degradation.

This bold and ruthless raid
Adversely hit our trade,
But Every was never brought to trial.
With a price upon his head,
To New Providence he fled,
Which was boring, so he only stayed a while.

Again, and yet again,
What was called 'The Spanish Main',
Was a place where life at sea was never dull.
For treasure, men were vying
With their 'Jolly Rogers' flying –
Or that flag which has the crossbones and the skull.

This ensign prompted fright,
But it didn't signal 'fight',
If the 'shot across the bows' was quickly heeded.
But a red flag on the mast,
Meant, 'Prepare for action fast!'
And pirates could show ruthlessness when needed.

Henry Every or Avery (1659–1696) operated in the Atlantic and Indian Oceans.

The main ship of the Indian Muslim fleet he captured was the *Ganj-i-sawai*, carrying a cargo worth between £200,000 and £600,000, including gold and gemstones. Reportedly, the ship was also carrying a relative of Emperor Aurangzeb, and the popular belief is that it was his daughter or granddaughter.

The East India Company's fortunes had already been badly, but not irredeemably, affected by a war with the Mughal Empire (Child's War, 1686–90).

New Providence is in the Bahamas, where there was very little for Every and his crew on which to spend their ill-gotten gains. He reputedly returned to England or Ireland, but there is no record of him after June 1696.

The Spanish Main was the name given to the mainland areas of North, Central and South America which surround the Gulf of Mexico and Caribbean, and which were Spanish possessions.

As well as treasure, pirate crews were often equally happy seizing provisions. Pirates, it will be recalled, attacked ships of any nation, including their own.

The white skull on a black background sometimes featured cross swords and/or an hourglass. Both signalled death. The Knights Templar were the first to use the skull and crossbones motif. Pirates had a range of flags, and often didn't hoist any of them until they were close to the targeted vessel. The black flag with a white emblem indicated a pirate ship, from which a warning shot would usually be fired. Attack only followed if the warning was ignored, when a plain red flag would then be raised. The term 'Jolly Roger' may derive from the French 'jolie rouge' (pretty red).

Henry Every and his ship, the *Fancy*
(17th century artist unknown)

George Anson's voyage around the world

How's this for a mission?
'Please lead an expedition,
To oust the wretched Spanish from Peru.
And also, for good measure,
Bring back a load of treasure.
That, dear George, is all you have to do.

Though you need to be prepared,
Proper troops cannot be spared
But invalids will probably suffice.'
Thus Anson had been tasked.
He set sail to do as asked,
And partially succeeded – at a price.

Of the eight ships in his fleet,
Most with problems were to meet,
The return of only one was celebrated.
To disease along the way,
Many souls had fallen prey,
And their numbers, in effect, were decimated.

But that one remaining vessel
With a galleon would wrestle:
A Spanish ship which carried loads of coin.
This was wealth beyond belief;
After all the woes and grief,
The prize was one George managed to purloin.

Anson's voyage was from 1740 to 1744.

The mission in Peru involved the capture of the port of Callao (which served Lima), plus Lima itself, and the instigation of a revolt of Peruvians against Spanish colonial rule. The treasure would come from the capture of Panama, and the seizing of a Manila galleon, (a Spanish trading ship).

Five hundred invalids, from the Chelsea Hospital, were provided. Although all were considered too old, sick or wounded for active duty, it was thought some might be capable of performing light tasks!

The fleet comprised six warships, plus two merchant vessels (one of which, the *Industry*, turned back early into the voyage). The only vessel to return was the *Centurion*, Anson's fourth-rate flagship.

The *Nuestra Señora de Covadonga*, carrying more than a million pieces of eight, was captured and its cargo sold in Macau (1743).

George Anson (artist unknown)

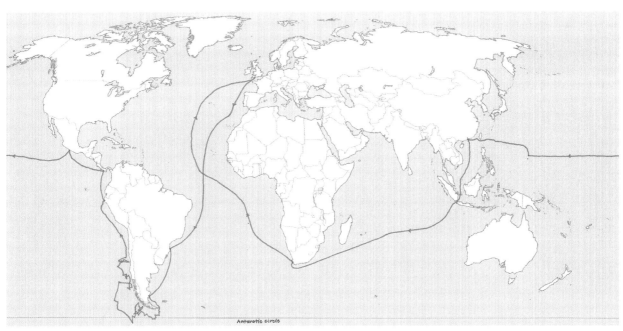

George Anson's voyage around the world, 1740–44

Beyond what he had captured,
The nation was enraptured
By his victory v. France at Finisterre.
Elevation his reward –
He earned the title 'lord',
Then in admin were his talents brought to bear.

The blockade he was behind
That France's ships confined;
Attacks elsewhere start proving Britain's dominance.
Though we fight both France and Spain,
More possessions we would gain:
Our navy now is on its way to prominence.

Improvements in navigational aids

Determining latitude

We've already had a look
At the juggling it took,
To calculate a ship's north/south position.
It needed lots of skill
As a deck does not stay still:
Improvements had been several people's mission.

The things that had been tried,
Left their users quite boss-eyed,
In their efforts to assess a bright sun's height.
Those at sea were more contented,
Once the back staff was invented,
Though it didn't work especially well at night!

A solution's needed fast:
By stars, no shadow's cast.
If the back staff works at all, it does so badly.
Using systems of reflection
Enter now a great confection...
Enter measured arcs and mirrors – and John Hadley.

This clever man presented,
The octant he'd invented,
In the dark, for navigation there was hope.
With a breakthrough now achieved,
Soon the sextant was conceived:
An instrument which offered greater scope.

A deficiency's been cured,
And this instrument's endured,
Although radio, then radar, took its place.
Now 'sat-nav' plots location,
But sextants aren't forsaken:
There is often one on board for 'just in case...'

After a major victory in the first Battle of Cape Finisterre (1747, during the War of the Austrian Succession – see verses 527–532), George was elevated to the peerage, and became 1st Baron Anson of Soberton. He masterminded the blockade of Toulon during the Seven Years' War (see verse 549).

In 1751, he became First Lord of the Admiralty. His many reforms included the transfer of the marines from army to navy authority (see verse 359), and a revision of the Articles of War (1749), which further tightened discipline throughout the navy.

See verses 197–199 for instruments designed to calculate latitude.

The cross-staff involved sighting two things at once. The back staff involved turning one's back on the sun, and calculating angles from the shadow cast. A variation on the back staff was invented by John Davis, an Elizabethan navigator (see verse 284). The Davis Quadrant would remain popular, even after more sophisticated devices had been developed.

English mathematician John Hadley (1682–1744) and Thomas Godfrey, a Philadelphia glazier, almost simultaneously, and independently, invented the octant (c.1731).

Sir Isaac Newton (1643–1727) had discovered the principle of the doubly reflecting navigation instrument, but never published it.

The octant could measure an angle of up to 90°. The sextant can measure up to 120°. The first was produced by John Bird in 1759. Octants continued to be used alongside sextants well into the 19th century.

Training in navigation still includes a knowledge of the heavens: in the event of a power-cut, mechanical methods would need to be used.

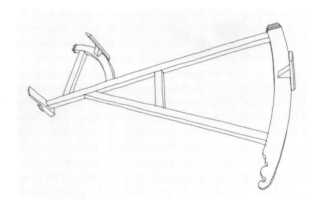

Davis Quadrant

Using the back staff

Meanwhile, Hadley's younger brother,
Was at work on yet another
Important thing, which could not be ignored.
He tried to put together
Certain data on the weather,
Though assumptions that he made were somewhat flawed.

The direction of a 'trade',
Can hinder, or can aid.
If it blows the way you're going, that is good!
To know which winds prevail
Is of use to those who sail,
But trades' properties weren't fully understood.

With his comet he'd found fame,
But Halley won acclaim
In many fields – this man was energetic.
He went to distant parts,
And drew many detailed charts,
Still used by those whose interest is magnetic.

Determining longitude

Whereas latitude was sussed,
There remained another 'must':
Longitude, to calculate, was next.
How far west or east you are,
Can't be plotted by a star.
All the scientists and boffins were perplexed.

Defective navigation
Had caused a situation,
Whereby many lives were lost when four ships sank.
By wicked winds all lashed,
On Scilly's rocks they'd crashed,
The quest to solve this problem drew a blank.

Galileo did his best –
On and off, lifelong his quest –
'We can use the moons of Jupiter,' he noted.
The theory was OK –
It's in use on land today –
But they couldn't make it work on ships that floated.

Halley then reports
That he's had some useful thoughts:
Try appulses. Try magnetic deviation.
With the former there were hitches,
Whilst the latter suffer glitches:
As solutions thus weren't met with acclamation.

George Hadley (1685–1768) was an amateur meteorologist who collected information from observational diaries sent to the Royal Society. He missed the point that the earth's rotation affects the direction in which winds travel. The word 'trade' comes from Middle English, and means 'track' or 'path'.

In 1698 Edmond Halley (1656–1742) led the first ever British expedition that was purely exploratory/scientific. Given command of the *Paramour*, he did not prove to be a particularly competent captain, and problems of insubordination on his first trip resulted in an early return from the South Atlantic. Halley worked out that the degree of deviation between true north and magnetic north was not constant, and he plotted isogonic charts accordingly. He also studied trade winds and monsoons, and his maps showing these remained the most definitive available until well into the 19th century. He is renowned, too, for a diving bell (see verse 1641).

In 1707, part of Britain's naval fleet, under the command of Admiral Sir Cloudesley Shovell, was involved in one of our worst ever naval disasters. 1,400–2,000 sailors perished off the Scilly Islands. The disaster was attributed to a number of navigational shortcomings.

The Italian, Galileo Galilei (1564–1642) was the first person to use a telescope for astronomical observation, though he didn't invent it. (Dutch lens maker Hans Lippershey had applied for a patent in 1608.) Galileo also studied, *inter alia*, tides and pendulums.

Using appulses relies on measuring the closeness of one heavenly body to another eg a star to the moon.

The deviation between the North Pole and the magnetic north had already been noted, but it was found that the variance was inconsistent.

Octant (Museo Naval, Madrid)

Sextant (Museo Naval, Madrid)

But it prompted very soon
Detailed study of the moon,
Better knowledge of its motion to produce.
(Not quite yet, a team's persistence
Would measure lunar distance,
And emerge with detailed data of real use).

King Charles had made it clear,
That he liked this whole idea.
An observatory would help to get things done.
An astute important move,
It can only serve to prove,
That he wasn't all frivolity and fun.

To help, a cash incentive
To attract the most inventive,
Would be offered by a most prestigious Board.
There was one who set his eyes
On this very worthwhile prize:
Though he waited many years for his reward.

Plotting lines from pole to pole,
Could not achieve the goal,
(Though on land it was quite easy not to err).
Folk had started now to think,
That there had to be a link,
'Twixt what time it was, and whereabouts you were.

John Harrison, self-taught,
Gave the problem careful thought:
'Yes, horology's the key,' he soon deduced.
But salt air... a boat that rocks...
Cause malfunctioning in clocks:
A better time-piece had to be produced.

Carpentry's John's trade,
So the first from wood were made.
He tested the escapement, cog and wheel.
Some ideas he had to scotch,
Thought, 'Let's try a biggish watch'.
By then, he'd started using tempered steel.

He succeeded with 'H4',
Which is proving quite a draw
At Greenwich. It no longer ticks away.
But it's there for all to see,
(As are versions one to three),
The engineering triumphs of their day.

The 'Board of Longitude' was set up by parliament in 1714, in response to the 1707 Scilly Islands naval disaster. It offered a prize of £20,000 (worth more than £2,000,000 today). This could be split between several recipients in proportion to their contributions to a solution.

It was already established that time equals longitude. Local time, relative to the time at any given reference point, will indicate where you are. For example, if your watch indicates 12 noon in London, and it is 12 midnight local time, you know you're halfway round the world.

Although a carpenter by trade, John Harrison (1693–1776) made and repaired clocks as a hobby. In his quest for something that could accurately tell the time at sea, he spent from 1730 to 1735 designing and producing his first, H1.

The Rev Dr Nevil Maskelyne (1732–1811), was the first person to scientifically measure planet Earth's weight. When he became Astronomer Royal (1765), this made him ex officio a Commissioner of Longitude. As such, he was closely involved in trialling contenders for the Longitude Reward.

The reference points for assessing the validity of the means to calculate longitude were the Greenwich Meridian (see verse 248) and Bridgetown, Barbados.

Using lunar distance tables, (favoured by Maskelyne, especially as their use could be rolled out more quickly), Tobias Mayer produced reasonably accurate results. Although these were less accurate than the timekeeping method, the Board was persuaded that Harrison's success was down to luck, and also needed to know that his sea watch could be replicated. He initially received only a £10,000 share of the reward. Later payments, (the last when he was eighty years old), increased the total to about £23,000.

The Royal Observatory at Greenwich was built in 1675, and opened in 1676. John Flamsteed was appointed the first Astronomer Royal. Charles II (r.1660–1685) founded the Royal Society to promote research into matters such as astronomy and navigation (see verses 356–357).

All now at the Royal Observatory, H1, H2 and H3 still work. H4 isn't kept running, as it requires oil for lubrication, and is liable to degrade. (For Greenwich, see also verses 246–248.)

Board Room of the Admiralty (Thomas Rowlandson, 1808)

H4

The location of a star,
Is still key to where you are
After Harrison has proved himself a hero.
How these glints of light are dotted
Was, for Greenwich, being plotted –
Thus establishing its longitude of zero.

Charts

To cope with coastal parts,
It is wise to have some charts,
With hazards such as wrecks and reefs all showing,
And water depths besides,
Plus the levels of the tides –
And a compass, so you know which way you're going.

This aid to navigation,
Was a 'DIY' creation,
And not always shared, so knowledge was erratic.
Then Dalrymple was appointed,
He made things less disjointed:
Collating charts was much more systematic.

Our own coast had been addressed
For, at Samuel Pepys' behest,
Greenvile Collins sailed around it and surveyed.
He had a detailed look,
Then produced a lovely book,
In which forty-eight great drawings are displayed.

The War of the Austrian Succession

Our relationship with Spain
Had been one of lessened strain,
But beneath the surface lurked the same old tension.
It needed just one spark
And on war we would embark,
Although Parliament was filled with apprehension.

Of smuggling accused,
Jenkins' person was abused –
His left ear by a Spaniard cruelly lopped.
This appendage was presented,
And resentment now fermented:
Such outrageous actions really must be stopped!

Most charts record high and low water marks, water depth, navigational hazards and aids, plus a compass – often in the form of an elaborate rose in early versions. These must be continually updated. Captains of vessels produced their own charts, and sometimes kept them secret.

Alexander Dalrymple was appointed in 1796 as the first hydrographer of the new Hydrographic Office (now the UKHO). He brought together existing charts.

The Admiralty's first official chart (of Quiberon Bay) was published in 1800, and charts were sold to the public from 1821.

For Samuel Pepys see verse 370.

Sir Greenvile Collins (1643–1694) was a Trinity House (see verses 238–239 & 1054–1059) pilot. *Great Briain's Coasting Pilot* was published in 1693: two samples of about forty-eight charts, (prepared between 1686–93), are shown below.

A further one – of Milford-Haven – features on Plate B on page 113.

A New and Exact Survey of the River Dee

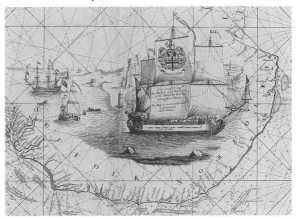

North Sea, Thames Estuary to the Wash

Jenkins' ear was severed in 1731, but was not used as a *casus belli* until seven years later, when this appendage was reportedly presented in the House of Commons. The War of Jenkins' Ear lasted from 1739 until 1748, and is regarded as one of several going on during the War of the Austrian Succession (1740–48).

To more fighting, Britain's doomed,
In a war that was subsumed,
In the one concerning Austrian succession.
It is maybe fair to say,
Things did not go all our way,
In the far-flung varied outbreaks of aggression.

Early triumph Britain gained,
But this wouldn't be sustained.
We failed at Cartagena. It was then
That we started to assess,
What was needed for success:
A navy that was more than ships and men.

All too rarely we'd exult
In a positive result.
Indecisive battles led to much frustration.
The Brits could not hold sway
If the foe refused to play,
And the game was one of tactical stagnation.

Aggressively quite sage,
We might hold the weather gage,
And the enemy outnumber and outgun.
But opponents soon were twigging:
They stayed leeward, shot our rigging,
Caused some damage, then were quickly on the run.

In The Battle of Toulon,
The British blundered on,
Though the signals they'd received were quite confusing.
At courts-martial men appeared,
And some captains were cashiered,
As we should have won, but ended up by 'losing'.

The French attacked Madras,
Briefly lost to us alas,
(Till for Louisbourg in Canada exchanged).
The final peace would show
Pretty much the 'status quo',
Although 'who owned what' was slightly rearranged.

All this European warring
Is getting somewhat boring
So an element of respite wouldn't hurt.
It's timely to suggest
This rhyme takes a little rest.
To other themes, it's going to divert.

Challenging Maria Theresa's right to the Habsburg (Austrian Empire) throne was the excuse used by France and Prussia to go to war over the contested area of Silesia. Britain sided with Austria.

In 1739, Edward Vernon (see verse 382) captured Porto Bello (Panama) with just six ships but in 1741, with a much larger fleet and a strong land force, attempts to capture Cartagena de Indias (Columbia) failed disastrously. In a reversal of fortunes, the British were repelled by 6 ships and a tiny garrison under the command of Blas de Lezo, who lacked one eye, one arm and one leg. Additionally, Spanish privateers inflicted serious losses on British merchant ships in the Americas.

A ship is said to hold the weather gage if it is upwind (windward) of opposing vessels, as this enables it to sail at will towards any downwind (leeward) point.

The 1744 Battle of Toulon was tactically indecisive but represented a strategic Franco-Spanish victory. After it, seven British captains were dismissed, including Admiral Thomas Mathews, whose retreat left Britain's Mediterranean fleet under Spanish control for long enough to ensure Spain's objectives in Italy.

In 1749, Parliament amended the 1661 Articles of War to increase the autonomy of naval courts.

The Treaty of Aix-la-Chapelle (1748), which ended the war, encapsulated its rather inconclusive outcome, although Britain had won two significant victories at Cape Finisterre, the first under Anson, (see verse 500), and the second under Edward Hawke (see also verse 551).

Return to Whaling – 'the Greenlanders'

In the year of forty-nine,
What was once in deep decline
With a 'bounty', almost instantly kick-started.
An activity's resumed.
'Greenland' whaling quickly boomed.
It was tough, and clearly not for those fainthearted.

From many ports now sail,
Men in cats, to hunt for whale.
These special ships had plenty of capacity.
Fifty chaps or more
Arctic waters would explore,
And secure their prey with lances – and tenacity.

Back at home, employment flourished.
Crews needed to be nourished.
And their vessels built… equipped… repaired… supplied.
Blubber first must boil
To extract the valued oil.
The range of onshore trades was very wide.

There were 'cons' as well as 'pros',
In the ice, some vessels froze,
And unlucky missions met with no success.
Great wealth masters could procure,
And the bounty was a lure,
But their crews were very tempting for 'the press'.

The industry would dip
If, men taken from their ship,
To the navy all would suddenly divert.
Only once more to increase,
In periods of peace,
When many whales their final breaths would squirt.

Seal hunting

It was not just whales. Instead
Men would kill the pinniped.
(Those creatures we more often call a seal,
Whose flippers are their feet),
They were sought for oil and meat,
And for fur, which had accessory-appeal.

What once clothed them now reshapes
Into bags and muffs and capes,
Which are worn with scant regard for the cetacean,
This the hunter blithely slaughters
In South Atlantic waters,
Until certain species face extermination.

The government bounty (1749) was 40 shillings (£2) per ship-ton. A 20 shilling bounty offered in 1733 had proved insufficiently attractive.

Both ships and men were known as 'Greenlanders', as Spitsbergen (one of the richest whaling grounds), was erroneously thought to be part of Greenland.

British whaling ports were mainly on the east coast, but there were others such as Exeter and Liverpool.

Cats were sturdy ships with three masts and were also used to carry cargo, when they were manned by crews of ten to twelve. As privateers during wartime, they might have up to one hundred men on board. Cats were not the only type of whalers.

Capacity was measured in burthen.

Farmers, butchers and bakers provided food. Rope-makers, canvas-spinners, sail-makers, carpenters, painters and chandlers were all required by the industry. Ships' chandlers were suppliers of specialised provisions, but the general trade of chandlers was making candles.

For impressment see verses 467–471.

Arctic whaling reached its peak in the 1780s.

In 1982, the International Whaling Commission (IWC) adopted a moratorium on commercial whaling. This is opposed by a number of nations, including Russia and Japan.

Pinnipeds include sea lions and walruses.

In addition to the South Atlantic, British sealers also hunted in Newfoundland.

A narrative of the cruise of the Yacht Maria among the Feroe Islands in the summer of 1854 (artist unknown, 1855)

On South Georgia Island's coast,
The fur seal suffers most:
Pursued with no real concept of 'sustainable'.
The activity – unceasing –
Soon means numbers are decreasing,
And this type is quickly almost unobtainable.

Round the British coast today,
Live the 'common' and the 'grey'.
The former are just what their name suggests.
Further north, greys congregate.
It is here some meet their fate,
As salmon farmers kill them off as pests.

In the UK and EU,
Legislation's been put through
Though for more protection certain groups campaign.
They say the law's not heeded,
And the culling isn't needed,
That what's done is neither timely nor humane.

The Seven Years' War, 1756–63

Back to what may well now seem
An old recurring theme:
Europe's fighting. (Why is largely immaterial.)
Our country opts to play
In this complicated fray,
Where the repercussions, once more, are imperial.

To the French, Menorca fell.
This event did not bode well
For the man sent to defend it – poor John Byng.
It was deemed he'd lost the plot.
He was sentenced to be shot,
And he sadly got no mercy from the king.

George the Second is that man;
He's the army's greatest fan.
The navy is a service he'll eschew.
William Pitt thought this was all wrong,
That for Britain to be strong
She'd need to take a wider global view.

The rules that served Byng ill,
Were intended to instil
A sense of conduct viewed as reprehensible.
The message must be heeded:
'One's utmost' is what's needed,
Even if this overrides what seems more sensible.

Seals are highly efficient predators and can cause damage to nets. They also tend to take a single bite out of each fish and leave it to die. Salmon farmers have a duty of care to protect their fish from harm and unnecessary suffering.

Deterrents such as screening blinds and acoustic devices are widely used. Legislation includes the UK Conservation of Seals Act 1970 and the Scottish Parliament's Licensing Act 2010. EU legislation (2009) banned the trade in seal products.

Objections to culling include the fact that cubs left motherless during the breeding season, are unable to survive without a source of high fat milk.

Minorca fell to the French in 1756. After an inconclusive battle, John Byng (1704–1757) sailed to Gibraltar so that his badly damaged ships could be repaired. Despite a 30 year record as a solid naval officer, he was shot by firing squad. His punishment for failing to 'do his utmost' was intended as an example to others. The Admiral Byng Campaign is actively seeking his exoneration.

The Articles of War, as revised in 1749 (see verse 501), gave naval courts-martial authority to act independently, but offered little discretion to vary the severe penalties prescribed.

The 1866 Naval Discipline Act, which remained in force for nearly one hundred years, in theory brought penalties more into line with enlightened practice. In 2006, the Armed Forces Act provided uniform disciplinary procedures for all Britain's armed forces.

William Pitt the Elder (1708–1778) held that France should be opposed at sea and not in continental Europe – a view with which the king disagreed.

> In this country, it is good to kill an admiral from time to time, in order to encourage the others.
>
> **Voltaire, from *Candide* (1789)**

We couldn't take much heart,
From this inauspicious start,
And must also note that Britain tried descents.
PM William Pitt had planned
To amphibiously land
Some troops in France – these missions non-events.

Now Boscawen blocks Toulon,
And further moves anon
Will stymie France from Marseille to Dunkirk.
Ports effectively are closed…
And French colonies exposed…
When trade's been stopped, economies don't work.

Thus the Brits have more success,
And the French are in a mess,
As progressively their ships become confined.
They may have no place to go.
They're obstructed. Even so,
Invading Britain's clearly on their mind.

France tries once, and with intent,
But Edward Hawke is bent
On thwarting this attempt to reach our shores.
Shoals and reefs he has to face,
But his British fleet gives chase,
And a very famous triumph thereby scores.

'Quiberon' (a bay) –
The 'Trafalgar' of its day –
Caused France's naval bubble to be burst.
At the start of that same year,
We'd cohabited with fear,
But now everywhere, our fortunes were reversed.

France had got it in the neck,
Losing places like Quebec.
The redrawn map, for us, was hunky dory
The Americans were friends,
But France longs to make amends:
A decade on will be a different story.

With triumphs meritorious,
Deservedly victorious,
Britain was the world's most mighty nation.
But the price we had to pay,
For things turning out that way,
Was to find ourselves in splendid isolation…

The idea of the planned descents was to attack the town of Rochefort, in the hope that this would divert French troops from Germany (Britain was allied with Prussia), and from France's global colonies.

After blockading Toulon, Admiral Edward Boscawen (1711–1761) successfully engaged France's Mediterranean fleet, which formed a major part of the plan to invade England and Scotland (The Battle of Lagos, 1759). He subsequently blockaded Cádiz, where five French ships had taken refuge.

On 20 November 1759, in the Battle of Quiberon Bay, Admiral of the Fleet Sir Edward Hawke (1705–1781) achieved one of Britain's greatest naval victories over the French. This finally ended for good the threat of French invasion. 1759 has been referred to as the *Annus Mirabilis*, the 'wonderful year' mentioned in the second line of *Hearts of Oak*, the official march of the UK's navy (and of the navies of some Commonwealth countries).

The French suffered massive losses elsewhere – in North America and in the Caribbean. (Britain took Guadeloupe and Antigua.) In the Siege of Madras, France's attempt to take the city failed, laying the foundations for eventual British supremacy in India.

The Marine Society

In the year this war began,
A philanthropic man
Knew the navy was in dire need of recruits.
Jonas Hanway's simple scheme,
Would ensure a steady stream,
And provided boys with bedding and with suits.

These lads, who must be 'stout',
Once duly kitted out,
Were sent to help the British win the war.
Thus the navy was enlarged,
And when they were discharged,
A merchant fleet career was next in store.

This old and well known charity,
Found instant popularity,
And in time became a training institution.
A merchant vessel's bought;
Aboard it, boys are taught,
And thus begins the school ship's evolution.

Soon this first is not alone,
For the movement's quickly grown.
The Admiralty joins in. So do others.
Thus there's training to be had,
For the would-be sailor lad,
Who'd choose this calling, if he had his druthers.

One such boy who took his chance,
Would later swim to France,
Though his first attempt by wind and waves was foiled.
Matthew Webb won much acclaim –
A matchbox bore his name –
Once he'd reached his destination (still well-oiled?).

As it seems an ideal fit,
We'll jump ahead a bit
To the Sea Cadets, (once Naval Lads' Brigades).
The orphaned and the poor,
Could join this well-known corps,
And learn all about the sundry naval trades.

Said to be the first person in London to carry an umbrella, traveller and philanthropist Jonas Hanway (1712–1786) became a governor of the Foundling Hospital, and was also, for more than twenty years, a commissioner for victualling the navy. He founded the Marine Society in 1756 and, by the end of the Seven Years' War in 1763, it had recruited more than 10,000 men and boys. Nelson became a keen supporter of the Society, and it is estimated that, by 1805, it was providing at least 15 per cent of British naval manpower (all volunteers).

The Marine Society is the oldest maritime charity in the world. It no longer provides training, but continues to offer practical and financial support and encouragement to those wishing to pursue a maritime career. The *Beatty*, purchased in 1786 and later renamed *Marine Society*, was moored on the Thames between Greenwich and Deptford.

In 1859, the School Ship Society was founded.

Matthew Webb (1848–1883) trained on board HMS *Conway*, a school ship stationed on the Mersey. Whilst serving in the merchant navy, he won the Royal Humane Society's Stanhope Medal for attempting (unsuccessfully) to rescue a man overboard from drowning. Coated in porpoise oil, he swam the English Channel, without aids, in 1875. He died attempting to swim through the Whirlpool Rapids below Niagara Falls.

The Sea Cadet Corps (SCC) originated in the Lads' Brigades formed by sailors returning from the Crimean War (1854–56). It is now a national youth organisation, and the UK's largest Naval Cadet Force.

The Boston Tea Party, 1773

This was not the sort of do
With a fancy cake or two,
Or the sandwich with a neatly cut-off crust
For the nibbling dainty picker.
And it wasn't 'more tea vicar?'
In the fragile cups that someone had to dust.

It was protest and near riot
That exemplified disquiet,
In a country that felt bitter and aggrieved.
Its folk weren't represented,
And resentment thus fermented
Over taxes which, as unfair, were perceived.

The tea tax – one such levy –
Was symbolic, more than heavy,
And importers had been turned away unpaid.
Now in Boston, one consignment,
Suffered major realignment:
It was thrown into the harbour to degrade.

Iconic this event,
Which told of discontent.
The British take some actions to chastise:
The Intolerable Acts,
A blockade that soon impacts
On Boston's trade. All this was most unwise.

The American Revolutionary War, 1775–83

Our colonies (thirteen),
Were progressively quite keen
To have the unfair British go away.
We'd not done as they'd demanded
So together they now banded,
Into what was dubbed a brand new USA.

Disproportionately harassed,
Our navy was embarrassed –
For which the Earl of Sandwich took the flak.
He should have paid more heed
To the navy that we'd need,
Instead of to a bread and butter snack.

Britain's thirteen American colonies (Georgia had been added in 1731) were subject to taxes, levied principally to fund their defence.

The Tea Act of 1773, aimed at protecting the interests of the East India Company, actually reduced the price of tea in the colonies, but was resisted on the principle that it had been passed without American input. Two ships, one carrying tea to Philadelphia and the other to New York, had been made to return to England with their cargoes.

In Boston, over 45 tons of tea were dumped from three ships, the *Dartmouth*, the *Eleanor* and the *Beaver*. A fourth ship, the *William*, bound for Boston, had encountered a storm and put aground at Cape Cod.

Some of the protesters wore Mohawk warrior disguises.

Thereafter, many Americans considered tea drinking to be unpatriotic, resulting in coffee's becoming the hot drink of preference in the USA.

Boston Tea Party (W.D. Cooper, 1789)

American Independence was declared on 4 July 1776.

Privateers acting on behalf of the Americans harassed British shipping.

Britain also suffered commerce raiding from the USA's newly formed Continental Navy, and John Paul Jones became America's first naval hero by capturing HMS *Drake* in British waters.

John Montagu, 4th Earl of Sandwich (1718–1792), during his third spell as First Lord of the Admiralty, ignored advice to send more ships to America, and favoured concentrating the British fleet in European waters.

A number of native American tribes fought alongside the British, but France (in 1778) and Spain (in 1779) supported the colonies by declaring war against Britain. Britain also went to war against the Dutch (1780–84) over the Dutch Republic's apparent trading support of Britain's enemies.

An account is needed not,
Of each battle and each shot
In a war in which we're almost on our own.
With a vengeful thirst to quench,
Suffice to say the French
For previous 'injustices' atone.

At Chesapeake, our fleet
With this enemy's would meet.
Our signalling resulted in morass.
Our ships got badly battered,
So retreat was all that mattered –
The victor, in a major coup, de Grasse

This forced us to withdraw.
We've America no more.
We capitulate, resign ourselves to failure.
To there, we had deported
Loads of convicts. Is this thwarted?
No, because we've just acquired Australia!

Now that retribution's wrought,
The French have just one thought
(Which wasn't simply sit back and enjoy).
Give the screw another twist
Was more or less the gist:
Great Britain's power they'd totally destroy.

To bring us to our knees,
Jamaica they would seize,
And this really would have been a knock-out blow.
Two fleets became embroiled
And this nasty scheme was foiled
By Rodney, setting British hearts aglow.

He'd already caused delight
In a battle held at night.
That supplies got through to Gib was consequential.
(Spain had joined in this affray
To take our rock away.
Fresh supplies and reinforcements were essential).

A Grand Assault was planned
To retake this chunk of land.
Floating batteries to help were engineered.
Faced with Britain's red-hot shot.
These did not achieve a lot.
Howe's fleet arrived. The threat soon disappeared.

The Battle of Chesapeake Bay took place in 1781. The opponents were fairly evenly matched. The British were under the command of Sir Thomas Graves and Sir Samuel Hood. Signals between the two admirals were at one point misinterpreted.

Following their victory, under the command of Comte de Grasse, the French were able to surround the British, resulting in the decisive surrender of Charles Cornwallis at Yorktown.

Between 1718 and 1783, about 50,000 convicts had been transported to British colonies in America.

George Brydges Rodney (1718–1792) secured a vital victory over a combined French and Spanish fleet at The Battle of the Saintes in 1782, thereby thwarting the planned invasion of Jamaica. Earlier that year at St Kitts, Admiral Samuel Hood (1724–1816) had beaten off attacks from De Grasse's much superior French force.

The Great Siege of Gibraltar (1779–83) followed an earlier unsuccessful attempt by the Spanish to regain it in 1727 (see verse 462).

The Battle of Cape St Vincent (1780) is also known as the Moonlight Battle because the fight lasted until after midnight. British success enabled the first relief of Gibraltar.

Vice Admiral George Darby provided a second naval relief in 1781.

Some of Spain's ten floating batteries were destroyed, and the rest were damaged beyond usefulness. The siege continued for some months after Howe's final relief, but the Spanish and French, (the 'Bourbon Alliance'), eventually gave up. Richard Howe (1726–1799), who had seen action in many conflicts, later became First Lord of the Admiralty.

The Defeat of the Floating Batteries at Gibraltar, 13 September 1782 (John Singleton Copley, _c._1783)

Illustrious careers
(Rodney's spanned full fifty years),
Could be forged by those whose origins were poor.
Once ability was proved,
Up the ladder they'd be moved,
Which could not be said for many jobs ashore.

Another here is noted:
Most deservedly promoted
Was Collingwood. Exceptional his skill.
He'd had a part to play
In the not-quite USA,
As a fighting sailor sent to Bunker Hill.

Our 'first empire's' in the past,
But we've not quite heard the last
Of America, that brand new fledgling nation.
In a very large locality,
She uses her 'neutrality',
And sometimes proved a cause of irritation.

The voyages of Captain Cook, and Australia

James Cook's first sailing role
Was the ferrying of coal,
On coasters down to London from the Tyne.
Whilst apprenticed, he learned much –
Navigation, maths and such –
All useful for the talents he'd refine.

Prior to voyages exploring,
He did a lot of drawing,
And mapped Newfoundland's coast with great precision.
This gained him recognition,
Then he led an expedition
Which required his skills, his knowledge and his vision.

To track a planet's motion,
From the vast Pacific Ocean
(Which didn't go as well as one might hope),
Was the first thing he would do.
There were further orders, too,
In the Admiralty's well-sealed envelope.

These were opened now and read,
To find out what lay ahead.
'Go discover' was the gist of what was written.
A landmass, supersized,
Had been hypothesized.
If found, it must be promptly claimed for Britain.

Cuthbert Collingwood (1748–1810) was part of a naval brigade (see verse 863), sent to augment British armed forces during the American War of Independence. He is probably best known for leading the second of two lines at the Battle of Trafalgar (see verse 693) aboard the *Royal Sovereign*.

James Cook (1728–1779) was commissioned by The Royal Society to track the transit of Venus. His observations were made from Tahiti, but were not as conclusive as had been hoped. The quest that followed was to find a hypothetical continent named Terra Australis. This would prove to be Antarctica. The theory, developed 2,000 years ago by the ancient Greeks, was that landmasses in the southern hemisphere should balance those in the northern.

On his second voyage, Cook crossed the Antarctic Circle and may have been as close as 150 miles from the mainland, the ice shelf of which was not sighted until 1820 (by a Russian expedition) (see verse 1275).

James Cook (Nathaniel Dance-Holland, *c*.1775)

On New Zealand, eyes were clapped,
And its coastline duly mapped,
After which the team continued on its way.
Ever mindful of the quest,
They travelled to the west,
To an area Cook first named Sting Ray Bay.

Up the eastern coast of Oz,
They had to halt because
The *Endeavour*, damaged, had to be repaired.
On a stop, when homeward bound,
Of the whole land that he'd found,
'That territory's British,' Cook declared.

As James travelled and explored,
A female was on board –
The first to go around the world afloat.
She was not of docile ilk.
Cook relied upon her milk.
This heroine was simply called 'The Goat'.

On voyage number two,
He takes something that is new –
A version of chronometer H4.
With the knowledge this imparts,
He made South Pacific charts –
So precise they would be used for ever more.

His achievements were admired.
He was fêted – and retired;
A state which wasn't easy to endure.
He wished not to stagnate,
And did not have long to wait:
The seas had irresistible allure.

The prospect was the thrill
Of the Arctic climate's chill:
The Northwest Passage once again was sought.
Perhaps this quest he'd not have chosen,
If he'd known it was still frozen:
His several tries to breach it came to nought.

It is through the Bering Strait
That the obstacles await.
Frustration maybe caused him now to change.
To Hawaii he returned,
As his crew became concerned
That their captain's conduct seemed to be quite strange.

In 1770, Cook (then with the rank of Lieutenant) landed at what he later renamed Botany Bay, due to the large number of plants discovered there. It is now Sydney's main cargo seaport.

The goat's first round the world trip had been aboard HMS *Dolphin* captained by Samuel Wallis. She butted a Tahitian royal when he stepped on 'her' deck. Cook was so fond of her, he gave her an inscribed silver collar, and the words of Samuel Johnson (that she was deserving of 'ease and perpetual pasture') became her epitaph when she died – just two days after Parliament awarded her a state pension.

For his second (1772–75) and third (1779–80) voyages, Cook was in command of HMS *Resolution*.

Cook's charts were in use at least until the middle of the 20th century.

See verses 274–275, 1278, 1298 & 1320 for the Northwest Passage.

On his third trip, Cook reportedly developed a stomach ailment and he also increasingly became irrational in terms of the commands he issued.

The *Resolution* and *Adventure* in Matavai Bay, Tahiti (William Hodges, ships' artist, 1776)

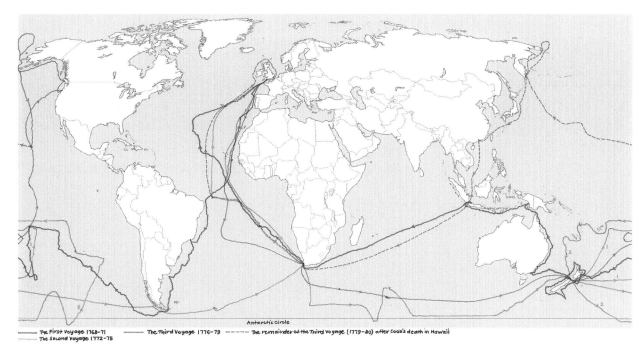

The voyages of James Cook

They reached their destination
At a time of celebration –
For worshipping a deity the season.
What a welcome there awaited!
Cook's this god, reincarnated,
(Though some dispute that theory as the reason).

One month later, Cook departed,
But the trip had barely started
When the foremast broke. He goes back for repairs.
Tensions suddenly now spring.
Cook abducts the native king,
Then turns his back, is struck down unawares.

First a blow upon the head,
Next stabs, till he was dead.
This episode makes very little sense.
On the globe, he'd filled in gaps,
With his surveys and his maps,
His legacy enduring and immense.

Matthew Flinders

Misfortune also hinders
A man named Matthew Flinders.
Australia, to him, would owe her name.
Though others had first found it,
He sailed all the way around it.
In that country, he's won popular acclaim.

The islanders were celebrating the Polynesian god Lono.

Cook was killed on 14 February 1779 at Kealakekua Bay on the western Kona coast of Hawaii Island.

Death of Cook (D.P. Dodd & others, 1784)

Matthew Flinders (1774–1814), an accomplished navigator and hydrographer, concluded that there was no Terra Australis, (see verses 1274–1277), which resulted in a loss of interest in finding it. He therefore gave this name to Australia. On the third of three voyages to the Southern Ocean, he sailed all the way round it. On the second, he had established that Tasmania is an island.

See verse 520 for marine chronometer H4.

See verse 418 for earlier visitors to Australia.

As homeward he was wending,
His vessel needed mending,
He dropped anchor at the French isle of Mauritius.
On his claim, 'My mission's science,'
He'd placed far too much reliance:
Was held captive, when the Guv'nor got suspicious.

This was maybe with good cause,
(The Napoleonic Wars),
But Matt suffered from enforced incarceration.
We'd been led a merry dance
From the so-called Isle de France:
With raids upon the shipping of our nation.

This is mentioned prematurely,
But we had to stop this, surely?
The Royal Navy was despatched to save the day.
But it sadly was to meet
Our worst (and sole) defeat.
Three months later, though, we drove the French away.

The Port of London

The Venerable Bede
Wrote a rather lengthy screed,
In which the Pool of London gets a mention.
It's the reason, he insists,
That our capital exists,
And no one disagrees with his contention.

Ever since the Romans landed,
The port had been expanded:
The largest in the world it would become.
Its business was colossal,
Many vessels there would jostle
To unload their tea and spices, wine and rum.

Coasters transferred coal and grain...
Bigger ships brought sugar cane,
Or tobacco, timber, furs and hemp (for rope).
There'd be long delays to face,
And theft was commonplace,
As the criminal enjoyed a lot of scope.

What merchantmen deliver
Is carried well up river –
To as far as masted ships could sail with ease.
Many wharves had been erected,
Customs duties are collected –
Hence the area is dubbed 'The Legal Quays'.

France took control of Mauritius in 1715 and renamed it Isle de France.

Flinders was held there from 1804, for a period of six years. His health was affected and he died the day before the publication of his acclaimed book, *A Voyage to Terra Australis*.

In 1809, a squadron under Sir Josias Rowley (1765–1842) successfully raided the neighbouring Island Réunion, and captured it in 1810. In the same year, led by Captain Samuel Pym, the British suffered heavy losses at the Battle of Grand Port. It was our only naval defeat during the Napoleonic Wars (see verses 690–719). A squadron under veteran Albemarle Bertie (1756–1824) arrived, after some fighting had already taken place, to secure the seizure of Mauritius from the French. The campaign involved an amphibious landing and the deployment of royal marines.

Bede (672/3–735) was an English monk whose works include *The Ecclesiastical History of the English People*.

The Pool of London was originally a stretch along Billingsgate on the north bank of the Thames and, later, a longer stretch from Rotherhithe up river as far as London Bridge, beyond which vessels with tall masts could not pass.

The Port of London was the biggest port in the world during the nineteenth century. It is now the UK's second largest port (after Grimsby and Immingham), and the second largest container port (having been overtaken by Felixstowe).

EIGHTEENTH CENTURY LONDON

In ev'ry Town where Thamis rolls his tyde,
A narrow pass there is, with houses low,
Where ever and anon the stream is eyed,
And many a boat soft sliding to and fro...

And on the broken pavement, here and there,
Doth many a stinking sprat and herring lie...

Hard by a sty, beneath a roof of thatch,
Dwelt Obloquy, who in her early days
Baskets of fish at Billingsgate did watch,
Cod, whiting, oyster, mackerel, sprat, or plaice:...

Such place hath Deptford, navy-building town,
Woolwich and Wapping, smelling stong of pitch...

Alexander Pope (1688–1744), from *Early Poems: Imitations of English Poets. Spenser: The Alley*

Legal Quays, 1757 (Louis Peter Boitard)

Here the lightermen await.
Their job's transferring freight
In the barges with flat bottoms that they row.
Before they can be hired,
An apprenticeship's required,
So they understand the river's ebb and flow.

The Thames got too congested,
And the lightermen protested,
When proposals for a brand new dock were made.
The objectionable scheme –
The West India, down stream –
Was a threat to all their profitable trade.

But it had to be conceded:
New facilities were needed,
And others very quickly were proposed.
Built for purpose, they were walled,
So the would-be thief was stalled.
Proper warehouses ensured goods weren't exposed.

Tactical thinking and technical innovation

The fighting ship had not
Really changed its shape a lot;
The dimensions were in force, as you'll recall.
But some technical advances,
Would enhance our sailors' chances,
When naval actions turned into a brawl.

Some saw it as derisive,
That engagements weren't decisive,
And held the view we ought to get stuck in.
With a free-for-all perhaps,
We might beat the other chaps.
At least, this way, one combatant would win.

Copper-bottoming

Ships were dry-docked or careened,
So their bottoms could be cleaned,
For barnacles and seaweed stuck to wood.
Free of debris, hulls were slicker.
Unencumbered boats are quicker.
A solution to this problem would be good.

To coat the underside,
Certain 'stuffs' had been applied.
Variously white and brown and black.
Initially protective,
They weren't all that effective,
Against the shipworm's burrowing attack.

The Company of Watermen and Lightermen was established by Act of Parliament in 1555.

Watermen carry passengers. The activities of both groups had been subject to regulation since 1193.

Lightermen relied heavily on tidal currents, and needed detailed knowledge of these. The period of apprenticeship was typically two years, but could be as long as seven.

In the second half of the 19th century, overseas trade more than doubled, and there was also a huge increase in coastal vessels using the Pool, most of them colliers.

The 1799 West India Docks Act enabled the building of this new dock. The lightermen managed to secure the important concession (the 'free water clause') of free passage into and out of this (and later) docks. Some ships avoided dock fees by hiring lightermen to transfer goods to and from the quayside, to the detriment of dock owners' profits.

The new docks were opened in 1802, followed by the East India in 1806. More followed during the century. From 1909, all London's enclosed docks (except the Regent's Canal Dock) were operated by the Port of London Authority (PLA).

Warehouses were erected if the commodity handled needed to be stored. The West India Dock originally comprised an import dock and an export dock, and the warehouses were located at the former.

See Plate B on page 113 for a map of the Port of London in 1837.

East India Dock, 1806

For dimensions see verses 372–374.

Sir John Clerk of Eldin (1728–1812) in his *Essay on Naval Tactics* (1779, first published 1790) controversially expounded the tactic of cutting the line. This involved attacking the rear of the enemy's line with the whole force, resulting in a close combat melée (see verse 699). There is some debate about whether Admiral Rodney deliberately broke the French line at the Battle of the Saintes (see verse 571): the line *was* breached, but reports indicate that a turn of the wind caused gaps in two places.

Careening is the practice of beaching a vessel at high tide to expose one side or the other of a ship's hull.

Shipworms (actually molluscs) invaded wood, causing huge damage.

Ships could also spend more time at sea if they did not need such frequent maintenance.

White stuff was a compound of whale oil, rosin and brimstone. Brimstone was added to tar and pitch (black stuff) to make brown stuff. Lead was also tried without success.

They sought to keep from harm,
A frigate, the *Alarm*,
With a lovely sheath entirely made of copper.
This was promising to start,
Then the ship near fell apart,
As all its iron bolts had come a cropper.

But this metal wasn't bad.
Britain's fleet was wholly clad,
Then the problem with the bolts was once more faced.
Soon an alloy's constitution,
Proved a workable solution,
And every single rivet was replaced.

On Anglesey, a mountain
Proved a veritable fountain
Of the copper that this exercise required.
Although it wasn't cheap
There'd be benefits to reap,
Thus Middleton (who'd pushed it) proved inspired.

Fire-power improved

Our warships will parade
The amazing carronade:
A short-range gun, whose balls all fitted snugly.
Without the windage gap,
This 'smasher' had more zap,
And proved useful every time the fray turned ugly.

We will also hit the mark,
With the flintlock's handy spark,
To fire the guns arranged through warships' hatches.
This provided quick ignition
For the British ammunition,
And was safer and more accurate than matches.

We add to these ingredients
The simplest of expedients,
Making Britain's cannons simpler to direct.
Repositioning the rope,
Provided greater scope
For swivelling, to where they'd best eject.

From the year of ninety-five,
More sailors stay alive,
Now that citrus juice is stopping them from dying.
The scene is being set,
For our biggest triumph yet,
When once more, against the French, our navy's vying...

The *Alarm* was copper-sheathed in 1761. Copper and iron react. Sir Humphry Davy (he of the miner's safety lamp), undertook a number of experiments aimed at minimizing copper corrosion.

The scheme to clad the whole fleet was pushed through largely due to the determination and, at times, blind faith of the Scot, Charles Middleton (1726–1813).

A copper, zinc and iron alloy was developed to resolve the problem with the bolts. Luckily, large scale copper production at Parys Mountain had just started, but the process was nevertheless expensive. The term 'copper-bottomed' has come to mean something that is genuine or trustworthy. The process increased speed and manoeuvrability, and merchant vessels thus clad were viewed as less of a risk and were therefore cheaper to insure.

Charles Middleton was later created Baron Barham. He became a full admiral in 1795, and was appointed First Lord of the Admiralty in 1805. He was also a keen supporter of the abolition of the slave trade (see verses 734–736).

HMS *Alarm* (artist unknown, *c*.1781)

The carronade is a lightweight gun, which could be mounted on the forecastle and quarterdeck of fighting ships. It was developed in 1778 by the Carron Company, a Scottish ironworks.

Any gap between a cannon ball and bore reduces efficiency.

Developed for naval use by Rear Admiral Sir Charles Douglas (1727–1789), the flintlock mechanism enabled instantaneous fire.

For scurvy see verse 389.

Mutiny on the *Bounty*, 1789

She'd had a modest role:
The carrying of coal.
Now 'The *Bounty*' is a name we've come to know.
She sailed with the entreaty
'Collect breadfruit from Tahiti,
Then take it to a place where it might grow.'

In charge was William Bligh,
He had been around, this guy.
He'd been master on Cook's sloop, the *Resolution*.
He liked everything kept clean,
Was on science very keen,
And he now set sail to make his contribution.

Near Cape Horn, the trip was thwarted.
That route had to be aborted.
He turned eastwards to collect his leafy freight.
Seedlings had to grow a bit
To make them travel-fit;
For the crew, this meant an unplanned five month wait.

So pots were duly tended,
And the natives were befriended,
Here, a sailor could be struck by Cupid's dart.
Fletcher Christian (Bligh's old pal)
Even wed a local gal,
But all too soon, the time came to depart.

Goodbye hedonistic life.
Farewell girlfriend. Farewell wife.
The loyalty of some began to shift.
Although Fletcher took the lead,
Eighteen other men agreed.
They mutinied, and Bligh was cast adrift.

It's alleged that he was cruel.
That his vanity he'd fuel,
By humiliating those who caused affront.
Though it's hard to comprehend,
He targeted his friend:
Poor Christian always seemed to bear the brunt.

Bligh now finds himself afloat,
In a little open boat,
With those whose strong allegiance hasn't wavered.
Thus the *Bounty*'s launch departs –
No chronometer, no charts,
Not much to eat – the prospect isn't savoured.

Originally called *Bethia*, after a refit the former collier was renamed, becoming HMAV (His Majesty's Armed Vessel) *Bounty*. She was rated as a cutter.

It was hoped to cultivate breadfruit trees in the West Indies, as food for slaves. Breadfruit, when cooked, resembles potato and tastes like bread!

The *Bounty*'s crew of forty-six included two civilian botanists.

William Bligh (1754–1817) had the rank of lieutenant. He'd joined the Royal Navy at the age of thirteen, and had subsequently also spent a period of four years in the Merchant Service.

Fletcher Christian (1764–1793) had joined the navy aged 17 as a cabin boy – relatively late, as the usual age for this role was 12 to 15. On the first visit to Tahiti, Christian developed a close relationship with a Polynesian woman and, on a second brief stop on the island, married the daughter of a local chief.

Bligh was a complex character, who certainly lacked people skills and found it difficult to tolerate inefficiency. There is one theory that, with unlimited access to the rum supply, he was a secret drinker, which could account for his violent outbursts.

Prior to the *Bounty*'s reaching Tahiti, there had been clashes between Bligh and crew members. These included the carpenter, the surgeon, and sailing master John Fryer, who remained loyal despite the considerable and enduring ill-will between the two men. In the three weeks after the departure from Tahiti, Fletcher Christian increasingly became a particular target of the captain's rages, to the point of despair. Having established that he had support, Christian decided to act. In a bloodless mutiny, Bligh was seized from the unlocked room in which he was sleeping, bound and set adrift in the ship's large boat. With a capacity of ten, this launch was overloaded.

Of the 'loyalists', 18 went with Bligh, and four others were forced to remain on the *Bounty*. Some of those who opted to join Bligh may have done so to avoid becoming *de facto* mutineers under the Articles of War (see verses 355, 501, 531, 545 & 663).

William Bligh (Alexander Huey, 1814)

There's a stop to find provisions;
Not the wisest of decisions:
The Tofuans soon grow hostile. What a scrape!
They've provided little food,
And are now in murd'rous mood.
Norton's stoned to death whilst trying to escape.

'Men are tastier than animals' –
The view of Fiji's cannibals –
Meant landing there just wouldn't be astute.
But on Restoration Isle,
There is refuge for a while.
Here are oysters, and supplies of native fruit.

To the west the boat now sails,
Through rolling seas and gales.
They ate little, due to stringent limitation.
Somehow, everyone survived,
And at Timor they arrived:
An extraordinary feat of navigation.

And for this, Bligh must earn praise:
After forty-seven days,
He had brought his men to where they could be safe.
His log's there for posterity,
But did he write with verity,
Given how he dealt with some began to chafe?

Back home, the tale was told.
The *Pandora* was enrolled,
To search for the dissenters of the time.
On Tahiti, some were found,
Then the vessel ran aground.
The survivors later answered for their crime.

The remainder were meanwhile,
On a (then) uncharted isle.
Pitcairn was the place they chose to stay.
As things soon turned acrimonious,
It may have been erroneous,
To burn their ship in what's called Bounty Bay.

Most were far from Fletcher-phylic,
So his life was not idyllic.
All was factiousness and drink-fuelled discontent.
Christian's dreams were unfulfilled:
It is likely he was killed,
But many now can rightly claim descent.

A stop at Tofua (one of the Tongan islands) led to a hurried escape from angry natives convening on the beach. In an act of great bravery, quartermaster John Norton was captured whilst trying to cut the rope that moored the party's boat. He was stoned to death.

Later in the journey, the launch was chased and nearly overtaken by natives in canoes off Fiji ('Fee Gee' according to Bligh's log: he charted the islands as they passed.)

Restoration Island was thus named by Bligh, as the boat landed there on the anniversary of the restoration of Charles II (see verse 354). Bligh cautioned the men against eating what they picked, in case it was poisonous, but it proved harmless and, as he conceded in his log, apparently beneficial. Although the overloaded boat was in danger of capsizing, the rainy weather proved a lifesaver in that it provided drinking water.

A journey of 3,681 nautical miles brought the men to the safety of Coupang in Timor, but the cook and the botanist died shortly after arrival. Four others died within the next few months.

The mutineers first attempted to settle on Tubai, but came into conflict with the natives and returned to Tahiti. By now disillusioned with Christian, two-thirds of his crew of twenty-four opted to remain there.

When the *Bounty* set sail for Pitcairn with the remaining nine mutineers, a number of Tahitians (six men and eleven women) were still on board, effectively kidnapped. This ultimately led to violent insurrection, resulting in the deaths of most of the men.

It is not known how Christian met his death. There are rumours (unlikely to be true) that he somehow found his way back to Britain. He had a daughter and two sons, Thursday October Christian and Charles Christian. His surname is especially common in New Zealand, and many of those who bear it are probably Fletcher's descendants.

Four former *Bounty* crew members, taken from Tahiti in 1791, perished when HMS *Pandora* sank. Once back in England, the remaining ten faced a court martial. Four were acquitted. Of the six found guilty of mutiny, three were hanged from the yardarm of HMS *Brunswick* in Portsmouth dock, and three received pardons.

A nautical mile (M, NM or nml) is a unit of distance. It is about one minute of arc along any meridian and equates to 1.15 land miles. A sea mile is a variable distance of about 6,000 feet.

The mutineers casting Lieutenant Bligh adrift (Robert Dodd, 1790)

Spithead and Nore Mutinies, 1797

It's appropriate right here,
To pick up on Bligh's career.
He led breadfruit expedition number two.
In Jamaica, these plants flourished,
But not many slaves were nourished:
As a foodstuff, it was something they'd eschew.

At Spithead we'll now note.
Bligh is once again afloat
When drastic action sailors there are taking.
He's a captain, what is more
At the anchorage of Nore,
Though these mutinies were not of William's making.

The pay that they were getting,
Caused these seamen to be fretting:
They'd had no rise since 1658!
After lengthy wage stagnation,
They'd been hit by high inflation.
There's another issue, too, concerning weight...

The two ounce purser's 'perk'
Had started now to irk.
(Their 'pound' of meat by this amount was short.)
Of this salary addition,
They were seeking abolition.
When talks fail, to other measures they'll resort.

Fewer stops in port they had,
Now that ships were copper clad...
All those 'landsmen' didn't know what they were doing...
Some lieutenants – just a few –
They wanted rid of too.
Such grievances had really got them stewing.

Spithead's action was restrained,
With discipline maintained.
It was settled when the 'powers that be' saw reason.
At the Nore the seamen's stand,
Got rather out of hand,
(Some were later hanged for piracy and treason.)

This bunch of mutineers,
Wakes the government's worst fears:
They might kindle revolutionary zeal.
Their demands have been expanded;
As radicals they're branded:
The response an unequivocal 'no deal'.

The second breadfruit mission (1791–93), when Bligh was master and commander of HMS *Providence*, was successfully accomplished.

Bligh was captain of HMS *Director* at the time of the Spithead (an anchorage near Portsmouth) mutiny. Bligh also caused antagonism when he was Governor of New South Wales, which ultimately prompted the Rum Rebellion. He finished his career as Vice Admiral of the Blue.

The word perk is an abbreviated form of the noun 'perquisite' signifying an incidental benefit. The 'purser's pound' weighed 14 (instead of 16) ounces.

The new population-based quota system (the Quod) was introduced in 1795, and was unpopular with experienced seamen, especially as counties sometimes provided financial inducements for men to join the undermanned navy as quotamen. The system was ended in 1815 after the Napoleonic Wars, along with impressment (see verses 467–471). Under the Quota Act, London had to provide 5,704 men.

Most demands emanating from Spithead were met under a negotiated settlement conducted by Admiral Lord Howe, (see verse 641), who ensured that all involved received a royal pardon. The complaints of the Spithead mutineers did not include flogging (or impressment).

The Nore (an anchorage in the Thames Estuary) mutiny was led by Richard Parker.

Richard Parker, President of the Delegates in the late Mutiny in his Majesty's Fleet (J.Harrison & Co; William Chamberlain, 1797)

Discontent was in the air:
There were episodes elsewhere.
To which nasty captains sometimes might fall prey.
But the protests got results,
And the sailor now exults
In less brutal treatment, better food and pay.

Rebellious distraction,
With our sailors out of action,
Could well have proved of benefit to France.
But there was no exploitation
Of this sorry situation,
And our enemies thus missed a gilt-edged chance.

An example of what happened elsewhere are the events aboard HMS *Hermione* in the West Indies, when unduly cruel Captain Pigot, and most of his officers, were killed (1797).

The Spithead and Nore mutinies paralysed Britain's Channel and North Sea fleets.

The majority of the men in the fleet of Admiral Adam Duncan (1731–1804), joined the Nore mutiny, and refused to quit their anchorage in Yarmouth. Although this left Duncan with only his own ship, *Venerable*, and Hotham's *Adamant*, it is to his credit that two crews agreed to continue with their duties. (See verses 676–682 **The Battle of Camperdown, October 1797**.)

ADMIRAL DUNCAN ADDRESSING HIS CREW.

Admiral Duncan addressing his crew, from *The Sea: its stirring story of adventure, peril & heroism* by Frederick Whymper (1887)

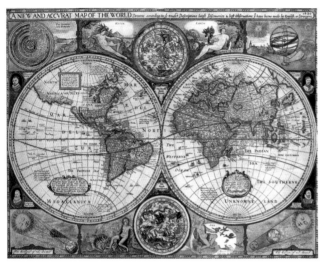

A New and Accvrat Map of the World (John Speed, English cartographer, 1627)

New and Accurate Map of the World (Nicholaes Visscher, 1690)

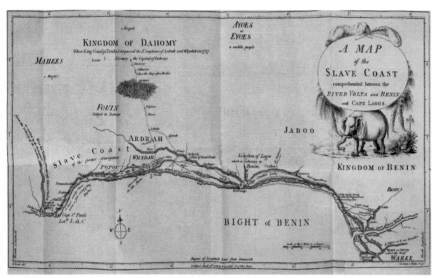

Map of part of the African Slave Coast (Robert Norris, British slave trader, 1789)

Map of Virginea Pars (John White, 1585)
(Roanoke Island shown coloured pink)

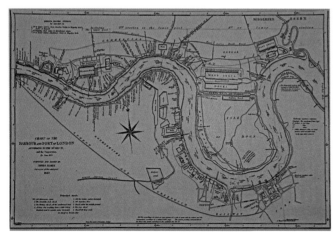

Port of London, 1837 (James Elmes)

Milford-Haven and the adjacent islands (Sir Greenvile Collins, 1686–93)

6 Early nineteenth century

6

Early nineteenth century

The start of the French Revolutionary Wars

In France, there is upheaval.
Privilege is evil!
The nobles face the fate they are deserving.
'Madame Guillotine' is busy,
And Europe's in a tizzy:
Revolutionary fervour is unnerving.

We can't sit by all flustered,
Whilst in France an army's mustered –
So huge, it quashes any opposition.
Expansion is the dream
Of that country's new regime.
To resist this, there is formed a coalition.

Our response was fairly prompt,
But Europe's quickly swamped.
Relentlessly, the French troops now progress.
On land, it's fair to say,
Things go pretty much their way.
Our navy, though, will meet with some success.

Toulon we briefly held –
Till by Bonaparte expelled,
So what Hood achieved was only really fleeting.
Outmanned, our force withdrew,
But we had a trick or two,
And burnt a lot of warships whilst retreating.

Hood's significant credential
Was in proving influential,
On how a well-known protégé progressed.
This mentorship bore fruit,
And a seasick raw recruit
Named Horatio, became one of the best.

We'll get to Nelson soon,
But the Glorious First of June,
Is down to someone else who found acclaim.
A convoy filled with grain
Howe tries to block – in vain.
But we're chalking up a triumph all the same!

The French Revolution (1789–1799) had the mantra 'liberté, égalité, fraternité'. The king himself (Louis XVI) was executed in 1793, an event which was followed by the Reign of Terror.

The French army vastly increased in size due to mass conscription. French expansionism meant that Britain's overseas possessions were at risk. These included India, the naval defence of which was, at the time, the responsibility of Admiral Peter Rainier (1741–1808).

After the War of the First Coalition (1792–98), there would be the War of the Second Coalition (1798–1802). During the Napoleonic Wars (1803–1815), alliances between the European powers fluctuated and there would be five more coalitions (usually financed and led by the UK), the last of which (the seventh) was in 1815. Essentially, we were fighting the French throughout and, until peace with Spain was declared in 1808, the Spanish too.

Toulon was France's principal Mediterranean port. Admiral Sir Samuel Hood (1724–1816), whose Mediterranean fleet had been blockading the city, was invited to occupy it on the invitation of the French royalists. The British were expelled late in 1793. Napoleon Bonaparte (1769–1821) was in command of the artillery force that regained the town. To prevent the French fleet from falling into the hands of the revolutionaries, Hood ordered that it should be burned. Captain Sidney Smith, who became a skilled inshore tactician, managed to destroy about half of the 58 French ships in Toulon harbour. Lord Hood's less famous cousin (confusingly also named Samuel) was involved in the British withdrawal from the port.

Horatio Nelson (1758–1805) was plagued by seasickness the whole of his career.

Most battles are named after a place near the location of action, but the Glorious First of June (1794) wasn't close to anywhere in particular and was therefore named for its date.

Admiral of the Fleet Richard Howe (1726–1799) had been involved in the amphibious landings during the Seven Years' War (see verse 548) and had also taken part in the Battle of Quiberon Bay (see verse 552).

Admiral Peter Rainier (unidentified British artist, c.1778-87)

On a mid-Atlantic stage,
He'd commanded, 'Rake! Engage!'
But not everyone complied with this suggestion.
To the message thus conveyed,
Attention wasn't paid,
Which brought discipline and training into question.

Cornwalliss's retreat, 1795

With more ships the French are blessed,
When they threaten us off Brest
In an action called 'Cornwallis's retreat'.
It seems we're doomed to lose,
So employ a cunning ruse,
And signal to a non-existent fleet!

Our men know for a fact
That our 'secret' code's been cracked,
And ensure their hoisted flags are in plain sight.
'Join us now' one message beckons,
And the French commander reckons
It is better to sail off, than stay and fight.

Signalling

How did ships communicate?
Our methods weren't so great;
To find a better way some had been trying.
(Signals, in the past,
Had related to which mast
A hoisted flag was prominently flying.)

But the book that we were using,
Quite often proved confusing,
One imagines sailors looking on askance.
So, at times, we would avoid
Needing flags to be deployed,
By working out our tactics in advance.

Howe's orders, as intended,
Had not been apprehended.
And befuddlement a battle plan encumbers.
(He had clearly not succeeded,
In devising what was needed
When he'd introduced a method using numbers.)

It will only be a while
Before (much more versatile)
A coded system Popham pioneers.
Whole sentences were 'voiced'
In a range of flags to hoist.
His method was in use for many years.

Raking fire is directed along the length of an enemy ship, from ahead or astern, rather than at its side. Whilst it is harder to hit the target, more damage is inflicted when a shot does connect.

The French had 12 ships of the line and 11 frigates. The British had 5 and 2 respectively. Sir William Cornwallis (1744–1819), Commander of the British Channel Fleet, was a friend of Nelson. His brother was Charles Cornwallis, British Commander at the siege of Yorktown during the American Revolutionary Wars (see verse 568).

The false signals were sent on the orders of Captain Robert Stopford aboard the frigate *Phaeton*. The appearance of sails on the horizon completed the illusion. What French commander, Villaret de Joyeuse, had seen was, in fact, a small merchant convoy. His withdrawal allowed Cornwallis to sail to Plymouth for repairs to his battered, but intact, squadron.

The earlier signalling system was introduced in 1653 by the generals-at-sea. In 1673, James, Duke of York, added further instructions in a single book. James was Lord High Admiral, and heir to the throne, the first to command a fleet in battle since the days of the Plantagenets. He became James II (see verse 427).

During the Anglo-Dutch Wars, the new signal to tack from the rear had caused difficulty at Lowestoft (1665), and the inadequacy of the system was exposed again at Solebay (1672).

Howe had had a spell as First Lord of the Admiralty (1783–88) when he oversaw innovations in signalling and also managed to secure a number of new ships, despite budgetary constraints. The numerical system was introduced in 1790.

Rear Admiral Sir Home Riggs Popham (1762–1820) produced a system which utilised 12 double-sided flags. This was adopted by the Royal Navy in 1803. He also recommended his idea of Sea Fencibles, a concept he'd first put into practice in 1793 when he had armed a local fishing fleet to help prevent the French from taking a British held garrison in Belgium. Around the English and Irish coasts, units of these anti-invasion volunteer forces were established between 1798 and 1810 (apart from a brief break during the Peace of Amiens (1802–3)).

For Britain's merchant fleet,
Things are not yet quite so neat,
Till the problem is by Marryat addressed.
Words (in sentences connected),
And a vocab (well selected)
Are the means by which a message is expressed.

Of schedules, there are more:
Two concerning men of war,
And another for the vessels on Lloyd's List.
And as safety is one goal,
The reef... the rock... the shoal...
Are in a fourth, as features to be missed.

On land Chappe has devised,
A system that comprised,
Structures which had arms, perched up on towers.
These contraptions could convey
News from very far away,
And what once took days was only taking hours.

This invention would produce
Two terms in common use.
Telegraphy and semaphore arrived.
Hand held flags – still waved today,
When transferring under way –
Mean longevity for that which Claude contrived.

Lord George Murray was impressed
As he ventured to suggest
To the Admiralty, something of appeal.
Soon a chain of fifteen stations,
Offered fast communications
From London all the way across to Deal.

Signal lamps

When the sun hits something bright,
It reflects a glint of light,
Which is visible from very far afield.
It is possible a Greek,
Used this very old technique
To signal in a battle with his shield.

The idea of using flashes to
Spell words with dots and dashes,
By a British captain first was pioneered.
Colomb's own code was soon dropped,
(Morse the navy would adopt).
The lamp devised by Aldis then appeared.

Royal Navy captain, Frederick Marryat (1792–1848), was also a writer and an early pioneer of the sea story. This genre of nautical fiction deals with the human relationship to the sea.

His system of flag signalling included four schedules covering (1) English and (2) foreign Men of War. A third listed English merchant vessels (see verses 942–946 **Lloyd's Register of Shipping**), and a fourth was a list of physical coastal features such as lighthouses, headlands and ports. A shoal in this context is a sandbank or similar linear landform composed of sediment and granular material (it is not a bunch of fish). Marryat's *Code of Signals for the Merchant Service* was published in 1817. Although supplanted in 1857 by the British Board of Trade's *Commercial Code of Signals*, it was still being used at least until the 1880s. These days, the *International Code of Signals* (ICS) is used by most navies.

In 1792, Claude Chappe (pronounced 'Shappey') (1763–1805) demonstrated a semaphore system. A network was established throughout France and beyond. It was used by Napoleon to run his empire and his army, and the system operated for sixty years until newer technology rendered it obsolete. Semaphore, using the red and yellow Oscar flag, is still used at sea.

Underway replenishment is a modern way of transferring stores, munitions and fuel from one ship to another whilst under way. It largely replaces coaling stations (see verses 969–971).

Lord George Murray (1761–1803) was an Anglican cleric. Using rectangular towers with six large shutters that could flip between vertical and horizontal, he established Britain's first optical telegraph in 1795. It took about 60 seconds for a message sent in London to reach its destination in Kent. This was followed by further chains (London – Great Yarmouth, and London – Portsmouth and Plymouth). Popham later suggested a more visible system, and a new London – Portsmouth link became operational in 1822. It lasted until 1847, when it was superseded by electric telegraph.

A heliograph (from the Greek meaning 'sun' and 'write') is a solar telegraph using flashes of sunlight reflected in a mirror. It has been used since ancient times and, more recently, was employed by the British army (and, less extensively, by the Royal Navy).

The story about battlefield signalling, relating to the Battle of Marathon, is more probably an urban myth.

Philip Colomb (1831–1899) was later a Vice Admiral. After working out a system for signalling, which was introduced into the Royal Navy in 1867, he then concentrated on naval tactics in the age of steam-powered warships. His code was used for seven years.

Arthur Cyril Webb Aldis (*d.*1953), of Aldis lamp fame, took out his first patent in 1910.

The way it was designed,
Was progressively refined.
There were large ones fixed on masts and these were static.
Smaller versions, too,
Could be carried by the crew,
And the shutter 'blinks' of late were automatic.

The invention's still retained.
New recruits were always trained,
To ensure that in its use they were adept.
Its wartime work was tireless –
For a message sent by wireless,
Was something that the foe could intercept.

The Powder Monkeys

Most were nobbut lads,
Who missed their Mums and Dads,
(Some were taken by 'The Press' and forced to serve.)
In their risky occupation,
They faced death or mutilation.
Their job required efficiency and nerve.

A battle's heat and noise
Must have terrified these boys.
Lethal splinters flew from wood which had been shattered,
Dismounted guns could crush,
Turning human flesh to mush,
And a misfire meant that scalding iron was splattered.

The gun crews would rely,
On these children to supply
The cartridges they needed to keep firing.
In the hold, the powder's stored
(The safest place on board),
And running up and down was very tiring.

The kids were energetic,
And their working place frenetic.
Sometimes speed of fire determined how fights ended.
There should be no diminution
Of the monkeys' contribution –
For upon their role a victory depended.

As if this is not enough,
The discipline is tough,
And the penalties, a product of the times.
Most accept them as the norm,
For those who don't conform –
Although relatively minor are some crimes.

Kerosene provided illumination at night and was later supplanted by electricity (mains or battery). The Begbie Lamp was kerosene-fuelled and was fitted with a lens to focus over long distances. Lamps were also used as simple spotlights.

In 1997, training in flash telegraphy was phased out by the Royal Navy.

Aldis lamps were used extensively by convoys during the Battle of the Atlantic (1940). (See verses 1449–1456.)

A sailor signalling aboard HMS *Shropshire* during the Second World War

'Nobbut' is northern English, from Middle English for 'nothing but'.

For impressment see verses 467–471. Many boys volunteered, only to find that a life at sea was not an attractive proposition.

The powder magazine was situated below the water level so that it could be flooded if the ship caught fire.

While most powder monkeys were boys, some were older youths or young men. Women accompanying their husbands also performed the task, although this was rare.

The Articles of War,
State what punishments are for:
These list every type of possible transgression.
The occasion must be logged,
If a miscreant is flogged,
(And on this, the captain uses his discretion).

Twelve lashes are the max,
(Unsupported by the facts:
Many more than this were really not that rare).
In the interests of redemption,
A young boy gets no exemption,
And is beaten on his naked derriere.

Another little monkey

In Hartlepool, some folk
Held a seaside trial – no joke.
A primate had survived a nearby wreck.
It must have looked quite cute,
In its small French sailor's suit.
'It's a spy,' they thought, and hanged it by the neck.

Nautical phrases and sayings

Sticking briefly now with primates,
The weather in cold climates
Might 'freeze brass monkeys' balls' – if bleak enough.
It's said cannon balls were stacked
On a base that would contract...
This is just not true and needs a firm rebuff.

Yet another thing to quash,
Is the origin of 'POSH',
Meaning upper class, and able to afford
To travel o'er the foam –
Port Out and Starboard Home –
In the cabins that were shadiest on board.

The members of CANOE,
Firmly hold it to be true,
That everything is nautical at source.
Explanations that they try,
Can leave them 'high and dry',
But nothing can induce them to 'change course'.

A 'shot across the bows'
Will a sense of threat arouse.
In such circumstances, yield or 'cut and run'!
But you may not feel chagrined
If you're 'three sheets to the wind'
(Just 'two sheets' is the stage of having fun!)

Offences included profanity, drunkenness, spying, cowardice, striking or threatening a superior officer, and attempting to stir up a disturbance upon the pretence of complaining about the 'unwholesomeness of the victual' or 'other pretence'!

Officially, a maximum of 12 lashes was permitted but captains' logs show that this was often exceeded, and as many as 72 were not uncommon. Captains' decisions would not normally be queried unless the number exceeded 72.

The degrading punishment of being beaten on the bare bottom, carried out in front of the assembled boys, involved leaning over a cannon. It was referred to as 'kissing the gunner's daughter'.

The locals in Hartlepool had never seen a monkey (nor indeed a Frenchman) before. This unfortunate creature didn't say anything in its own defence. The town's football club, Hartlepool United, is nicknamed 'The Monkey Hangers'.

Iron cannon balls on sailing ships were supposedly stacked in a pyramid on brass triangles (called monkeys). The theory is that brass contracts faster than iron (true), but a drop of 100°C would cause only a miniscule difference. The navy never stacked cannon balls in this way, (they would tumble off at an angle of 30°), using instead planks, called shot garlands, with holes cut into them.

The Victorians didn't go in for acronyms, so this explanation of 'posh' was dreamed up retrospectively. There is no evidence that passengers' luggage tickets were marked PO/SH, although it is true that the left hand (port) side of ships travelling to India in the days of the Raj was cooler, and that the same applied to starboard berths on the return trip.

The acronym CANOE stands for 'The Committee to Ascribe a Nautical Origin to Everything'!

'High and dry' relates to a vessel that has been beached for some considerable time. It means to be in a helpless and hopeless situation.

'Change course' means to move from one side of a ship to the other.

'Shots across the bows' were used to signal readiness to engage in battle. The term is largely used metaphorically to indicate a warning (see verse 495).

'Cut and run', meaning 'scarper', may refer to ships' cutting the anchor rope and running before the wind to make a hasty getaway.

Sheets are the ropes used to manage a ship's sails. If they come loose, the ship becomes uncontrollable. The phrase 'three sheets to the wind' means very drunk. One or two sheets represent lesser stages of inebriation.

Back to the French Revolutionary Wars

Something clearly must be done:
Europe's being overrun.
Napoleon becomes a central figure.
Alliances may shift,
But overall the drift
Is an empire that progressively gets bigger.

The Battle of Cape St Vincent, 1797

Spain with France has now aligned:
(They spell danger when combined).
Invasion is a prospect we don't savour.
Cape St Vincent is the place,
Where this enemy we face
With odds of two to one – not in our favour.

This at first we do not log:
Her fleet's shrouded in thick fog,
But we must engage in battle, all the same.
This particular endeavour,
Needs some tactics that are clever...
One Horatio's about to make his name.

A good man in the clutch,
He applies 'the Nelson touch':
His idea of heeding orders only partial.
His 'loose interpretation'
Proves to be an inspiration.
(If it hadn't worked, he might have faced court-martial.)

The scheme he would devise
Takes the Spanish by surprise.
It was later viewed as somewhat unconventional.
As events start to unfold,
His ship can't be controlled,
And his 'patent bridge' was maybe not intentional.

As *Captain* starts to labour,
Nelson's sailors board its neighbour –
Then cross this Spanish first-rate to the next.
He was not rebuked by Jervis,
(Who went on to be of service,
When reformatory muscle would be flexed.)

The British Fleet numbered about 500 vessels at the start of these wars and had increased to 950 by 1805.

Napoleon was on a quest for personal power, but also sought to introduce liberal reforms such as religious toleration and the ending of feudalism throughout Europe.

The damage to Nelson's ship *Captain* occurred in the attempt to 'wear ship': ie turn away from the wind – a difficult manoeuvre for square riggers requiring a high level of seamanship (which, great tactician though he was, Nelson arguably did not possess). The move was later feted in Britain and referred to as 'Nelson's patent bridge for boarding first-rates'. Both of the Spanish ships involved were captured.

Admiral of the Fleet John Jervis (1735–1823) was a strict disciplinarian. In the wake of events at Spithead and Nore (see verses 627–635), he put in place measures to prevent mutiny in the Mediterranean Fleet. Appointed First Lord of the Admiralty in 1801, one of his achievements was the introduction of block making machinery in the Portsmouth Dockyard, resulting in the standardization of this component.

Admiral Lord Nelson (Lemuel Francis Abbott, 1799)

Battle of Cape St Vincent (Richard Brydges Beechey, 1881)

The Battle of Camperdown, October 1797

We would be in such a scrape,
If the Dutch choose to escape:
They'd cause havoc if they reached the open sea.
'Blockade them' the proposal.
Duncan has at his disposal
Only two ships to ensure they don't break free.

He produces the illusion
Of vessels in profusion:
By disguising those he has, there seem like more.
To his fleet that's nowhere near
Nonsense signals would appear,
To imply it's close, not emulating Nore.

The objective is achieved:
Dutch De Winter's been deceived,
In believing lots of British are involved.
He has not been right to waver
Whilst the wind was in his favour.
Then the mutiny is finally resolved.

But the Dutch are disinclined,
To remain in port, confined.
They wait some months, and then get a reprise.
With our onboard stocks expended,
The vigil's briefly ended,
When our ships return to Yarmouth for supplies.

Here's his chance. De Winter's naughty
And embarks upon a sortie.
No longer are his ships at home stagnating.
Of this, the British learned,
And they hurriedly returned.
As the Dutch neared land, they found us there and waiting.

A battle would ensue.
We out-fire them three to two.
On unplanned tactics Adam Duncan gambles.
As might have been predicted
Heavy damage is inflicted,
(Though our signalling, as often, is a shambles.)

But they get a thorough trouncing;
Back the Dutch will not be bouncing.
Their force is spent, and that's how it will stay.
Demoralised, their men
Will refuse to fight again,
And overboard their ammo's thrown away.

The Dutch Republic had by now become a client state of the French Republic, and was renamed the Batavian Republic. The Dutch Fleet was blockaded in their harbour in the Texel (an island in the northern Netherlands).

Each day, Admiral Duncan disguised his two vessels to look like different ships. As the Nore mutiny crumbled, (see verses 632–633), he was progressively joined by more ships.

Camperduin (or Kamperduin) is a Dutch coastal village. The Dutch Fleet, (with 30,000 troops on board for a planned invasion of Ireland), was under the command of Vice Admiral Jan Willem de Winter. Duncan's original battle plan had to be abandoned due to proximity to the shore. There were extensive casualties on both sides but, whilst 11 Dutch ships were captured, no British vessel was lost. Camperdown was one of our most significant actions against an evenly matched force, confirming British superiority. However, its importance would be eclipsed by later naval victories.

Two years later, in the Vlieter Incident, the Dutch sailors surrendered en masse.

Wooden block used for pulling ropes (Museu Nacional de Arqueológico, Lisbon)

The Battle of the Nile, 1798

The war continues raging,
Pesky Bonaparte's rampaging,
And thinking Egypt's worthy of a punt.
At The Battle of the Nile,
Britain triumphs, Nelson-style;
France's army's trapped, a victim of this stunt.

To fete Nelson, people clamour:
Wounded heroes have their glamour,
Are attractive, (even though their teeth have rotted).
A very famous beauty,
Thinks to nurse him is her duty.
With Emma, he is readily besotted.

Thence this very famous pair,
Embark on an affair.
To his paramour, his wife can't hold a candle.
Poor Fanny is discarded,
Her feelings disregarded.
And thus is caused the age's biggest scandal.

The Battle of Copenhagen, 1801

As we're thwarting France's trade,
Checks on others' ships are made:
If their goods are seized, this gives rise to frustrations.
To the Baltic Nelson's sent.
Where there's mounting discontent,
And the chance of flak from disaffected nations.

Copenhagen is the set
For his toughest battle yet:
The outcome versus Denmark not emphatic.
The parties called a truce,
And his efforts proved of use:
We achieved our goals through methods diplomatic.

It was in this very year
That the 'UK' would appear:
Ireland and Great Britain were now linked.
The Union held true,
Until 1922,
When Eire detached as somewhere quite distinct.

In addition to Gibraltar,
In the Med we now have Malta,
An island where we're told we cannot stay.
But the treaty of accord,
Was something we ignored.
And the British somehow never went away.

The invasion of Egypt was to be the first step in Napoleon's planned campaign against British India. The Battle of the Nile (1798) was also known as the Battle of Aboukir Bay. Nelson's 14 ship fleet captured 6 and destroyed 7, of France's 17 ships.

Lady Emma Hamilton was a one-time artists' model and wife of British Envoy to Naples, Sir William Hamilton. She and Nelson had a daughter named Horatia, born 1801. The cover story was that she was someone else's daughter, and she was later 'adopted' by the couple as an orphan. She never acknowledged Emma as her natural mother.

At the Battle of Copenhagen, the now Vice Admiral Nelson was second in command under Admiral Sir Hyde Parker (1739–1807). Parker's father (of the same name) was a Vice Admiral who was lost at sea en route to the East Indies, where he was due to take command.

Denmark, Sweden, Russia and Prussia were the major complainants of the Royal Navy practice of searching neutral ships.

Under the terms of the 1800 Act of Union, The United Kingdom of Great Britain and Ireland was formed in 1801. The union remained until 1922, when 26 of the 32 counties in Ireland seceded to form the Irish Free State (later the Republic of Ireland). 'Eire' is both a poetic term for the whole island of Ireland, and (as in this context) a name for the Republic of Ireland.

Malta volunteered to join the British Empire in 1800. The island of Cyprus would also come under British rule, when it became a protectorate in 1878. It was annexed by the UK in 1914, at the start of the First World War.

The Napoleonic Wars, 1803–1815

The Battle of Trafalgar, 1805

From the fighting, there's relief
But the calm is only brief:
The Peace of Amiens does not last long.
France's emperor's ambitious,
And his progress expeditious,
For his formidable army's very strong.

To invade our isle he planned,
But the French first need to land.
His fleet's geared up for what will lie ahead.
And now here's a bit of botching:
Villeneuve thought, 'The Brits are watching'
So sailed south, and stopped near Cádiz bay instead.

Cape Trafalgar is the place
Where this enemy we'll face.
And Nelson has devised a cunning plan.
In these foreign swollen waters,
We'll engage them at close quarters,
Which means getting there as quickly as we can.

Our two columns now approach,
As we're seeking to encroach:
To split their line in three is the intent.
Just a gentle wind doth blow,
Making progress rather slow
In reaching what's to be the main event.

What England now 'expects',
With John Pasco, Nelson checks.
'Confides' had been the word he'd first intended.
The flags were duly raised,
With their message (as rephrased).
It's a famous quote that had to be amended.

For 'close action' next the call,
So begins the five-hour brawl:
With the French and Spanish ships ours are embroiled.
We are practised, routines slicker:
Our rate of fire much quicker.
And 'Boney's' scheme is going to be foiled.

By then they'd figured out,
What the British were about:
And up the rigging, French with guns ascended.
From there, they had a go,
At the British decks below.
A single shot, and Nelson's life was ended.

The Peace of Amiens held from October 1801 to May 1803.

Napoleon had become First Consul (and in effect dictator) of France in 1799. In 1804, he re-established a hereditary monarchy, with himself as Emperor.

The combined Franco-Spanish Fleet at Trafalgar was under the command of Admiral Pierre Villeneuve. John Pasco (1774–1853), who became a Rear Admiral, was signal officer aboard HMS *Victory*. Nelson wanted to say, 'Nelson confides (ie has confidence) that every man will do his duty.' For the sake of speed, Pasco suggested substituting the word 'expects' for 'confides', as the former was in the code book and the latter would have to be spelt out. The next signal was, 'Engage the enemy more closely'.

'Boney' is the nickname by which the British referred to Napoleon. Small children, when they misbehaved, were told he would come and get them.

Nelson, in his admiral's regalia, was an obvious target. A month after the event, a competition for the best 'Death of Nelson' painting was announced. The 500 guineas prize was won by Arthur William Devis. The work depicts Captain Thomas Hardy in attendance, though he was not present at the moment of death.

Flag signal 'England expects…'

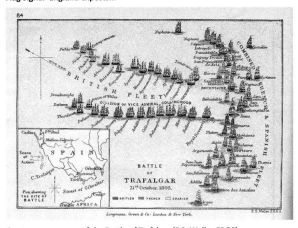

Contemporary map of the Battle of Trafalgar (F.S. Weller FRGS)

Britain mourned, and she exulted
In a triumph that resulted
In the foes' fleets in a very sorry state.
The French – aims unfulfilled –
Started once more to rebuild.
By the time they had, they'd find it was too late.

How would other men have fared
If they'd been so well prepared?
Nelson's sailors were all disciplined and trained.
The attack he could well presage
With the means to send a message.
He had firepower that was readily sustained.

Though he'd thought the whole thing through,
His tactics weren't brand new.
That the old ones didn't work to all was plain.
The means were thus in place
To our enemies erase.
He was well set up to win this key campaign.

This niggling thought let's perish,
He's a hero whom we cherish.
He'd already had his share of strife and war.
Charismatic, he had charm,
He had lost an eye and arm,
Then he gave his life. We couldn't ask for more.

Who'd been fighting on our side?
Sailors came from far and wide.
Many foreigners were found amongst our crews.
Former slaves... nabbed privateers...
Plus pressed men, who'd changed careers,
And criminals, with nothing much to lose.

The Peninsular War, 1807–14

Napoleon's assault
Hasn't yet come to a halt
Most of Europe by this emperor's controlled.
He's installed his puppet kings,
And is pulling all the strings.
But he hasn't brought the Brits into the fold.

Around Europe there's a buffer,
And our trade begins to suffer;
On importing British goods there is a ban.
This the Portuguese defy.
They're refusing to comply:
A stance which surely undermines his plan.

The Battle of Trafalgar resulted in the Franco-Spanish fleet's losing 22 of its 33 ships of the line. Britain lost none of her 27.

France suffered a further blow when Spain (by then an ally of the British and an enemy of the French) captured her Rosily Squadron in 1808.

Melee tactics, similar to those adopted by Nelson, had been used to great effect by Admiral Adam Duncan, at Camperdown against the Dutch in 1797 (see verses 676–682).

See verses 602–612 **Tactical thinking and technical innovation**.

Nelson lost the sight in his right eye after it was hit by debris from a sandbag during the assault, led by Hood, on Calvi in 1794. His wounded right arm was amputated after the British defeat at the Battle of Santa Cruz de Tenerife (1797).

Crews included a number of landsmen (men unfamiliar with the sea or sailing). Those serving aboard HMS *Bellerophon* included a former button maker. Counties, unable to fulfil their quotas (see verses 627–633) in any other way, would offer those convicted of petty offences the option of going to sea instead of going to jail.

> 'You need not be sorrowful. Have I not often told you who was almost as little, as pale, as suffering as you, and yet as potent as a giant, and brave as a lion?'
>
> 'Admiral Horatio?'
>
> 'Admiral Horatio, Viscount Nelson, and Duke of Bronti; great at heart as a Titan; gallant and heroic as all the world and age of chivalry; leader of the might of England; commander of her strength on the deep; hurler of her thunder over the flood.'
>
> **Charlotte Bronte, from *Shirley* (1849)**

The Death of Nelson (Arthur William Devis, 1807)

The ban on British goods, aimed at securing the economic collapse of Britain, was the Continental System. Despite some damage to British trade, the blockade proved largely ineffective. In addition to the Portuguese, our (by now) ally Sweden similarly refused to comply with it, as later (1810) did Russia, thus prompting Napoleon's disastrous decision in 1812 to invade that country.

Napoleon failed in his attempt to occupy Portuguese ports, and the King of Portugal transferred his court to Brazil under Royal Navy escort.

For this non-cooperation,
Let the price be occupation!
Then Bonaparte does something he'll bemoan.
A key alliance ends:
He and Spain no more are friends.
And he's put his brother Joseph on her throne.

Spanish disaffection's
Giving rise to insurrections,
Guerrilla tactics, panic and hysteria.
With this partnership dissolved,
Our army gets involved:
Soon we're fighting for the Spanish in Iberia.

At Coruña sabres rattle:
Versus France, we're doing battle.
This is really not the safest place to stay.
We must evacuate.
The navy turns up (late).
Many thousand troops embark and sail away.

Wellington was key:
He fought hard to set lands free,
On Belgium's plains, in Pyrenean highlands.
In the war that's being waged,
Britain's army's now engaged,
Which amounts to more than 'filching sugar islands'.

Yes, that's just what we were doing.
Quite a haul we'd been accruing,
Of 'properties' – from Holland, France and Spain.
Some of these, like Guadeloupe,
Former 'owners' would recoup,
But other places Britain would retain.

The Battle of Lissa, 1811

The contested Adriatic
Sees a triumph that's emphatic,
Near an island which is off Croatia's coast.
Here at Lissa, we've been based.
Now the enemy is faced
By a frigate captain, name of William Hoste.

Quite a lot of French ships loomed.
His three frigates could be doomed,
In a 'David and Goliath' type affair.
His plucky men rejoiced,
In the message that he'd hoist:
'Remember Nelson' helped them to prepare.

Reinforced by a treaty of mutual assistance signed in 1793, Portugal's refusal to cooperate was in accordance with her longstanding alliance with Britain (see verse 93), as was Britain's support of Portugal during the Peninsula War.

Joseph Bonaparte was Napoleon's older brother. In 1808, he was transferred from being King of Naples and Sicily, which he'd enjoyed. His role in Spain was always tenuous and, during his reign, the Spanish possessions of Mexico and Venezuela declared independence. He abdicated in 1813.

After the Battle of Corunna (or A Coruña) (1809), about 26,000 troops managed to embark, although some were too ill to do so and had to be left behind. In 1589, the year after the defeat of the Spanish Armada (see verses 292–311), English forces had attacked the city, but Galician heroine María Pita successfully rallied the defenders. She was honoured with a large statue which, improbably, depicts her slaying Drake.

Field Marshall Arthur Wellesley, 1st Duke of Wellington (1769–1852).

The Battle of the Pyrenees was in 1813. The vast majority of the Duke of Wellington's battles, most of them victories, were fought in Spain but his most famous and decisive was at Waterloo.

The 'sugar islands' comment was made by Richard Brinsley Sheridan (playwright, politician and Treasurer of the Navy 1806–7). He considered that the government was not putting enough effort into hitting Napoleon where it would make a real difference.

Guadeloupe remains part of France to this day and, as such, is within the Eurozone. Britain retained places such as Trinidad (which combined with Tobago in 1889 to become a single Crown Colony) and Guiana (now Guyana) on the South American mainland. Cape Colony and Sierra Leone in Africa were also retained, plus Malta (see verse 689). The Seychelles (a source of cinnamon, vanilla and copra) were acquired from the French in 1810 and administered from Mauritius (see verses 594 & 1174).

Statue of María Pita, Plaza de María Pita, A Coruña

France had gained coastal control of the Adriatic, which the British were attempting to counter. Also known as the island of Vis, the British had been disrupting French shipping from Lissa.

Sir William Hoste (1780–1828) was one of the great frigate captains of his day. Others include James Gordon who, it has been argued, was the model for Horatio Hornblower in C.S. Forester's series of novels. In these books, another notable frigate captain, Edward Pellew (see verse 746) makes fictional appearances.

The Gunboat War, and the Anglo-American War

The Norwegians and the Danes
Were going to great pains
To attack the British cargo ship or brig.
For the campaign they conducted,
Many gunboats were constructed,
Though these couldn't deal with frigates (far too big).

This was economic war.
Brigs again came to the fore
In America – The Battle of Lake Erie.
Here we suffered quite a rout,
In a conflict which broke out,
Over matters which are getting rather dreary.

We'd impressed some of their men,
So the US had a yen,
To expand to parts which lay north of their border.
We'd imposed some trade restrictions.
And, compounding all these frictions,
Our support for native tribes was out of order.

Once war had been declared,
Britain sent what could be spared
But this only really stretched to port blockades.
Privateering on the Pond
Was running rife beyond:
On British merchant ships were lots of raids.

Thwarting commerce hurts both nations,
Merchants vocalize frustrations.
To call a halt's the only way to go.
To terms both sides consent,
And a treaty's signed in Ghent:
The outcome, a resounding status quo.

The last of Napoleon

For all the power he wielded,
The British have not yielded
To Napoleon's attempts to block our trade.
In attacking Russia's Tsar,
He now goes a step too far
And the price for this grave error will be paid.

On Elba he's confined;
With absconding on his mind,
He eluded all the guards and then sneaked through.
Back in France, support he'd get,
And once more present a threat.
Until finally he met his Waterloo.

The Gunboat War (1807–14) took place during the Napoleonic Wars.

A brig is a highly manoeuvrable two-masted sailing vessel, often used by the Royal Navy during the 19th century as a small warship carrying 10–12 guns.

Following the invasion of Holstein by British ally Sweden in 1813, Denmark-Norway sued for peace, ceding Heligoland to Britain. These islands were returned to Germany in 1890.

There had already been spats between American and British ships in 1807, prior to the outbreak of the Anglo-American War in 1812. The war lasted until 1815. The naval theatres were the Great Lakes and the Atlantic. The Battle of Lake Erie took place in 1813. Although this gave the Americans control of the lake, their attempts to seize Upper Canada failed, as too did their bid to capture Montreal in Lower Canada.

The trade restrictions involved British blockades, aimed both at denying neutral carriers access to colonial trade, and at preventing American trade with Europe (especially France). Britain's North American squadron, based in Halifax Nova Scotia, had been plagued by mutinies and desertions. It was not large enough to cover both the coast and the Atlantic.

The war, which had demonstrated the need for 'blockade-breakers', did stimulate American shipbuilding and other industrial activities.

The disruptive force has vanished:
The Corsican's been banished.
In exile, life could not have been much meaner.
It came as quite a shock,
When he saw that 'curséd rock' –
The Atlantic isle that's known as St Helena.

His escape we seek to hinder.
Near his rock, there is a 'cinder'
Where a garrison is placed to aid prevention.
The Brits were there to stay:
We still govern it today:
This is how we gained the Island of Ascension.

Redesigning ships

Though our navy's been rejoicing,
Those in charge had started voicing
Their concerns – about our ships and their design.
Those of France (it's sad to tell)
Unlike ours manoeuvre well –
So new principles we'll learn, and then enshrine.

Teaching how ships should be crafted,
An expert has been drafted:
French architect Barrallier's the maven.
The man whom we've recruited,
To town planning seemed well suited –
At the would-be Royal Docks at Milford Haven.

Just why this place was chosen
In the mists of time is frozen.
Maybe Hamilton had influenced the plot?
With ships still made of wood,
This location wasn't good.
Is oak plentiful? The answer's, 'No it's not!'

Even so, it was intended
As a model, oh so splendid;
The dockyard which all others would eclipse.
This the navy tried to buy,
But the price set was too high,
So in Pembroke they then started building ships.

After his defeat at Waterloo, Napoleon sought asylum in England, and asked for a house, large enough to accommodate his entourage, north of London. He spent several days aboard a British warship off the coast of Devon while his request was considered, and ultimately rejected. Exiled to the island of St Helena, Napoleon died there in 1821.

On a visit in 1836, during the *Beagle* voyage (see verses 893–895), Charles Darwin concurred with the view of the inhabitants of St Helena that they lived on a rock, but the poor people of Ascension Island lived on a cinder. The two islands are 804 miles apart.

In 1815, a garrison was established on Ascension Island, which was designated HMS *Ascension*, the navy's only stone frigate at the time. The island went on to be used as a Royal Navy victualling station (see verse 1220), and played a part in the struggle against the Slave Trade (see verses 739–741). As well as being a supply station during the Second World War, it had a role during the Falklands conflict (see verses 1648–1664) as a launch base for RAF Vulcan bombers.

It was recognised that success in recent naval campaigns had solely been down to the superior skills of British sailors. In order to improve ship design, the first School of Naval Architecture was established in Portsmouth (opened 1811).

Emigré naval architect Jean-Louis Barrallier from Toulon, assisted by his son Charles, was brought in to design and construct warships. Seven royal ships were constructed at Milford Haven, and Barrallier also designed the grid pattern on which the town was built.

The large natural harbour of Milford Haven had been the base for several English invasions of Ireland. It was also where Henry VII landed in 1485 prior to his bid to wrest the crown (see verse 223). Sir William Hamilton founded the town in 1790. His wife Emma was Lord Nelson's lover, and the three controversially lived together (see verses 684–685). This could explain Nelson's affection for the place (verse 995).

A Royal Navy Dockyard was established at Pembroke in 1814.

The Transportation of Convicts

The growth of towns and cities,
(Incidental to these ditties),
Mean the population's suddenly displaced.
This leads to increased crime
And – a subject of this rhyme –
Is what befalls those caught and thus disgraced.

Most convictions are for theft.
In the jails there's no room left...
One alternative is harsh. It's execution!
For most, this fate does seem
To be overly extreme,
And to pack them off to Oz the best solution.

(Another system tried
Was to squeeze them all inside
The prison ships. These hulks could still be floated.
Now, not fit to sail the seas,
They were crammed with detainees,
Whose deplorable existence must be noted.

There is barely room to stand.
Disease gets out of hand.
To keep costs low, they're very poorly fed.
Mouldy biscuits, maybe soup,
Are issued to this group,
Who labour hard and often end up dead.)

To Australia transported,
(Some by wives and kids escorted)
The first lot left in 1787.
Others travelled too,
In addition to the crew.
Officials and marines attained this 'heaven'.

Captain Cook's botanic bay
Was not where they would stay,
Despite its metonymic connotation.
Port Jackson was the place,
For the first established base,
This colony the basis of a nation.

With the First Fleet's safe arrival,
There were scant means of survival.
Of farming expertise, there was a dearth.
So now the penny drops.
'We need livestock. We need crops.
We need to tend this new land's fertile earth!'

By the end of the 18th century, 220 offences attracted the death penalty. Most of these were crimes against property, grand larceny's being defined as theft of goods worth more than one shilling (about £50 today).

On prison ships, any meat was usually ox-cheek, which might be served boiled. Peas were also a common addition to the diet. Hard labour always formed part of the sentence.

The first Australia-bound fleet of 11 ships, under the command of Arthur Phillip (1738–1814), assembled at Portsmouth in 1787. There were 780 convicts aboard, about 20 per cent of whom were women.

Botany Bay was considered unsuitable due to a lack of fresh water, a safe harbour, useable timber and good soil. Port Jackson was chosen instead. The arrival date there of 26 January (1788) is now celebrated as Australia Day.

The first settlement became the city of Sydney, and Phillip became the country's first governor.

> The Question comes to this, which has the better right, the savage born in a country, which he runs over but can scarcely be said to occupy or the civilized man, who comes to introduce into this unproductive country, the industry which supports life.
>
> **Charles Griffiths, Australian settler, 1845**

The prison deck of a convict ship (deck height shown is higher than it would have been)

They were wholly unprepared,
For this new life that they shared.
Perhaps the second fleet their fortunes would reverse?
But this hope would prove misguided,
Their requirements unprovided:
More mouths to feed would only make things worse.

This alternative to jails
Would spread from New South Wales,
Despite those early problems with nutrition.
An assisted passage scheme,
Helped free settlers live the dream,
(Most were driven by despair, not by ambition).

Europeans brought disease
To the Aborigines.
Smallpox halved the native population.
It's OK for this to ravage
The Antipodean 'savage':
We're civilised, with rights to domination!

Slave Trade – the Abolitionist Movement

Once the plight of slaves they'd learned,
Folk began to be concerned.
They thought the trade a gross abomination.
'It really must be stopped',
Was the stance they would adopt,
Which led to a society's formation.

One who this bad practice knocks,
Is a man named Charles James Fox,
But others, too, were seeking abolition...
Clarkson, Sharp and others –
There were sisters, not just brothers –
Then came Wilberforce, persistent politician.

He put pressure on. At last
The long called-for act was passed.
Woe betide those noncompliant with cessation.
Those refusing to align,
Faced a very heavy fine,
And also risked their vessels' confiscation.

Now this horrid trade we've ended
We must see that ban extended:
Inhumanity is something we berate.
(Yet the chimney sweep employs
His climbing girls and boys,
Though by law they must have reached the age of eight.)

The second and third fleets arrived in 1790 and 1791 respectively. Further penal colonies were established in Tasmania (1804), Queensland (1824), Western Australia and Victoria (both 1826). The journey to Australia initially took about eight months, and conditions aboard transport ships were often cramped, as companies sought to maximise profits. The first free settlers arrived in 1793. Appalling conditions in overcrowded British cities prompted many to emigrate.

By 1730, Britain had become the biggest slave trading country. 'The Society for Effecting the Abolition of the Slave Trade' was formed in 1787. A considerable number of women joined the society.

The Slave Trade Act (1807) abolished this trade in the British Empire with effect from 1808, and its objective was achieved fairly quickly. However, the French, Spanish and Portuguese filled the vacuum left by British ships.

Well known parliamentary campaigner William Wilberforce (1759–1833) continued to push for the jurisdiction of the 1807 act to be expanded. (It had not covered the territories in the possession of the East India Company, or Ceylon and Saint Helena). He died just a month before the 1833 Slavery Abolition Act received royal assent.

A sweep wasn't allowed to send an apprentice up the chimney if the fire was lit.

Last Tuesday, the smallpox began to rage, and we hauled 60 corpses out of the hold... The sights which I witness may I never look on such again. This is a dreadful trade... I am growing sicker every day of this business of buying and selling human beings for beasts of burden...
On the eighth day (out at sea) I took my round of the half deck, holding a camphor bag in my teeth; for the stench was hideous. The sick and the dying were chained together, I saw pregnant women give birth to babies whilst chained to corpses, which our drunken overseers had not removed. The blacks were literally jammed between decks as if in a coffin; and a coffin that dreadful hold became to nearly one half of our cargo before we reached Bahi (Brazil).

Richard Drake, from *Revelation of a Slave Smuggler* (1860)

To supervise conformity,
(A task of some enormity:
Three thousand miles of coast must be patrolled),
A squadron was created,
Whose orders clearly stated,
'Use every means' this new law to uphold.

Once parliament had spoken,
British effort's more than token,
Those engaging in illegal trade were hunted.
We would catch them (if we could,
For our ships were not that good);
Next, a suspect vessel had to be confronted.

Traders had a lot to lose
So resisted British crews,
Sometimes having first thrown overboard their 'shipment'.
This fact was borne in mind:
When new treaties were designed,
When evidence enough would be equipment.

More than violence, even scarier
Were diseases like malaria.
With dangers such as these our men contended.
But the seas were duly policed
And many slaves released:
It took sixty years before the practice ended.

The West Africa Squadron was established in 1808 with just two ships. The first Commodore of this squadron was Sir George Ralph Collier, who had six ships in 1818. The task was interrupted between 1812 and 1815 due to the American War (see verses 712–715). The ships allocated to the West Africa Squadron could often be outrun.

Throwing slaves overboard was partly to avoid the payment of 'head money' – a £100 fine for each captive. Britain paid heavy subsidies to other countries in return for their co-operation. The various treaties ultimately stated that the presence of shackles etc on board would be enough to prove a ship's participation in illegal slave trading. Royal Navy captains were also charged with negotiating treaties with local African chiefs.

In 1829, 204 of 792 officers and men died mainly as a result of malaria or yellow fever.

Only about 10 per cent of slave ships were captured. This still amounted to well over 500 vessels by 1868, and an estimated 150,000 captives were liberated.

> The unweary, unostentatious, and inglorious crusade of England against slavery may probably be regarded as among the three or four perfectly virtuous pages comprised in the history of nations.
>
> **William Lecky (1838–1903), Irish historian and political theorist**

William Wilberforce (Karl Anton Hichel, *c.*1794)

The Bombardment of Algiers, 1816

'From the Halls of Montezuma'
Uncle Sam's been in ill humour,
Along a coast where trouble often flares.
Goods – and crews – were being seized
And the USA, displeased,
Waged war against the Barbary Corsairs.

For many a long year,
These pirates had struck fear.
Extensive was the scope of their predation.
From their homes they would go forth,
To the south and to the north.
In England, they'd once caused much aggravation.

They said 'tributes must be paid',
Or they'd interfere with trade
In the Med. Their prisoners could be held to ransom.
Or the people that they snatched
As white slaves might be dispatched:
But either way, the pay-off would be handsome.

On these states we had depended,
But hostilities have ended,
And from piracy the Berbers must refrain.
Diplomacy was tried,
Then agreement brushed aside.
Two hundred blameless fishermen were slain.

Negotiation's failed.
Back to Gib Lord Exmouth sailed
Where, to help, a small Dutch squadron volunteers.
An Algerian fired first,
(In the protocol unversed);
Thus started the bombardment of Algiers.

As might have been predicted,
Lots of damage was inflicted,
Enough to force the town into submission.
Exmouth will withdraw,
Then threaten worse and more –
A bluff, as he'd run out of ammunition.

The Dey to terms agreed.
Many hostages were freed.
But the dastardly activity persisted.
Although once France had invaded,
The practice quickly faded,
Which Europe's bans on slavery assisted.

The American Marines' Hymn begins with the words 'From the halls of Montezuma' and continues, 'to the shores of Tripoli' – a reference to the Barbary Wars.

The term 'Uncle Sam', signifying the USA, was first used in 1812.

The First Barbary War (1801–05) was fought by the alliance of the USA and the Kingdom of the Two Sicilies, against Tripoli and Algiers. The second, extended to include Tunis (the third of the 3 Muslim states), was in 1815.

The pirates travelled as far north as Iceland, plagued the West African coast and even went as far as South America. In England, they'd once plagued the South West (see verse 333).

During the Napoleonic Wars, Britain had obtained supplies from the Barbary States for Gibraltar, and for her Mediterranean fleet.

Stopping the practice of enslaving white Christian Europeans was the principal British aim. Diplomacy was seen to have failed when 200 fishermen from Corsica, Sardinia and Sicily, who were under British protection, were massacred by Algerian troops.

Edward Pellew, 1st Viscount Exmouth (1757–1833) is probably best remembered for his action in 1797, when his frigate and one other were attacked by a French ship-of-the-line in Audierne Bay, and he successfully ran her aground.

When, in contravention of an earlier agreement, an Algerian fired the first shot, the bombardment began immediately. The Dey (the ruler of Algiers) agreed to the repayment of ransom money and the release of the British Consul and 1,083 Christian slaves. A further 3,000 were later freed.

France invaded Algiers in 1830, and Tunis in 1881.

The Bombardment of Algiers (Martinus Schouman, 1823)

Smuggling

Why turn to smuggling?

Waging war does not come cheap:
Taxes rise and prices leap.
Excise is a levy on consumption.
For what's eaten and what's supped,
The costs have all been upped.
Getting round this merely takes a bit of gumption.

If there's conflict, it is then
That the navy needs more men,
But many to such service weren't resigned.
By the goods that they transported,
Napoleon was thwarted,
His 'Continental System' undermined.

And when peaceful times return,
A living folk must earn,
Now employment with the navy has been stopped.
Not required by Britain's fleet,
They need to make ends meet,
And smuggling's the solution some adopt.

In Conwy... Buckie... Mull...
Fishing could seem rather dull.
The adventurous, their boring lives bemoaned.
The bootleg trade's alluring,
And – so very reassuring –
This was something most communities condoned.

Some men's motives were financial:
Profits could be quite substantial;
Some just dabbled with the odd cross-channel dash.
Day job wages were not high,
And that's the reason why
Risks were taken for a bit of extra cash.

It is not just here and there,
We find hooky gin to share.
The practice round our coastline is ubiquitous.
In buying what's illicit,
Almost everyone's complicit,
And don't view dodgy imports as iniquitous.

Thus Will Owen, Pembroke born,
Would ferry sacks of corn.
Round Solway, Captain Yawkins brought in tea.
The Carters' business throve
At a place called Prussia Cove,
A secluded spot, and near a handy quay.

Customs duty is levied on goods brought into the country. Excise is a 'purchase' tax. Most people didn't know the difference. They knew only that what they bought was getting more expensive. Compounding this, income tax was introduced for the first time in 1799, to fund the wars against France. Apart from a brief respite during the Peace of Amiens, it was not abolished until 1816.

Smuggling was rife during wartime. Those who got caught were often handed over to the navy because of their valuable seamanship skills.

For the Continental System see verse 703.

Compliance was either willing or enforced. In many places, the locals were beneficiaries and happily colluded, but this was not always the case. Where the particularly violent gangs operated, communities lived in terror.

The Corn Laws, which applied to any type of grain that required grinding (notably wheat), imposed high import duties in order to protect the interests of aristocratic landowners. The laws, brought in during the first half of the 19th century, were repealed in 1846.

Yawkins features as the smuggler Dirk Hatteraick in Sir Walter Scott's novel *Guy Mannering*.

At Cawsand. John Carter – self-styled 'King of Prussia' – and his two brothers, Harry and Charles, ran a profitable smuggling business for many years in the late 18th century. John was a devout Methodist, who would not allow swearing on his ship, and whose dealings were conducted fairly.

> Why, look ye; this very baccy had a run for 't. It came ashore sewed up neatly enough I' a woman's stays, as wife to a fishing smack down at t' bay yonder. She were a lean thing as iver you saw, when she went for t' see her husband aboard t' vessel, but she coom back lustier by a deal, and wi' many a thing on her, here and there, besides baccy. An' all that were I' t' face o' coast-guard and yon tender, an' a'. But she made as though she were tipsy, an' so they did nought but curse her, an' get out on her way.'

Elizabeth Gaskell, from *Sylvia's Lovers* (1863)

(Clear of where the mainland ends,
Almost everyone depends,
On contraband: their fishing is but seasonable.
The Scilly Islands' coast,
Was a useful staging post,
And participation seemed entirely reasonable.)

At sea

Smugglers sometimes use a craft
That is rigged both fore and aft,
So it doesn't matter whence the wind is blowing.
And although it's not permitted
A bowsprit might be fitted:
Thus swift passage for the tax-free stuff they're stowing.

These boats, packed to the hilt,
Are often purpose-built.
Sleek their carvel planks, which give them added pace.
The customs' coastal cutter,
Scarcely prompts a heart to flutter,
As it rarely wins when trying to give chase.

But smaller boats (the norm),
Often brave the raging storm –
From 'the revenue' and weather, scant protection.
Those on board get wet and chilled,
But these seamen – highly skilled –
Know the elements can help avoid detection.

As the British coast they near,
They must signal, 'We are here',
For the landers cannot see them in the dark.
Those waiting for the stash,
Might see a bright blue flash,
Or a tinder-box's fleeting little spark.

On the whole, this system worked,
But what if danger lurked?
The penalties for warning ships were stiff.
Banned are beacons to alert,
'It's essential you divert,
And put in on the safe side of a cliff.'

If the coast's not clear to land,
A solution was to hand:
And this was sinking goods in weighted tubs.
When safe, or so perceived,
These would later be retrieved,
And find their way to houses or to pubs.

When smuggling was eradicated in the Scilly Islands, the population became destitute. A cash injection to boost the fishing industry was helpful in partially relieving the situation. Like the Scillies, the Channel Islands also played an important staging post role.

Warren Lisle, Surveyor of Sloops of the South Coast (1740–1779), had succeeded in getting larger and better armed revenue ships, which had very long bowsprits. At one time, only revenue vessels were allowed to use this type of spar.
   Smugglers' boats, (these were often small luggers), were usually built of fir, (cheaper than oak), and might be painted black to make them less conspicuous. The customs clippers (clinker-constructed and more heavily armed than the smugglers' vessels) were slower, and their crews often lacked skill. The first customs patrol vessels had been introduced in the 1680s (see verse 424).
   The Royal Navy, when available, assisted in patrolling the British coast.
   The business of smuggling involved far more people on land than at sea. 'Batmen' stood guard and fought off the revenue men. 'Tub carriers' and others unloaded and transported the goods.
   Smugglers' signals were initially answered by a lantern until harsh penalties for signalling ships at sea were introduced. Lighting furze beacons was also prohibited. Devices such as the spout lantern, which could be seen only by those at whom it was pointed, were developed.
   The 1718 Hovering Act had made it illegal for small vessels to wait within 6 miles of the shore.

(The great exponent here
Was Jack Rattenbury, from Beer:
In the Channel Islands tubs were what he bought.
A well-known escapee,
He'd managed to get free,
Every single time he had been caught.)

Cutting tax did not suffice;
That on tea was lowered (twice).
This did not impact as might have been desired.
For the smugglers just a glitch,
To more spirits they would switch.
For the government, the tactic had backfired.

It was not just stuff like booze
That was brought in without dues:
In one case, there's bewildering taxation.
So it's all 'the system's' fault.
The commodity was salt,
Which was utilised in food stuff preservation.

To stop shady importation,
Not much use is legislation:
Though strict laws were passed to thwart the racketeer.
Who sometimes lacked morality,
And acted with brutality:
There's nought to lose when punishment's severe.

A few famous smugglers

The famous Hawkhurst Gang,
Whose leaders were to hang,
Of vicious types were *the* most quintessential.
Well organised, efficient,
And in cruel acts so proficient,
Their fearsome reign was very influential.

If you choose to read this story,
Be warned that it is gory...
In the customs' house at Poole was bootleg tea,
Which the revenue had seized,
So the gang were most displeased.
'We must get it back,' is what they all agree.

They have waiting clientele;
With the break-in, all goes well.
Through a village, they triumphantly parade.
They progress along the road,
And a bag of tea's bestowed
On a friend, and thus a big mistake is made.

Rattenbury was the leader of a gang of smugglers in Beer, an east Devon village. Spirits were contained in small barrels or 'tubs' called half ankers, which held about 4 gallons. Tea and tobacco were packaged in oilskin, which made watertight bundles, in case they had to be thrown overboard to prevent detection. These were small enough to be carried.

Import duties on tea had been kept artificially high to protect the profits of the East India Company. A heavy excise duty was also imposed, making the illegal import of tea more profitable than gin or brandy. Considerably more tea was smuggled than was brought in legally. The Commutation Act of 1784 reduced the tax on tea from 119 per cent to 12.5 per cent.

Fish such as herring were regarded as a delicacy in northern Europe, and exported in large quantities from ports like Montrose in Scotland, where preservative salt was the main contraband product.

The 1736 Act of Indemnity had made it a capital offence to injure a preventive officer in the course of his duty.

Hawkhurst Gang leaders Arthur Gray and Thomas Kingshill were hanged in 1748 and 1749 respectively.

There were other famous gangs eg The Blues of Kent (or Adlington Gang), The Hadleigh Gang from Suffolk and The North Kent Gang, a murderous mob that operated in the Medway.

If you wake at midnight, and hear a horse's feet,
Don't go drawing back the blind, or looking in the street.
Them that ask no questions, isn't told a lie.
Watch the wall my darling while the Gentlemen go by.

Five and twenty ponies, trotting through the dark –
Brandy for the Parson, 'Baccy for the Clerk.
Laces for a lady, letters for a spy.
Watch the wall my darling while the Gentlemen go by!

Running round the woodlump if you chance to find
Little barrels, roped and tarred, all full of brandy wine;
Don't you shout to come and look, nor use 'em for your play;
Put the brushwood back again – and they'll be gone next day...

From *A Smuggler's Song* (1906) by Rudyard Kipling, who lived in Burwash near Hawkhurst, both villages in Kent

This pal, called Daniel Chater,
Would brag about it later.
As a witness, he's thus quickly singled out.
His evidence would damn,
And expose the smugglers' scam,
So he'd pay the price for being such a snout.

As the process is judicial,
With Dan there's an official
Called William Galley. Both are plied with liquor.
As they'd proved antagonistic,
What they suffer is sadistic:
There've been many deaths less painful and much quicker.

The details here we'll spare
But such incidents weren't rare.
All sorts of torture smugglers would connive.
Daniel's body, sad to tell,
Was hidden down a well.
As for William, he was buried whilst alive.

Tom Johnstone as a boy
Quickly turns real life 'Rob Roy'.
He's a smuggler, then becomes a privateer.
When convicted of his crimes,
He's imprisoned several times,
But escapes – in all, a colourful career.

With a price upon his head,
He volunteers instead
As a pilot for a British navy scheme.
He's so skilled in navigation
That this meets with approbation:
He is pardoned and he starts to live the dream.

A substantial cheque he gets,
But before long runs up debts,
And once again his life becomes chaotic.
Next, Lymington's famed son
Undertakes the guinea run.
Gold – to pay French troops – is hardly patriotic.

But he does then draw the line,
And an offer he'll decline:
He refused to lead Napoleon's invasion!
This costs nine months of anguish,
In the clink he'll once more languish.
(It takes longer to break free on this occasion.)

Fordingbridge was where the tea was thrown to Chater, a shoemaker, whose tale reached the authorities.

Thomas Johnstone (1772–1839) was from near Lymington, Hampshire. When his creditors caught up with him, he was sent to London's notorious Fleet Prison, from which he managed to escape.

ON LYMINGTON, HAMPSHIRE

I do not find they have any foreign commerce, except it be what we call Smuggling and rouging, which I may say, is the reigning commerce of all this part of the English coast, from the mouth of the Thames to the Land's End in Cornwall.

Daniel Defoe, 1724

Sketch of Thomas Johnstone, 1834

Once he's seen the last of jails,
To the USA he sails,
Where inventor Robert Fulton he will meet.
No more living on his wits,
Tom's forgiven by the Brits,
Who are working on Napoleon's defeat.

Fulton's name will feature later,
As a versatile creator
Of the many clever objects he designs.
All that we must defer.
He helps Tom turn saboteur,
And blow up ships by using limpet mines.

When first put to the test,
These would not explode at Brest,
But they later proved a workable invention.
At Flushing three years later,
His success is so much greater.
Our hero, for his efforts, gets a pension.

His story's ended not.
Johnstone next devised a plot
To rescue Boney. Picture please the scene.
The ex-emperor's protected,
But they'll reach him undetected,
Because it's planned to use a submarine!

The idea was really daft:
In their infancy such craft.
And miles of ocean had to be traversed.
The scheme was never tried,
As Bonaparte had died.
But at least he didn't do so when submersed.

A new career comes next,
Which makes fellow smugglers vexed:
For the revenue, Tom's happily employed.
As part of HM's force,
He knows all the tricks of course.
It's no wonder former comrades were annoyed.

In Cornwall, smuggling's rife:
One might say a way of life.
And so was taking cargo from a wreck.
On one ship which plunged and rose,
A man took off his clothes,
Then jumped into the maelstrom from the deck.

For Robert Fulton see verse 925.

The American David Bushnell had invented the first practical mine for use against the British during the War of Independence. A limpet mine is attached to the target vessel by a magnet.

Flushing is the English name for the important Dutch harbour of Vlissingen.

Double agent Johnstone supposedly began devising the plot to rescue Napoleon in 1820. He may have planned to use a better-developed version of Fulton's *Nautilus* (see verse 925) for his plan. Napoleon died in 1821. (See verse 719 for St Helena). Johnstone ended up in command of the revenue cutter HMS *Fox*.

His vessel lurched and trembled.
On the beach, folk were assembled.
In that dreadful storm, the huge man swam ashore.
This was how the Dane arrived,
And only he survived:
His broken craft was sadly seen no more.

He seems friendly – quite the charmer.
He ends up with a farmer,
Imposing on the offered hospitality.
Along with warmth and food,
There's a daughter to be wooed:
Plus scope for what he does in the locality.

As soon as he's entrenched,
The nice persona's quenched.
'Cruel Coppinger's' a name that's wholly suited.
He is smuggler... pirate... thief...
And is bad beyond belief,
As were the vicious thugs he had recruited.

Throughout surrounding parts,
He strikes terror in all hearts.
By everyone, this blackguard's greatly feared.
Brutal was his reign,
No one dared to cross the Dane.
And then, one day, he simply disappeared.

Wrecking

Did folks go out at nights,
And flash misleading lights,
To lure ships onto rocks where they'd be doomed?
There's no proof that this occurred,
Except the whispered word,
So the practice cannot safely be assumed.

The goods wrecked ships once bore,
Would be washed up on the shore.
For looting these, the penalty was death.
For those who did get caught,
A smuggling charge was sought –
At least, that way, they'd still be drawing breath.

The end of smuggling

The Preventive Water Guard,
Whose job was often hard,
Did their very best to stop illegal trade.
They were now worthwhile opponents,
For they had the right components:
Competent their men and highly paid.

The tales of this stranger are founded in reality, but it is uncertain who he actually was. He might have been John Coppinger, who was of Danish stock, or Daniel Coppinger who was shipwrecked in 1792. The accounts that have emerged are possibly an amalgam of both. He and his gang even controlled local transport, to the extent that people were forbidden to move at certain times. He married farmer's daughter Dinah Hamlyn. They had a son, who was deaf and who was as cruel as his father, torturing animals and reputedly murdering a six-year-old playmate.

Cornwall's Wonderland by Mabel Quiller Couch contains an evocative account of Coppinger's activities. This is partly based on the legends that surrounded him.

> Will you hear of Cruel Coppinger
> He came from a foreign land;
> He was brought to us by the salt water,
> He was carried away by the wind.
>
> **Revd Robert Stephen Hawker, from *Cornish Legends* (1866)**

The practice of looting wrecks is called 'wrecking'. There are tales of shining false lights to lure ships to their doom. Legends about this emanate from Cornwall, Scotland, Ireland, France, Spain, Newfoundland, the Jersey shore and the Carolinas. Whether or not there is any truth in these, (no proof has ever been found), coastal communities in Devon and Cornwall certainly looted ships that had been wrecked.

It was preferable to be charged with smuggling, which (certainly in times of war) usually only carried the penalty of impressment, unless violence against revenue forces was involved.

The Preventive Water Guard, also known as the Preventive Boat Service, was established in 1809. The service was under Admiralty control from 1816 to 1822. The uniforms of its officers were very similar to those worn in the Royal Navy. Based in Watch Houses around the coast, boat crews patrolled inshore.

The service's work complemented that of the land-based riding officers and the offshore revenue cutters. Renamed the Coast Guard, all three were amalgamated in 1822 under the control of HM Customs. Control switched to the Admiralty in 1856, and back again to HM Customs in 1891.

With the hunt for those who smuggled,
Another role was juggled:
This was helping ships in trouble on the water.
With a vessel that was wrecked,
Now a gadget can connect:
The recently invented Manby's Mortar.

The Coast Blockade then came,
More unity its aim.
It operated on the coast of Kent.
It was still fragmented, yes –
But successful nonetheless,
And becoming very hard to circumvent.

Stranded souls can be retrieved,
So the Coastguard was conceived,
It now operates round Britain from its stations.
'Search and rescue' is its function,
And it does this in conjunction
With the RNLI (funded by donations).

With improvements in detection,
And the revenue's inspection,
On how to hide their goods the smugglers mulled.
Certain cunning ways appealed,
With contraband concealed
In hollow masts, or vessels double-hulled.

Adam Smith's 'The Wealth of Nations'
Had important implications:
Free trade the British government embraced.
So when import duties tumble,
Most smugglers quickly rumble
That the profit in their game has been erased.

Though not carried out this way,
Smuggling still persists today,
With drugs and weapons, booze and cigarettes.
Though their import is forbidden
Sometimes animals are hidden,
For those who want to keep exotic pets.

The activity is rife,
When it comes to human life:
There's huge money in illegal immigration.
Overcrowded ships go down.
People suffocate or drown –
The risks they take outweighed by desperation.

Captain George William Manby (1765–1854) was an eccentric inventor who claimed to have been a boyhood friend of Horatio Nelson. Having helplessly witnessed a Royal Navy ship, the *Snipe*, run aground off Great Yarmouth, he devised an apparatus that could fire a line to a stricken vessel. Its first recorded use was in 1808, and it continued to be deployed for many years. It saved countless lives – almost 1,000 by the time of Manby's death.

The Coast Blockade Service pre-dated the amalgamation of anti-smuggling forces. It was established, and commanded, by Captain Joseph McCulloch. Formed in 1816, it operated on the Kent and Sussex shores and was intended to coordinate the land, inshore (Water Guard) and preventive forces, but there was still scope for confusion and duplication.

The Coast Guard that came into operation in 1822, absorbed the Coast Blockade Service in 1831, thus acquiring authority over the whole UK coastline. The first Coast Guard Instructions, issued in 1829, included a section on lifesaving and lifesaving equipment, although the Water Guard had always had a supplementary role in giving assistance to shipwrecks.

Today, HM Coastguard is responsible for coordinating all maritime search and rescue (SAR), and (from 2015), land based SAR helicopter operations.

For the RNLI see verses 1038–1046.

The Wealth of Nations was first published in 1776. Its author, the Scot Adam Smith (1723–1790), is often referred to as 'the Father of economics'.

The term 'free trade' is used here in the context of international commerce, rather than as a euphemism for smuggling.

Smuggling, as described, died out in the 1840s as a result of a combination of factors. Improved detection had already led to ever more ingenious ways of bringing in contraband, eg hiding silks in hollowed out legitimately imported legs of ham. More significantly, the re-introduction of income tax (as a temporary measure!) in 1842 produced more revenue than expected, and enabled the reduction of import duties on a large range of goods.

Manby's Mortar in use

SHIPWRECK

'What is the matter?' I cried.
'A wreck! Close by!'
I sprung out of bed, and asked, what wreck?
'A schooner, from Spain or Portugal, laden with fruit and wine. Make haste, sir, if you want to see her! It's thought, down on the beach, she'll go to pieces every moment.'...

I was so confused that I looked out to sea for the wreck, and saw nothing but the foaming heads of the great waves. A half-dressed boatman, standing next to me, pointed with his bare arm (a tattoo'd arrow on it, pointing in the same direction) to the left. Then, O great Heaven, I saw it, close in upon us! One mast was broken short off, six or eight feet from the deck, and lay over the side, entangled in a maze of sail and rigging; and all that ruin, as the ship rolled and beat – which she did without a moment's pause, and with a violence quite inconceivable – beat the side as if it would stave it in. Some efforts were even being made to cut this portion of the wreck away; for, as the ship, which was broadside on, turned towards us in her rolling. I plainly described her people at work with axes, especially one active figure with long curling hair, conspicuous among the rest...

But, a great cry, which was audible even above the wind and water, rose from the shore at this moment; the sea, sweeping over the rolling wreck, made a clean breach, and carried men, pars, casks, planks, bulwarks, heaps of such toys, into the boiling surge. The second mast was yet standing, with the rags of a rent sail, and a wild confusion of broken cordage flapping to and fro. The ship had struck once, the same boatman hoarsely said in my ear, and then lifted in and struck again. I understood him to add that she was parting amidships, and I could readily suppose so, for the rolling and beating were too tremendous for any human work to suffer long. As he spoke, there was another great cry of pity from the beach; four men arose with the wreck out of the deep, clinging to the rigging of the remaining mast; uppermost, the active figure with the curling hair.

There was a bell on board; and as the ship rolled and dashed, like a desperate creature driven mad, now showing up the whole sweep of her deck, as she turned on her beam-ends towards the shore, now nothing but her keel, as she sprung wildly over and turned towards the sea, the bell rang; and its sound, the knell of those unhappy men, was borne towards us on the wind. Again we lost her, and again she rose. Two men were gone. The agony on the shore increased. Men groaned, and clasped their hands; women shrieked, and turned away their faces. Some ran wildly up and down along the beach, crying for help where no help could be. I found myself one of these, frantically imploring a knot of sailors whom I knew, not to let those two lost creatures perish before our eyes.

They were making out to me, in an agitated way... that the lifeboat had been bravely manned an hour ago, and could do nothing; and that as no man would be so desperate as to attempt to wade off with a rope, and establish a communication with the shore, there was nothing left to try...

Another cry arose on shore; and looking to the wreck, we saw the cruel sail, with blow on blow, beat off the lower of the two men, and fly up in triumph round the active figure left alone upon the mast...

The wreck, even to my unpractised eye, was breaking up. I saw that she was parting in the middle, and that the life of the solitary man upon the mast hung by a thread. Still, he clung to it...

Charles Dickens, from *David Copperfield* (1850)

Plate C / **139**

7 The end of the 'Age of Sail'

7

The end of the 'Age of Sail'

The Industrial 'Revolution'

We'll go briefly now inland.
Revolution's being fanned
By developments in farming and production.
For making stuff, the means
Are increasingly machines.
And for transport, there is waterway construction.

Each industrial locale,
Is near to a canal,
And by boat is carried everything that's needed:
Raw materials and coal...
This network, on the whole,
Worked well – and then by rail was superseded.

There can't be any doubt
That the British had huge clout,
Which increased, with each and every new invention.
We thought, with such great might,
That our country had the right,
To treat others with deservéd condescension...

That we're correct and they are wrong...
With our views must go along...
Those who hold beliefs that differ are moronic.
We genuinely feel,
With a missionary's zeal,
All will benefit from rule that's hegemonic.

We had different types of powers.
In those countries that were 'ours',
There were colonies, protectorates, dominions.
Some were self-ruled in a sense,
But we saw to their defence,
And ensured that all they thought were our opinions.

Although termed a 'revolution', the transformation of Britain into an industrialised nation took about a century.

The development of railways in the 19th century led to many disputes with canal owners, who had previously enjoyed a monopoly in carrying Britain's (then) plentiful supplies of coal and iron.

The British, including those on evangelical missions (see verse 876), often had scant knowledge of, or regard for, the mores of indigenous peoples.

The Battle of Navarino, 1827

All our erstwhile foes are weak,
Britain's on a winning streak,
There is just one left that has the power to crush her.
We are wise to be suspicious,
For this country is ambitious,
And there will be times we have to cope with Russia.

We are on her side however,
In a jointly run endeavour.
The Ottomans are threatening the Greeks.
They're in Navarino Bay,
Where they're not allowed to stay.
Their departure is what Codrington now seeks.

In he sails – a show of force –
(Not belligerent of course).
Turks open fire, which wasn't in the script.
Down the barrel of a gun,
He can either fight or run.
And very soon in battle all are gripped.

The enemy was slated,
Though our vessels were outdated:
New technologies we hadn't yet embraced.
These had largely been ignored
(That's a risk we can't afford:
We must think again and modernise with haste.)

We don't use exploding shells,
Our fleet the wind propels,
It's built of wood, as everybody knows.
The Brits can only dream,
Of a warship powered by steam:
Though even Greece possesses one of those.

By the public, Edward's feted.
But behind the scenes berated,
(From the powers-that-be got nothing but reproach).
Soon we'll make friends with the Turks:
It's from Russia danger lurks,
Now on Greece she'll find it easy to encroach…

Although not known for his diplomatic skills, Admiral Sir Edward Codrington (1770–1851) was charged with enforcing a peaceful solution to the anarchic situation in Greece during its War of Independence. Britain, France and Russia had joined forces to assist the Greeks against the Ottoman Empire (and its ally Egypt).

Greek ship the *Karteria* had, in addition to sails, steam-powered paddles.

The *Scipion*, Battle of Navarino (George Philip Reinagle, 1827/8)

Singing, dancing and recreation

Setting off in any craft
Takes coordinated graft.
The sails must first be hoisted and then hung.
Prior to progress being made,
The anchor must be weighed,
And when ropes were hauled, a shanty would be sung.

There was thus a rhythmic guide,
As huge effort was applied,
And the songs would always fit the task in hand.
The 'Shantyman' would call,
A reply would come from all.
The lyrics spoke of booze, girls – and dry land.

On their schooner or their brig:
Sailors oft performed a jig.
The hornpipe took more energy than grace.
A partner's needed not…
You can do it on the spot,
So it suits the lack of women and of space.

Tars always wore hard shoes,
When they danced away the blues,
And to life on board their movements would equate.
A shading hand there'd be,
As though looking out to sea,
Plus the rubber legs that feigned a seaman's gait.

A boatswain's not heard, is he?
When life on deck gets busy,
So he'll use a pipe – its sound can't be ignored.
The most basic of his calls,
Was in regulating hauls,
But it's used these days for welcoming aboard.

Playing card games such as euchre,
One might win a bit of lucre:
To make a lot of tricks would do the job.
Some to board games are more suited.
Though the rules seem convoluted;
Uckers uses tactics like the 'blob'.

When in work there was a lull,
Life on whalers could be dull,
And for occupation many had a craving.
The patient man would hone,
His skills in carving bone,
And produce the most elaborate engraving.

There were short and long drag shanties for rope pulling, and 'capstan' or 'windlass' shanties for raising and lowering anchor. When sailors were relaxing, in their quarters, (the fore bitts or the forecastle), they would sing ballads or humorous songs for entertainment.

The crews of warships were not permitted to perform tasks to work songs (shanties).

In rough weather, visiting senior officers were hoisted aboard by 'side boys' using a 'bosun's chair'. The pipe is now used ceremonially to welcome aboard flag officers and VIPs.

Pronounced 'you-ker', this game for four players was responsible for introducing the joker into packs of cards.

Uckers is a board game for two or four players and is similar to, but more complicated than, ludo.

HMS *Warspite* cadets dancing the hornpipe, 1928 (see verse 1481)

Scrimshaw is the word,
By which this work's referred,
The first piece dates from 1817.
By candlelight from dusk,
Men would scratch a tooth or tusk,
Or use the stuff we've met before – baleen.

Steamships

Paddle wheels weren't new:
The Romans had them too,
And a Greek devised an engine run by steam.
But to move a ship along,
The force must be quite strong,
And how all this developed is our theme.

Men are looking for new means,
Of powering machines.
By wind or water industry's sustained.
These require the right locations,
So they have their limitations,
Though of very great importance they remained.

We come now to James Watt,
A rather famous Scot,
Who made instruments. In this, he was proficient.
He mended things as well,
And that's how he could tell
That the early steam contraptions weren't efficient.

Water cooled once it was heated –
A cycle oft repeated –
A separate condenser the solution.
Beyond this innovation,
Double-action and rotation,
Were elements of James's contribution.

What was once to no avail –
An alternative to sail –
Was something which no longer seemed remote.
All this hard work and devotion
Would refashion locomotion.
Steamships started, on a small scale, with the boat.

If conditions are ideal,
Boats can use a paddlewheel,
Instead of what came later – giant screws.
(Such vessels are still run,
But mainly just for fun,
Curiosities that function to amuse).

Hull Museums have the best collection of scrimshaw in Britain. Originally done using the by-products of whales and other marine mammals, the earliest authenticated decorative piece of sperm whale was recorded in 1817, though the practice dates back to the mid-18th century. Soot, tobacco juice or candle black were used to highlight the etched design.

For baleen, see verses 402–403.

Scrimshaw depicting HMS *Royal George*, c.1759

Greek mathematician Hero of Alexandria (Egypt) is thought to have produced a steam-powered device in the first century AD.

English engineers Thomas Newcomen (1664–1729) and Thomas Savery (c.1650–1715), both developed early steam engines and attempted to apply them to powering boats. The latter, who also worked for the Sick and Hurt Commissioners, invented the first commercially used steam-powered machine (a pump) for use in draining mines, but it had serious problems.

James Watt (1736–1819) was the son of a prosperous shipbuilder in Greenock, Scotland. The instruments he made included reflecting quadrants, and parts for telescopes and barometers. Watt is also credited as the first to apply a screw propeller to an engine at his Birmingham works.

So now there's a 'PS'
('Paddle Steamer' – did you guess?)
If it's in too deep, performance quickly drags.
On canals such craft were routed,
(To choppy seas unsuited);
It did not take long to overcome the snags.

From (where else?) north of the border,
Lord Dundas placed an order.
He had businesses in Scotland on each side.
For quick travel east and west,
A steamboat would be best,
To traverse the link that went from Forth and Clyde.

It was named after his daughter,
But it churned up all the water:
Some complained the banks were being worn away.
From service it's removed,
But now, well and truly proved,
Is that steam power has a massive part to play.

With Trevithick things evolved.
Certain problems had been solved.
Low pressure gizmos now seem quite outmoded.
But high pressure, he'd conceded,
Meant that safety valves were needed,
(When an engine that was stationary exploded).

Here's another Scottish peer,
Whose remarkable career
Took him far away, to Chile and Brazil.
In their quests for independence,
Thomas Cochrane's in attendance,
Deploying all his knowledge and his skill.

These causes he embraced,
As he'd left our shores disgraced
Even though, against Napoleon, he'd striven.
But after many years,
Back at home he reappears,
Reinstated in our navy and forgiven.

This rhyme Tom Cochrane mentions,
Because of his inventions:
The most notable, an engine and propeller.
On steamships he was hooked:
At bitumen he looked
As a type of fuel. He was a canny fella.

The prefix designation 'SS' stands for 'Screw Steamer' (and not 'Steam Ship' as many believe).

Early steamboats went on rivers and lakes.

Thomas Dundas, 1st Baron Dundas (1741–1820) was governor of the Forth and Clyde Canal. He commissioned the *Charlotte Dundas*, which is widely regarded as the world's first practical steamboat (though there had been several experimental projects elsewhere earlier). The boat was designed by William Symington. After one false start, Symington patented a horizontal engine. It had one large paddle wheel at the stern – a feature designed ironically to avoid damaging canal banks. On its second journey (1803), and towing 2 heavy barges, the new boat took 9 and a quarter hours – an average speed of 2 mph – to travel almost 20 miles along the canal. Due to a strong breeze at the time, all other canal traffic was stopped. It was eventually broken up in 1861.

The first 'sea-going' steamboat (Richard Wright's *Experiment*) sailed from Leeds to Yarmouth in 1813.

Richard Trevithick (1771–1833) was a Cornish mining engineer who developed the steam locomotive *Puffing Devil*.

The tragic explosion of a pumping engine at Greenwich in 1803 killed 4 men. Although Trevithick blamed this on human error, the perceived dangers of high-pressure steam were exploited by competitors.

In common with the likes of William Hoste (see verse 709), Thomas Cochrane, 10th Earl of Dundonald (1775–1860), had been a very able frigate captain, one of a breed on whom the British Empire heavily depended. He then turned to politics. Disgraced after being convicted for involvement (probably unwitting) in a stock market fraud (1814), he went to Chile, Brazil and then Greece, where he spent time organizing the Greek navy during that country's struggle for independence (see verse 804). In 1832, he was reinstated by the royal navy, and ended his career as Admiral of the Fleet (Red).

The *Charlotte Dundas* (drawn by William Symington, *c.*1803)

Now that trees were not widespread,
We had turned to iron instead
For producing things that once were made of wood.
There was soon a metal ship:
Aaron Manby took a trip –
And the English Channel happily withstood.

The Atlantic's been traversed,
And the U.S. did it first,
But what exactly did this feat entail?
The Brits can take good heart:
Steam played just a little part:
The remainder of the trip was under sail.

Out of Deptford soon will chug,
A wooden ferry/tug.
She's a steamboat and the Admiralty bought her.
Though this vessel they're parading,
They had taken some persuading:
Steam-powered fighting ships have yet to hit the water.

When it comes down to the crunch,
They're a very leery bunch
And the innovator has to prove his case.
No surprise that they were chary:
New technology is scary!
But by degrees it's something they'll embrace.

Maybe caution made good sense:
When it comes to ships' defence,
A paddle is not easily protected.
The space these wheels consume,
Means for guns there's far less room –
All good reasons why these vessels were rejected.

The propeller would arrive,
And by 1845,
No longer were they voicing reservations.
Britain couldn't lag behind,
And steamships one could find,
In the navies that belonged to other nations.

Soon an arms race had begun.
For a decade it would run.
The French built the *Napoléon* and *Gloire*.
To put all this concisely,
At times France won't play nicely –
And we need to heed the forces of the Czar.

Shipbuilding had depleted Britain's stock of suitable timber (see verse 869). Capstans, bridge-ways and pulleys made of iron could now be found in places like Liverpool docks.

Aaron Manby was the first iron steamship to go to sea (1822).

American hybrid vessel SS *Savannah* ('SS' although she was paddle-powered) crossed from Savannah Harbour to Liverpool in May 1819. No passengers were prepared to risk their lives, so the voyage was purely experimental. Her journey took 633 hours (over 26 days).

The British-built (Dutch owned) *Curaçao* was possibly the first to cross the Atlantic substantially under steam power (Rotterdam to Surinam), but a Canadian ship is also a contender.

HMS *Comet* was designed by Henry Bell and engineered by John Rennie (another Scot) and Marc Brunel (father of the more famous Isambard Kingdom Brunel). Made of wood, she was the first steam-powered vessel purchased by the Royal Navy (in 1822), though she wasn't added to the Navy list until 1831.

By 1845, other steamships had been purchased, including paddle wheel steamships such as the *Nemesis* that was so instrumental during the First Opium War (1839–42) (see verses 888–892).

The French, so often more innovative than the British, were the first to combine steam power and iron hulls capable of withstanding explosive shells. The breakthrough was the advent of the screw propeller. However, the British were quick to follow.

The Russians had built an armed steam frigate (the *Izhora*) in 1836.

Russia later started wintering her Atlantic and Pacific fleets in the USA. She could use her navy more easily against the British and French from there, but her home ports were vulnerable to enemy blockade.

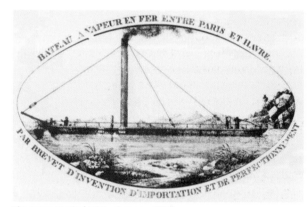

The *Aaron Manby* (artist unknown, *c*.1825)

SS *Savannah* (Hunter Wood, 1819)

Any foe would be the sorrier,
Confronting our ship *Warrior*:
An armoured frigate clad in iron plating.
But she'd soon be obsolescent
For progress was incessant,
And ever-modern vessels we're creating.

By 1871,
We'll find the mast has gone,
That the hybrid wind power/steamship is no more.
We now have the *Devastation*,
Which has undergone mutation,
Growing turrets where the sails had been before.

Developments came fast:
Ships were quickly of the past,
Almost out of date before they were complete.
Our 'outdoing France' obsession...
New designs in quick progression...
Resulted in a mishmash of a fleet.

Those steam engines – clean they ain't,
So money's spent on paint
As, for wind power, old-style captains really hanker.
With gold trimmings, ships are furnished...
Fire doors taken off and burnished...
In a quest for admiration whilst at anchor.

Isambard Kingdom Brunel (1806–1859)

A vessel by Brunel,
Had braved the ocean's swell.
The *Great Western*'s made her first Atlantic crossing.
Her sails were at the ready,
To keep this huge ship steady,
As paddles cannot cope with too much tossing.

Fourteen days was all she took:
The first record's in the book!
Which a contest for an honour set in motion.
The 'Blue Riband' competition,
Engendered the ambition,
To make the fastest passage o'er this ocean.

Would these verses lie to you?
For the last one's not quite true.
Sirius the recognition stole.
Though the 'first trip' claim she earned,
All her furniture was burned,
As she hadn't got enough supplies of coal.

HMS *Warrior* and her sister ship HMS *Black Prince* were the first 'ironclads'. They were built between 1859 and 1861 in response to the French *Gloire*, which was wooden-hulled. Superseded about a decade after their launch, *Warrior* was put on the reserve list in 1875 and is now, as part of the National Historic Fleet, a museum ship in Portsmouth.

Wind, unlike coal, is a free resource, and early steamships would travel under sail in favourable conditions. The presence of masts and rigging meant that guns had to be mounted broadside.

As HMS *Devastation* (1871) was built without masts, this allowed the introduction of two turrets and the installation of more versatile swivel guns.

While, during the 1850s, the French were engaged in an arms race with Britain (they dropped out in the middle of the 19th century), their innovations were sometimes adopted by the Admiralty, despite an inherent disinclination towards new ideas.

By the end of the Victorian era, captains had little to do except obsess about the appearance of their ships. Rigorous attentions to fire doors meant that they were no longer fire resistant!

Brunel's *Great Western* was made of wood with iron sheathing. She was the first steamship purpose-built for Atlantic crossings and was launched in 1838. A fire broke out in the engine room almost immediately, and Brunel was badly injured in a fall from a burning ladder. In April 1838, the *Great Western* sailed from Bristol to New York in 14 days, 12 hours.

The term 'Blue Riband', which was not widely used until 1910, applies to Atlantic crossing times by passenger liners. It is an unofficial accolade, the rules of which are unwritten. Of the 35 ships which have held it, 25 were British. In 1935, British MP Harold K. Hales commissioned and donated a gilded four foot high solid silver trophy, currently held by the USA.

SS *Sirius*, built in 1837, was a side-wheel driven wooden-hulled steamship, and was chartered in 1838 for a passenger service to New York. She arrived there one day ahead of the *Great Western*. She was one of the earliest ships to use a condenser, but this resulted in high coal consumption. She was ultimately wrecked and sunk off Ireland in 1847.

HMS *Devastation* as featured on a Bryant & May matchbox

Isambard Kingdom Brunel against the launching chains of the *Great Eastern* (Robert Howlett)

Soon the world took close regard,
Of a fellow named Cunard,
Whose new shipping line is still in operation.
His *Britannia*'s maiden sortie,
Took place in 1840,
Her speedy trip an awesome demonstration.

A further five short years,
And *Great Britain* then appears.
Two features of importance she combines.
To iron Brunel's committed...
A propeller has been fitted...
Both improvements on his earlier designs.

And now, for all you swots,
She could travel at 12 knots.
On a thousand tons of coal her engine gorged.
Round the clock this would be burned,
And the crankshaft thereby turned:
This was (then) the largest object ever forged.

Being driven by a screw,
Was not entirely new:
The SS *Archimedes* was the first.
The downside of the paddle –
At the rear or hull astraddle –
Was the need for this large wheel to stay submersed.

If by ships you are now smitten,
You can visit the *Great Britain*.
She's a member of our land's Historic Fleet.
Bristol Harbour's where she rests,
To welcome paying guests,
Who can stroll around, the deck beneath their feet.

By comparison, she's small,
On the biggest of them all
Work had started. This was just a decade later.
The *Great Eastern* was laid down
At Millwallon (London Town).
For four thousand, she could comfortably cater.

With long distance routes in mind,
She'd been cleverly designed
So she didn't have to stop at coaling stations.
On her first trip, six were killed;
Her berths were never filled,
Though she's still the most impressive of creations.

Samuel Cunard (1787–1865) was British Canadian. His company was originally called the British and North American Royal Mail Steam Packet Company.

Britannia was paddle-driven, with three masts. She was built in Greenock and her home port was Liverpool. Her return voyage from Halifax, Nova Scotia, took just under 10 days (her outbound trip took 12 days and 10 hours). She was sold in 1848 to the German Confederation Navy.

SS *Great Britain* was the world's first great ocean liner. Completed in 1845, she was designed for speed and comfort, though an inspection of her cabin accommodation suggests that 'comfortable' is a relatively generous description. Refitted in 1853, she could carry up to 630 passengers, and she operated an efficient service between London and Australia for almost 20 years. She could carry 1,200 tons of coal. 200 tons of sea water, held in the largest boiler in the world, produced the steam. Four cylinders drove an 18' 3" (5.56m) diameter chain wheel, which powered the crankshaft (at 18 rpm) and the propeller shaft (at 53 rpm).

Greek mathematician Archimedes first developed the principle of moving water with a screw in the third century BC. SS *Archimedes* was designed by British engineer Francis Petit Smith. Despite initial problems (including an exploding boiler and a broken crankshaft), she impressed the Admiralty and greatly influenced Brunel.

The National Historic Fleet is a list of more than 1,000 historic vessels located in the UK. It includes fishing boats, lifeboats, barges, light ships and various naval and cargo craft. Some are operational. Others are museum exhibits or, like SS *Great Britain*, museum ships.

Work on the *Great Eastern* started in 1854. She combined side paddle wheels with a single screw, and had auxiliary sails. It was planned that she would take passengers to Australia and the Far East, and be able to do so without refuelling. In the event, she never sailed these routes. By far the biggest ship ever built at the time, she was launched sideways, with difficulty, in 1858.

There was a huge explosion during her short maiden voyage. Five stokers died as a result of steam scalding, and a sixth leapt overboard and was lost. She had only 35 fare-paying passengers on her first trans-Atlantic run, the departure of which was delayed as the crew were drunk. Thereafter, she lost out to competition from companies such as Cunard (see verse 1111).

William Fairbairn and David Napier (cousin of Robert Napier – see verses 1108–1110) had developed Millwall Iron Works into a centre for iron shipbuilding on the Thames during the 1830s. Financially unsuccessful, in 1848 the works were bought by John Scott Russell, who built Brunel's ship, and fell victim to the 1866 financial slump.

A knot is one nautical mile (see verse 623) per hour.

SS *Archimedes* (William John Huggins)

She's the largest of all ships,
Which no other would eclipse
Until more than half a century has passed.
Her huge size means she's able
To lay trans-Atlantic cable.
But she didn't make much money to the last.

Engines

To generate their power,
Lots of fuel these ships devour:
(To tend a blazing fire the stoker's role).
The navy then decided,
That this should be provided
From Glamorgan. Welsh was best in terms of coal.

The engines they were using,
Can be horribly confusing:
The early types were driven by a lever.
To propellers these weren't suited,
So something else was mooted,
And on direct-acting versions boffins beaver.

Soon improvements were occurring,
To keep those large screws whirring;
New compound types used every scrap of pressure.
Through three cylinders steam passed,
'Twas recycled from the last
(The water must be free of salt and fresher.)

Post 1815: 'Pax Britannica' and Empire

All the fighting that occurred,
In the reign of George the Third
Has ended, and hostilities now cease.
People dance. The church bells ring.
Soon another George is king,
And we're seeking to impose 'The British Peace'.

Then in brotherly progression,
It's 'The Sailor King's' accession.
William joined the Royal Navy at thirteen.
Though high status he possessed,
He mucked in with all the rest:
Showing willing, he would blithely cook and clean.

In New York our prince once served,
And the Brits were quite unnerved
By a kidnap plot, which happily was thwarted.
Guards were rapidly assigned,
So William would now find,
That no longer could he walk round unescorted.

For trans-Atlantic cable, see verse 1132.

The Navy used the rank structure Ordinary Stoker, Stoker, Leading Stoker, Stoker Petty Officer and Chief Stoker.

South Wales produced several different types of coal such as anthracite, house coal and, relevant here, steam coal. Following trials, a British Admiralty report (1851) concluded that this was the coal most suitable for use in Royal Navy ships (in preference to coal supplied from Newcastle-upon-Tyne).

Variants of early beam (side-lever) engines persisted during the first half of the 19th century, but these could only operate paddle wheels. Paddles, it should be noted, don't work very well if they're not in the water ie in rough seas.

Compound engines, which increased efficiency, were introduced in the early 1860s. In 1881, the triple expansion marine steam engine was adopted, with a further improvement in efficiency, although sea water could no longer be used to produce the steam.

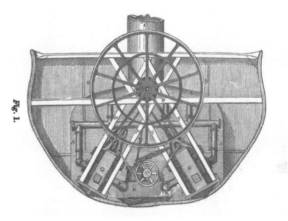

Transverse section through the hull of the *Great Britain*, from *History and Description of the Steamship Great Britain* (J. Smith Homans, 1845)

SS *Great Eastern* (Charles Parsons, 1858)

George III (r.1760–1820) and George IV (r.1820–1830).

William IV (r.1830–1837), began as a midshipman and was treated no differently from his shipmates, except that he was accompanied by a tutor. The plot to seize William, which also included the kidnapping of Admiral Digby, was endorsed by George Washington.

Despite some youthful pranks,
He moved up through the ranks:
(To the highest post of all in fact was heading).
He knew his stuff, worked hard,
And earned Nelson's high regard:
(Will was best man at his friend's ill-fated wedding).

Let's try to set the scene,
For when next we have a queen,
As the age of the Victorians is looming!
William's health is in decline.
His niece is next in line.
In the nation she'll inherit, all is booming.

As our fortunes keep ascending,
On the navy we're depending.
(We have trade routes going north, south, west and east).
It patrols the oceans' waves,
Checking no one deals in slaves.
Against piracy the seas are also policed.

Though there's been a little break,
We've corrected our mistake:
In building ships, no longer are things static.
Naval strength is fundamental,
When your world position's central:
It adds great weight in matters diplomatic.

Keeping dominance at sea,
Isn't how it used to be.
For ship-to-ship engagements are no more.
But our sailors still have roles
In achieving Britain's goals –
Even though most of the conflicts are ashore.

Fighting seamen we shall meet,
Who, of late, are in receipt
Of training in a very special place.
In the past, not all that skilled,
In shooting they are drilled,
So they're expert when the enemy they face.

A stone frigate's where they learn,
And all must take their turn:
Both officers and men thus spend their weeks,
In gaining by degrees,
Much needed expertise,
By practising their gunnery techniques.

William was swiftly released, once his identity became known, after being arrested with others for involvement in a drunken brawl in Gibraltar. He was promoted to Rear Admiral in 1789. In 1827, he was made Lord High Admiral, but was forced to resign the following year, after putting out to sea with a squadron for 10 days without telling anyone where he was going. During his short tenure, he commissioned Britain's first warship and abolished the use of the cat-o-nine tails for all offences except mutiny.

The last confrontation between sailing ships was at Navarino (see verses 803–808).

The only ship-to-ship action in the second half of the 19th century took place in 1877 between HMS *Shah* (along with the corvette HMS *Amethyst*) against Peruvian vessel *Huáscar* (the Peruvians were harassing British merchant shipping). It was the first occasion on which a self-propelled torpedo, recently introduced into the Royal Navy, was used. Conventional guns had failed to pierce the *Huáscar*'s armour shield. The torpedo missed.

Fighting seamen formed part of naval brigades, along with Royal Marines. They had already fought in several campaigns on land, including during the American War of Independence and the invasion of Isle de France (Mauritius) in 1810 (see verses 594 & 1174).

A stone frigate is a shore establishment (see also verse 719 on Ascension Island).

The first gunnery training ship was HMS *Excellent*. She was converted and moved to Whale Island near Portsmouth in 1830. The original ship has been replaced several times by others – all renamed *Excellent*.

Canada

From one empire we once held,
We had firmly been expelled,
But with Canada that fate was not applied.
She remained within the fold,
(Although largely self-controlled),
And in two World Wars would fight on Britain's side.

In that land, we'd long been nestled,
And with France had often wrestled
For supremacy, until at last she cracked.
Via a trade-off she'd withdrawn –
Guadeloupe the crucial pawn,
In one of those old wars' concluding pact.

Bermuda

Bermuda we kept too.
She's pro-British through and through,
Since James the First – a solid acquisition.
In the wars that we have fought,
We've relied on her support,
A fact which surely warrants recognition.

The fast Bermuda sloop,
On French privateers would swoop,
With its single mast and rigging fore-and-aft.
(With two spars on which sails stretch,
Boats become a yawl or ketch,
Or possibly a schooner type of craft).

Building ships had, by degrees,
Meant we're running short of trees.
Of timber, Britain hence became a needer.
In Bermuda not much grows,
But – assuaging British woes –
Were lots of forests, full of scented cedar.

We've built a dockyard there,
For construction and repair.
Plus a garrison to make sure it's protected.
Stone's in rather short supply,
But we'll solve this by and by:
The problem, with a floating dock, corrected.

There's a triangle near here,
Where vessels disappear,
But enquiries often find an explanation.
Craft may vanish without trace.
Maybe whisked to outer space?
The evidence can't stop the speculation.

The USA has been referred to as Britain's 'first empire'. Canada became a dominion within the British Empire in 1867.

The very first English settlements were fishermen's bases in Newfoundland (see verse 213), where Harbour Grace, (a thriving seasonal community by 1550), became the first permanent settlement in North America in 1583. Under the Treaty of Paris (1763), which concluded the Seven Years' War (see verses 544–554), there was a trade-off which returned Guadeloupe to France. Although it was a hugely productive sugar island, the British government decided that Canada was strategically more important.

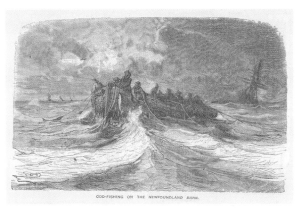

Cod-fishing on the Newfoundland Bank (artist unknown, 1876)

Bermuda (see verses 320 & 409), which had become a maritime nation, often assisted Britain in conflicts with America.

Like sloops, cutters are also single-masted, (but with a different sail plan). Schooners have two or more masts.

The Royal Navy began commissioning vessels from Bermuda in 1795.

Because of a shortage of manpower, Bermuda was, uniquely, exempt from impressments.

Cedar could be used for ship construction as soon as it was felled, and had a natural resistance to rot and woodworm. In efforts to conserve forests, acts were passed to restrict its export and use, despite which forests were depleted by the 1830s, and only recovered with the advent of steel-hulled ships. (Until 1783, the British had been using American timber.)

In 1795, the Royal Navy began purchasing land in the East End of the island chain for a dockyard and naval base, then relocated to Ireland Island at the western extremity. The first of HMD Bermuda's floating docks was installed in 1869. (HMD stands for His/Her Majesty's Dockyard.)

HMD Ireland Island, Bermuda (engraving by Thomas Chisholm Jack, c.1860)

Settlement

After spats at Nootka Sound,
There is now some common ground,
On how land can be claimed by any nation.
The notion can't be nursed,
Of 'it's ours: we found it first'.
There must be a degree of occupation.

Many Britons grasp the nettle:
And move elsewhere to settle,
And forever to their homeland bid goodbye.
Due to hardships they've endured,
Or by better prospects lured,
There are 'push and pull' components as to why.

Trade was often key,
To our acquisition spree.
Thus, in India, our presence seemed secure.
Then Nepal we had to get,
To gain access to Tibet:
The wool of Kashmir goats had great allure.

(We've a fair chunk of Nepal,
Though we didn't win it all.
We're dominant in India of course.
Bangladesh and Pakistan,
Both capitulate to plan:
The 'EIC's' a very potent force.)

It is missionaries who,
Chanced ending up in stew,
For by tales of pagan lands they'd been inspired.
In their wish to spread the word,
By the risks they're undeterred
Now their zeal to convert heathens has been fired.

One group – the CMS –
In New Zealand gained success
With the Māori, who liked European stuff.
The Hohi mission station,
Was our first base in that nation,
Though others followed rapidly enough.

Of Australia we've heard,
And the settlers who transferred.
Very many, for the passage, had enrolled.
With departing, more were smitten
When six ships arrived in Britain,
Carrying their loads of new-found gold.

Nootka Sound is in the north Pacific on the west coast of Vancouver Island. An incident in 1789 involved the seizure of British fur trading vessels by Spain, who claimed exclusive rights in the area. Subsequent agreements under the Nootka Conventions (1790–94) weakened the notion that sovereignty could be claimed without establishing settlements.

Emigration 'push' factors include escape from religious persecution, as was the case with the Pilgrim Fathers (see verse 321). In the 18th and 19th centuries, the Highland Clearances deprived many small farmers of their livelihoods. Many also sought to escape overcrowded cities (see verses 724 & 732).

'Pull' factors include the prospect of better weather, or of wealth (eg the 'Gold Rushes' which enticed people to places like Canada, Australia, New Zealand and South Africa).

The main trading bases in India were Madras, Calcutta and Bombay. Robert Clive (1725–1774), or 'Clive of India', had established the supremacy of the East India Company (EIC). Due to financial difficulties, this company had effectively been taken over by the British Government by an act passed in 1773. (The company was dissolved in 1858, and India became a Crown Colony.)

Indian cotton was becoming less important, as it was regarded as inferior in quality to that produced elsewhere (notably in Egypt). However the prized wool of the shawl goat, which would breed only in Tibet, was an attractive prospect. EIC negotiations to gain access to Nepal had failed, which led to the Anglo-Nepalese War (1814–16). Following British success in that war, about one third of Nepal was ceded to the company. This area became part of India in 1947, when that country gained independence.

The discoveries made by explorers such as James Cook prompted many to travel to the south Pacific and elsewhere to spread the Gospel, often with great success. They faced not only a hazardous sea journey, but other risks, such as cannibals. Missionaries John Williams and James Harris were murdered and eaten on the island of Erromango (New Hebrides) in 1839. In 2009, Williams' descendants travelled to the island, and received the apologies of the cannibals' descendants.

The Church Mission (or Missionary) Society (CMS), a group of evangelists, was founded in 1799. Operating worldwide, they often imported useful techniques eg irrigation.

The Māori are of eastern Polynesian origin, and they settled in New Zealand in the second half of the 13th century. Relations between the Māori and Europeans were usually amicable, though they fought amongst themselves, and were therefore eager to trade for muskets and tools such as axes.

The first ships bearing prospectors' gold arrived back in Britain in 1852.

For settlement in Australia see verses 728–732.

East India House and docks (French engraving, 1844)

The British Empire flowers.
Cape Colony is ours,
But for Africa, the scramble's not begun.
There is plenty more to get,
But the time is not quite yet
That all Europe wants its own 'place in the sun'.

Ceylon (1817), Singapore (1820) and Malaya (1824)

Now Dutch influence has gone,
We nick their part of Ceylon,
Then take the rest – the Kingdom known as Kandy.
Unconcerned with the morality,
We seize power with brutality.
The tea and rubber grown there come in handy.

Chests for tea with tin are lined.
In Malaya this is mined.
There, we'd leased Penang, a very useful place.
By the Sultan of Johore,
We were given Singapore.
Soon other parts the empire would embrace.

Burma (in phases from 1824 to 1886)

The Burmese start to poach.
There's a danger they'll encroach
On areas where Britain's holding sway.
So in 1824
There starts a two-year war.
The 'East India' will make them go away.

In 1852,
Hostilities renew.
On a fragile pretext, Lambert blocks Rangoon.
Despite the parts they cede,
We've not satisfied our greed:
And will take the rest whenever opportune.

In 1885
The curséd French arrive.
Their interference sets our hearts aquiver.
In dense jungle now we're fighting
With our troops, who are alighting
From the steamships on the Irrawaddy River.

Under this land's fertile soil,
There's a product known as oil,
Which comes from wells which people have hand dug.
Though some of it's for sale,
Production is small scale:
Bigger companies elsewhere must feel quite smug.

Cape Colony (The Cape of Good Hope) was acquired from the Dutch in 1814. The first British settlers arrived in Port Elizabeth in 1820. Britain had also progressively acquired bases in the Gambia and the Gold Coast (now Ghana) – plus Sierra Leone (ceded by France 1808). These areas were combined in 1821 to form British West Africa.

The so-called 'Scramble for Africa' took place between 1881 and 1914, by which time about 90 per cent of the continent had been partitioned between the European powers (as opposed to about 10 per cent in 1870).

Penang was leased from 1786.

Sir Stamford Raffles founded Singapore in 1820. He hoped to challenge the Dutch, who had been stifling British trade in the region, by creating a new port along the Straits of Malacca, the main shipping route for the India-China trade. It is now one of the largest ports in the world.

There were three Anglo-Burmese Wars in the period 1824–1885. Lower Burma was annexed in 1853. The French consul arrived in the Burmese capital (Mandalay), and began negotiations with the Burmese government. Expansion in Indo-China had brought the French too close for comfort. The whole of Burma (now Myanmar) was annexed by the British in 1886, but resistance continued for a further decade.

Commodore George Lambert (1796–1869) was privately referred to as the 'combustible commodore' by Lord Dalhousie (Governor General of India).

Yenangyaung oil wells, Burma (photograph by Arnold Wright, 1910)

Some has reached our own fair isle.
And has done so for a while;
Burmah Oil will prove to be a firm that flourished.
Though we don't yet have the tanker,
Soon for more and more we'll hanker,
When our navy's ships on liquid fuel are nourished.

Afghanistan (First Anglo-Afghan War, 1839–42)

Of the Russians, we're afraid.
Will they India invade?
Should they want to, through Afghanistan they'd pour.
Was this threat exaggerated?
Perhaps we should have sat and waited.
But we took it, though some asked, 'Whatever for?'

The First Opium War, 1839–42

Where would the British be,
Without their cup of tea?
From the Chinese came the drink that all delights.
But to fill our breakfast mug,
We part paid them with a drug,
Which made half their population high as kites.

China vetoed such corruption.
Trade thus suffered a disruption.
The *Nemesis* was part of Britain's scheme
To ensure things were restored.
The Chinese junks were floored,
For happily, our boat was powered by steam.

'It's the "devil ship",' they claim,
And appropriate that name,
For the likes of it have not been seen before.
Of iron this ship was made,
And all others she out-played.
The Chinese our demands cannot ignore.

We consider it worthwhile
To claim a coastal isle –
A request with which the Chinese go along.
A fairly humble plot,
Developed it is not,
But it will be soon. That place is called Hong Kong.

This has sketched out the position,
In terms of acquisition,
And we'll get to how we kept hold in good time.
But as yet we haven't heard,
Of what else has just occurred,
So let's move a little backwards with this rhyme.

Early exports of 'earth-oil' were to India, for conversion into kerosene. Britain began importing oil from Upper Burma in the early 1850s. Initial imports were carried on conventional ships in earthenware containers. As the British Admiralty moved away from coal to fuel-oil-powered vessels, Burma oil fields were the only major producer during the 1900s (see verses 1351–1352 for the development of oil tankers).

The Afghan invasion force comprised Indian troops under British command. There were two Anglo-Afghan wars.

In 1822, the tea bush was introduced into India, and plantations were established in the 1840s, but until then, China had a monopoly. Opium was, at that time, legal in Britain and grown extensively in the cotton-producing areas of India.

The *Nemesis*, unlike sailing ships of the line, had a shallow draught (the draught is the distance between the waterline and the bottom of the hull). This enabled her to give chase to the retreating Chinese vessels into shallower water. She fought alongside a number of conventional sailing warships.

A number of agreements would be signed with western powers by China (and also by Japan) during the 19th and early 20th centuries. Dubbed 'unequal treaties' they allowed, *inter alia*, free access to ports.

The colony of Hong Kong was established in 1841. British ownership was confirmed by the 1842 Treaty of Nanking.

There would be a Second Opium War (1856–60) over similar issues. This involved 173 allied (British and French) ships. Southern Kowloon was ceded to the UK by the concluding Treaties of Tientsin. Under an agreement of 1898, Britain was given possession of this, Hong Kong, and a number of neighbouring islands for a period of 95 years, ending in 1997.

HMS *Nemesis* (Edward Duncan, 1843)

The second voyage of HMS *Beagle*, 1831–36

Charles Darwin

Aboard a famous vessel,
A smart man starts to wrestle
With a problem. He will find his own solution.
There were differences between
Some mockingbirds he'd seen.
The theory that explained these? Evolution!

Whole new thinking this would shape.
Man's descended from the ape!
A concept many viewed with consternation.
If a species is to thrive,
The fittest will survive,
Which goes against the idea of creation.

The *Beagle* was the ship
On which Darwin took his trip.
The Galápagos were where such thoughts were triggered.
His heretical conclusions
Shattered everyone's illusions,
But he proved to be quite right in what he'd figured.

Charles Darwin (1809–1882) published his theories in *On the Origin of the Species* (1859). During his voyage aboard the *Beagle*, he'd noted small but significant differences between these birds from island to island. The same applied to markings on tortoises' shells.

Beagle's first voyage (1826–30) was a hydrographic survey mission to Patagonia and Tierra del Fuego under the command of Captain Pringle Stokes, who committed suicide.

Charles Darwin (John Collier, 1881)

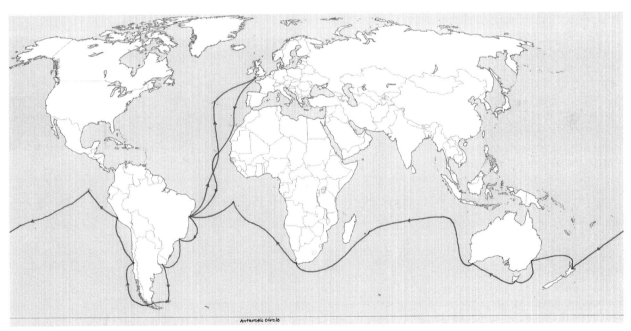

The second voyage of HMS *Beagle*, 1831–36

Robert FitzRoy and the weather forecast

On the *Beagle*, who's in charge?
Someone else who must loom large.
Charles and Robert FitzRoy often dined together.
The captain's late career
Dealt with what the Brits hold dear:
It was he who started forecasting the weather.

The force of storm or gale,
Is measured on a scale,
Which Francis Beaufort steadily refined.
His protégé was Rob,
And he gave his friend the job
Of heading up a team he had in mind.

FitzRoy was thus charged
With a role (since much enlarged)
Of prediction. Would the seas be rough or calm?
The 'Met Office' was born.
Its function was to warn
Of conditions in which ships might come to harm…

… A much needed grand design,
For in 1859,
Royal Charter by northeasterlies was lashed.
Many drown, as they'd kept hold
Of their precious Aussie gold.
Others perish when against cruel rocks they're dashed.

New telegraph he'd use
To convey the latest news.
It was also how he gathered information.
It's now heard four times a day,
In the same unvaried way,
Only war would cause its temporary cessation.

Viking… North Utsire…
Some parts distant, others nearer…
Forth… Tyne… Dogger… Fisher… German Bight…
For insomniacs, terrific:
A poetic soporific –
Is that shipping forecast read out in the night.

Restless they may lie,
Then the strains of 'Sailing by',
Are followed by conditions in the deep.
Come Biscay, eyes are closing,
By Fastnet, folk are dozing
And by south-east Iceland, some are fast asleep.

The wind force scale rises numerically from calm (0), through increasingly strong breezes (2–6), high wind (7), gales (8–10), storms (10–11) and hurricane (12).

Rear Admiral Sir Francis Beaufort (1774–1857). At the age of 55, he was appointed British Admiralty Hydrographer of the Navy, a post he held for 25 years. He did not invent the wind force scale, but did develop it into a standardized means of classifying sailing conditions (1805).

Vice Admiral Robert FitzRoy (1805–1865) was appointed Meteorological Statistician to the Board of Trade.

The steam clipper *Royal Charter* was returning from Melbourne and bound for Liverpool when she was wrecked in a strong storm off Anglesey with the loss of about 450 lives. Among her passengers were many gold miners, who had struck it rich and carried their treasure about their persons. Much of this ended up on the beach, making the locals who found it very rich. A further 200 ships were also wrecked in the same storm.

For telegraph, see verses 652 & 1129–1132.

The BBC started broadcasting weather forecasts in 1922, and shipping forecasts in 1924. There are 31 sea areas, most of which are named after towns, islands (and islets) and sandbanks. In 2002, Finisterre was renamed FitzRoy, both in honour of the first professional weatherman, and to avoid confusion with a smaller sea area of the same name used by the Spanish and French.

FitzRoy, who suffered from depression, found it difficult to accept criticism when he got the forecast wrong, and committed suicide at the age of 59.

'Sailing by' was composed by Ronald Binge in 1963. This piece of music has introduced the late night (0048 hours) shipping forecast since 1967.

Robert FitzRoy
(Herman John Schmidt, *c.*1910)

Francis Beaufort
(Stephen Pearce, *c.*1855)

The *Royal Charter* sinking (artist unknown)

The soft voice never falters.
The order never alters,
And the meaning of the terms used is precise.
It's a British institution:
Any change means revolution!
Some wouldn't have it tweaked at any price.

Sailors these days might agree
They don't need the BBC,
To inform of what they soon might be enduring.
Be it hurricane or squall,
Clever gizmos tell them all,
But the radio's still there: it's reassuring.

Ranks, flags and uniforms

Into three our fleet's partitioned,
And Admirals commissioned,
To take charge of the Red, the White, the Blue.
Below them would appear,
The 'Vice' and, next, the 'Rear',
And Commodores would hold a flag rank too.

(In 1864,
This system was no more:
With those coloured flags, what were they going to do?
To the navy, white's assigned.
Red on merchant ships we find,
And auxiliary vessels fly the blue.)

Under flag ranks come positions,
For those who hold commissions
From whomever is the reigning king or queen.
A captain's at the top,
A commander's down one drop,
Then lieutenants in their guises can be seen.

Sub-lieutenants/masters' mates,
Feature higher than the rates,
As do warrant holders: ancient their creation.
This rank was first devised,
For a man who's specialized,
In carpentry, with sails, or navigation.

The man who works with wood,
Does repairs and makes things good,
The boatswain – who's assessed the wind that's blowing –
Rigs according to the breeze,
Whilst the master's expertise,
Is determining where vessels should be going.

The forecast has a limit of 370 words. 'Soon' means expected within 6 to 12 hours. 'Poor' means visibility of between 1,000 metres and 2 nautical miles (a nautical mile is 1,852 metres by international agreement).

A proposal to change the timing of the early morning broadcast by twelve minutes from 0048 hours to 0100 hours led to a mass protest.

The fleet was partitioned in 1620. The same three squadron colours had been introduced during the reign of Elizabeth I, with the Red under an Admiral, the White under a Vice Admiral and the Blue under a Rear Admiral. 'The Red' was the most senior squadron. The promotion ladder for a Rear Admiral of the Blue (the most junior flag rank in the most junior squadron) would be to Rear Admiral of the White and then the Red, followed by Vice Admiral of the Blue etc. There was no Admiral of the Red as he would be deemed to be in charge of the whole navy (ie Admiral of the Fleet). This changed after the Battle of Trafalgar in 1815, when the rank was introduced, largely in recognition of the navy's achievements in the Napoleonic Wars (see verses 690–715).

With the advent of steamships, the Admiralty decided to end the ambiguity of the white ensign's being used for both naval and civil (ie merchant) ships. The white ensign is flown on Royal Navy ships and shore establishments. It is also flown by the Royal Yacht Squadron, and from ships of Trinity House when escorting the monarch. The red ensign, used by the Merchant Navy is also known as the 'Red Duster'. The blue ensign is used by ships in public service, or by those commanded by an officer in the Royal Naval Reserve (see verse 950).

There is also a rank of Lieutenant Commander, which was introduced to replace the 'time served in rank' distinction between lieutenants. Previously, those with fewer than eight years' service were the equivalent of an army captain, and those with more than eight held a rank equivalent to an army major.

A 'master' is a professional seaman and specialised navigator. His 'mate' would learn and assist. In 1840, would-be masters became 'masters' assistants', and a 'mate' equated to what (in 1860) was renamed the rank of Sub-Lieutenant. A 'rate' or 'rating' is an enlisted member of the navy who does not hold a commission or warrant.

The concept of warrant officers dates back to 1040, when the Cinque Ports (see verses 166–170) were charged with supplying to the king ships and men capable of fulfilling skilled roles (which also included cooks).

Because they no longer worked solely with wood, carpenters were renamed Warrant Shipwrights in 1918.

The master was the highest ranking warrant officer and was billeted in the wardroom, (the exclusive mess-cabin), along with other senior warrant officers. From 1808, they (and also surgeons), were considered the equivalent of commissioned officers.

Certain warrants would stay vested,
Even when a ship was rested,
('In Ordinary' means that it's been docked).
It still needs to be maintained
By the suitably well trained,
And presumably its cupboards must stay stocked.

As the former 'clerk of burser'
We also find the purser.
His post once offered scope for the corrupt.
A 'mark up' oft applied,
On what this man supplied:
Candles, bedding, food and what was supped.

If the surgeon's on-board crew
Have had a fling or two
And, because of this, contracted a disease,
For every hundred treated
With the 'remedies' he meted,
An extra fiver supplements his fees.

The chaplain, clerk and teacher
With their warrants also feature,
And the gunner, too, the navy has been hiring.
His knowledge he'll apply,
To ensure the powder's dry,
And whatever else to keep those cannons firing.

And when steam-powered ships appear,
There's the role of engineer,
To ensure that the machinery won't fail.
(If it broke or it exploded,
All could end up incommoded,
Especially if the vessel had no sail).

Warrant status gives some clarity,
Though the 'engineman' lacks parity,
Until the 'E.R.A.' grade's introduced.
For his role to be fulfilled,
He must be highly skilled,
And a training college gives careers a boost.

(New type 'sailors' now arrive:
To keep the fires alive
Are the stokers. Only strong tall men are hired.
Greasers oil the moving parts,
And a trimmer's one who carts
Coal from bunker to the furnace, as required.)

A warrant was issued by the Board of Admiralty. 'Standing warrant officers' were attached to a ship throughout its lifetime, whether in commission or 'in ordinary' (ie laid up). These included the master, the boatswain, the carpenter and the purser.

As well as general provisions, the purser also supplied luxuries such as tobacco. He would get credit on most items (except food and drink). The cost of the clothing and hammocks issued to the men would be deducted from their earnings, although the purser was not responsible for pay.

Ships' surgeons were appointed by The Sick and Hurt Board. The 1866 Contagious Diseases Act was prompted by concern about the number of soldiers and sailors contracting venereal diseases. The surgeon was also paid an allowance for equipment and could, all in all, enjoy a substantial income.

The master, the chaplain and other 'wardroom' warrant officers were awarded commissioned status in 1843.

The school in a ship was the responsibility of the chaplain. Teachers were called seamen's schoolmasters whilst serving on ships, and were later renamed 'Naval Instructors' in shore establishments. From 1861, the latter were appointed by commission.

Warrant Officers, whatever their specialism, had to (and still must) be capable of carrying out instructional duties both afloat and ashore. Initially, those responsible for keeping engines running were sometimes derisively referred to as 'engine drivers' or 'enginemen' by the rest of the crew. In 1868, the Engine Room Artificer (ERA) came into being. This title was not changed until the late 1960s.

A number of new categories of warrant officer were introduced in 1913 to reflect new technology. These included Warrant Telegraphist, Warrant Engineer and Warrant Electrician. By 1935 yet others appeared eg a category specialising in submarine detection and a Warrant Photographer.

The Royal Navy Engineering College opened in 1880 at Keyham, Devonport. Larger premises at Manadon were purchased (1937). These days, 'engineers afloat' train at civilian universities, and then at specialized establishments in the Portsmouth area.

After an absence of 21 years, in 2014, the RN proposed to re-introduce its Maritime Reserves Engineering Branch.

Stokers needed to be a minimum of 5 feet 9 inches (1.75m) tall to qualify.

Those responsible for keeping the fires burning eventually replaced those who had worked sails and ropes. Merchant and Royal Naval captains were initially puzzled about how this new breed fitted into the traditional ranking system.

Before any person can hereafter be received on board Her Majesty's ship *Excellent* as a candidate for a appointment as Naval Instructor, he will be required to produce a certificate of his age, and testimonials of good character; and both laymen and clergymen when appointed to act as Naval Instructors must pass an examination as to their qualifications to instruct the young Officers in the following branches:-

1st   Common Arithmetic, including Vulgar and Decimal Fractions.
2nd The first six and the eleventh books of Euclid.
3rd Algebra, progressing to the highest order of Equations, and its application to the solution of Geometrical Problems.
4th Plane and Spherical Trigonometry, theoretical and practical.
5th Nautical Astronomy, particularly the principles on which the various rules for finding the latitude and longitude are founded.
6th Mechanics.
7th Hydrostatics.
8th A competent knowledge of the Classics.

Extract from *Regulations of the Qualification, Pay and Half Pay of Naval Instructors*, issued by the Admiralty (10 September 1842)

Further down one rung are those
Who are classed as CPOs:
Then plain petty ones, who haven't made it yet.
To this rank is now equating
The midshipman, once a rating,
Who'll become in time an officer cadet.

On ships, the vast majority,
Had no real seniority.
The enlisted chap – what do we know of him?
If experienced, his label
Denotes that he is able:
He knows his stuff, but probably can't swim!

As well as these gradations,
There are social demarcations:
There are 'gentlemen' whose status is discrete.
There's an etiquette that cites,
Those who 'qualify' have rights
Regarding where they walk and where they eat.

Both for day-to-day and 'best',
Long had officers been dressed
In uniforms, to show they served the crown.
Ratings didn't have such props:
They were merely clothed in 'slops',
Though one captain had each man garbed as a clown!

Perhaps this made the navy twig
That they really need a rig,
In a service that is held in high repute.
The collar that's devised,
Is somewhat over-sized,
And distinctive on this brand new sailor suit.

Chief Petty Officer is a non-commissioned rank. Specialised roles such as quartermaster (helmsman) were ranked as petty officers. In the 17th century, the term midshipman, which comes from amidships (where he either worked or was berthed), referred to an experienced seaman. By the turn of the 19th century, he was an apprentice officer, gaining experience aboard a ship for at least three years. With the establishment of an officer training college at Dartmouth in 1863, a midshipman meant either a naval cadet, or the most junior commissioned rank.

Prior to becoming an able seaman, a sailor would have been an ordinary seaman. There were boys on board, and there might also have been landsmen (see verse 631), who served as labourers.

Only those officers who qualified as 'gentlemen' were permitted to eat in the wardroom. Similar rules applied to permission to walk on the Quarterdeck.

Uniforms for officers were first introduced by Lord Anson (see verses 496–501) in 1748. The white tunic and trousers used in tropical climates were introduced in 1877 (replaced by a white shirt and shorts in 1938). Epaulettes, used by all officers from 1846, first appeared in 1705. Midshipmen received a white patch on the collar (1758), the oldest badge still in use.

In 1853, the commanding officer of the *Harlequin* dressed his boat crews as harlequins (at his own expense). The Admiralty established uniforms for ratings four years later in 1857.

The naval rig (or Number One uniform) is now primarily ceremonial. It has undergone many changes since it was first introduced.

The blue denim collar was not, as is sometimes thought, introduced because sailors wore tarred pigtails, the last recorded incidence of which was in 1827. Bell-bottomed trousers were designed to be easily rolled up for tasks such as scrubbing the deck.

Submarines

Bourne and Drebbel we have met,
Plus their plans to not get wet
Under water, in a vessel that submerged.
Others since had tried.
Of the mark they'd fallen wide.
Interest waned, but now it suddenly resurged.

How to move it they must nobble,
And overcome the wobble.
New technology at last some answers held.
This would finally enable
Such craft to be more stable,
And provide the means by which they'd be propelled.

Their combatant potential,
Which would prove so influential
For a long time, and by many, had been seen.
But for battleship assaults,
They still had many faults:
They remained a wholly human-powered machine.

Robert Fulton did suggest,
(Though the French were not impressed),
The construction of his *Nautilus* design.
The aim? Hit British shipping,
So his boat would need equipping,
With something that exploded, like a mine.

The scheme would come to naught:
With problems, subs were fraught.
Folk tried water bugs and variants of *Turtle*.
Some trials were tales of woe:
Like these boats, the pace was slow.
(A people-pedalled craft can scarcely hurtle).

Experiments galore
Always seemed to show a flaw,
And problems with design loomed ever large.
They tried diesel, they tried steam,
They tried every sort of scheme,
They tried batteries – with no means to recharge.

Then a man from the UK,
Began to show the way.
John Holland, engineer, from County Clare.
In one prototype – his second –
This inventor always reckoned
All the necessary elements were there.

For Bourne and Drebbel see verses 285–286.

The *Rotterdam Boat*, designed to attack English shipping, was built in 1654. Underpowered, it went nowhere.

In 1747, Nathaniel Symons had patented and constructed the first known submersible, using a ballast tank. Leather sacks filled with water caused it to sink and these were emptied by a twisting mechanism, thus allowing the boat to resurface.

In 1776, David Bushnell built the *Turtle*, which failed in an attempted attack on a British ship in New York harbour.

American engineer Robert Fulton (see verses 777–778) made several changes to his 1796 design, and eventually constructed a version in 1800, at his own expense. He made several attempts to attack British ships, but they saw him coming and moved out of the way. He eventually fell out with the French government. He then tried to sell 'torpedoes' (nowadays referred to as mines), to the British government.

Wilhelm Bauer's *Brandtaucher* (Incendiary Diver 1850) and Lodner J. Phillips' two trial vessels, (the second of which was hand-cranked, (1852)), still relied on human effort to propel them, as did Bauer's 1855 *Seeteufel* (Sea Devil), and several others constructed during the American Civil War (1861–65).

For his designs, Irish born inventor John Holland (1840–1914) is widely regarded as 'the Father of the modern submarine'. He emigrated to the USA in 1873. His first small prototype *Holland No 1*, (1878) was constructed in New York, and built in secrecy, as it was funded by The Fenian Brotherhood, a militant anti-British organisation. Its gasoline-fuelled Brayton-cycle engine didn't work, but an improvised external steam supply functioned well enough for a second larger prototype to be commissioned.

ON THE SUBMERSIBLE

1. Tis private: a man may go thus to any coast in the world invisibly, without discovery, or prevented in his journey.
2. Tis safe, from the uncertainty of Tides, and the violences of Tempests, which do never move the sea above five or six paces deep. From Pirates and Robbers which do so infest others voyages, from ice and great frost, which do so much endanger the passages towards the Poles.
3. It may be of great advantage against a Navy of enemies, who by this may be undermined in the water and blown up.
4. It may be of special use for the relief of any place besieged by water, to convey unto them invisible supplies, and so likewise for the surprisal of any place that is accessible by water.
5. It may be of unspeakable benefit for submarine experiments.

Bishop John Wilkins, from *Mathematical Magick* (1648)

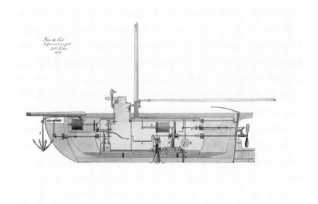

Cross-section of Fulton's 1806 submarine design

By this certainty he's spurred,
There were setbacks. Undeterred,
He made sure his basic concepts were refined.
He worked with sheer persistence,
Till a sub would go the distance,
(Two methods of propulsion were combined).

It performed well under water,
And the US navy bought her.
And though Britain never did things in a rush,
(Still not keen on what was new),
We commissioned these craft too:
An investment that we tried to keep hush-hush.

Lest the secret be betrayed,
The first of these was made,
In a 'yacht shed', which was meant to be misleading.
Component parts, once done,
Were labelled 'pontoon one'.
Via such ruses, her construction was proceeding.

If subs get in a scrape,
How on earth do crews escape?
Nobody's yet thought to make provisions.
To danger they're exposed,
With a hatch not fully closed,
Not to mention the explosions and collisions.

So for stealthy operations
We were making preparations:
The seeds of covert warfare had been sown.
In new vessels we've invested.
Their potential's being tested.
Meanwhile, Germany's developing her own...

Trade in the Victorian Era

Steam power, iron and coal,
Begin to take their toll:
In the countryside now fewer people dwell.
Though farming's more efficient,
We're no longer self-sufficient,
As overcrowded towns and cities swell.

From this, you will conclude,
That we had to import food.
We are shipping in more butter and more meat.
(Once the Corn Laws are repealed,
We can look to far afield,
And buy enormous quantities of wheat).

The *Fenian Ram* (1881) was more successful. Holland considered it to have all the necessary ingredients, and continued to develop his ideas. The privately built *Holland VI*, launched 1897, was the first submarine to have enough power to travel submerged for a considerable distance by means of an electric motor. The batteries for this motor were charged by a generator which was powered by the diesel engine (used for surface travel). She was bought, tested and commissioned in 1900 by the US Navy.

The Royal Navy followed suit, and the first (*Holland 1*) of 5 *Holland* class submarines was assembled (in secrecy) at the Vickers shipyard in Barrow-in-Furness (1903), which went on to specialise in submarine building (see verses 1099–1100). It is now in the RN Submarine Museum, Gosport.

Japan, Russia and Sweden also adopted Holland's design.

Prior to the start of the First World War, there were 68 submarine accidents – including 7 battery gas explosions, 12 gasoline explosions, 13 sinkings due to hull openings' not being closed, and 23 collisions.

John Philip Holland standing in the hatch of a submarine

Wood was increasingly expensive as a fuel, and was largely replaced by coal, which was in plentiful supply. The steel industry was started by Bessemer's 1856 converter, but did not outstrip iron production until 1918.

The so-called 'Agricultural Revolution' of the mid 17th century to the late 19th century, resulted in a massive increase in agricultural production, and during the 18th century, 50 per cent more land was brought under cultivation. Britain was able to feed itself until the 19th century. In 1801, the population was 11 million. It had almost doubled by 1851, and more than trebled by 1901 to 37 million.

The Corn Laws (see verse 755) restricted the import of grain. The years following their repeal in 1846 saw a dramatic increase in grain imports (mainly from the USA), and a corresponding decline in British wheat and barley growing acreage.

Sugar... coffee... tea...
Long have reached our shores by sea.
Sweet-toothed we are, which makes our molars rotten.
Our textiles' sector booms,
Involving mills and looms,
For this we need an awful lot of cotton.

Rubber's had a mention
And a Scottish man's invention
Has resulted in the (not yet plastic) mac.
Thanks to vulcanizing fires,
It will soon be making tyres,
So in quantity we bring this substance back.

What's imported has near doubled,
But the balance sheet's not troubled:
What we export is much more than keeping pace.
The distant foreign client,
Is on British goods reliant,
For pianos, arms and fripperies in lace.

The world's a giant store
Of our foodstuffs and much more.
And no one (yet) can burst the British bubble.
But this leaves us unprepared,
If war should be declared:
Our dependence then might get us into trouble.

Of steam, we've seen the coming...
Ever better engines thrumming...
These, to some extent, the power of wind replace.
But machines are not compact:
They eat coal, which must be stacked.
And all this takes up precious cargo space.

Agamemnon's the solution.
Engine size, a diminution.
And the pressure in the boiler is now higher.
The hull's been redesigned,
To a stronger sleeker kind,
And this reduced the power she would require.

British sugar consumption increased five-fold between 1700 and 1800. This was mainly taken in tea. In addition to all that sugar, the need for industrial raw materials, such as cotton and dyestuffs from plantations, was the driving force behind our Atlantic trade.

For rubber see verse 880. Made of rubberised fabric, the first waterproof raincoats were sold in 1824. English inventor Thomas Hancock took out a patent for vulcanization in 1844, 8 weeks ahead of the American Charles Goodyear.

Between 1809 and 1839, British imports doubled and exports tripled. America was Britain's biggest market. In 1800, it accounted for 60 per cent of the export trade, but this reduced as the USA industrialised. Asia and the colonies accounted for much of the rest. Exports included luxury items (gloves, stockings etc), engineered products such as portable engines, and cast iron items (anything from cooking pots to whole houses!).

Built by Scotts of Greenock (see verse 1106), in 1866, SS *Agamemnon* of The Blue Funnel Line became the first of the long-distance merchant steamships to sail non-stop from Liverpool to Mauritius.

By the 1890s, the British merchant ship, with its triple expansion engine was so efficient, it could carry a ton of cargo for a knot on little more than the energy released by the burning of a couple of sheets of writing paper.

See verses 817–854 **Steamships**.

> The plains of North America and Russia are our corn fields; Chicago and Odessa our granaries; Canada and the Baltic are our timber forests; Australia contains our sheep farms, and in Argentina and on the western prairies are our herds of oxen; Peru sends her silver, and the gold of South Africa and Australia flows to London; the Hindus and the Chinese grow tea for us, and our coffee, sugar and spice plantations are all in the Indies. Spain and France are our vineyards and the Mediterranean our fruit garden; and our cotton grounds... are now being extended everywhere in the warm regions of the earth.
>
> **William Stanley Jevons, English economist and logician, 1865**

State Library of Queensland
John Oxley Library

SS *Agamemnon*

Registers and Reserves

Lloyd's Register of Shipping

Those in shipping used to meet,
In a place on Lombard Street:
A coffee shop was where they all convened.
Here both drinks and deals were brewed:
Lloyd, the owner was quite shrewd
In circulating info he had gleaned.

When it came to risk assessing
His report sheets proved a blessing:
Men rushed to read the data he collected.
His name has had endurance,
In the business of insurance,
And is one which, to this day, is well respected.

Lloyd's Register existed,
But not every ship was listed.
Those that were had all been surveyed and assessed.
Hulls and fittings, viewed objectively,
Were graded. Used respectively,
A letter and a number. 'A1's' best!

So from 1764,
There were records. What is more,
These came to be an annual compilation.
As the 'Green Book' it is known.
Soon it isn't on its own:
The 'Red Book' is a rival publication.

The competition stems
From ships built on the Thames:
A higher class to these would be accorded.
Though the lists in time were merged,
Points of view were so diverged,
That the whole affair was damaging and sordid.

Registrations of Seamen

Once Napoleon was finished,
The need for men diminished,
And the spectre of the Press Gang was no more.
So what could Britain do,
If her navy needed crew,
Because we'd somehow found ourselves at war?

Originally established in Tower Street (1686), Edward Lloyd's Coffee House moved in 1691. (These second premises are now occupied at street level by a Sainsbury's supermarket.)

Ship owners, merchants and mariners involved in the slave trade and underwriters used to convene there. It became the place for obtaining marine insurance. Lloyd's had a reputation for paying up fully and promptly. Its effective monopoly in marine insurance was reviewed in 1810, and was ended in 1824.

Lloyd's Register, originally called the Registry of Shipping, first appeared in 1764, following the formation of the Register Society by Lloyds' customers in 1760. Ship surveyors were usually master mariners or master shipwrights. Surveys were conducted on ships calling at British ports.

The grading of ships is how the term 'A1' for the top classification of anything originated. It first appeared in the 1775–6 edition of the Register. The first two lists were dated 1764–66, and 1768–71. Lists were issued annually from 1775.

A dispute (1799–1833) between owners and underwriters led to the publication of 2 lists. These were merged in 1834. The list became more comprehensive in 1874 and included all vessels over 100 gross tons.

What didn't yet exist,
Was a comprehensive list,
Of those who served as onboard personnel.
But an Act in time was passed.
Were there records now at last?
No. It wouldn't be complied with all that well.

But the theory was sound:
Seasoned mariners abound
And, in part, that's why the register appeared.
But when extra men were needed,
The call was barely heeded,
And a mere four hundred seamen volunteered.

This left ships understaffed,
Which Charles Napier thought daft:
In the Baltic he had struggled, so complained.
A commission this debated.
And a new force was created,
Which, every year, in gunnery was trained.

The next back up for the navy,
Acquired the nickname 'wavy':
Civilians for the first time were recruited.
Then, as World War Two approached,
A new idea was broached:
To their new roles, leisure yachtsman proved well suited.

Ideal one role would be,
For those who trawled the sea,
And who much about their local waters learned.
All this expertise combines,
In the task of sweeping mines,
And from fishing, to new dangers, many turned.

Those who volunteered to serve,
Needed watchfulness and nerve.
In wartime, boats galore were requisitioned.
These were sturdy, these were strong,
And it didn't take that long
For the nation's chips to lack their normal 'fish and'.

(In all, five registrations
May just help you trace relations,
But for lengthy spans you might not have much luck.
For more than fifty years,
Are no records, it appears.
If your ancestor served then, you could be stuck.)

There were some muster rolls for individual ships from 1747, when it became a legal requirement for masters of vessels to compile a list of the crew engaged over a voyage. There were also some records of indentured apprentices.

The *First Register of Merchant Seamen* (1835–44), introduced under the 1835 Merchant Shipping Act, was initially compiled using ships' crew lists. Seamen were then issued with a numbered register ticket.

When the Crimean War broke out (1853), very few men volunteered. Despite a chronic manpower shortage (especially of experienced seamen), and despite contradictory orders from the Admiralty, Admiral Sir Charles Napier (1786–1860) managed to contain Russia's Baltic Fleet without the loss of a single ship. This prevented the reinforcement of the Tsar's Black Sea Fleet, and also contained 30,000 Russian troops. He was, however, made a scapegoat by the Admiralty for not achieving more than a successful blockade (see also verse 1176). Elected an MP in 1855, Napier (who, throughout 60 years' naval service, had vigorously campaigned to improve the treatment of common seamen) took his dispute to the House of Commons.

In 1858, a Royal Commission on Manning the Navy was set up, and the new Royal Naval Reserve (RNR) was created by Act of Parliament the following year. It had 12,000 volunteers by 1862, when the scheme was extended to include officers.

In 1903, The Royal Naval Volunteer Reserve was created. RNVR officers wore wavy sleeve rings to distinguish them from RNR/RN personnel. King George VI ultimately decreed that these be replaced by straight rings. By 1914, there were 30,000 officers and men in the reserves.

Amateur sailors, after intensive training, played a key role in the reserves, and often found themselves in positions of command.

The benefits of recruiting and training fishermen in minesweeping were recognized in 1907 by Admiral Lord Beresford (Commander-in-Chief of the Home Fleet), with the result that the RNR (Trawler Section) was set up in 1910. All 371 new trawlers built on Humberside during the First World War were commissioned for minesweeping, but most were afterwards sold back as fishing vessels.

In 1958, the two reserve services were amalgamated, the RNR absorbing the RNVR.

There were second and third registrations of seamen (1845–54 and 1854–56) but then followed a period (1857–1913) when these weren't required. Fourth and fifth registrations appear from 1931–1941 and 1941–1972.

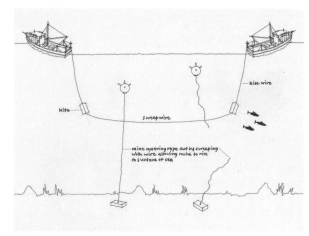

Trawlers minesweeping in pairs

Clippers and merchant sailing ships

We all know the *Cutty Sark*:
And the clipper made its mark;
For three decades, it was firmly on the scene.
Its concave bow was sleek,
And to start with quite unique,
When the *Scottish Maid* was built in Aberdeen.

Synonymous with speed,
It went very fast indeed,
'Clipping' waves across the oceans as it raced.
Rapid transit was the key
For foodstuffs such as tea,
Which over time begin to lose their taste.

Though this beautiful creation
Can inspire such admiration,
Its role requires a timely word of caution.
Quite a minor part it played
In the volume of world trade:
It carried just a very small proportion.

Once Suez was created,
The clipper's role abated:
With hefty towage costs such ships were lumbered.
But though steam's in the ascendant,
On sail we're still dependent.
It will be a while before its days are numbered.

They need be but lightly manned
O'er the distances they spanned,
For wind-powered ships by now are much improved.
They don't eat coal with voracity,
And thus have the capacity
To accommodate whatever must be moved.

A master who's adroit,
Can prevailing winds exploit,
These – and currents – have been analyzed by Maury.
Ships' logs this man collected –
These had been too long neglected –
And his studies found they told a useful story.

'Windjammers' some were named.
Their hulls were metal framed.
On the longest trips these vessels were enrolled.
Often round the world their route,
Filled with rice... wheat... lumber... jute...
All commodities in bulk these ships could hold.

The term 'clipper' derives from the verb 'to clip' (now synonymous with speed). It was probably first used in connection with the American Baltimore clippers of the late 18th century, and may also have been applied to the pre-1830 small British 'opium clippers'.

The first true British clipper, *Scottish Maid*, was built by Alexander Hall & Sons and launched in 1839. Its design, later widely copied, was in part intended to reduce liability for tax and harbour dues. The clipper had three masts and a square rig. It sailed day and night in all conditions.

Often referred to as 'tea clippers', these ships also carried spices, opium and people. They had an advantage over steamships in that space was not taken up by coal, fresh water supplies or, indeed, by the engines themselves. Despite this, they only carried about 0.5 per cent of world trade. Unless towed, (the charges were prohibitively expensive), sailing ships could not shortcut through the Suez Canal (see verse 1195). By the time the canal opened (1869), they were already being less extensively used and the steam clipper, which had an auxiliary engine (eg *Royal Charter* – see verse 899), had been developed.

However, not until the 20th century did steam truly dominate, largely thanks to the 'Windjammer', a type of large merchant sailing ship with three to five masts. The iron (later steel) hulls of these vessels took up less space, and thus enabled a greatly increased cargo capacity (usually of between 2,000 and 5,000 tons, whereas the typical capacity of clippers was 1,000 tons). The world's first was the Glasgow-built *County of Peebles* (1875).

Cargos also included iron, nitrate fertilizer, guano (excrement from certain birds and animals used as a fertilizer) and, of course, coal.

American Matthew Fontaine Maury (1806–1873) was nicknamed 'Pathfinder of the Seas'. His detailed study of winds and currents enabled better use to be made of prevailing climatic conditions.

Simpler rigging was devised.
Some were semi-mechanised.
Certain heavy tasks by 'donkeys' were assisted.
In the mercantile marine,
Both sail and steam were seen;
For a while, two types of vessel co-existed.

The Great Tea Race, 1866

Tea, the drink we Brits so relish,
Isn't something that will perish,
For swift transit there is quite another reason.
With 'freshest' much enamoured,
The merchants always clamoured,
To buy the very first crop of each season.

Speeding back with this is normal.
Competition is informal,
But one contest Britain's public would transfix.
Four ships leave on the same tide,
And there's nothing to divide
First and second, in the race of '66.

It is such a close-run thing.
The winner is *Taeping*,
But the premium she earns must be divided.
In a further compromise,
Two captains share one prize
'Such payments must be stopped,' it is decided.

Harbours and coaling stations

On distant shores, it's wise
To ensure you have supplies,
And somewhere ships can undergo repair.
Ideal harbours don't abound:
Once good places have been found,
Those who occupy them aren't too keen to share.

They'll be sheltered, not exposed
(But they won't be too enclosed:
Ease of getting out's a prime consideration).
Where they're few and far between,
They have often been the scene,
Of intense defence – and naval confrontation.

One haven such as these,
Was eastern Ceylonese.
Trincomalee was often in the news.
For this refuge Suffren hankers,
There the French can drop their anchors,
But contesting it is Britain's Edward Hughes.

Steam 'donkey' engines were used for hoisting sails, raising anchors and working pumps. Relatively small crews were therefore needed to man these ships.

The tea route was from China to London via the Indian Ocean and round the Cape of Good Hope. The neck-and-neck situation in the thrilling 1866 race was widely reported in newspapers. After 99 days' sailing from Shanghai, three ships (*Ariel*, *Taeping*, and *Serica*) arrived on the same tide. The fourth, *Fiery Cross*, was not far behind. Less than half an hour separated *Taeping* and *Ariel*. A premium of 10 shillings per ton was paid to the first clipper to dock in London. The circumstances of the 1866 race were such that this benefit was subsequently abandoned.
The captains' prize was £100.
The situation was further complicated by the fact that a steamship had arrived two weeks earlier with a consignment of first crop tea.
The fast Aberdeen-built clipper *Thermopylae* beat the *Cutty Sark* by 7 days in the 1872 tea race, after the latter lost her rudder.

A fighting ship, HMS *Trincomalee*, was named for the contested Ceylon (now Sri Lanka) harbour. Part of Great Britain's heritage fleet and the National Museum of the Royal Navy, it can be visited at Hartlepool's Maritime Experience.
Pierre André de Suffren (1729–1788) and Sir Edward Hughes (c.1720–1794) vied for naval supremacy in the Indian Ocean during the American War of Independence. Their fleets were involved in several fiercely contested, and largely inconclusive, encounters during 1782 and in April 1783.

ON LANDLOCKED HARBOURS

Certain it is that these ships are purposely to serve His Majesty and to defend the kingdom from danger, and not to be so penned up from casualtie as that they should be less able or serviceable in times of need.

Walter Raleigh

A ship on a foreign station, moving from port to port, offers continual opportunity for diversion, and, as an abundance of leave is granted to men of good character, they have ample opportunity to visit the different towns, see the sights, and study the ways of the natives.

From the log of HMS *Argonaut* (1900–04)

Steam power brings another need:
The fuel on which to feed.
And, world-wide, British harbours are now mapped.
Most of these have the potential
To stock what's so essential,
And as coaling stations readily adapt.

The process of refuelling,
Was slow and very gruelling:
'Black diamonds' must be passed to ship from land.
Men got dirty. Men got tired,
Moving all that was required,
For they shovelled it, and carted it by hand.

They might work around the clock,
But ships remained in dock
For days, and crews could spend some time ashore.
In their pockets, coins would jingle,
With local folk they'd mingle,
And encounter ways of life not seen before.

The only place to which Britain did not ship coal was America's Atlantic coast, but Britain did have coaling stations in places that were not within the British Empire.

The coal passers' main role was on board, keeping the furnaces supplied, ensuring that ashes were cleared out and that everywhere else was kept clean.

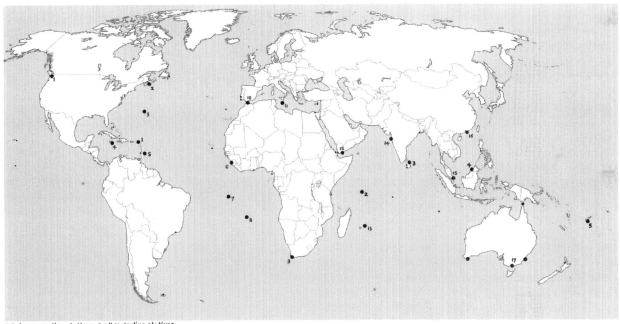

● Primary coaling stations ● other coaling stations

Major coaling stations at the end of the nineteenth century
1 Esquimalt (Vancouver Island) **2** Halifax (Nova Scotia) **3** Bermuda **4** Port Royal, Jamaica **5** Carlisle Bay, Barbados **6** Freetown, Sierra Leone **7** Ascension Island
8 St Helena **9** Simon's Town, Cape Town, South Africa **10** Gibraltar **11** Malta **12** Aden, Yemen **13** Port Louis, Mauritius **14** Bombay (now Mumbai) **15** Singapore
16 Hong Kong **17** Australia generally (King George Sound WA, Melbourne, Sydney and Thursday Island, Queensland
1 English Harbour, Antigua and Barbuda **2** Seychelles **3** Trincomalee, Ceylon (now Sri Lanka) **4** Labaun **5** Fiji

The steam coal that's required
For engines to be fired,
Is something which the sailing ship supplies.
The irony don't miss:
Such ships, by doing this,
Contribute to their very own demise.

Plimsoll Line

If it carries too much freight,
A ship is overweight,
And too deeply in the water is immersed.
To stay buoyant, the propensity
Depends on water density,
And on how the onboard cargo is dispersed.

Before a ship embarks,
The captain checks two marks:
For the prevalent conditions these are coded.
He'll have done some careful thinking
To prevent his craft from sinking –
Which was happening, when ships were overloaded.

If you ever thought of him,
It was maybe during gym,
And prompted by those shoes you had to wear.
Samuel Plimsoll's name they bore.
It was he who pushed the law,
That forced owners into taking better care.

Through persistence and concern,
All the credit he would earn,
But it wasn't really his idea at all.
From the history books deposed,
The scheme was first proposed
By a ship owner from Newcastle, James Hall.

The new mark must be visible.
What happened next was risible.
It did not prevent ships crammed full to the gunwales.
It had not been specified
Where the line should be applied,
And sometimes it was painted on the funnels.

Parliament had appointed a committee in 1836 to investigate the growing number of shipwrecks, and the Marine Department of the Board of Trade was created in 1850 to enforce the laws governing the manning, crew competence and operation of merchant vessels. However, the government avoided direct interference with ship owners.

Still widely used today, the Plimsoll mark is located midship on both sides of the hull. It indicates safe levels for various conditions. For example, 'TF' stands for 'Tropical Fresh Water' and 'WNA' for 'Winter North Atlantic'. The marks are one inch wide.

Overloaded, and often heavily insured, vessels were referred to as 'coffin ships'!

Samuel Plimsoll (1824–1898) pushed through the Unseaworthy Ships Bill (1876).

Where the marks should be wasn't initially specified – a loophole that was used by unscrupulous owners until 1894, when the positioning of the line was fixed.

Pronounced 'gunnels', the original meaning (15th century) of the word was probably 'gun walls' ie the upper edge of a ship's side.

Plimsoll marks

Fishing up to the late nineteenth century

The seas that lap our coast,
Have for centuries played host
To a range of creatures harvested by men.
Some consistently abound,
Whereas others move around,
And life's pattern rests on what is where – and when.

When prey is not abundant,
The boat becomes redundant,
There's no option but to tend the land and wait.
And breeding is the reason
Why some species are 'off season' –
Although cockles, whelks and mussels don't migrate.

Brixham trawlers

There has been a quantum leap,
With fishing in the deep.
Off Devon, stocks were low and looking bleak.
Brixham trawlers were devised:
They had gaff rigs oversized,
And their underwater lines were very sleek.

The fact they were so slick
Made them relatively quick,
This would prove to be of very great assistance.
Those who fished weren't now confined:
They left local shores behind,
In vessels that could travel longer distance.

Coastal folk are soon acquainted
With the sails which have been painted.
They're distinctive and consistently get noted.
They are not a whitish spread,
But a brightly coloured red
For with ochre, for protection, they've been coated.

The design was so astute,
Others elsewhere followed suit,
And into deeper waters ventured forth.
In the new-type craft they went,
From ports like Ramsgate, Kent,
And from all along the east coast further north.

Some towns' fortunes would now change,
With new fishing grounds in range,
Which had plentiful supplies for men to trawl.
For the boats that they would need,
Building carried on at speed.
Soon Grimsby had the largest fleet of all.

See section/verses 1677–1691 **Shellfish** (non-fin fish).

The gaff is a spar going upwards and outwards from the mainmast at an angle of 45-50°.

Made of wood, Brixham trawlers, which had distinctive red sails, (a protective coating), emerged at the end of the 18th century. They could travel beyond the Bristol Channel into the Irish Sea, reaching fishing ports such as Fleetwood in Lancashire. They also went eastwards into the English Channel. Some based themselves in other ports as far away as Northumberland.

Scotland's East Coast Fishery and beyond

By 1718,
In Scotland fishing's seen
As an industry which clearly needs a boost.
The government takes heed:
'An incentive's what we need!'
So a bounty payment's duly introduced.

Fair to say that some are lured.
Bigger catches are procured:
The money offered surely has its pluses.
They forgo the line and bait,
And the Dutch then emulate,
By building types of vessels known as busses...

... From which nets are left to drift,
But most fishermen don't shift:
From the old ways these inducements can't dissuade.
They don't venture very far,
And they like things as they are,
So from fragile deck-less craft still ply their trade.

For years, most rode their luck,
But a sudden storm then struck
In the Moray Firth. One hundred lost their lives.
Many boats had been submersed.
The event – one of the worst –
Made widows out of forty-seven wives.

So why did that fishing fleet,
Such a tragic ending meet,
After what had seemed just one more routine mission?
An enquiry then took place.
Its report soon made the case
For measures to prevent a repetition.

This says, 'Better harbours needed' –
A message that was heeded.
And Washington's committee also called
For no open hulls on boats.
These are dangerous, it notes,
So it recommends that decks should be installed.

'We'll lose space,' is the reply,
But in time most boats comply,
And get larger, too, by way of compensation.
The lug rig's still in favour:
Such sails require skilled labour,
Plus men of strength, and close cooperation.

The bounty (1718), initially paid for using (and even just building) larger boats, was later based on volume of herring catch (1820).

Until the later part of the 19th century, line fishing (of various types) was the usual method of catching white and flat fish off Scotland's east coast.

Since the 16th century, the Dutch had fished the area on a large scale, staying at sea for several weeks, and curing their catch on board. They used driftnets.

The fishermen argued that their traditional boats were lightweight, and easy to haul onto the beach.

The Moray Firth disaster was on 18 August 1848. Conditions had been promising that afternoon, when 800 boats set out, but deteriorated towards midnight. 124 boats sank, many of them close to harbour. 161 children were left fatherless.

The ensuing enquiry was headed by Captain John Washington of the Admiralty, and reported in 1849. A programme for improvements to harbours was soon underway. The first decked boat was built in Eyemouth, Berwickshire (1856).

The names of Scottish luggers,
Have been very awkward beggars:
Rhymes for 'skaffies'... 'fifies'... 'zulus' don't abound.
From the Isle of Man, the nickey
Has proved itself less tricky,
But for sgoths and baldies little could be found.

Of the rig type's variations
Here you'll find no explanations:
The minutiae no verse like this discusses...
How a dipping lug sail hangs...
Why some gaffs had added vangs...
Such refinements had their minuses and pluses.

With a three or four man crew,
Luggers sailed from Tenby, too.
And for Brixham trawlers, South Wales had allure.
Then, by tourists overtaken,
Fishing largely was forsaken,
In favour of the round bay trippers' tour.

Just a few miles further west
Milford Haven had been blessed
With a harbour which to steamships was well suited...
When other ports seemed doomed,
In 'the Haven' fishing boomed.
(During 'Suez', oil supplies to here were routed.)

Nets and rope

While the menfolk plied their trade,
Back at home, the nets were made
By women, who would deftly weave and knot.
With hemp, this had begun,
(Fibres first were stripped, then spun).
Later, cotton proved less liable to rot.

All hand-crafted and hand-twisted,
This domestic art persisted,
And a young man was obsessed with what he'd seen.
The device he would produce
Didn't work: a bolt was loose!
But then Paterson perfected his machine.

In Bridport, you will find
Rope and nets are intertwined:
Royal navies it exclusively supplied.
This town's layout was designed
With its industry in mind:
'Rope walk' alleys – and a main street, extra wide.

Zulus (named as a result of the Boer War) were introduced in 1879. The Manx nickey was the predecessor of the nobby. Until the 1860s, when mackerel fishing grounds off Ireland were opened up, herring was the main catch. The Lancashire nobby (gaff rigged) was primarily a shrimp trawler. Sgoths fished in the Scottish islands, and baldies (c.1860) were smallish craft used on Scotland's east coast.

Luggers' crews were usually three men, plus a boy to do the dirty work.

Nelson called Milford Haven harbour 'one of the finest!' In 1906, it was the sixth largest fishing port in Britain. After Milford Haven was no longer the site for the new Royal Dockyard (see verses 721–723), it became an increasingly important commercial dock and fishing centre. Following the construction of an oil refinery there in the 1960s, it developed into one of the largest terminals for liquefied natural gas (LNG) in the world.

It took about five weeks' work to complete one net. Ninety per cent of nets and ships' sail canvas and rigging at one time relied on hemp. Hemp is a common plant belonging to the genus cannabis, from which the word canvas is derived.

Hemp nets lasted 5–6 years. Cotton ones lasted 9–10 years and were increasingly used during the nineteenth century. Flax was also used.

James Paterson from Musselborough patented a net making machine circa 1820. In 1849, he sold his firm and patents to Messrs J. & W. Stuart, whose company is still manufacturing nets today in Eyemouth.

The hangman's noose was referred to as the 'Bridport dagger'. Inter alia, the town's firms have won contracts for supplying the British army (hammocks etc), and nets for Wimbledon's tennis courts and the English Football Association.

In the 18th century, there was a drop in demand for ships' ropes once the ropery (still being operated by Master Ropemakers Ltd) had been established at the Chatham Royal Dockyard. The town also faced competition from abroad.

Having commissioned in 1211 large supplies of 'hempen thread' to produce ships' ropes and cables 'according to Bridport weight', the king ordered that there be 'made at Bridport by day and by night, as many ropes for ships both large and small as they could.'

King John, 1213

All hemp grown within five miles of Bridport must be at the sole disposal of the navy.

Henry VII Statute, 1505

All cordage for the English Navy should, for a limited time, be made at Bridport or within five miles of it and nowhere else.

Henry VIII Statute, c.1512 (and reaffirmed for 60 years thereafter)

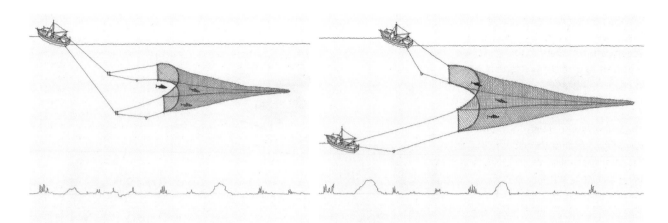

Pelagic single trawling **Pelagic pair trawling**

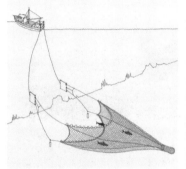

Dermersal otter trawling

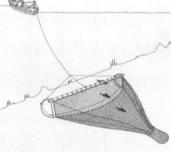

Dermersal beam trawling

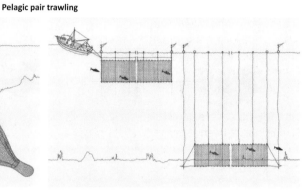

Drift gill and Set gill drifting

The Herring Industry

Scotland's herring had appeal...
Guaranteed a tasty meal...
And this was down to how the fish were cured.
Standards had been set
And invariably met,
So quality could always be assured.

But no rule like this prevails
In England and in Wales,
So the end result too rarely proves seductive.
Here the government had sought
To increase the numbers caught,
Though the measures taken weren't all that productive.

But the industry's sustained.
In time Dutch interest waned,
And the railway age in Britain was fast looming.
Fish were taken at great speeds
To meet inland cities' needs.
Ports like Grimsby and like Hull would soon be booming.

The Herring Act 1808 did not apply south of the border. There was more regulation in Scotland, which ultimately made the introduction of steam-powered fishing vessels less easy than it was around the English and Welsh coasts.

The rival Dutch turned their interest away from trade, and towards finance, around 1830.

Where herring could be found,
(As we've seen, they moved around),
Vast quantities were landed on the quays.
And waiting with their knives
Were the 'lassies' (and the wives),
To split and gut with dextrous expertise.

Their hands would be red raw,
Would be cut and chapped and sore,
Yet they'd travel where the 'silver darlings' beckoned.
With just 'thumb rags' for protection,
They'd spend hours on fish dissection:
The fastest processed almost one per second.

When the herring trade had dwindled,
Unrest was being kindled
And, in Scotland, fisher women went on strike.
Such action, when repeated
Over pay and how they're treated,
Resulted in a price per barrel hike.

Thus far, you'll have detected,
Fishing hasn't been subjected
To very much by way of regulation.
But boats now go far afield,
And much greater is their yield:
Something's needed to control the situation.

Disputes have been quite vocal –
International and local –
Over rights to grounds where fishermen competed.
And concerns were being aired,
About the catches snared,
With evidence that stocks had been depleted...

See verse 150 for herring mobility.

Lassies began their careers at the age of about 15, though some were as young as 13. Their working year started in winter/spring with the Scottish season, (which lasted about 2 months), after which they progressively travelled south as far as Yarmouth and Lowestoft. They were contracted to work by signing for, and accepting, 'Arles' money, and they were organised by 'teamies'.

The Scottish strike was in 1936. In 1938, the lassies went on strike in East Anglia, gaining an increase from 10 to 12 pence per 'cran' (a barrel containing about 1,000 spirally-arranged salted fish).

Prior to the First World War, 80 per cent of herring were exported to places like Russia and Germany. The collapse of this market resulted in a decline for the industry.

See section/verses 1569–1575 **The Anglo-Icelandic Cod Wars**.

SONG OF THE FISH-GUTTERS

Come, a' ye fisher lassies, aye, it's come awa' wi' me,
Fae Caimbulg an' Gamrie an' fae Inverallochie:
Fae Buckie an' fae Aiberdeen an' a' the country roon,
We're awa' tae gut the herrin, we're awa' tae Yermouth toon.

You rise up in the morning wi' your bundles in your hand,
Be at the station early or you'll shairly hae to stand,
Take plenty to eat and a kettle for your tea,
Or you'll shairly die o' hunger on the way to Yermouth quay.

The journey it's a lang ane and it taks a day or twa,
And when you reach yout lodgins sure it's sound asleep you fa,
But ye rise at five wi' the sleep still in you e'e,
You're awa tae find the gutting yairds alang the Yermouth quay.

It's early in the mornin' and it's laye into the nicht,
Your hands aa cut and chappit and they look an unco sicht,
And you greet like a wean when you put them in the bree,
And you wish you were a thousand miles awa' fae Yermouth quay.

There's coopers there and curers there and buyers, canny chiels,
And lassies at the pickling and others at the creels,
And you'll wish the fish had been aa left in the sea,
By the time you finish guttin' herrin' on the Yermouth quay.

You've gutted fish in Lerwick and in Stornoway and Shields,
Warked along the Humber 'mongst the barrels and the creel;
Whitby, Grimsby, we've traivelled up and doon,
But the place to see the herrin' is the quay at Yermouth toon.

Traditional

8 They built great ships and sailed them

8

They built great ships and sailed them

Tramp steamers and ocean passenger liners

The tramp ship could be hired
For journeys, as required.
It would take goods to wherever, which was handy.
But the liners worked to plan:
Full or not, to schedule ran –
A different type of *modus operandi*.

Packet boats, it's noted,
Were named for what they toted:
They carried mail. Their use was then expanded
To passengers and freight.
They ran to time and date.
As the 'packet trade' these services were branded.

It's dependent on the breeze,
So one can't predict with ease
What a sailing ship's arrival time will be.
And foreign postal traffic
Hadn't been too systematic –
But this will change to 'everywhere by sea'.

1840 was the year
A new prefix would appear:
If it ferried mail, a ship was 'RMS'.
Of this status it could brag
With a very special flag:
An added crown was certain to impress.

One company we know –
Its name is P and O –
At first took mail to Portugal and Spain.
Several decent contracts later,
It then began to cater
To the British Empire's further-flung terrain.

Though not for the faint-hearted,
With the Black Ball Line it started:
Trans-Atlantic ships for passengers set sail.
These took sheep and pigs in pens,
Plus cows, ducks, geese and hens:
The journeys were twice monthly, without fail.

The so-called 'tramp trade' began in Britain in the mid 19th century, mainly for the transport of coal. Ships could be hired for a voyage, or for a period of time, under varying terms contained in a contract called a charter party.

The Royal Mail was established in the reign of Henry VIII with the office of 'Master of the Posts'. The original function of the 'packet trade', (which began in Tudor times), was to carry post office packets which, in turn, initially referred to important or valuable items for urgent delivery, (latterly usually to British embassies and colonial outposts). Once their journeys had extended to America and Britain's colonies, the use of the term then came to mean any regularly scheduled ships carrying passengers.

In the 1820s and 1830s, the majority of passengers were 'steerage' (see below), but there were a few cabins (typically 10–20) for better off passengers. Mail to India was conveyed by the East India Company.

In 1756, the first mail brigs started operating a service from Falmouth to New York.

'Everywhere by sea' (*Per Mare Ubique*), was the motto of Cunard from 1839. Later it was adopted by Royal Mail Services.

The Admiralty was responsible for running overseas mail services from 1823–1861, when the Post Office took over.

Ships that carried mail for part of their journeys were entitled to use the designation RMS whilst doing so. Otherwise, they reverted to 'SS'. The last ship used for delivering mail, RMS *St Helena*, was retired in 2016 after an airport was built on the island.

The Clyde-built RMS *Segwun* operates short sightseeing excursions in Ontario, Canada. Cunard's flagship, *Queen Mary 2* was designated RMS as a courtesy.

P and O started as the Peninsular and Oriental Steam Navigation Company. The company was founded in 1822, and a mail service commenced 1837. P&O were awarded the mail contracts for Alexandria (1840), India via Aden (1842), Ceylon, Penang, Singapore and Hong Kong (1845), Shanghai (1849) and Australia (1852), including the Philippines and Mauritius.

> The very imperfect state of the communication between Great Britain, Spain and Portugal, for Passengers, Mails and Goods, has led many persons... to contemplate a more efficient and regular establishment of Packets than has yet existed.
>
> **Peninsular Steam Navigation Company Prospectus, 1834**

The well-off can lay claim
To the whale-oil lamp's weak flame,
And some candles, when the ocean they are crossing.
These were comforting and yet,
If by storms their ship's beset,
No one's spared the rolling, and the tossing.

Secure, this line's position,
For it had no competition,
Until steam-power showed it had a part to play.
Then some big names came along,
(One or two are going strong):
Cunard still runs a service to this day.

A journey made by sea,
To get from A to B,
Was not pleasant – even for a millionaire.
Fairly basic was the trip
In a trans-Atlantic ship,
But this now became a sumptuous affair.

The 'Blue Riband' had found fame,
And the Germans staked their claim
With a large four-funnelled vessel they created.
This wasn't only fast,
But it offered at long last,
The luxury, so eagerly awaited.

Others, not to be outdone,
On the US/Europe run
Responded. To the rich their vessels pandered.
Some aboard were thrilled to bits,
To be sailing in the 'Ritz',
As increasingly deluxe became the standard.

In 1899,
The famous White Star Line
With their second *Oceanic* had replied.
There followed the 'Big Four',
The last of which, what's more,
Offered swimming in a pool that was inside.

From John Brown's Clydebank yard,
Came a vessel for Cunard,
Conforming to the 'bigger/better' trend.
Lusitania had style,
And a sister ship, meanwhile,
By Swan Morton was constructed at Wallsend.

The Black Ball Line was an American line, founded in 1817 by a group of New York Quaker merchants. The first company to operate a scheduled trans-Atlantic service, its New York to Liverpool sailings were on the 1st and 16th of each month.

Competition from the Red Star Line, which also offered a regular service, began in 1822. Thirty years later, and much to the annoyance of the New York company, another Black Ball Line was established by James Baines and Co of Liverpool. This operated a service to Australia, as well as to the USA. Surviving names in shipping have been through many ups, downs and changes in focus.

Cunard was acquired by the USA-based Carnival Corporation in 1998. It is currently the only company to run a scheduled passenger service between Europe and North America.

In 1870, White Star's first *Oceanic* broke new ground by affording first class passengers more space on the top deck, and the luxury of running water (in most of their cabins).

The German liner *Kaiser Wilhelm II der Grosse* entered service in 1897.

In line with the concept of 'floating hotels', the interior of the USS *Amerika* was modelled on the Paris Ritz.

The 'Big Four' were *Celtic* (1901), *Cedric* (1902), *Baltic* (1903) and *Adriatic* (1907). The *Adriatic* also boasted Turkish baths.

The *Lusitania* (1906) was known as 'the Scottish ship'.

See section/verses 817–854 **Steamships**.
See verse 842 for Blue Riband.
See verse 1110 for John Brown.

MAIN VICTORIAN BRITISH/PART-BRITISH LINER COMPANIES

Peninsula and Oriental (P&O) (1822–date)
Mail service initially to Iberia.

Great Western Steamship Company (1838–46)
Provided first scheduled steamship Atlantic crossings.

British and American (1838–41)
Company collapsed after the *President* was lost with all hands.

Royal Mail Steam Packet Company (RMSP) (1839–1932)
Service between Britain and West Indies. Became the largest shipping line in the world when it took over White Star in 1927. Liquidated 1932 after financial scandal.

Cunard aka British and North American Royal Mail Steam Packet Co. (1840–date)
Won North American mail contract to the annoyance of Great Western.

White Star Line (1845–1937)
Taken over by RMSP in 1927 and later merged with Cunard.

Inman Line aka Liverpool, Philadelphia and New York Steamship Co. (1850–1893)
Liverpool to North America. Absorbed into American Line (1893).

Eastern Steam Navigation Company (1851)
Passenger service to India, China and Australia.

Black Ball Line (British) (1852–1871)
Liverpool to Australia. The original Black Ball Company objected to the use of its name.

British-India Steam Navigation Company (1856–1972)
Then the largest shipping line in the world. Amalgamated with P&O in 1914 but retained its own identity until 1972. Many of its 500+ ships were built on Clydeside. Initial service between England and India, Australia, Kenya and Tanganyika.

Union Castle Line (1900–1977)
Service between Europe and Africa.

These additions to the fleet
Meant our country could compete,
(For White Star was no longer British-owned),
The government agreed,
To some funding they would need.
With conditions, a substantial sum was loaned.

Mauretania's career
Lasted many a long year.
In peace and war, her functions would adapt.
The Blue Riband this ship took –
For two decades in the book –
Until finally this heroine was scrapped.

But her hapless running mate
Meets a really dreadful fate,
In an act of war that cannot be excused.
With passengers on board,
Her bow is badly gored –
She is listing, so her lifeboats can't be used.

Steerage

New ships' space and light and glass...
'À la carte' meals in first class...
Were attractive to the wealthy and the peerage –
Who relaxed and dined in style,
But lower down meanwhile,
Conditions weren't so good for those in 'steerage'.

Many millions made the trip
To America by ship.
For this promised land, so full of hope, they yearned.
Opportunity, they reckoned,
Alluringly now beckoned –
Although quite high numbers later on returned.

The North Atlantic run,
Was never that much fun,
In the age of sail and early days of steam.
Many weeks must be endured,
By the sub-third class immured,
Who had nothing but their one pervading dream.

These folk simply can't afford
Any comfort whilst on board,
In the bygone days of large-scale emigration.
Those who seek a brand new life
Eat poor food; disease is rife:
They are crowded in, with little sanitation.

In 1902, White Star had been bought by the American company International Mercantile Marine (IMM), headed by financier J.P. Morgan.

To kick start the British luxury liner business, the government made a £2.6 million low interest loan, repayable over 20 years on condition that the ships could convert to armed merchant vessels if required. *Mauritania* (1906), (and another sister ship *Aquitania*), were variously troop carriers and hospital ships during the First World War. Withdrawn from service in 1934, the *Mauritania* was scrapped in 1935. Her fastest crossing record of 1909 stood until 1929, when the German ship *Bremen* finally beat it.

The *Lusitania* held the Blue Riband accolade from 1907 to 1909. In 1915, after she'd been hit by a torpedo, only 6 of her 48 lifeboats could be launched successfully. Others overturned or broke apart. 1,198 lives were lost (see verses 1398–1399).

The cargo hold was called 'steerage' because a ship's rudder control strings originally ran through this area. Conditions for steerage passengers did improve on the new luxury liners, especially British ones.

Between 1815 and 1932, about 60 million Europeans emigrated. 71 per cent of these went to North America. Argentina, Brazil, Australia and New Zealand were also popular destinations.

A crossing took an average of 6–7 weeks under sail, but could last as many as 14 weeks in adverse conditions.

Life was also grim for the ships' crews, especially those stoking the boilers.

... The 900 steerage passengers crowded into the hold... are positively packed like cattle... The food, which is miserable, is dealt out of huge kettles into the dinner pails... The stenches become unbearable... On the whole, the steerage of the modern ship ought to be condemned as unfit for the transportation of human beings... In providing better accommodations, the English steamship companies have always led, and while the discipline on board of ship is always stricter than on other lines, the care bestowed upon the emigrants is correspondingly greater.

Alfred Steiglitz, American photographer, on conditions aboard the *Kaiser Wilhelm II*, 1907

In the ship's bowels where they camp,
It is often dark and damp.
There are families, and people who are single.
There may be segregation,
In this cramped accommodation;
With the better off, they aren't allowed to mingle.

The ingloriously shipped
Must ensure they are equipped
With utensils, plates and bowls, and even bedding.
Scarce water they might sup
From just one communal cup –
Kept going by the thought of where they're heading?

On *Titanic*, the elite
Could book a parlour suite
If nine hundred pounds or so they had to spare.
But it needn't cost the earth,
To buy an open berth
And cross for just three quid – the cheapest fare.

Cruising

Wall Street crashes. Gloom descends.
And mass migration ends;
For cheap passage in the hold there's no more clamour.
To replace trade ships are losing
Is the holiday spent cruising,
With the special clothes, the deck games and the glamour.

This concept still holds sway;
It's persisted to this day:
A life on board for some holds fascination.
Just sailing on a ship
Is the purpose of their trip –
Maybe more so than each scheduled destination.

A personal 'PS'

Your author wants to mention,
That it seems a strange invention –
All this sailing for the purposes of leisure.
It's weird that people choose
To embark upon a cruise,
And, what is more, are paying for the 'pleasure'.

At the mercy of the seas,
Into cabins they will squeeze,
And re-circulated viruses inhale.
Then, their visit all too short,
They'll help inundate a port,
Ever mindful of the deadline to set sail.

There are many personal accounts of experiences in steerage. At one time, some lines (not British) even required passengers to take their own food, which invariably ran out too soon.

A parlour suite on the *Titanic* cost £870 (about £95,000 in today's money), a first class berth £30, a second class berth £12, and third class (the term steerage was no longer used) travel cost between £3 (about £350 today) and £8. Strictly speaking, there were no open berths in third class. All 700+ passengers had private cabins, though some of these accommodated 10 people. By the standards of the day, conditions were excellent.

The crash of the US stock market in 1929 triggered the Great Depression of the 1930s. The British government instituted pay cuts for the navy, which resulted in the Invergordon Mutiny of 1931. This event in turn prompted a run on the pound, and led to the abandonment of the Gold Standard.

Grace Darling and the RNLI

Midst the North Sea's chilly water,
Lived a lighthouse keeper's daughter,
Her home a rock full six miles from these shores.
Grace Darling was her name,
And she found unwanted fame
For her courage, and her skill with boat and oars.

After one wild stormy night,
She had seen a steamer's plight.
It was tossed by waves and lashed by howling gale.
It had broken quite in two,
Risking passengers and crew.
Grace knew the local lifeboat wouldn't sail.

Though conditions were so bad,
This brave girl and her Dad
Launched their small boat, which was always at the ready.
All the dangers they ignored:
Dad hauled stranded souls aboard,
Whilst Grace made sure she held their vessel steady.

Her fearless act was fêted;
Grace was famous, which she hated.
The world knew how courageously she'd rowed.
Celebrity... euphoria...
Some cash from Queen Victoria...
And an RNLI medal were bestowed.

This lifeboat institution
Makes a vital contribution:
Its inception was in 1824.
It was on the Isle of Man
That its history began –
Here many ships were wrecked in days of yore.

William Hillary, its founder,
Had seen lots of vessels flounder,
And in rescue missions sometimes got involved.
With authorities he pleaded:
'Boats and proper crews are needed'.
On preserving life this way he was resolved.

There were some boats around,
Aiding folk who might have drowned:
In South Shields one of these was 'purpose-built'.
Ten yards long and ten feet broad,
And by ten short paddles oared,
A coat of cork helped right it, should it tilt.

Grace Horsley Darling (1815–1842). Her father had persuaded Trinity House that the original lighthouse on Brownsman Island was not well positioned to guide shipping, and a new lighthouse on Longstone Island was constructed in 1826.

Grace often looked out to sea and, in the early light one morning, noticed that the SS *Forfarshire* was in trouble at Big Harcar, a nearby low rocky island. The survivors were on this island. The rescue took place in 1838. Grace was 23 years old.

The Royal National Lifeboat Institution (RNLI), was originally called the National Institution for the Preservation of Life from Shipwreck. Its name was changed in 1854, and its flag was designed by Miss Leonora Preston 30 years later. The RNLI has awarded medals for bravery since the year of its inception, and continues to do so.

There were 30 independent lifeboats around Britain when the RNLI was founded, but Hillary envisaged a national service for Britain.

Designed by Henry Greathead, the first purpose-built lifeboat was stationed in South Shields from 1790. Also used as an early lifeboat was Lionel Lukin's 'unimmergible' (1785).

Short oars are easier than long ones to manipulate.

Grace Darling at the *Forfarshire* (Thomas Musgrave Joy, 1840)

Grace, aged 24 (Thomas Musgrave Joy, 1839)

Jackets issued to each crew,
Were made of this stuff too,
And invented by a Brit called Captain Ward.
They weren't comfy, one suspects:
Cork is rigid, has no flex,
So the need to put one on was oft ignored.

This wasn't very shrewd,
And tragedy ensued.
A boat capsized, and lost were twelve brave seamen,
Who'd thought their kit dispensable.
One colleague was more sensible
And worn his – sole survivor Henry Freeman.

(In 1928,
Came a rig that could inflate;
Of her figure any wearer would feel proud.
This special type of vest
Is nicknamed a Mae West,
After someone who was very well endowed!)

A price is sometimes paid,
Helping folk in need of aid,
And when lifeboat crews are out on rescue missions.
Though they've trained and been to school,
(There's a centre now in Poole),
They often venture forth in dire conditions.

A memorial exists.
Very many names it lists,
Of rescuers who never made it back.
And it honours, in its way,
Those who save lives every day,
As well as those who feature on the plaque.

Things keep moving on of course:
Boats (no longer launched by horse)
Are more modern and designed for their location.
And prevention is, for sure,
Much better than a cure,
So the charity gives safety education.

The earliest PFDs (Personal Flotation Devices) were simple blocks of wood used by Norwegian seafarers. The first cork lifejacket was patented by Dr John Wilkinson in 1765. However, the cork vest created in 1854 by Ward, an RNLI inspector, is generally regarded as the forerunner of the modern lifejacket. Kapok was used in later versions, and synthetic foams were developed in the 1960s.

The tragic capsize happened in 1861 off Whitby.

The Lifeboat College was opened by HM Queen Elizabeth II in 2004.

Twenty-seven lifeboat men from the Southport and St Anne's station lost their lives in 1886. More recently (1981), the 8 crew of the Penlee lifeboat *Solomon Browne* perished.

778 names are inscribed on the memorial, a sculpture by Sam Holland, designed as a 'beacon of hope'. It is in Poole, Dorset.

The RNLI rescues a daily average of 23 people round the coast of Britain and Ireland. It also operates a service on the River Thames. The biggest rescue (of 456 people) took place off Cornwall in 1907.

The first steam-driven lifeboat was launched in 1890. Petrol power was trialled in 1905, and 1930 brought the first motorboat. The last horse-powered launch was in 1935. There are two main categories of boat: all-weather and inshore.

The RNLI also provides a seasonal lifeguard service.

Launching the lifeboat at Brighton, 1875 (artist unknown)

Lighthouses

These structures are employed
So that vessels can avoid
The shoals... the rocks... the reefs all sailors fear.
Trigonometry's applied
In order to decide
The height required, so ships don't come too near.

The Pharos at Dover – first century AD

Once the Romans had come over,
They developed Dubris (Dover) –
Which is close to France and in a handy place.
It was not yet blocked by silt,
And two lighthouses were built,
To guide ships to this major naval base.

Roman sailors, through the night,
Kept these pharoses alight.
To this very day, the eastern 'twin' still stands.
Not as tall now as it was,
It was needed there because
Of the perils of the nearby Goodwin Sands.

Though impressive, this creation
Was without sophistication:
Just a tower – plus fire upon its highest floor.
No rotation and no flashes;
Clearing out a load of ashes
Was tricky – and was not a favourite chore.

St Catherine's Oratory, 1328

Someone's conscience had been pricked,
By the casks of wine he'd nicked,
From a stricken ship that floundered in Chale Bay.
This the church did not condone:
The pope forced him to atone
With a lighthouse, which has lasted to this day.

Walter built The Pepperpot,
On a very lofty plot,
But the siting of this beacon wasn't right.
Ships continued to be lured,
For the light was oft obscured
By the fog which can affect the Isle of Wight.

There are three broad classifications of lighthouse: 'tower or rock', 'island' and 'shore or land'.

The estuary of the narrow River Dour silted up in medieval times, necessitating the reconstruction of the harbour. The river now enters the sea via a culvert.

The Roman Fleet was called the *Classis Britannica*, and it had another base in Boulogne.

Wood, and probably also coal, were used for the lighthouse fires.

The original main purpose of lighthouses was to mark the entrance to harbours, rather than to warn of dangerous promontories and other hazards.

The two pharos were probably constructed in the first century AD to a height of about 80 feet (24.4m). The Goodwin Sands, to the north of Dover, are an area in which many ships have been wrecked. However, the shallow Varne Bank is closer to the route from Boulogne, and also presents dangers.

Walter de Godeton, Lord of Chale Manor (*d*.1327), created the first Isle of Wight lighthouse, as a penance. The ship was wrecked on the treacherous rocks at Atherfield Ledge in 1314. The wine in question was church property. Walter narrowly avoided excommunication by agreeing to the Pope's demands. The original St Catherine's lighthouse, built 1328, is affectionately known locally as 'The Pepperpot', and de Godeton's ghost is often seen standing at its base.

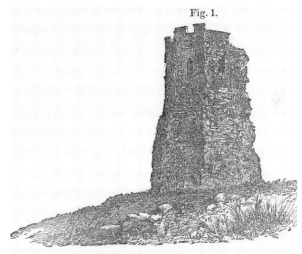

Roman pharos in Dover Castle.
Drawing by George Henry Elliott, 1875

St Catherine's Oratory, Isle of Wight

The fire those old monks tended,
Was unseen when mist descended –
And the same mistake's repeated with the second.
The 'new' tower's thus made shorter,
(Height was lowered by a quarter)
To alert those out at sea that danger beckoned.

The Corporation of Trinity House

Two centuries passed by,
Since that wine ship went awry
And, together with its alcohol, was grounded.
Safety's given some priority,
There is thus a new authority:
The enterprise that's Trinity was founded.

This important corporation
Offers aids to navigation,
Helping massive ships, and those that are quite tiny.
Lighted vessels… beacons… buoys…
Are what Trinity employs,
To keep all craft from harm upon the briny.

From the year sixteen-o-nine,
Two lit up towers align:
These guide small boats when Lowestoft's approached.
For a century or so,
Their candles' welcome glow
Gives safe passage – but the North Sea then encroached.

And thus, upon the shore,
The Low Light is no more
Causing those who'd been reliant to complain.
Conditions then improved,
With a light that could be moved,
(In case the sea came pillaging again).

Where a lighthouse is unsuited,
Things that float might be recruited.
Over sands or in deep water, ships can moor.
With two lanterns on the yard,
A vessel now keeps guard –
The 'world's first' has been stationed at the Nore.

Lightships' numbers have diminished,
But their role has not yet finished,
(Though round Scotland, sad to say, their time is done).
Once, in labour terms, intensive,
They were really quite expensive.
Today, unmanned, they're powered by the sun.

The oratory adjacent to the tower was closed down in 1547, following the dissolution of the monasteries, and the lighthouse ceased to function. Built in 1838, and sited closer to the sea, the second tower was lowered by 43 feet from its original height of 130 feet (1875). This was because it was sometimes capped with mist. In ideal clear conditions, its light is visible for 30 nautical miles.

Exactly 200 years after the Chale Bay wreck, Trinity House's Royal Charter was granted in 1514 (see verses 238–239). Trinity House is responsible for lighthouses around England and Wales, plus the Channel Islands and Gibraltar. The Northern Lighthouse Board (NLB), established in 1786, is responsible for navigation aids around Scotland and the Isle of Man. See Plate D on page 195.

Lowestoft was the first lighthouse established by Trinity (1609). It was originally lit by candles. The principle of two fixed and continuous lights in alignment was used extensively for more than three hundred years.

Discontinued in 1706, the Low Light was reinstated in 1730 with the use of a whale oil burning open flame. This could be moved in the event of further encroachment by the sea, or if the Stamford Channel, into which ships were guided, changed direction. The Channel no longer exists.

In 1854, Trinity House began using buoys with chains at the centre of gravity (designed by Robert Herbert).

The first lightvessel (or lightship) was designed by Robert Hamblin (1730). Sea Reach No1 Buoy is located there today. Trinity House now operates eight lightvessels (on the east coast of England and in the Bristol Channel). The Northern Lighthouse Board's last, the North Carr lightship, left service in 1975 and then served as a museum in Anstruther Harbour. She is now awaiting restoration as an exhibition space on Dundee's waterfront.

Other devices, such as LANBYs (large navigational buoys) are also used.

Nore lightvessel

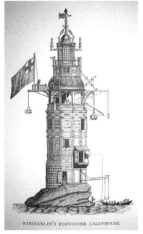

Winstanley's lighthouse

Rudyerd's lighthouse

The Eddystone lighthouses, 1698 to date

Eddystone's a reef.
Many ships there came to grief.
When the tide is high, then most of it submerges.
Even when the sea is calm,
It retains the power to harm,
For water hits the rocks in sudden surges.

Beacons not built on dry land,
Must be able to withstand
The pounding waves, when at their very worst.
And to get the towers erected,
Was much harder than expected,
As Winstanley found when working on the first.

To construct his strange confection,
He's in need of some protection
From our enemy. What happened makes him blench.
For the ship that does appear.
Is a hostile privateer.
Our designer has been captured by the French!

Henry must be feeling scared,
But by Louis he is spared.
The job gets done – extensions follow later.
The result is quite ornate,
Though too soon will meet its fate,
Dispatched by storm – along with its creator.

Rudyerd's Tower appears,
And it lasts for fifty years.
Like Winstanley's it was built of stone and wood.
John Smeaton's version's stronger,
Is in service for much longer,
But eroded were the rocks on which it stood.

The techniques the man had found,
Meant his building was still sound,
But with every wave this awesome structure trembled.
It was robustly cemented –
A technique John reinvented –
Now on Plymouth Hoe, the top's been reassembled.

Made of red granite and known locally as the 'Stone', the Eddystone Rocks are an extensive reef lying to the south of Cornwall and Devon on the sea route to Plymouth.

Henry Winstanley (1644–1703). England was at war with France, and those working on the lighthouse project were protected by a Royal Navy ship. When one such ship was recalled to the fleet, a French vessel turned up instead of the expected English replacement.

Winstanley's lighthouse was extended in 1698. The interior featured carvings by Grinling Gibbons. It was swept away in the great storm of 1703. Completed in 1709, the second lighthouse burned down in 1755. Immunity from the Press Gang was given to those who worked on it (mainly Cornish tin miners). Designer John Rudyerd (1650–c.1718) was a silk mercer with no engineering experience, but proved himself a 'gifted amateur'.

Civil engineer John Smeaton FRS (1724–1792), was involved in many maritime projects, including harbour design. Having been called to testify in a legal case following the silting up of the harbour at Wells-next-the-Sea, he is considered to be the first expert witness to appear in an English court. His lighthouse design was modelled on an oak tree, and featured the now classic wide base. Structural stability was improved by the use of dovetail joints, securing the granite building blocks.

The Romans had discovered hydraulic lime (a cement that will dry under water). Smeaton's rediscovery of this led to the development of the highly versatile Portland cement. The stub of his creation can still be seen alongside the fourth Eddystone lighthouse (1882 to date), which was designed by James Douglass (1826–1898).

THE KEEPER OF THE EDDYSTONE LIGHT

Me father was the keeper of the Eddystone Light
And he slept with a mermaid one fine night.
Out of this union there came three,
A porpoise and a porgy, and the other was me.
Chorus:
With a yo-ho-ho, let the wind blow free,
It's all for a life on the rolling sea!

One night, as I was a-trimmin' the glim
And singing a verse from the evening hymn
I see by the light of me binnacle lamp,
Me kind old father looking jolly and damp:
Chorus:

A voice from starboard shouted, 'Ahoy!'
And there was me mother sittin' on a buoy,
Meanin' a buoy for ships what sail,
And not a boy what's a juvenile male.
Chorus:

'Well, what became of me children three?'
Me mother then she asked of me.
Well, one is an exhibit as a talking fish,
The other was served on a chafing dish.
Chorus:

The phosphorous flashed in her seaweed hair.
I looked again and me mother wasn't there,
But her voice came echoing out of the night,
'To hell with the keeper of the Eddystone Light!'
Chorus:

Traditional shanty

Bell Rock, 1810

Though designers had a model,
Building others was no doddle,
As evidenced by Bell Rock further north.
The challenges were many,
Facing Stevenson and Rennie,
In the fairway to the Firths of Tay and Forth.

Each tower, by definition,
Marks a hazardous position:
This place was far more dangerous than most.
But so well their beacon's fared:
It has never been repaired,
And functions still off Scotland's Angus coast.

Technology and Light Dues

But a problem is afoot:
Fires produce a lot of soot:
Dim lights will fail to meet their prime objective.
So engineers were turning,
To something cleaner burning:
The Argand lamp, which proved much more effective.

Once technology advanced,
Any brightness was enhanced
By dishes with small mirrors which reflected.
And a one-time privateer,
Who'd turned lighting engineer,
Discovered how a beam could be projected.

The beacons must be staffed.
It's a solid stint of graft:
That of keeper is a most important role.
How much fuel he will require,
Depends on type of fire –
And some got through a huge amount of coal.

So mariners must pay
To be guided on their way:
For every lighthouse passed there is a debt.
Not all ships put into port
In conditions where they ought –
An economy some don't live to regret.

Though the upkeep can be high,
If a lot of ships pass by,
Private operators' profits could be large.
There was therefore some resistance
When, at Parliament's insistence,
A 'buy out' deal put Trinity in charge.

The first mention of a lighthouse in Scotland was in 1635, when Charles I granted a patent to erect one on the Isle of May.

Tradition has it that a floating warning bell, said to have been carried off by pirates, was at one time attached to Bell Rock.

On-site engineer Robert Stevenson is generally credited with the lighthouse's design, though chief engineer John Rennie (1761–1821) insisted on what may well have been crucial adaptations to the base. There were two fatalities during its construction, plus several casualties, two of whom later went on to become Bell Rock lighthouse keepers – John Bonnyman (amputated finger) and Michael Wishart (crushed feet). There are controversial proposals for siting a 140 turbine (some sources say 213) offshore wind farm in the vicinity, (see verses 1734–1738 under **The sea as a source of energy**).

In 2014, a Lidar unit was attached to the lighthouse to gather information on wind direction and velocity.

Bell Rock lighthouse (J.M.W. Turner, 1819)

Michael Faraday (see verse 1075 opposite) later devised for lanterns, a special chimney which didn't get dirty from the products of combustion. This was universally adopted.

Introduced in the late 18th century, Argand lamps were widely used for more than one hundred years. They were superseded by paraffin vapour burners (PVBs) or, in some cases, by electricity.

In 1776, the world's first parabolic reflector was installed in the Old Hunstanton lighthouse (built 1665).

William Hutchinson (1732–1814) rose from cabin boy to privateer captain, and then became Dock Master in Liverpool. He kept the first sustained set of tidal measurements in the UK. His giant reflector, developed in 1763, was erected at Bidston.

Though the majority were men, there were some female lighthouse keepers. Fires could be open or enclosed. The hours of darkness, the weather and the skill of the keeper also affected fuel consumption. The Isle of May lighthouse used 350–400 tons of coal in 1799.

Light dues were collected at ports. They are now calculated on net tonnage, and are paid into the UK's General Lighthouse Fund.

Under the 1836 Lighthouses Act, Trinity House took control of lighthouses by compulsory purchase where necessary. The leaseholders of Skerries held out until 1841. They were reluctant to relinquish an annual profit of £12,525 (worth just over £1 million in today's money).

This was 1836.
From the paint used to the wicks,
From the type of glass enclosing each candela,
To schemes for ventilation
And electric operation –
All progressed apace beneath this one umbrella.

The Fresnel lens came in...
Those rays can flash and spin...
Distinctive are the patterns of rotation.
This uniqueness is of use,
Because sailors can deduce
What they're looking at, and hence their own location.

Many problems get resolved,
Once Faraday's involved.
The electric light is something he'd enable.
In due course, the carbon arc
Would lend brightness to the dark,
Though the first he looked at proved to be unstable.

Michael quickly got embroiled;
In his workshop daily toiled
Till his dream came true in 1858.
At South Foreland this success...
There were more (like Dungeness)...
But the programme as a whole would have to wait.

All children, listen here:
When you're choosing a career,
The job of keeper's very much outdated.
An address in the Atlantic,
Might seem quirky or romantic,
But every lighthouse is now automated.

Many others, decommissioned,
Have alternatives positioned,
Such as beacons, solar powered with LED.
Others simply are not needed,
(By 'SATNAV' superseded)...
Or fell victim to the predatory sea.

And the foghorn's almost gone.
(In Scotland, there are none,)
With such high tech means to find your way around.
Less important now that wail,
Which was heard by those who sail:
Each one possessed its own distinctive sound.

A candela is a unit of luminosity equivalent to the light emitted by one candle.

There were proposals to merge the NLB (Northern Lighthouse Board), the Commissioners of Irish Lights and Trinity House but this didn't happen.

Fresnel (pronounced Fre-nel with a silent 's') lenses increased light intensity by rendering the light rays parallel.

A 1834 Royal Commission on lighthouses had recommended the appointment of a Scientific Adviser. The chemist and physicist Michael Faraday (1791–1867) held the post for almost 30 years (1836–1865). From the time of his appointment, 17 per cent of his extant correspondence concerns lighthouses. His base was London's only lighthouse, Trinity Buoy Wharf, sited at the confluence of the Thames and Bow Creek.

Dungeness was adapted to electricity in 1862. In 1871, Souter was the first lighthouse purpose-built to use electricity. Conversion to electricity was abandoned for a while in 1880, due to the expense and given that paraffin had become available as a good alternative illuminant. St Mary's Island lighthouse (deactivation in 1984) was the last to convert to electricity (1977).

All Trinity House and NLB lighthouses had been automated by 1998.

Hartland Point, north Devon, for example has an LED beacon.

For 'SATNAV' at sea, read Global Navigation Satellite System (GNSS).

Following a review by Trinity House in 2009, such systems were deemed not sufficiently reliable and, as a result, a number of lighthouses were reprieved. The power of the light at Southwold, (one of those which had been under threat of closure), had been increased to compensate for the deactivation of Orfordness, which was decommissioned because it is so perilously close to the sea.

Scotland's last foghorn (at Skerrymore lighthouse) was switched off in 2005. As at 2014, Trinity House still operated 24 foghorns.

Scotsman Robert Foulis (1796–1866) invented the first automated steam-powered foghorn, after realising that lower notes were more audible than higher ones.

The Guernsey foghorn is known as the 'Lowing Cow', and the Whitby foghorn, operational from 1902 to 1988, was called the 'Hawsker Bull'.

Where foghorns still exist, they are activated automatically when a light beam hits fog.

Michael Faraday (photograph by John Watkins, *c*.1861)

Shipyards

We have ore here, pleased to tell.
This was really just as well:
You'll have heard of 'wooden walls' from years gone by.
Building fighting ships like these,
Used at least two thousand trees,
And we didn't have an infinite supply.

Engines cause vibrations,
So wood has limitations;
Planks can work apart, then ships begin to leak.
But iron (and later steel)
Didn't suffer this ordeal,
And lent to hulls a sturdier physique.

Even with just sail
Too-long wooden ships will fail:
Due to hogging, they will droop at either end.
Though cross-bracing added strength,
And enabled greater length,
There were limits on how far they could extend.

Metal came in by degrees
Reinforcing joints like knees,
Then plates were used. With rivets these were joined.
But the method was the same –
These encased a wooden frame –
And the appellation iron clad was coined.

The resources we'd been gifted,
Meant that shipbuilding had shifted
To where its needs were readily supplied.
Most centres, though not new,
With this impetus now grew
On the Mersey, Tees, the Tyne and Wear and Clyde.

For example, Buckler's Hard
Was a once productive yard,
From which ships for 'Nelson's navy' had come forth.
But its fate was quickly sealed,
Once craft were iron-keeled,
And the focus of the industry moved north.

Tyne and Wear

The entrance to the Tyne
Was, for sailors, unbenign.
The Black Midden rocks provoked their deepest fears.
'And the river,' folk complained,
'Isn't properly maintained.'
So it's deepened, and erected are two piers.

Steel began to supplant iron for shipbuilding in the second half of the 19th century.

For further reading on the term 'iron clad' see verse 837.

In many of the river locations, the construction of ships had taken place since medieval times and, in addition to those listed in northern England and Scotland, the same applied to Belfast in Northern Ireland with the Harland and Woolf shipyard.

Buckler's Hard was a shipbuilding village on the River Beaulieu, Hampshire where, from 1748, Master Shipbuilder Henry Adams and his sons built, for example, *Agamemnon*, *Euryalus* and *Swiftsure*. All three served at the Battle of Trafalgar (see verses 690–696). Nelson had captained *Agamemnon* for three years from 1793. *Euryalus* was released as a prison hulk in 1825 (see verses 726–727), and *Swiftsure* became a target ship for HMS *Excellent* (see verse 864).

Shipbuilding in Hampshire did revive in the early 20th century, when John I. Thornycroft moved from Chiswick to Woolston (Southampton) in 1908. In 1966, the company merged with Vospers of Portsmouth, a builder of small vessels, to form Vosper Thornycroft (later VT Group).

The improvements to the River Tyne were carried out following the River Tyne Improvement Act (1850) and the establishment of the Tyne Improvement Commission, (which became the Port of Tyne Authority in 1968). New docks were also built on the river.

The Mouth of the River Tyne, North Bank (Duncan Fraser McLea, 1875)

These are each side of its mouth.
One's called 'North', the other 'South'.
Now the worries of the mariners have gone.
Soon, six miles or so upstream,
Two famous names will team:
Burton Hunter joins the widow, Mrs Swan.

And this marks the beginning
Of the firm that will be winning
The contract for a brand new ocean liner.
Swan Hunter's Wallsend yard,
Produced it for Cunard,
To the plans of Leonard Peskett, chief designer.

That inter-war recession,
Which we call 'Great Depression',
Hit the industries of northern Britain hard.
Many big concerns would close
And, sadly, one of those,
Was the long-established Palmers Tyneside yard.

With livelihoods destroyed,
Many now were unemployed:
The figure was some seventy per cent.
The men, no longer paid,
Embarked on a crusade,
The 'Jarrow March' a sign of discontent.

For many a long year,
There'd been building on the Wear
Where the mineral-polluted waters swirled.
Sunderland's location,
And its iron/coal combination,
Mean the town's 'the largest shipyard in the world'.

'The black squad' are the toilers
Whose job is making boilers:
They're paid 'piecework' – very lucrative for them.
Any man who turns up late,
Must stand outside the gate,
Which is always promptly closed at 6 am.

It wasn't all prosperity:
There'd be hardship and austerity.
With lay-offs when the orders didn't flow.
Strikes – a sign of discontent –
Were a regular event.
Trade unions in time began to grow.

George Burton Hunter (1845–1937). Like many other shipbuilders, he had spent time (1867–73) working for Robert Napier (see verses 1108–1111).

Charles Swan had managed the Wallsend yard, formerly owned by Charles Mitchell, since 1874. Swan was killed in a paddle steamer incident in 1879, and Hunter formed the partnership with his widow in the following year. Their company merged with Wigham Richardson in 1903, specifically to bid for the contract to build RMS *Mauretania* – see verse 1021.

Leonard Peskett (1861–1924) was the Cunard Line's senior naval architect.

Palmers Shipbuilding & Iron Company (established in 1852) had been the first company in the world to manufacture armour plate. Like Armstrong Whitworth, it had manufactured oil tankers, along with merchant ships and naval vessels.

The Jarrow March, or Jarrow Crusade, started on 5 October 1936 when 200 men walked to London in an attempt to highlight the town's plight. The Labour Party was opposed to the march, and the Conservative Prime Minister, Stanley Baldwin, refused to meet the 'Crusaders'.

Thomas Melville's yard at Hendon on the River Wear, for example, dates back to 1346. Due to iron mining in its upper reaches, the Wear still suffers from heavy metal mineral pollution. Despite this, there have been more than 400 registered shipyards in Sunderland. For the Second World War, the town produced more than a quarter of Britain's total merchant and naval tonnage.

Being paid on a piecework (productivity) basis made it possible for toilers to earn much more than the shipwrights, who were paid for the time they worked. Latecomers were docked a quarter of a day's pay.

There were great depressions in 1884–87, 1908–10 and in the 1930s, and those lucky enough to remain in employment had their wages reduced.

The Sunderland engineers' strike lasted from 1883–85.

'Health and Safety' don't forget
Hadn't been invented yet,
And wouldn't be till 1974.
Unawareness must be blamed
For the injured, killed and maimed:
In the workplace, there were accidents galore.

Merseyside

Ships were made around 'The Pool'
But life can be so cruel:
Two docks were built. The yards were all displaced.
By 1846,
They have all again upped sticks,
And are further downstream subsequently based.

They're not just nudged along:
Certain other things go wrong.
From competitors, they start to feel the squeeze.
They had everything to fear,
From England's Tyne and Wear...
And from Canada, (with more, and cheaper, trees).

We know many firms have closed,
It might almost be supposed
That complete has been the industry's demise.
Ships are still built and repaired
To this day at Cammell Laird,
In that company's contemporary guise.

It has launched a thousand ships
And weathered all the dips;
Like others, it has not been unaffected.
But with contracts newly won,
A resurgence has begun,
And this 'big name brand', it seems, is resurrected.

Barrow-in-Furness

The dig-and-smelt exertions,
Of some long ago Cistercians
Near to Barrow, showed that hematite abounded.
A prospector came along,
And proved those monks weren't wrong:
On iron and steel huge enterprise was founded.

Building ships gets underway
To the north of Morecambe Bay:
Every necessary process here convenes.
To our navy some would sell,
Or to foreign clientele.
Yards specialized in making submarines.

Prior to the comprehensive Health and Safety at Work Act (1974), and starting with the widely evaded 1802 Factory Act, there were various pieces of legislation relating to the safety of workers (eg the Shipbuilding Regulations under the 1901 Factory and Workshop Act).

The Lyver Pool (now filled in) was a natural tidal inlet of the River Mersey, and ships had been built there from the late 17th century. The Old Dock (1715) was the world's first commercial enclosed dock. Salthouse Dock followed in 1739, and the more famous Albert Dock was opened in 1846.

Industrial unrest on the Mersey compounded the problem of finding a secure waterfront tenancy. The Mersey Docks and Harbour Board (MDHB) purchased and relocated many shipyards, until there were none on the Liverpool shore. The last large vessel launched from there was HMS *Britomart* in 1899.

The founder of Cammell Laird, William Laird, started as a boiler maker in 1828 at Wallasey Pool. Shipbuilding there currently delivers aircraft carrier flight deck sections.

The company has actually launched 1,100 ships, including two *Ark Royal* aircraft carriers in 1937 and 1950. It has been nationalised, re-privatised, taken over, closed, and reborn in various forms. As the preferred bidder, against global competition, it recently built the new £200 million polar research ship (see verse 1439).

The Furness peninsula was controlled by Cistercian monks during the Middle Ages, and Furness Abbey was constructed in 1123.

Hematite is the mineral from which iron is extracted, and speculator Henry Schneider discovered large deposits in 1850. The Furness Railway (from 1846) brought mined ore into the town, and this was smelted at steelworks which, by 1876, had become the largest in the world.

The *Jane Roper* was the first ship to be built in Barrow-in-Furness in 1852.

The Barrow Shipbuilding Company (1871) was taken over by Sheffield steel firm Vickers in 1897. Because of Barrow's relatively isolated position, several capabilities that would often be contracted out, such as a foundry and an engine shop, were included in the town.

The Clyde

Both Leith and Aberdeen,
For centuries had been,
Centres for the building of fine ships.
Major yards – there would be three –
Based their business in Dundee,
But one place all these others would eclipse.

Once new markets were accessible,
The Scots proved irrepressible:
And from Glasgow many trading vessels sailed.
But its famous River Clyde,
Was in parts not deep or wide:
So an awful lot of hassle this entailed.

Goods cannot arrive by sea
Straight to where they need to be:
All that sediment means large ships cannot enter.
At some distance they unload
Cargo's carried then by road,
Or in shallow boats to reach the city centre.

Handling effort is thus doubled.
The tobacco lairds are troubled.
They insist that all the obstacles need clearing.
The powers that be then pledged
That this waterway be dredged,
Which took a lot of clever engineering.

Groynes provided the solution
To the silt's redistribution,
And vast industry in time would be begotten.
Into water there'd be slipping
A million tons of shipping ,
From a once small town that mainly dealt in cotton.

River traffic was still barred,
When Scott opened up his yard
And built fishing boats, and craft for coastal sailing.
His enterprise grew bigger
With the specially strengthened rigger,
When Greenland opened up for big-time whaling.

Not every builder thrived
But some, like Scott's, survived –
It constructed ships till 1993.
While it prospered and grew strong.
Others didn't last for long:
One never even sent a ship to sea!

It is known that three ships were fitted out at Aberdeen as early as 1475.

The major Dundee yards were the already well-established Alexander Stephen & Sons, Gourlay's (1854) and W.B. Thompson (1866). Other smaller yards also existed.

By the early 20th century, one fifth of the world's ships were made on the Clyde. Fewer than 2 per cent are now made in Britain.

New markets became accessible to Scottish entrepreneurs following the 1706 and 1707 Acts of Union (see verses 449–453). The voyages out of Scotland were usually the triangular trade route (see verse 272), involving trips from Britain to Africa to deliver goods and collect slaves, a second leg to the Caribbean or North America to trade slaves for sugar, rum or tobacco, and a return third leg.

Between Bowling and Dumbarton, it was possible to wade across the River Clyde at low tide, and cargo was transported on packhorses.

In 1662, the Magistrates had bought 13 acres of land on which harbours and the first graving dock, (a dry dock in which ships' hulls are repaired and maintained), in Scotland were built. A quay was added in 1688.

The first large scale measure was engineered in the 1770s by John Golborne; other engineers involved included John Smeaton (see verses 1064 & 1641), John Rennie Senior and Thomas Telford. Regular dredging began in 1852.

John Scott opened his shipyard in Greenock in 1711. It is often regarded as marking the start of Clyde shipbuilding and notably built herring busses. It expanded in 1752, three years after the doubling of the whaling bounty in 1749 (see verse 399). The company's final incarnation was Scott Lithgow. During its long history, it built more than 1,250 vessels and became the oldest shipbuilding organisation in the world. By contrast, the short-lived Morton Wylde & Co (1870) never completed a ship.

> ... the council agreed that a trial be made this season of deepening the river below the Broomielaw, and remitted to the Magistrates to cause to do the same, and go to the length of £100 sterling of charges thereupon, and to cause build a flat-bottomed boat, to carry off the sand and chingle from the banks.
>
> **1740**

Robert Napier, engineer
Started up in business here,
And did much to help the wind-to-steam transition.
Right man, right time, right place,
But he also had to face
The Admiralty's sticking with tradition.

Though his engines were outstanding,
No contracts was he landing:
Seems the dockyards on the Thames were still preferred.
He asked the question, 'Why?'
And Parliament's reply
Proved the Navy, in their former choice, had erred.

From then on things progressed:
Robert clearly was the best,
And the seeds of major industry were sown.
Expertise he handed down –
For example to 'John Brown' –
Many protégés themselves became well known.

Of enormous ships Rob dreamed,
With Cunard he'd therefore teamed:
They, and others, shared an ocean-going vision.
The project was ambitious:
Made some English yards suspicious,
For 'provincial' towns were viewed with some derision.

The de-silting wasn't slowing.
(As a process, it's ongoing);
New steam dredgers have now put in an appearance.
All the sludge and clay and sand,
Was scooped up, and dumped on land
In a programme of progressive river clearance.

Fairfield, Lithgows, Denny
And others (there were many –
By 1880, seventy or more),
All did business near the Clyde
And for long were Scotland's pride,
Most especially when Britain was at war.

London and the South East

London's had a major share,
Both of building and repair.
In the capital, firms thought themselves superior.
With Napoleon defeated,
And the EIC unseated;
Now their business prospects start to look much drearier.

Robert Napier (1791–1876) has often been referred to as 'the Father of Clyde shipbuilding'. In 1823, he built his first steam engine for the paddle steamer *Leven*, (now exhibited at the Scottish Maritime Museum in Dumbarton). Although he had been contracted by the Admiralty in 1838 to build two engines, orders had ceased thereafter. It was only later that they were found to be cheaper than those of his London competitors, as well as more reliable.

One of his protégés was George Thomson, a marine engineer, who founded a shipbuilding company with his brother James. J. & G. Thomson's Clydebank yard was taken over by John Brown & Company in 1899, and went on to produce hundreds of ships, including RMS *Lusitania*, HMS *Hood*, HMS *Repulse*, the *Queen Mary*, *Queen Elizabeth* and the *QE2*.

John Elder, founder of the Fairfield Shipbuilding & Engineering Company, was another of Robert Napier's apprentices. Like his father David, John made many improvements in marine machinery.

Ravenscraig steel works in Motherwell provided much of the steel for Clyde shipbuilders.

Cunard was formed by Canadian Sir Samuel Cunard (1787–1865) and, as well as Napier, he worked with James Donaldson, Sir George Burns and David MacIver.

Steam dredgers appeared for the first time in 1824. A number of firms, especially in Paisley and Renfrew, specialised in building them. Nowadays, they are mainly built elsewhere, notably in the Netherlands. The dredged materials were initially transferred to the river banks by barges called punts. The spoil was later disposed of at sea.

HMSs *Repulse, Rowena, Romola* **and** *Erebus* **at the John Brown shipyard, July 1916**

In 1803–4, 2,500 ships were being built on the Thames. A decade later, this number had been decimated (to 250) and, by 1825, the number of private yards had reduced from 20 down to only 6.

All the East India Company's ships were built and repaired at the Blackwall Yard. The Charter Acts of 1793 and 1813 had begun to whittle away the EIC's monopoly of trade with India and the Far East. (Its monopolies were abolished altogether in 1833.) The EIC was also using ships for more voyages before replacing them. Despite this, and in various guises, Blackwall continued in operation until 1987.

Had the River Thames been deeper...
The cost of labour cheaper...
And the workforce less intent on demarcation...
Had the changes to be faced
Been more readily embraced...
Then there wouldn't perhaps have been this situation.

With the switch from wood to metal,
New companies would settle
And, importantly, Thames Ironworks was founded.
This very large concern,
A full order book did earn,
And its premises with hammering resounded.

On the Medway, Chatham flourished.
By huge investment nourished,
It's extended by a hundred million bricks.
Thus this Royal Dockyard grows,
While two others have to close,
As does Millwall, post the slump of '66.

Whilst the north is on the rise,
London faces its demise:
Shipyards folded, and some others merely dwindled.
They simply can't compete
In providing Britain's fleet:
Here, this industry would never be re-kindled.

Sheffield

Sheffield's well inland.
Its rivers are not grand:
(It has several but you'll miss them if you blink).
Not your typical vicinity
For maritime affinity?
It has more to do with ships than one might think.

There's certainly no doubt
That a steely hand reached out:
Some famous firms had interests far from narrow.
There were Cammell... and Firth Brown
(Which linked up with Glasgow town)...
And the Vickers' name is active still in Barrow.

Yet another Sheffield bloke,
Who first dealt in coal and coke,
On other ventures quickly made a start.
Thomas Ward was well renowned
For the industries he'd found –
And was very good at taking things apart!

In 1802, there were strikes in London for higher wages. Notably, in the demarcations disputes, there was no flexibility between shipwrights and caulkers.

Wigram & Green's (one of the later incarnations of the Blackwall Shipyard) was the only major London yard to successfully make the transition from wooden to iron-built ships. The company built its last ship in 1894.

Barnard's, a great 18th century builder of wooden ships in Rotherhithe, did make the transition to steam.

Thames Ironworks was founded in 1835 by shipwright Thomas Ditchburn and engineer/naval architect Charles Mare. It became the Thames Ironworks & Shipbuilding & Engineering Company in 1857. As well as British contracts (eg for HMS *Warrior* – see verse 837), the firm won much overseas business. The Thames Ironworks football club was re-formed in 1900 to become West Ham United. 'Thames Ironworks' closed in 1912, financially ruined by the company's last contract, HMS *Thunderer*, which went on to fight in the Battle of Jutland (see verses 1386–1395).

Chatham Royal Dockyard (founded c.1570) was vastly expanded from 1862–1885, when an estimated 110 million bricks were used. From late Victorian times, it couldn't cope with larger warships but did produce submarines during the First World War. It finally closed in 1984, its gradual decline punctuated by periodic reinvestment. Similarly unsuitable for increasingly large vessels, both Woolwich and Deptford dockyards closed in 1869.

In addition to Chatham, the Admiralty had also invested heavily in the expansion of Portsmouth and Plymouth Dock (now renamed Devonport). Development of the latter caused the demise of the village of Hallsands – see verses 1149–1150.

Construction of the dockyard at Rosyth began in 1909. The associated naval base closed in 1994.

Cammell is as in Cammell Laird (see verses 1097–1098).

Vickers Shipbuilding & Engineering is, though, now part of BAE and has accordingly been re-named – twice – to reflect this. Since 2007, it has been BAE Systems Submarine Solutions.

Thos. W. Ward Ltd was founded in 1878 and, in 1894, diversified into ship-breaking.

To ships this was applied:
His yards were nationwide,
The dismantling business clearly kept him busy.
All this took place round the coast,
But the man's remembered most
For the elephant he hired. Her name was Lizzie.

Ship-breaking

Recycling 'twould appear,
Is not a new idea.
Sometimes sailing craft were stripped of useful wood.
But it's clear that many weren't.
Most were 'lost' at sea or burnt,
Especially if their timbers were no good.

With an image we're acquainted:
It's a picture Turner painted
Of a ship which looks so splendid and unbowed.
The once 'fighting' *Temeraire*,
(By now deemed not worth repair),
To her final berth by tug is being towed.

Does ill-fortune impregnate
Ships which met some dreadful fate?
And linger once dismantling is completed?
Lest this awful thought be true,
There was just one thing to do:
The last letter of their names would be deleted.

Ships in time all reach the stage,
When they're suffering from age,
Their workings, through the years, get less reliable.
Parts aren't easy to obtain…
Metal rusts and suffers strain…
In short, to keep them going is not viable.

Though their hulls might now be old,
Steel can always be re-rolled.
Almost all a ship in some form is reusable.
There are dangers to be faced,
For what's left is toxic waste!
So a lack of care is always inexcusable.

It's one of life's sad facts,
That some countries are quite lax,
In the ways by which such hazards are controlled.
As the work is so intensive –
And labour's inexpensive –
It's to places such as these most ships are sold.

Ward had 9 yards in England, Wales and Scotland, and his Inverkeithing yard was operational until the 1960s. RMS *Mauretania* (built in 1938) was broken up there in 1965. When his horses were requisitioned for the First World War service, he acquired the elephant from a travelling menagerie to transport goods around Sheffield.

The stripping of wood is known to have happened since Tudor times.

The *Temeraire* was taken from Sheerness to John Beatson's yard in Rotherhithe by means of two hired tugs. Castle's, another well known ship-breaker on the Thames, has often incorrectly been credited with the breaking of her.

It was common practice in Victorian times for the final letter to be chiselled off the name of damaged vessels.

The average lifespan of a modern ship is 26 years. The salvage operation of a ship can allow 97–98 per cent to be reusable. Non-ferrous metals are melted down and furniture, equipment and artefacts are sold. The remaining 2–3 per cent is hazardous waste (such as oils, mercury and asbestos).

The 2003 Basel Convention laid down strict technical conditions for dismantling ships, but compliance is far from universal. Labourers in some countries are paid a pittance for the hot, dirty and highly dangerous work involved in ship-breaking. During the 1950s, the scrappage industry shifted to Asia. Ten per cent of India's domestic steel requirements are met from scrapped ships. China, Bangladesh, Pakistan (and increasingly Turkey) have large ship dismantling industries.

Since Leavesley International discontinued its facility in Liverpool, Able UK of Hartlepool is the only major British company specialising in this field.

The Fighting *Temeraire* on her final journey (J.M.W. Turner, 1839)

Developments in communications

Telegraphy we've met.
It's mechanical as yet...
Electricity begins now to inspire.
And soon the most intelligent,
Have started to experiment:
Could messages be sent along a wire?

They work on what they'll need
To communicate with speed:
Something quicker than a liner – or a horse.
So the boffins spend their days
On a quest for better ways:
One such person is ex-artist, Samuel Morse.

On land they've got things sussed,
So a sea link is discussed,
And a trans-Atlantic cable is uncoiled.
But a lack of right techniques,
Means it works for just three weeks:
By a too-big surge of power the scheme is foiled.

Five more attempts are made,
Till a robust version's laid,
And at last the dodgy hook-up is no more.
Then it's just a few short years,
Until radio appears,
Linking ship to ship, and also ship to shore.

From a vessel in distress,
Can be signalled 'SOS'.
That appeal for help has many times been made.
The *Slavonia*, when wrecked,
Was the first to thus connect –
And two other ships then hastened to her aid.

In the year of 1910,
That most murderous of men,
Dr Crippen, killed his wife and tried to flee.
But a timely wireless message,
Would our villain's downfall presage:
It was sent when he was some miles out to sea.

As radio's upgraded,
Plotting where ships are is aided,
And a massive leap is made with navigation.
On two stations get a fix,
And this readily depicts
Your position – by what's called triangulation.

Communication between various parts of the world was by ship. (The first regular mail ship runs between Britain and her colonies had begun in 1755.)

In 1824, British scientist William Sturgeon invented the electromagnet and, in 1837, English inventor Edward Davy demonstrated his electric telegraph system. The first commercial electrical telegraph (patented in 1837) was co-developed by Britons William Cooke and Charles Wheatstone. Their system was widely used in the growing railway network.

Samuel Morse was an American who had developed the Morse code signalling alphabet with his assistant Alfred Vail. The ensuing Morse/Vail overland telegraph connected the USA's east and west coasts in 1861, thus ending the Pony Express.

Having studied the proposed specification of the undersea cable, William Thomson, 1st Baron Kelvin, expressed reservations about whether it would work, and his calculations proved correct. Nevertheless, the project began in 1854 and was completed in 1858. Half of it was laid by HMS *Agamemnon* and half by USS *Niagra*. Then it was joined in the middle. The final, successful, version was laid in 1866 by the *Great Eastern* (see verse 851).

A cable across the English channel had been laid in 1845.

Welsh born David Hughes developed the printing telegraph in 1855 and, in 1894, Guglielmo Marconi improved wireless telegraphy and demonstrated its use.

'SOS' is not an acronym for 'Save our souls' or 'Send out succour'. It is simply a nine digit Morse code signal meaning 'help'. The signal can be repeated continuously.

The *Slavonia* was wrecked in 1909 when the Cunard liner got into trouble off the Azores. 1,700 lives were saved.

Crippen and his mistress, who was disguised as a boy, were aboard the liner SS *Montrose*. The captain recognised the fugitives and, just before the ship was out of wireless range, sent a telegram to British authorities. Crippen was arrested in Canada, (then still a British Dominion), and returned to Britain, where he was tried and hanged for murder.

Triangulation could be created by strings of radio beacons that were set up near harbours (and airports) specifically for the purpose of plotting positions.

Submarine cable on a ship

More potential was presented
Once radar was invented,
And automation came with the transponder.
Today all can assess,
With the aid of GPS,
Their whereabouts, whichever way they wander.

Telegraph and the British Empire

Perhaps too far ahead we zoom.
With those cables let's resume.
The trans-Atlantic link was just the start.
To the empire's distant lands
A network soon expands,
With the 'mother country' Britain at its heart.

Special vessels were devised,
So the lands we'd colonized,
Could be contacted with super-fast connection.
We could instantly get through
To all but very few,
Post-completion of the trans-Pacific section.

Such a jolly good resource
Brought anxieties of course,
So redundancies were part of its design.
Just on 'British' soil it's grounded,
But the fears were all unfounded,
For no one breached the famous 'All Red Line'.

We had built in safeguards but
The Germans' lines were cut.
They were severed by our cable ship *Alert*.
So on wireless they rely
And that's the reason why
We could listen in, and certain plans pervert.

(Hostilities had started,
When a German ship departed
From Melbourne. There's a shot it can't ignore.
Back it turns. The crew's arrested,
When they scarcely have digested
What was news to them – their country is at war!)

Radar was invented in the 1930s. A transponder is both a transmitter and receiver. British science fiction writer Arthur C. Clarke published the concept of using satellites as communication relays in 1945. The first communication satellite was launched in 1963, and the USA began to develop the GPS (Global Positioning Satellite) system in 1973.

The specially designed vessels were known as cable ships and prefixed CS.

The All Red Line involved an estimated 100,000 miles of submarine cable. As well as being connected to Britain, some countries – eg Australia and New Zealand – were also connected to each other.

'Instant' is used as a relative term in this verse, as what once took up to six months was now achieved in a matter of hours. The trans-Pacific section was completed in 1902.

A redundancy is the inclusion of extra components which provide back-up if others fail. Every effort was made to ensure that the cables only made landfall in British colonies.

One of the first actions of the First World War was to commission CS *Alert* to locate and cut the five German communication cables which provided links ultimately to North America. Subsequently, others were found and either cut, or lifted with grappling hooks, and diverted to British use.

The Australian authorities had been informed of the outbreak of the First World War by telegraph, and the RAN (Royal Australian Navy) fired a warning shot across the bows of German cargo ship SS *Pflaz*, and forced it to return to port, where the ship was confiscated.

In 2016, concern began to be expressed about the possibility that submerged internet cables would be sabotaged by Russia.

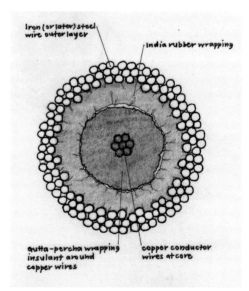

Typical cross-section through a trans-Atlantic cable

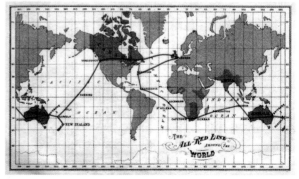

The All Red Line (George Johnson, 1902/3)

Current operational lighthouses (as at 2015)
• **Trinity House lighthouses 64** (including 4 in the Channel Islands and one, Europa Point in Gibraltar, not shown)
• Trinity House lightvessels 8
• Northern Lighthouse Board lighthouses 206

9 Wider still and wider

9

Wider still and wider

Coastal Erosion and Sea Defences

Our coastline isn't static
And the change can be dramatic,
For whole chunks of cliff can suddenly collapse.
Many factors are in play,
Which can cause rock to give way –
Like how soft it is, and whether there are gaps.

Pounding waves can be invasive;
And churned-up sand's abrasive;
The acidity of water can liquesce.
Any stone containing lime
Will dissolve if given time,
Which is why our seaboard's often under stress.

Attrition and corrosion
And corrasian cause erosion;
All are mainly due to how the sea behaves.
Its habitual predation,
Can result in the creation
Of landforms: arches, tunnels, stacks and caves.

England's north-east coast,
Is affected more than most:
Holderness is just soft boulder clay.
Winds create a longshore drift,
Which material will shift:
Five millimetres vanish every day.

Mappleton's a village,
Which the sea had sought to pillage:
The erosion rate just there was even faster.
Two million pounds expended
So the place could be defended,
Means its residents no longer face disaster.

But an engineered creation,
Aimed at damage limitation,
Will often have the caveat 'Beware!'
One location it protects,
But there may be side effects:
By aggravating what occurs elsewhere.

The study of erosion and sediment redistribution is called coastal morphodynamics. Fault lines and fissures, when filled with water under high pressure, will widen, thereby weakening the structure.

Calcium carbonate rock, such as chalk and limestone, is alkaline and the 'White Cliffs of Dover' are thus affected.

Corrasian is the term for the transport of materials, leading to abrasion.

The soft boulder clay was deposited about 18,000 years ago on top of chalk. Longshore drift is the transportation of sediment along a coast at an angle to the shoreline, (dependent on wind direction, and on swash and backwash ie the water that advances and retreats on the beach when a wave has broken). The Holderness coastline is retreating at a rate of 1–2 metres each year, and parts of the East Anglian coast (eg Hunstanton) are also particularly affected.

The coast at Mappleton, (3 miles south of the town of Hornsea), was eroding at an average rate of 7–10 metres a year. The construction (in 1991) of revetments and two groynes, plus the creation of a more gradually sloping cliff face to prevent undercutting, has saved the village. Unfortunately, erosion rates further down the coast have increased as a result of the measures taken to save Mappleton.

Durdle Door, West Lulworth, Dorset Jurassic Coast

Old Man of Hoy, Scotland (William Daniell, *c*.1817 Aquatint on paper)

So where the coast is battered,
Land is worn away or shattered,
And human beings too have played their part.
Sand and gravel from one bay,
By the ton was dredged away,
To extend some docks – which didn't prove that smart.

With its ever lowered beach,
Now Hallsands is in reach.
Its inhabitants are driven to complain.
They fear their homes are fated,
But the digging's unabated:
Only later does the company refrain.

There's a strengthened new sea wall,
But that doesn't help at all,
When it proves itself quite easily traversed.
Now there's not much to be seen,
For in 1917,
The elements combined to do their worst.

Another place that thrived,
Has also not survived.
It was once the seat of Anglo-Saxon kings.
Dunwich was a port,
Where wool was sold and bought.
Now it's from the deep a sunken church bell rings.

When its river northwards wended,
Its raison d'être ended:
As a major centre, Dunwich ceased to be.
Though its buildings still remained,
The defences weren't maintained,
And the town was at the mercy of the sea.

The North Sea's stomach's hollow;
Yet more land it seeks to swallow
To assuage what seems a never-ending thirst.
But schemes of reclamation
Can effect an alteration,
And the balance of the struggle is reversed.

When the Romans here were reigning,
In the Fens they started draining:
The area was sogginess and slosh.
Now there's solid fertile ground,
In the counties that surround,
The square-mouthed shallow bay that's called The Wash.

Dredging in Start Bay, (easterly south Devon), began in 1897. Material was being removed at the rate of up to 1,600 tons a day. It was needed for the expansion of the naval dockyard at Keyham, near Plymouth (see verse 1118). By 1900, the level of Hallsands' shingle beach, which had once kept the sea at a safe distance by dispersing wave action, had dropped by 12 feet, and water was now routinely within 3 feet of the houses. The dredging contract had been awarded to Sir John Jackson. By the time the licence was revoked, in 1902, about 665,000 tons had been removed. When an easterly wind and exceptionally high tide combined, most of the village was destroyed, and what had once been a thriving and close knit community was abandoned.

Dunwich may or may not have been 'Dommoc', which has been described as the capital of East Anglia. By the 11th century, it was the tenth largest place in England, and a major centre of religion, trade, fishing and shipbuilding. Dunwich was no longer the sheltered port it had once been when, due to coastal processes, the River Dunwich had diverted two and a half miles north. Storm surges during the 13th and 14th centuries destroyed almost all the town, but locals claim that the bell of one of its many churches can still be heard.

The Romans were responsible for many innovations, including the building of walls underwater for harbours and breakwaters.

Infilling is used to reclaim land, and the silting of estuaries means that, in some cases, what were once coastal towns are now situated some miles from the sea (see verses 53 & 169).

In 1966, Irish poet Seamus Heaney posed the question of whether sea defined the land, or land the sea.

Hallsands, Devon, 1885

What the sea seeks to purloin
Can be thwarted by the groyne,
A structure that projects out from the land.
It can act as an impediment,
By trapping drifting sediment.
Its height must be meticulously planned.

Revetments... tetrapods...
Aim at lengthening the odds
Of success, when tidal forces come a poaching.
'Hard' methods such as these,
(Plus the walls that block the seas),
Have all been tried to stop the waves encroaching.

But they can look quite unsightly,
So aren't undertaken lightly
And, by engineers, aren't favoured as they were.
Sand dune augmentation
By the growth of vegetation,
And reshaping beaches: they're what some prefer.

Different methods man might juggle,
In this never-ending struggle:
Global warming has a lot to answer for.
With water levels rising
Clever measures need devising,
To repel the sea that's knocking at our door.

The rise and fall of the Seaside Resort

If you had sufficient wealth...
Took the waters for your health...
Then the spa town was a favoured destination.
It was just the sort of place
The nobility would grace,
For meeting friends and other recreation.

Then the seaside proved a draw,
As it offered something more:
The lure of shore and waves was irrepressible.
All those frivolous pursuits,
Would gather more recruits.
When the railways made our coast much more accessible.

From the 1840s on,
The 'elite' description's gone,
And the beach resort's no longer so genteel.
Coming now, upon a spree
Are the nation's bourgeoisie;
Thus the seaside has acquired its mass appeal.

If groynes (breakwaters) are too low, they are often not effective. Too high, they trap too much sediment. Poorly designed, or inappropriately located, structures can result in problems elsewhere, sometimes a long distance away.

Revetments are sloping structures, projecting from banks or cliffs. They are designed to absorb the energy of incoming water. Tetrapods, strangely shaped concrete structures which have four projections with blobs at their ends, are also used to dissipate wave energy.

'Soft' management methods are increasingly being used, but need to be regularly repeated. Vegetation traps and stabilises blown sand, and encourages dune growth. Beach nourishment involves importing compatible sand, and piling it on top of existing sand.

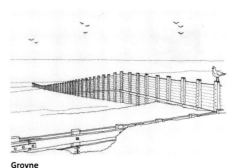

Groyne

Revetment

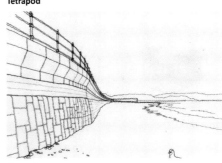

Tetrapod

Sea wall

To escape the urban grind,
Here the workers can unwind.
They'll have saved all year to fund their week's diversion.
It's their chance to get away –
Maybe only for a day –
On some Sunday School, or other group excursion.

The promenade has stayed.
Here the toffs would still parade.
But the lower classes' lives could be austere:
All too brief their spells of leisure;
They deserve a bit of pleasure;
And what better than a stroll along a pier?

Unseen forces sometimes mean
Water's nowhere to be seen,
Though it might have left some rock pools to explore.
But if a pier there be,
One can walk above the sea,
Even *when* it has decided to withdraw.

(Some weren't built to be enjoyed:
There's the 'working pier', employed
As a place where ships their cargoes could discharge.
A landing stage is needed,
When the ocean has receded,
Especially where the tidal range is large.)

The longest – had you heard? –
Is a mile long plus one third.
It had suffered fires. Its structure was unsound.
It seemed doomed, but was retained
After residents campaigned;
Southend is where this edifice is found.

There are other piers elsewhere,
Some of these too need repair:
By infernos or by storms they've been beset.
They're no longer in commission...
Might be facing demolition...
And our heritage is therefore under threat.

As for food, there's a solution:
That great British institution,
The fish and chip shop always comes in handy.
Whilst your dentist may get cross,
If you don't routinely floss,
One invented what some know as 'cotton candy'.

Initially, the seaside's widening popularity extended mainly to the middle classes, giving rise to jokes about clerks and shopkeepers. From the 1870s, working class families from the mills in the north increasingly took their annual Wakes Week (unpaid) holidays at the coast, saving up all year to pay for them. Cheap day excursions were also organised by various bodies such as Sunday Schools or commercial promoters.

The pleasure pier is an English and Welsh phenomenon, but there are some working piers and jetties in Scotland. Brighton's Old Chain Pier, built in 1823, was originally constructed as a landing stage for passengers going to, or coming from, Dieppe. The pier at Southend-on-Sea, extending 1.34 miles, is the longest pleasure pier in the world. The original was opened in 1830. During the Second World War, it served as 'HMS *Leigh*' and was (1) a mustering point for convoys and (2) a Naval Control for the Thames Estuary. In 1980, the council announced it was to close, but it has since been reprieved and redeveloped.

Gravesend pier, built in 1834, is the oldest cast iron pier in the world. In addition to fires on Southend's pier, there have been others at Weston-super-Mare, Hastings, Brighton (West Pier), Blackpool (North Pier), Southsea and, most recently, Eastbourne (2014). There were almost one hundred piers by the end of the Victorian era. This number has since halved. The National Piers Society, founded in 1979, is dedicated to their preservation.

The first shops selling both fish and chips came into being in the early 1860s. A very British institution, the fish and chip shop provided a unique domestic market for fish. A machine for making candy floss was invented in 1897 by a dentist from Tennessee, USA.

See verses 24–30 **Tides**, and verses 1722–1723 on tidal range.

Oh! I do like to be beside the seaside
I do like to be beside the sea!
I do like to stroll along the prom, prom, prom!
Where the brass bands play:
'Tiddely-om-pom-pom!'
So just let me be beside the seaside
I'll be beside myself with glee
And there's lots of girls beside
I should like to be beside
Beside the seaside!
Beside the sea!

Popular music hall song by John A. Glover-Kind (1907)

Southend Pier

Those who liked to take a dip.
In privacy could strip:
The machines they used for bathing could be hired
For a one-and-sixpence levy –
The 'bathing dress' was heavy,
But ensured a girl was modestly attired.

Punch and Judy were in action,
A popular attraction.
There were donkey rides, and bands which entertained.
One could paddle, frilly knickered,
But families still bickered,
And then – as now – it very often rained.

Cheap flights in time would foster,
A preference for the 'costa',
For in Spain there's much more chance of clear blue skies.
This less popular would render,
Our hotels in all their splendour,
And bring about the seaside town's demise.

Naval Brigades

Be it fisherman or trader,
Be it convict or crusader,
Be it simply those who chose to live elsewhere,
With the whole world, we've a link –
All our bits are coloured pink.
It's an empire with which others can't compare.

Our influence is wide,
But with no wish to misguide,
The picture didn't always lack hostility.
There's no European threat,
(Or at least there isn't yet),
But the scene is not all calm subdued docility.

In the year of 1810,
We had seen some groups of men
Engage in the amphibious assault.
French offensives from Mauritius,
Had been proving quite pernicious,
Rowley's squadron helped to bring these to a halt.

Once again on terra firma,
Fighting sailors were in Burma.
Then Russia had a grandiose idea.
War was land-based on the whole,
But the navy had a role
In our struggle to dislodge her from Crimea.

Sea bathing was initially done for health reasons and not for pleasure. Bathing machines were introduced around 1730, and the cloth awning (the 'modesty hood') was invented in 1750 by Benjamin Beale, a Quaker who lived in Margate.

Punch and Judy date back to the 16th century and were originally adult entertainment.

Little fishing villages began to cater for those with a taste for the picturesque.

Even in their heyday, some seaside resorts struggled, and attempts (such as Blackpool's illuminations) were made to extend the season.

ON THE BATHING MACHINE

'You have never seen one of these machines. Imagine to yourself a small, snug, wooden chamber, fixed upon a wheel-carriage, having a door at each end, and on each side a little window above, a bench below. The bather, ascending into this apartment by wooden steps, shuts himself in, and begins to undress, while the attendant yokes a horse to the end next the sea, and draws the carriage forwards, till the surface of the water is on a level with the floor of the dressing-room, then he moves and fixes the horse to the other end. The person within being stripped, opens the door to the sea-ward, where he finds the guide ready, and plunges headlong into the water. After having bathed, he re-ascends into the apartment, by the steps which had been shifted for that purpose, and puts on his clothes at his leisure, while the carriage is drawn back again upon the dry land; so that he has nothing further to do, but open the door, and come down as he went up.'

Tobias Smollet, from *The Expedition of Humphrey Clinker* (1771)

Bathing machines at Llandudno (Francis Bedford, *c*.1880)

For decades after the Napoleonic Wars, Russia was the only European power that presented any threat.

In 1802, 'His Majesty's Marine Forces' were designated 'Royal Marines' in recognition of past services to the nation. Two years later, The Royal Marine Artillery (RMA) was raised to replace artillery units assigned to ships. The Royal Marines and fighting sailors of the naval brigades were under army officer command whilst in action.

Originally called Île de France, the renamed Mauritius became part of the British Empire until 1968. See verses 592–594.

Sir Josias Rowley (1765–1842).

The Crimean War (1853–56) was fought, in support of Ottoman Turks, by a Franco-British alliance against the Russians.

Naval brigades also saw action during the Boxer Rebellion (1900) in China. A multi-national expedition to protect Beijing (then Peking) was led by Vice Admiral Sir Edward Hobart Seymour (1840–1929).

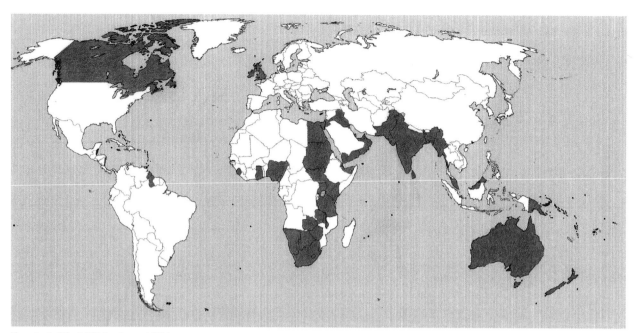

The extent of the British Empire as at 1914

On this conflict's Baltic stage,
The gunboat comes of age,
And for decades hence will prove a useful craft.
It could reach a tricky coast,
(Inaccessible to most),
As it wasn't big, and had a shallow draught.

In 1854,
Russia's Black Sea fleet's no more:
It's been scuttled to protect the harbour there.
Our foe went on to use
As marines, its former crews;
Its artillery was utilized elsewhere.

(We'd also used this ploy,
And the *Sapphire* did destroy,
When the French in Bay Bulls Harbour had her trapped.
Her captain, not enraptured
By the thought she might be captured,
Decided that to sink her would be apt.)

Our brigades, too, were in action,
To face Indian reaction,
Over coating on the bullets they must bite.
Lard or tallow – just a smidgen –
Didn't fit with their religion,
And to native soldiers thus did not seem right.

Between 1854 and 1856, in an effort to eliminate the threat posed by Russia's Baltic Fleet in Finland, naval defences and much of Finland's merchant fleet were destroyed. At the outset of the campaign, British ships (part of a combined Anglo-French fleet) were deplorably undermanned (see verse 949).

Later attaining the rank of Rear Admiral, midshipman Charles Davis Lucas was the first person to be awarded the Victoria Cross. Serving aboard HMS *Hecla* in the Gulf of Finland, he picked up a live shell, which had landed on the upper deck, and then threw it into the sea. It exploded before it reached the water. The Russians were also deploying new torpedoes (mines).

Using larger ships to re-coal, gunboats could steam close to shore defences and batter them into submission. They could also negotiate rivers, and thus access places distant from the open sea. They proved useful until the 1900s, when Admiral Fisher (see verses 1327 & 1344) dispensed with many.

Scuttling is the act of deliberately sinking one's own ship. The British had sunk the *Sapphire* in 1696, during one of the frequent disputes with France over Newfoundland fishing grounds. A scuttle is an opening or hatch (with a removable lid) in a ship's hull.

The Indian Rebellion (or 'Indian Mutiny') took place in 1857. Loading the recently introduced Enfield rifle necessitated holding a bullet greased with animal fat between the teeth. Eating pork (unclean) was offensive to Muslim Indian soldiers, whereas the cow is sacred to Hindus. The rebellion resulted in the Crown's taking over the EIC's (see verses 407, 563, 874, 882, 1009 & 1114) possessions and armed forces in India, and to the establishment of the British Raj. India became independent in 1947, following a campaign of non-violent resistance led by Mahatma Gandi.

> The gunboats, without being models of elegance, move easily through the water, turn deftly, and have a blunt, determined look, with a spice of mischief.
>
> ***Times* Correspondent, 23 April 1856**

In New Zealand, Māori Wars
Were yet another cause
In which sailors sought to quell a distant quarry.
These 'justified' disputes,
In land rights had their roots:
(For the greed of settlers, Britain's since said, 'Sorry').

The *Euryalus* (screw steamer),
Led the way at Kagoshima:
When talking didn't work, the town was hit.
After that, negotiations
Produced the reparations
We'd been seeking for the killing of a Brit.

Gunboat Diplomacy

At sea, a show of force,
Can achieve a wanted course.
Such diplomacy creates a big impression.
We shouldn't need to fight:
By displaying naval might,
This 'gunboat' method gets us our concession.

In other countries' wars,
Britain thought she had just cause
To become involved, and send the navy in.
When regimes are autocratic,
Trade becomes more problematic,
And the 'liberal' side we'd therefore want to win.

In a Middle East dispute,
We helped to free Beirut,
(When Charles Napier his orders disregarded).
We wanted Egypt out,
And, with firepower of some clout,
Acre (her last stronghold) was bombarded.

The Don Pacifico Affair, 1850

He was Portuguese, a Jew.
But by birth, was British too.
And Greece was where he daily plied his trade.
A mob his house destroyed:
Understandably annoyed,
Don said that compensation must be paid.

Because he was a Brit,
Our government saw fit
To help him out, and get him satisfaction.
But this the Greeks evaded –
So Athens was blockaded!
(And war with France was almost a reaction).

The First Māori War was in 1845. Disputes continued until 1872. Conflicts in the Pacific and elsewhere were supported from British naval bases in Australia. For example, the Naval Brigades of flagship HMS *Pelorus* of the Australia Station (and those of other ships) were involved in the Māori conflicts from 1860–64.

The *Euryalus* was a wooden screw-frigate acting as flagship to a squadron of 7 British warships. Under the command of Admiral Sir Augustus Leopold Kuper (1809–1885), the campaign did not involve the landing of British troops. The Bombardment of Kagoshima (1863) was also known as the Anglo-Satsuma War. It followed the Namamugi Incident (1862), in which one British national was killed (and two injured) by Satsuma samurai, for failing to show proper respect to their leader.

Britain got involved in the disputes of others, when it suited. This did not usually take the form of direct action. For example, the mere presence of British warships in the River Tagus (1825) helped persuade Portugal to recognise Brazilian independence.

The Second Egyptian-Ottoman War (1839–41) was occasioned by Egypt's occupation of the Turkish possession of Syria. British support for the Ottoman Empire was principally to prevent Russian influence on the Bosphorus.

Admiral Sir Charles John Napier (1786–1860) was, at the time, second in command of the British Mediterranean Fleet. He had, however, been asked to lead the land force because of the illness of the Army's commanding officer. Asked to return control when the Brigadier-General recovered, he refused because this would mean losing a tactical advantage. His hard-fought victory at Boharsef is one of only a very few land battles won by a naval officer.

The British Bombardment of Acre (1840) took place under the command of Admiral Sir Robert Stopford (1768–1847).

Following the establishment of the HMS *Excellent* gunnery school (1830), firing had become increasingly accurate (see verses 1250–1251).

David 'Don' Pacifico was born in Gibraltar, and was therefore a British subject. He had originally gone to Athens as a Portuguese diplomatic consul, then became a money lender. His house was burned in 1847, and his family were injured. Athens was blockaded in 1850.

> 'Every country that has towns within cannon shot of deep water will remember the operations of the British Fleet on the coast of Syria in... 1840, whenever such country has any differences with us.'
>
> **Lord Palmerston, the then Foreign Secretary**

> **JUSTIFICATION**
>
> '... as the Roman, in the days of old, held himself free from indignity, when he could say *Civis Romanus sum*; so also a British subject, in whatever land he may be, shall feel confident that the watchful eye and the strong arm of England, will protect him against injustice and wrong.'
>
> **Lord Palmerston, House of Commons speech, 25 June 1850**

In a fight that first began,
'Twixt the U.S. and Japan,
The Shimonoseki Straits were in contention.
To this channel's being closed,
The British were opposed,
And others, too, were keen on intervention.

Kuper led the allied fleet.
And defiance it would meet,
Though his squadron had superior potential.
To resist's a foolish move,
As events would quickly prove –
Much better to be wholly deferential.

The Two-Power Standard

To maintain superiority –
A government priority –
There came an act in 1889.
The British warship fleet
Would be large enough to meet,
The next two biggest, were these to combine.

To ensure we're well positioned,
Many new ships are commissioned,
To prevent the risk of ending up as losers.
Ten warships came to pass,
(Eight of these *Royal Sovereign* class),
Plus torpedo gunboats, and a lot of cruisers.

But we maybe should have figured
That a contest would be triggered,
As others sought to even up the score.
To what the Brits aspired,
Would be seen to have backfired
When elsewhere the quest was bigger... better... more.

Campaigns in Africa, and the Suez Canal

The sailor and marine,
On land would next be seen
On the Gold Coast. The Ashanti we were fighting.
Next the Zulus in Natal...
The Boers in the Transvaal...
Then in Egypt, where some troubles proved inciting.

After British intercession,
In effect we're in possession
Of that country and its neighbour, the Sudan.
Soon we're given the protection,
Of a waterway connection,
Though we didn't want it built when work began.

The Shimonoseki Campaign (between 1863 and 1864) was a series of engagements against the Japanese Chōshū clan, who were acting in defiance of their own government. The allied forces comprised the British, the Dutch, the French (who were mainly concentrating on events in Mexico) and the United States (who were mainly diverted by their own Civil War). The rebels attacked, even after an impressive allied show of force. Two days later, they were forced to surrender and pay reparations of three million dollars.

The Naval Defence Act formally adopted the 'two-power standard', which called for the maintenance of sufficient battle ships to at least match those of the next two largest navies added together. At the time, these were the French and Russian fleets. In 1885, when there appeared to be a real prospect of war with Russia, a large squadron destined for the Baltic had been assembled. Its commander, Sir Geoffrey Phipps-Hornby (1825–1895), described it as 'a menagerie of unruly and curiously assorted ships' (see verses 836–838 for the earlier development and acquisition of warships).
The *Royal Sovereign* class was the most formidable type of battleship of its day, surpassing any vessel in the French or Russian navies. The 18 gunboats were to support the main fleet, and the cruisers (42 of them) were to protect supply lines.

Naval brigades played a part in the Abyssinian Campaign (1868), which was a rescue mission to free British captives (and a punitive expedition) against the Ethiopian Empire. The Third Anglo-Ashanti War (1873–4) involved the West Africa Squadron. Britain was fighting the Zulus in 1879, and the First Boer War ran from December 1880 to March 1881.
Immense foreign debt had forced the Egyptian ruler to abdicate in favour of his son Tewfik, whose subsequent mismanagement led to revolt. He appealed to Britain for help (1882). The British bombarded Alexandria, (Egypt's primary seaport) and Sudan (a campaign in 1884), in effect taking control of both countries (until 1932), and thereby significantly reducing French influence.
The Convention of Constantinople (1888) declared the Suez Canal a neutral zone under British protection. In 1954, Britain agreed to remove her troops. The British Government had objected to the use of forced labour throughout the 10 years it took to excavate the canal.

There is now a shipping link –
Not as wide as one might think –
That runs between the Red Sea and the Med.
The conceiver of this trench
Was de Lesseps, who was French.
By the free flow of salt water it is fed.

It's called Suez, this canal,
And quite plain the rationale:
It's a shortcut for the Europe – Far East trip.
But the ways the winds prevail,
Aren't compatible with sail,
So it isn't used by every type of ship.

Much traffic to Bombay
Starts to go this shorter way;
There's a consequence because of what diverts.
Stops at British ports aren't made:
(Known as entrepôt such trade),
Which the business of the part-way warehouse hurts.

For a decade there's a pause,
Till we next take on the Boers,
(Reasons complex, but a gold mine's at the root).
Ladysmith's in trouble:
We need cannons at the double,
And the navy plays a part in this dispute.

To save our soldiers' bacon,
Some weaponry is taken,
When the *Terrible* and *Powerful* respond.
A brigade transports six guns,
(In total several tons),
From where they land to many miles beyond.

The 'Field Gun Competition'
Would commemorate this mission.
No Royal Tournament without it was complete.
It's a fitting celebration,
Of men's grim determination
In performing an extraordinary feat.

There is evidence to suggest that various canal links (both east-west and north-south) were built in ancient times. The Venetians (see verse 120) had contemplated digging a waterway after their monopoly on trade in luxury items had been lost (as a result of access round Africa to the Far East).

The Suez Canal (opened 1869) was a single lane, with two passing places, and no locks. Work on a second canal along half its route, (completed in 2015), doubled capacity from 49 to 97 ships a day.

Unless towed, sailing vessels couldn't navigate the canal, and therefore still had to go the long way round Africa, via Cape Horn (see verse 958).

Merchant shipping did not necessarily do the entire journey from collection point to final destination, and sometimes dropped off goods part way (where duty was payable) for onward transmission. 'Entrepôt' is the term for the intermediary centres. The business was highly profitable for Britain.

The global 'Panic of 1873' and resultant 'long depression' produced a British trade slump, which lasted until 1897.

During the Second Boer War (1899–1902), both protagonists wanted control of the lucrative Witwatersrand mines. The British garrison at Ladysmith was under siege for 120 days. The guns had first been brought 800 miles by sea, and a further 190 miles of sometimes difficult terrain had then to be covered. Full-sized field guns (smaller versions used for training are 'cadet sized') weigh about 900 pounds.

The last Royal Tournament was held in 1999, but the Field Gun Run is still re-enacted by enthusiasts.

The mechanisation of fishing

David Allan had a dream
Of fishing under steam:
A whole industry in time this would transform.
In the early days, his mission
Was viewed with some suspicion:
His boats were so much bigger than the norm.

Pioneer was screw-propelled.
(The belief is widely held
That this vessel was the first one of its kind.)
From his Leith yard, others poured,
But were mainly sold abroad.
Innovation marked the way they were designed.

Steam boats must be coaled.
This means less space in the hold.
And such vessels do cost more to buy and run.
But for distances they cater.
Their 'pulling power' is greater –
Big advantages, when all is said and done.

If they travelled far afield,
They'd secure a larger yield,
For the fish and chip shops popular in Britain.
This indifferent supply
Folk were happy still to buy –
Wrapped in paper on which last week's news was written.

The steam boat's huge expense,
For short 'local' trips made sense,
And by bigger, fresher catches was offset.
As the century was closing,
Out of harbours more were nosing,
But most of them still kept their sails – as yet.

Once wind power's in the past,
Boats still need to have a mast –
There's a reason why this feature will remain.
With a sail, a mast is able
To help keep a vessel stable –
But, above all else, it functions as a crane.

Fishermen aren't keen,
(As already has been seen),
To discard the old in favour of the new.
Oil's not readily embraced,
(Coal but slowly was replaced.)
Though, bit by bit, the changes filtered through.

David Allan began by converting a sailing drifter in 1875. At 80–90 feet in length, his boats were at least twice as long as traditional craft. *Pioneer LH854* (1877) was made of wood, and had two masts. Ten boats were produced at Leith between 1877 and 1881, and a further 21 were built at Granton. His boats featured tall narrow funnels (to keep the smoke away from the crew), which were nicknamed 'woodbines' because of their resemblance to cigarettes. The steam capstan, or 'iron man', was introduced onto boats in 1876, and assisted with pulling ropes (though this was still labour intensive).

Steam-powered trawlers were operating out of Aberdeen, Grimsby and Hull from the 1880s.

Arctic ice had been used from about 1830 to keep long distance catches cold, but not frozen. Fish were sometimes not therefore in ideal condition by the time they reached the consumer. Moreover, the product itself was regarded as coarser than fish from the North Sea. For fish and chips see verse 1168.

Because steam-powered vessels could return to port faster, the fish were fresher and could command higher prices. The last sailing fishing trawler was built in Grimsby in 1925.

The retention of sails was due to several factors. Initially, engines provided only auxiliary power. A mizzen sail helped steady the boat when its nets were out, and masts were used as cranes, initially for lifting the catch ashore, rather than for lifting nets from the sea.

For the conservatism of fishermen, see verse 987.

Lining was a cinch,
When they mechanized the winch
And the gurdy: quite a load these gizmos took.
But for automated baiting,
Some years they would be waiting –
And miles of line mean lots of fish to hook.

Handling catches was a tussle,
And it needed strength and muscle
To heave full nets – but help in time would come.
Some no longer had to maul,
To drag on board their haul,
Once they'd introduced the clever powered drum.

Not long after World War Two,
Along came something new –
Now of nylon, or of plastic, nets were made.
Unlike hemp and unlike cotton,
These synthetics don't go rotten,
So some float around as 'ghosts' that won't degrade.

There were bigger drums on board.
On these, nets were hauled and stored...
There's the brainchild of a man who was Croatian.
His mechanized large pulley,
(Developed since more fully):
The power block helped a fishing transformation.

Imperial Defence

Everyone agrees
That the British rule the seas,
That there can't be any challenge to our fleet.
On our island, nice and snug,
We're entitled to feel smug:
With our industry, no other can compete.

It must therefore have seemed strange,
When things began to change.
It was thought the French were planning to invade.
Perception is reality:
To preserve our insularity,
Plans for 'Fortress Britain' must be made!

Imperial defence,
Was a very large expense
Which, by and large, the Mother Country bore.
Wherever Britain swoops,
We garrison some troops,
But decide now most aren't needed any more.

Compartmentalised steel hulls in due course replaced wooden ones. The winch was mechanised in 1918. Gurdies are wheels which wind in baited fishing lines. They are typically used in mackerel trolling (pulling a line from a slow-moving boat). Increasingly, lures are being used instead of live bait eg for bass fishing. Lines can be many miles long (see verse 1701).

The powered gillnet drum was introduced in 1931. Nets made of nylon or plastic have the added advantage of becoming almost invisible in water. Because ghost nets are an entanglement problem for sea life, some now include degradable components.

Hydraulically-powered seine drums came in during the 1950s. These could handle most nets, including purse seines and large trawl nets. Croatian fisherman, Mario Puratić, patented his pulley in 1953.

Fish-finding sonar detection has also helped transform fishing in recent years.

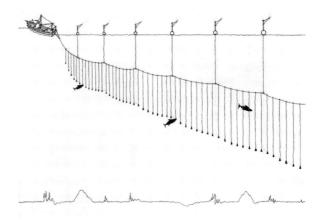

Pelagic long lining

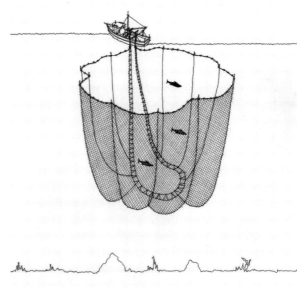

Purse seining

Louis Napoléon Bonaparte was elected president of France in 1848. Alarmed by his expansionist plans, the British commissioned a series of forts in southern England. Napoléon was, however, pro-British and Lord Palmerston agreed peaceful relations between the two countries.

Since the end of the Seven Years' War in 1763 (see section/verses 544–554), it had been Britain's practice to station a garrison in every new acquisition.

In the countries that we own,
Where self-government has grown,
Self-reliance is expected to keep pace.
Should a threat to us appear,
We would need our soldiers near,
Not located in some very distant place.

Then Germany united...
Her expansion dreams ignited...
As for industry, we cannot be complacent.
We are all too well aware,
Manufacturing elsewhere,
Has grown apace, no longer merely nascent.

But our vessels still patrolled
All the parts that we controlled,
And some argued this was how things should remain.
'Forget your bricks and mortar.
Our ships should be "blue-water",'
Was the keystone of the navalists' campaign.

In the past we've been engrossed
In warfare near a coast.
What's required is much more distant capability.
The message, widely heeded,
Was that battle fleets were needed,
That could cope far out at sea with all hostility.

Great Britain, by and large,
Would solely be in charge,
Though the countries in the empire must help pay.
Our Dominions weren't amused,
And most of them refused.
Collaboration's not achieved this way.

It can only make things worse
That the Empire's so diverse,
In spite of its prosperity and splendour.
It doesn't help one bit
That, at home, opinion's split
On how best to meet a very big agenda.

We had no 'naval bases':
As such, there weren't these places.
We'd 'establishments' with varied types of role.
Their functions might include,
Providing on board food.
Some had dockyards. Most refuelled our ships with coal.

An ardent free trader, the 3rd Earl Grey (as colonial secretary) did much during the 1840s and 1850s to promote colonial self-government, especially in Australia and Canada. From the late 1850s, there was a gradual withdrawal of British troops, though these were retained in places, eg Malta.

German unification was completed in 1871.

Navalists are advocates of the navy and naval power. Counter arguments to their stance place more emphasis on the army, and on building fortifications. Opinions were divided and, as noted by naval strategist John Colomb, the Admiralty and War Office did not cooperate with each other.

A 'blue-water navy' is one that has the capability to operate independently in open ocean, as opposed to one principally concerned with littoral defence, to which the term 'green-water navy' has, in more recent times, been accorded (to distinguish it from the 'brown-water' vessels of riverine warfare).

Australia and New Zealand refused to pay towards imperial defence. Canada ignored the debate. Only the Cape (of South Africa) assisted, contributing a cruiser (later converted into an annual payment).

Victualling yards were, for example, located on Ascension Island and at Gibraltar. The latter was destroyed during the Great Siege (see verse 573). Antigua was a rendezvous point.

For convenience, the term 'naval base' has occasionally been used in this book.

To make enquiry into the condition and sufficiency of the means of the naval and military resources provided for the defence of the more important sea-ports within our Colonial possessions and dependencies.

Remit of the Carnarvon Commission on Imperial Defence (1879–82)

The Royal Navy is not maintained for the purpose of affording direct protection to sea-ports and harbours, but for the object of blockading the ports of an enemy, of destroying his trade, attacking his possessions, dealing with his ships at sea, and we may add of preventing an attack in great force against any special place.

Second Carnarvon Commission report

There were also quite a few
That were points of rendezvous...
Some where medical facilities awaited...
Some for squadrons were headquarters,
In the Empire's distant waters,
And yet more were simply handily located.

Wherever they were scattered,
To our navy each one mattered.
Unprotected who knows what might be their fate?
How's defence to be achieved,
Now our troops have been relieved?
These are not the only factors to debate.

'Just what's our navy for,
Both in peacetime and in war?'
'How to fund it?' British citizens now ask.
'Is it getting overstretched?'
This does not seem that far-fetched.
'Are we certain it is equal to the task?'

That we need to be prepared
Is a view that's widely shared:
For with others' fleets in time we may be vying.
No matter what we spend,
There'll be savings in the end:
Once they twig they can't compete, they'll give up trying!

Though in retrospect naïve,
This some really did believe,
And the 'Two-Power' standard promised our salvation.
But it proves a short-term fix.
Soon the two are five or six:
We can live no more in splendid isolation.

The Mystery of *Mary Celeste*, 1872

She's not British, that's for sure:
The connection's quite obscure,
Though the myths began with Sherlock Holmes' creator.
He changed 'Mary' to 'Marie',
But spoke not of lukewarm tea
Or abandoned meals – these fictions grew up later.

This merchant brigantine,
Sailing all alone is seen,
Those aboard a passing vessel note she's yawing.
So they go and take a look.
There's no first mate. There's no cook.
There is nobody at all – not reassuring.

Hong Kong (Pacific Squadron) and Simon's Town (South Africa Squadron) were, *inter alia*, headquarters. King George Island, Western Australia, Mauritius and the Falkland Islands were all strategically important.

There were no official criteria for determining the relative need for naval protection. The Naval Defence Act of 1889 (see verse 1189) was looking increasingly unhelpful. In 1898, Germany (see verse 1323), the USA and Russia decided simultaneously to expand their navies, and France did the same two years later.

'It is quite true that policy determines armaments, but armaments also have something to do with determining policy. We still have the Two-Power standard for the navy but... (this) does not mean what it did when it was first introduced. When we first heard of the Two-Power standard, we only contemplated two considerable navies... almost equivalent to saying not only two Powers, but any probable combination against us.

Now the number of considerable navies in the world is growing. There is Japan with a large navy. Russia... will not be content for long to be without a considerable Navy: France has a considerable Navy: Germany is sure to have an important Navy: Italy also has a considerable Navy: and also the United States... With the great increase in the navies of the world, it is, in my opinion, necessary to depart from our old policy of splendid isolation.'

Sir Edward Grey, June 1904

The *Mary Celeste*, originally named *Amazon*, was launched under British registration in 1861. Her early career had been beset by problems, including the untimely death of her first captain at the start of her maiden voyage, two collisions with other vessels, and a fire.

In 1884, Sir Arthur Conan Doyle published *J. Habakuk Jephson's Statement*, a fictional first-hand account of what happened on board the *Marie Celeste*. It was so convincing, the British and American governments responded with formal denials.

'Yawing' means twisting or oscillating about the vertical axis of a moving ship (or aircraft).

Her cargo seems intact –
With alcohol she's packed –
There's sufficient food to see the journey through.
The ship's condition's fine.
Of a struggle, there's no sign.
So what's happened to her passengers and crew?

Have they sailed off? Have they jumped?
This has all the experts stumped,
And no one has been able to explain.
It seems – a cause for worry –
They departed in a hurry.
And none of them was ever seen again.

Possessions left behind,
Mean investigators find
It unlikely pirates went on board to plunder.
Had alcoholic fumes,
Pervaded 'Mary's' rooms?
Empty barrels give inquirers cause to wonder.

For our vessel, what comes next?
It seems she might be hexed.
In an accident, her owner's father drowned.
Yet another life she's claimed.
The famous ghost ship's blamed.
She's sold, as bad luck follows her around.

She changed hands plenty more.
Her condition now was poor.
The last to own her did a thing he shouldn't.
Worthless cargo he insured,
(His objective's being fraud),
Then tried very hard to sink her, but she wouldn't.

In a courtroom he appeared,
And of barratry was cleared;
He is guilty but the jury won't convict.
This verdict had arisen –
He faced death instead of prison –
As the penalty was thought unduly strict.

These days, 'ghost ship' has new meaning,
If to crime its crew is leaning,
And they want to sail the waters undetected.
If there's contraband on board,
Safety laws will be ignored:
There are risks to all, with Sat Nav disconnected.

She was found beyond the Azores by the crew of the *Dei Gratia*, who later came under suspicion of piracy at the Admiralty Court of Enquiry in Gibraltar, which adversely affected their salvage award.

The four general seamen who'd been aboard the *Mary Celeste* were German. The remainder of the capable crew of 7 were American, including her master, Benjamin Spooner Briggs. Accompanying him on the voyage were his wife, Sarah, and two-year-old daughter, Sophia Matilda. The cargo of 1,701 barrels of commercial alcohol (used to fortify wine) was being transported from America to Genoa, Italy.

When the *Mary Celeste* was eventually unloaded, it was discovered that nine of the barrels were empty. The alcohol was not palatable as a drink, but could be explosive.

When boarded by members of the *Dei Gratia* crew, and although in good condition, everything inside the abandoned vessel was very wet. Personal possessions, including valuables, had been left behind. There were no lifeboats on board, and it is not known how many there should have been.

The ship changed hands 18 times during the following 13 years, often at a considerable loss. Her last registered owner was Captain Gilman C. Parker, who filled her with scrap, old boots and cat food, then ran her aground and set fire to her.

In maritime law, barratry is gross misconduct relating to the wilful (as opposed to negligent) damaging of a vessel or its cargo. It is a crime against the ship's owner. Parker *was* the owner in this instance, but his attempted insurance fraud led to his trial (in the USA) for the offence.

'Ghost ship' is now a term that can be used to refer to a vessel on which the GPS system has been deliberately (and unlawfully) disabled to prevent detection. This dangerous practice is employed by those attempting to smuggle goods or people.

Engraving of the deserted *Mary Celeste*

Naval Artillery

In ship-to-ship engagements,
Were what now seem odd arrangements
Which already, in this book, have been revealed.
Men would grapple hand to hand –
Fighting as they would on land –
And the deck became a floating battlefield.

We then witnessed the departure
Of the sturdy onboard archer.
Change affected how a boat was powered and built.
It was farewell to the oar,
Now the heavy cannons score:
These are placed low down, or else the ship might tilt.

Cannons had their many guises:
Came in varied types and sizes.
Over time, their power extended longer range.
They're set up for broadside shooting,
This in turn meant instituting
New tactics, so the battle plan would change.

To thicken up the plot,
There are different types of shot,
The choice of which depends on the objective.
If a hull you want to pound,
Use the classic heavy 'round'.
But for cutting rigging, chain shot's more effective.

'Proper training? There's no need,'
The Admiralty decreed.
'Waste gunpowder? Oh no, it's too expensive!'
So our sailors weren't acquiring
Proper skills in real-life firing –
It's fingers crossed they'll cope in an offensive.

The cannon long held sway
But, in time, had had its day:
Shells the army used were in the wings, just waiting.
Their naval application,
Led to damage limitation:
The armoured ship, complete with iron plating.

The Armstrong Gun

In 1854,
When our country was at war,
Tales of cumbrous field guns duly got reported.
Our stoic British fighter,
Was in need of something lighter.
William Armstrong thought, 'We'd better get this sorted.'

For the 'galley tactics', (hand-to-hand fighting) prevalent until the 16th century see verses 173 & 233.

The first recorded use of naval artillery was during the Battle of Arnemuiden in 1338, which was fought between England and France at the start of the Hundred Years' War (see verse 172).

See verse 236 for cannon placement.

Types of cannon included the unwieldy full cannon, the demi-cannon, the culverin and (from 1778) the carronade (see verse 609). France and Spain preferred to use longer range methods to destroy the rigging. The English (and Dutch) favoured closer range rapid fire, aimed at ships' hulls. Battle plans changed to the 'line of battle', which was adopted from the 1650s (see verse 344).

One type of shot, 'hot shot' (see verse 573), was designed to set fire to opposing vessels. Spherical cast iron shot came in various weights, the largest of which were the 42-pounders.

Some owners of privateering vessels, who were dependent on their crews' skills for capturing prizes, did invest in explosives for more thorough practical training. The Admiralty ultimately rectified its mistake of not using the real thing.

The high trajectories of explosive shells made them unsuitable for naval combat until the Paixhans gun (French) was developed in 1822.

See verse 837 for armour plating.

Sir William Armstrong (1810–1900), dubbed 'the Father of modern artillery', responded to problems reported from the Crimean War by developing the Armstrong Gun.

A man now with a mission,
He put a proposition
For a weapon he could readily envision.
What he had in mind,
Was cleverly designed
To fire at longer range, with more precision.

It was rifled and breech-loaded,
And once the charge exploded,
After recoil it was quick to realign.
With Charles Mitchell he next teamed;
Of its naval use both dreamed.
Their armed warships would be built upon the Tyne.

As we've seen, guns sideways faced,
They're now differently placed
On turrets, which are round and can rotate.
The development as well,
Of the armour-piercing shell,
Rendered vulnerable those suits of iron plate.

Steel hulls then came along,
Impervious and strong...
But torpedoes had the power of penetration.
From small vessels these were fired...
Counter-measures were required...
In this cycle of response to innovation.

The Naval Ram

A weapon, long neglected,
Would now be resurrected
From the distant past, when ships were powered by oar.
To batter an opponent
Is a lethal bow component –
As the naval ram comes briefly to the fore.

Quite some havoc it can wreak,
This strange underwater 'beak':
For a while, it is an almost standard fitting.
But its use soon fizzles out,
When firepower gains more clout –
And too many of our own ships it was hitting!

Target Practice

Faster guns were then acclaimed
But were rarely that well aimed,
And made splashes which confused the onboard spotters.
War at sea has complications:
To compute the calculations,
Were mechanical machines to act as plotters.

Armstrong's company at Elswick (Tyne and Wear) merged with Mitchell's in 1882. Mitchell's firm had built the first purpose-built cable-laying vessel (CS *Hooper*, later renamed *Silvertown*) in 1873. The round shape of turrets was designed to deflect shots. Swivelling was initially achieved using steam-powered donkey engines. Developed by Cowper Phipps Coles, turret mounting was first used on the raft *Lady Nancy*, and later trialled (1861) on HMS *Trusty*.

Palliser shot (1867) had iron tips, hardened by a chilling process. It was replaced by new forged steel rounds, which were capable of penetrating the steel hulls introduced in the 1880s.

In the Age of Sail, ships could not be steered into position with enough accuracy to make rams effective. Steamships once again enabled manoeuvring, and the appendage gained popularity in the second half of the 19th century.

Quick-firing guns were relatively small, and became a characteristic feature of pre-dreadnought battleships. If fired at the same time as the larger artillery, it was difficult to detect which splashes were caused by which. Ships in battle move! Their speed and direction, the impact of prevailing weather conditions, and the physics relating to how shot behaves are amongst the factors which must be taken into account. 'Aim and shoot' is insufficient.

Today's Royal Navy guns have a range of 17 miles. The Navy's Harpoon missiles have a range of about 80 miles. These reached their 'out of service' date in 2018, and there are no immediate plans to replace them, leading to concerns about a capability gap. The government relies instead on nuclear submarines as a deterrent.

An advantage was obtained,
When guns were better 'trained'
(And these weapons, too, got more sophisticated.)
Each improvement – always needed –
Meant a version superseded:
What went before was rapidly outdated.

Oft dismissed as too progressive,
Percy Scott's thoughts proved impressive,
Though the powers that be weren't readily convinced.
His successes weren't believed:
It's no wonder he was peeved...
And expressed himself in words that were not minced.

He'd devised new ways of training,
And his gun crews were obtaining
An unprecedented four hits out of five.
What he did made quite a dent
In the twenty-eight per cent –
The average that the navy could contrive.

Aircraft and Torpedoes

There's another thing that's new.
It didn't float, it flew!
And in combat roles would soon become entangled.
To deal with aviation,
Guns with greater elevation
Could point skywards; some of these were quite high-angled.

Nothing's ever done and dusted:
Things move on. Things get adjusted...
Armour thickened, to protect from being shelled.
There's a new way to be hit
For, developed by a Brit,
Are torpedoes – still quite slow but self-propelled.

Ships must stay beyond their range,
So artillery would change
To 'all-big-guns', so cleverly aligned.
Protection was one need.
Of essence, too, was speed:
In the dreadnoughts, all these features were combined.

Innovation then would pause
And between the two world wars,
The emphasis would be upon disarming.
To the treaties, Britain sticks
But, by 1936,
The Nazi threat began to look alarming...

Two men, Arthur Pollen and Frederic Dreyer (1878–1956), worked independently on developing a mechanical computer to help improve the accuracy of gunnery. The work of the latter eventually prevailed with his Mark IV Fire Control Table. By the middle of the First World War, the addition of director control, and bigger optical range finders, meant most RN ships had a decent fire control system.

Many of the ideas of Captain (later Admiral) Sir Percy Moreton Scott (1853–1924) were eventually implemented, despite the Navy's conservatism and resistance to change. Scott was able to put his theories into practice when he was given command of HMS *Scylla* – the third ship of that name (for the fifth, see verse 1634).

See section/verses 1329–1336 **The Birth of the Fleet Air Arm**.

Initially, the angle of most guns was limited to 45° but some had a 70° elevation. The first aggressive firing of a self-propelled torpedo was by HMS *Shah* in 1877 (see verse 862). Torpedo boats, from which these could be fired, also came into being. The first (1878) was HMS *Lightning*, built by John Thornycroft in Chiswick.

See verses 1324–1325 (dreadnought) and section/verses 1440–1446 **Inter-War Naval Arms Agreements**.

The *Challenger* Expedition, 1872–76

Lying now beneath the waves
Are countless seamen's graves,
And chilly waters skeletons embrace.
But is there something more
On that secret sunken floor?
Or is it just a cold and lifeless place?

Two biologists insist,
That *something* might exist –
The darkness and high pressure notwithstanding.
The government agreed
To the funding they would need,
And human knowledge soon would be expanding.

This project set in motion
The study of the ocean.
Prior to then, there'd been no surveys far from shore.
Scientists would reap,
Many life forms from the deep,
And find creatures which had not been seen before.

Their borrowed navy ship
They'd been careful to equip,
With microscopes and other apparatus.
Some of this comprised
Items specially devised,
Because the venture had such novel status.

That the depths of the ocean were lifeless, had long been held to be the case. The mission was proposed by two biologists – Professor William Benjamin Carpenter and Charles Wyville Thomson, who had surveyed the North Atlantic in 1868, aboard paddle steamer HMS *Lightning*. The trip was very expensive (more than £10 million in today's money), and the government balked at funding a second expedition.

The venture began the science of oceanography. Small scale expeditions in the North Sea and around Scandinavia had led to the discovery of 'new' creatures, and fossil evidence of extinct life forms. Added to Darwin's theories (see verse 894), this had prompted great excitement, and the *Challenger* project attracted huge public interest and pride.

HMS *Challenger* was a steam-assisted Royal Navy corvette – an armed fighting ship smaller than a frigate. All but two of her 18 guns were removed prior to the expedition.

Temperatures were taken at various depths with thermometers, which could take maximum and minimum recordings. The crew also tested the reversing thermometer, which can measure temperature at specified depths. There were dredges and trawls to collect specimens.

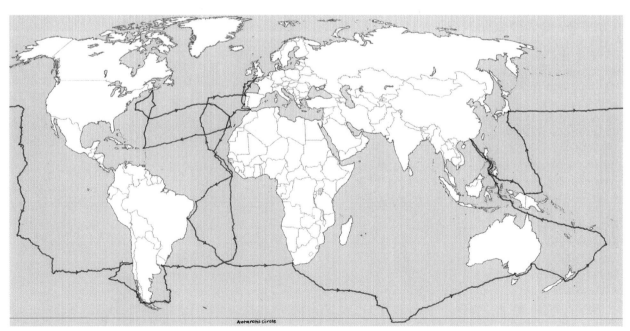

The route of the *Challenger* Expedition, 1872–76

There were miles and miles of rope,
Plenty long enough to cope
With enormous depths that needed to be sounded.
A platform was in place.
Plus laboratory space;
And bottles, jars, and alcohol abounded.

There is J.J. Wild (an artist),
Plus five scientists – the smartest –
Who take soundings in the various positions.
Though at first excitement's soaring,
The routine becomes quite boring,
But they're entertained between times by musicians.

At three sixty different stations,
They performed investigations,
And found the deepest place on planet Earth.
The ocean bed was rife,
With many forms of life:
Of new species there was certainly no dearth.

The Further Development of Oceanography

As we've seen, the day has dawned:
Oceanography's been spawned!
(It's been around a while, though not as such).
Though their knowledge had big gaps,
Men assessed winds and drew maps...
But maybe even now, we don't know much.

This broad subject is designed
For the scientific mind:
In the study of the sea, such satisfaction.
Its chemistry, geology...
Its physics and biology...
All such facets, and their complex interaction.

It's with how the sea behaves –
The currents, tides, winds, waves –
That this discipline has such a strong affinity.
Where warm water meets with cold,
It forms energy we're told,
And the same applies with changes in salinity.

Not so long ago,
Taking measurements was slow:
For assessing depth, long weighted ropes were needed.
Soon the seabed could be mapped,
If by sound waves it was zapped,
(Single sonar beams have now been superseded).

In addition to the inevitable rum for the crew, alcohol was needed to preserve specimens.

The scientific team included a Belgian geologist and a German naturalist. Such international collaboration has remained an important part of oceanography. As well as an artist, there was also a photographer, who had his own darkroom. Collecting, recording, cataloguing and storing specimens became tedious, and was physically hard work for the crew, 61 of whom deserted.

For entertainment, *Challenger* had its own band. There were also various pets – including ostriches, spiders and tortoises – aboard.

Earth's deepest place is in the south-west Pacific (sample station number 225), which is now named the Challenger Deep.

More than 4,000 previously unknown species were collected. These are now in the Natural History Museum, London, and are still studied today.

'What? Two thousand fathoms and no bottom!'

Robert the Parrot, bought by *Challenger*'s crew from a ship docked in Madeira

---

HMS *Challenger* under sail, 1874

Sir John Murray, who took part in the *Challenger* Expedition, and later surveyed the North Atlantic (1910), is considered to be 'the Father of modern oceanography'.

The Gulf Stream was first identified in 1513. William Dampier (see verses 415–416) collected data on currents, tides and winds. James Cook (see verse 584) gathered information on currents in the Pacific Ocean. British geographer James Rennell (1742–1830) has a channel named after him, following his studies of Scilly Island currents. Sir James Clark Ross (see verse 1278) took the first modern deep sea sounding in 1840. Robert FitzRoy (see verses 896–898) was a weather pioneer. Edward Forbes undertook dredging in the Aegean (1841–2), thereby founding marine ecology.

Britain's National Oceanography Centre was opened in April 2010. It comprises the National Oceanography Centres at Southampton and at Liverpool. The latter's origins date back to 1840, when it was established as the Proudman Oceanographic Laboratory (POL).

The use of sonar for bathymetry first began in the early 1930s. New multi-beam technology, introduced in the last 25 years, enables an even more accurate picture.

The Great London Dock Strike, 1889

We've met those who rode the waters.
There were coopers, and deal porters,
(Who handled wood, and put it into stacks),
The tallymen notched figures,
There were stevedores and riggers,
And the many who lugged barrels, crates and sacks.

With more new docks on the go,
Sometimes business could be slow,
And the peaks and troughs weren't easy to predict.
Shipments came in as and when:
Each consignment needed men,
Who would turn up with the hope of being picked.

They were called on as required
And, some days, would not be hired.
No work = no pay = no certainty in life.
For these 'casuals' this meant,
There was mounting discontent,
In an area where poverty was rife.

Then the match girls went on strike,
(There's a pun here if you like!)
Their demands were met. A decent deal was struck.
Their conditions had been dire,
And this outcome would inspire
All those hard up unskilled men to try their luck.

Their major strike was born,
When a bonus was withdrawn.
The company had cut this well-earned perk.
The dock owners' position
Was to starve into submission,
Those who'd had the nerve to say they wouldn't work.

Two weeks later many others,
Had staunchly joined their brothers,
In a rapid, and soon widespread escalation.
A committee supervised.
The docks were paralysed,
And the ship owners were voicing their frustration.

Both sides refuse to shift.
Then a huge financial gift
From Australia, helps the dockers to stand firm.
The power that they now wield
Forces companies to yield,
And decisive is the turning of the worm.

See verses 599–600 for lightermen and watermen.

Deal porters were nicknamed 'Blondins' after a famous acrobat, because they needed a head for heights. There were other specialised porters such as those who handled corn. Stevedores were responsible for putting cargo into ships: considerable skill and knowledge were required to ensure a balanced load. The stevedores were top of the unofficial hierarchy of dockers, and their union supported the strike .

See verses 600–601 for new docks.

The capacity of the docklands began to outstrip demand. There was also a worldwide price recession referred to as 'The Great Depression' (1873–1896). In a period of four successive weeks during 1861, the West India Dock handled 42, 131, 209 and 85 ships. The 'call on' system operated twice a day, and labourers might be taken on for just a few hours. According to the manifesto issued by the Stevedores' Union in support of the strike, dock labourers worked an average of only 3 hours a day. Although unskilled labourers were joining trade unions in increasing numbers, in 1888 only about 5 per cent of the national labour force were members, and these tended to be skilled workers.

In 1888, industrial action was taken at the Bryant & May match factory.

The dock strike began on 14 August 1889, triggered by the non-payment of 'plus money' for the speedy unloading of the *Lady Armstrong* at the West India Docks. Following the stevedores' lead, the strikers were joined by carmen (drivers of horse-drawn carts), seamen, firemen, rope makers, fish porters, lightermen, watermen and others working in East End factories and workshops.

Key members of the strike committee were Ben Tillett, Tom Man and John Burns.

In support of the strike, the first instalment of £150 was from the Brisbane Wharf Labourers' Union. In all, £30,000 was raised by Australian dockers (and other sympathizers, including cabinet ministers).

The Lord Major of London formed the Mansion House Committee to resolve the dispute.

Almost all the dockers' demands were met. The men returned to work on 16 September 1889.

> We are driven into a shed, iron-barred from end to end, outside of which a foreman or contractor walks up and down with the air of a dealer in a cattle market, picking and choosing from a crowd of men, who, in their eagerness to obtain employment, trample each other under foot, and where, like beasts, they fight for the chances of a day's work.
>
> **Ben Tillett, from *A Brief History of the Dockers' Union* (1910)**

The Antarctic

There is growing fascination
With a landmass, whose location
Is at the world's most southerly extreme.
Captain Cook had come quite close,
Now this cold place will engross
Certain others, who all focus on one dream.

Bransfield was delighted
When an icy shelf he sighted,
But another's exploration was synchronic.
Land a Russian also saw,
A mere two days before!
The timing of these glimpses was ironic.

For – a long long time ago –
(Two millennia or so),
This vast expanse of ice was first suggested.
To be then 'pipped at the post'
As the first to see this coast,
Cannot have been that easily digested.

So the ancient Greeks prove correct:
They were quite right to suspect
A 'balanced' Earth. This clever supposition
As true has been confirmed:
'The Antarctic' (as now termed)
Must be checked out, so 'Let's send an expedition!'

Appointed as the boss,
Was a man named James Clark Ross,
The ships that sailed well suited to thick ice.
Bomb vessels had been chosen:
They could cope with 'deeply frozen',
So the *Erebus* and *Terror* should suffice.

Then in interest there's a lull.
It is thought, 'The place is dull,
There's nothing there we need to ascertain.
It's boring. Lacks variety,'
Decreed the Royal Society.
But after sixty years, they think again.

The 'Heroic Age of Antarctic Exploration'

Science... exploration...
In this untouched destination,
Are what these learnéd folk are busy planning.
With these purposes in mind,
A ship has been designed:
Discovery is now in need of manning.

On Cook's second voyage, (see verses 580 & 584), he travelled south of the Antarctic Circle on three occasions, but never went far enough to sight land.

Irish born Royal Navy officer Edward Bransfield (c.1785–1852) had previously been involved in the Bombardment of Algiers (see verses 742–748). He had also been appointed to survey the South Shetland Islands, which are in the South Atlantic, following their discovery (1819) by merchant trader William Smith.

Russian explorer Fabian Gottlieb von Bellingshausen recorded a glimpse of icy shoreline on 28 January 1820, and is therefore generally credited with the discovery of the continent. Bransfield's first sighting was two days later on 30 January 1820.

Matthew Flinders had concluded that what was then called Terra Australis didn't exist (see verse 591).

Francis Beaufort (see verse 897) was a supporter of the idea of an expedition.

Sir James Clark Ross (1800–1862) was also an Arctic explorer. His first voyage had been with his uncle (Sir John Ross) in 1818. This was in search of the Northwest Passage (see verses 274 & 586).

A strong hull is useful in tough conditions. Two Antarctic volcanoes are named after *Erebus* and *Terror* (see verse 1320). For bomb vessels, see verse 174.

The new planned expedition was a joint enterprise with the Royal Geographical Society (RGS).

The Southern Cross Expedition (1898–1900) was the first British financed venture. It was led by the Anglo-Norwegian explorer Carsten Borchgrevink. The expedition was organized by a joint committee of the Royal Society and the RGS.

RRS (Royal Research Ship) *Discovery* is now a museum ship in Dundee, where she was constructed. She was the last traditional three-masted ship to be built in Britain, had auxiliary steam engines, and a rudder and propeller that could be hoisted out of the way to prevent ice damage.

So who will join the team
To the southerly extreme?
(A few of those they'd thought of were too old).
There are two, of whom you've heard,
Whose enthusiasm's stirred,
And both are very keen to be enrolled.

Ernest Henry Shackleton (1874–1922)

Restless scholars such as he,
Who want to go to sea,
Must train for this and need to choose a way.
Naval college is one route
But it costs a lot of loot,
And Ernest's father can't afford to pay.

For a lad of just sixteen,
The mercantile marine
Has training ships, to which he might be suited.
The *Worcester*'s one of these,
But it also charges fees.
As a shipping line apprentice he's recruited.

The young man surely hopes,
He will quickly 'learn the ropes',
And he isn't slow in proving his potential.
Next he does a Cape Town run...
Ferries troops, and meets the son
Of someone who is very influential.

Scott and the *Discovery* Expedition, 1901–04

Ernest claimed the title master.
Robert Scott's way had been faster.
His family had prospered thanks to beer.
But tradition was ingrained.
As an officer he'd trained,
And Dartmouth's where he started his career.

Though Scott's background was fortuitous,
His progress less circuitous,
Both men found they needed to pull strings.
They had each made their petition,
To join the expedition,
For adventure was there waiting in the wings.

To commander rank promoted,
As leader, Scott is voted.
And Ernest is responsible for stores.
With a chance to make their mark
To great cheering they embark,
And head for the Antarctic's chilly shores.

Shackleton was born in Ireland, but his family moved to London when he was ten. His father was a relatively newly qualified doctor, and not well off. His younger brother Frank was a suspect (later exonerated) in the 1907 theft of Ireland's Crown Jewels.

The Admiralty loaned HMS *Worcester* as a training ship for the Thames Marine Officer Training School (opened 1861). Its Mersey rival was HMS *Conway*. For training ships, see verses 557–558.

Shackleton's father secured for him an apprenticeship 'before the mast' with the North Western Shipping Company.

'Learning the ropes' is almost certainly a nautical saying (see verses 666–669) from the days of sail, although there is a suggestion that it might be theatrical in origin.

In 1898, Ernest attained master mariner status, which entitled him to command a British ship anywhere in the world. He met Cedric Longstaff whilst serving on a troopship during the Boer War, and used this acquaintance to contact Cedric's father, Llewellyn W. Longstaff, who was the main financial backer of the National Antarctic Expedition.

Robert Falcon Scott (1868–1912) was born near Devonport. His father owned a small brewery in Plymouth. His grandfather and four of his uncles had served in the army or in the navy.

Preparatory to his entrance examinations for the training ship HMS *Britannia* at Dartmouth, Robert had first been sent to Stubbington House School in Hampshire. He passed out of *Britannia* as a midshipman in 1883. Scott followed up a chance encounter with Sir Clements Markham, President of the RGS, by visiting him at home and volunteering to lead the expedition. Markham was himself an Arctic explorer and a navy man. He fought hard against opposition from the scientific community to secure Scott's appointment.

Following the sale of the brewery and the death of Robert's only brother, the Scott family's circumstances had deteriorated. Whereas during wartime there were plenty of opportunities in the navy for advancement, this was not the case during the more peaceful Victorian era.

Shackleton was third officer on the *Discovery* Expedition, and in addition to his other duties, was responsible for entertainment. Second officer was Albert Armitage.

Ernest Henry Shackleton   **Robert Falcon Scott, aged 13**

Within the ship's confines,
Things were run on naval lines,
Which most of those on board considered normal.
Shackleton concurred,
Though by nature he preferred
A regime that tended more towards informal.

After five long months spent swaying,
They arrive and start surveying,
Then drop anchor with a winter stay in mind.
It's discovered, come the spring,
They can't budge the wretched thing:
She's locked in ice and solidly confined.

They'd brought sledges, dogs and skis,
Plus a want of expertise
In using these resources to effect.
They had practised. Even so
They lacked prowess in the snow,
As a trio ever southwards slowly trekked.

The doc was getting nervy:
Men were showing signs of scurvy,
Some had frostbite, or their eyes were sore and blurry.
They needed meat for meals,
But Scott balked at killing seals
As these animals were much too cute and furry.

The dogs, all twenty-two,
Fail to see the long trip through,
But the record for the 'farthest south's' attained.
Stuff is mainly hauled by hand,
Across the frozen land.
Relationships, some said, got rather strained.

But at least all three survived.
A relief ship has arrived.
The *Discovery*'s still well and truly stuck.
Shackleton is ill,
He's sent home, against his will.
Others stay a second year and ride their luck.

This time, their dogged quest
Takes them further to the west.
To blizzards, slips and falls they might succumb.
On this dodgiest of sallies,
They find strangely snow-free valleys,
And are forced to find their way by rule of thumb.

The majority of the crew had been released from the Royal Navy but some, like Shackleton, had served in the merchant marine. Scott asked his team to agree voluntarily to work under the Naval Discipline Act (see verse 545).

Shackleton deemed the *Discovery* a bad sailer. She had a flat shallow hull, designed to work well in ice, but her stability in open seas was poor.

Scott, and on a second flight, Shackleton went up in a tethered observation balloon, from which they could see only a vast expanse of ice.

Scott, Shackleton and physician Edward Wilson (1872–1912) headed south with a supporting party. Shackleton collapsed with scurvy (see verses 313 & 380–383) on the way back. Unlike humans, animals can process vitamin C (which had not yet been discovered as a means of preventing scurvy), and fresh meat is therefore helpful in treating the disease. Some in the party suffered from snow blindness.

The dog food had become contaminated.

Their 'furthest south' was reached on 30 December 1902.

On the return journey, they were relaying half their supplies forward, then going back for the rest, thereby tripling the distance travelled.

There are accounts of a rift between Scott and the more popular Shackleton, but other evidence refutes this.

The relief ship was the *Morning*. *Discovery* eventually had to be freed by means of controlled explosives.

The Scottish National Antarctic Expedition (1902–04), overshadowed by the *Discovery* Expedition, completed its allotted programme of work, including the establishment of a manned weather station of dry stone construction.

The party's navigational tables blew away in a gale during the westwards expedition.

The *Discovery* in the Antarctic

For the cold place Ernest's yearning,
And dreams only of returning.
On the *Nimrod* trip, he has one major goal.
Successful he is not,
Though his teams achieve a lot,
And one made it to the south's magnetic pole.

The *Terra Nova* Expedition, 1910–13

The quest is not yet over,
And aboard the *Terra Nova*,
Scott sets sail upon his second chilly mission.
Maybe Shackleton's near miss
Was the impetus for this.
This time, there's Norwegian competition.

Roald Amundsen went forth,
On the basis he'd head north,
But supposedly that pole had been attained.
So en route he 'changed his mind':
Leaving scientists behind
He travelled south, completely unconstrained.

On his well thought out excursion,
He allows for no diversion.
He can focus his attention on this quest.
(He'd already scored one 'first':
Had successfully traversed
The Northwest Passage, going east to west).

But Scott's *not* gone all that way
With no other part to play:
There are eggs to find and readings to be taken.
Of his team he can't ask more:
They collect specimens galore.
Not one single scientific goal's forsaken.

Scott's already been apprised,
That Roald's plans have been revised.
As his rival's heading south with no compunction,
The ponies Scott's recruited,
To their task seem quite ill-suited,
And his sledges, which are mechanised, don't function.

Of supplies there is a lack,
So the dogs are all sent back.
On the final stage, five men their sledges drag.
At last the pole's in sight,
But the scene is not all white.
That black speck Bowers sees is Norway's flag.

The aim of the *Nimrod* Expedition (1907–09) was to reach the South Pole. The party that reached the Magnetic Pole was led by geology professor Edgeworth David. See verse 1322 for claims of reaching the North Pole.

'The only comment he made to me about not reaching the Pole was "a live donkey is better than a dead lion, isn't it?" and I said, "Yes, darling, as far as I am concerned."'

Emily Shackleton reporting the only conversation she had on this subject with husband Ernest

The southern party on board the *Nimrod*, 1909

Roald Amundsen (1872–1928) telegrammed the scientists he had promised to collect in San Francisco, and told them not to bother. A meticulous planner, he had already traversed the Northwest Passage from the Atlantic to the Pacific (1903–06).

It was thought that studies of Emperor penguin embryos might provide clues to the evolutionary history of all birds. To reach the breeding colony, a trio (Cherry-Garrard, Bowers and Wilson) had to endure the dark Antarctic winter and conditions of −60°C.

Scott's dogs were a success, but there was insufficient food to enable them to undertake the entire journey.

Amundsen's team reached the South Pole on 14 December 1911. Scott's party arrived about five weeks later on 17 January 1912.

So cheerfully they'd started,
But this makes them feel downhearted.
Being first to reach the pole had clearly mattered.
They'd come second in the race,
And must now return to base –
A daunting trek when spirits have been shattered.

With eleven miles to go,
They're holed up in blinding snow.
Already Edgar Evans has succumbed.
The remaining four are weak.
Their prospects must be bleak.
They have little food. Extremities are numbed.

Of all memorable quotes,
Surely that of Captain Oates,
Who had gangrene in that chilly Antarctic clime,
Must count amongst the best.
He was hindering the rest,
So went outside, and said he'd be 'some time'.

The gallant, the heroic,
The dutiful, the stoic,
Those who think about the loved ones left behind,
Those who simply want to live
Now have nothing more to give…
Their writings show to death they are resigned.

The Imperial Trans-Antarctic Expedition, 1914–17

Back once more from the sub-zero,
Ernest found himself a hero,
Much honoured (also heavily in debt).
He began to feel constrained…
Though the Pole had been attained,
One major challenge hadn't been done yet.

To the Weddell Sea he's bound,
And thence McMurdo Sound:
The plans for this were far from embryonic.
Some had tried before and failed,
Ernest southwards blithely sailed
But his ship's name, the *Endurance*, proved ironic.

In an ice floe she got stuck,
And there followed more bad luck:
After drifting for ten months, her hull was battered.
This made her structure weak…
She started then to leak,
And 'abandon ship!' was all that really mattered.

The ill-fated party's final camp was just 11 miles short of One Ton Depot.
    Petty Officer Edgar Evans (1876–17 February 1912) was the first to perish.
The second was Army Captain Lawrence Oates (1880–17 March 1912).

Scott's group at the South Pole on 17 January 1912

As the name suggests, the first land crossing of the Antarctic continent was the aim of Shackleton's 1914 expedition.
    The Weddell Sea is named after British whaler James Weddell, who discovered it in 1823.

Endurance **trapped in pack ice**

Into action men were stirred:
What they needed was transferred
To the place on solid water where they camped.
And now the task in hand
Was to get to proper land.
The journey wasn't one which could be tramped.

When their ice floe broke in two,
There was not much they could do
But go by sea. The island that they found
Didn't meet with approbation:
It had little vegetation,
But at least beneath their feet was solid ground.

They made a shelter here,
But no shipping lane was near,
And the chance of being rescued was remote.
The place was inhospitable.
No cry for help transmittable,
So they started to adapt a little boat.

A South Georgia whaling station
Might represent salvation.
To get there, stormy seas must first be crossed.
Eight hundred miles and more,
Was the distance to the shore.
For fifteen days their vessel lurched and tossed.

They make landfall on the side
That isn't occupied.
So they must traverse the island now on foot.
It's mountainous, they'll cope
With just fifty feet of rope.
Three men set off. The other three stay put.

By an effort unsurpassed,
Habitation's reached at last,
But those left behind will have to be retrieved.
A Chilean tug was lent.
Off to 'Elephant' it went,
And a bunch of men were mightily relieved.

The Ross Sea Party

One further group was stranded
At Cape Evans they had landed.
A steam yacht, the *Aurora*, was their base.
(They'd laid depots. It transpired
These would never be required,
As the trans-Antarctic march did not take place).

Following the loss of *Endurance*, the attempt to reach a supply depot on foot failed, and a further camp was established.

After 5 days spent in three small boats, the 28 men reached Elephant Island.

The boat adapted for the journey to South Georgia was named the *James Chard*, after the expedition's main sponsor. Shackleton chose five others to accompany him on this hazardous trip.

The twenty-two men left behind on Elephant Island spent four and a half months there. Shackleton's initial attempts to reach them were blocked by ice floes, and they were eventually rescued by whaler and a borrowed tug.

The land crossing via the South Pole was not achieved until 1957, when British geologist Vivian Fuchs, with New Zealander Edmund Hillary leading the back-up party, achieved the feat.

As they did what they must do,
Their ship (with eighteen crew)
From her moorings, in a gale, had broken free.
In ice she was cocooned...
Leaving ten poor souls marooned,
The helpless vessel headed out to sea.

For three hundred days she drifted,
Till her frozen cladding shifted.
One month later, in New Zealand she'd arrive.
Repaired, she went once more
To Antarctica's bleak shore,
And rescued those who'd managed to survive.

Three had perished by that stage.
In a true 'heroic age'
Those who ventured met with hazardous conditions.
Sometimes progress was arrested,
As their transport was untested:
They lacked all that helped more recent expeditions.

We've met Shackleton and Scott
But some names have featured not:
They're lesser known but do deserve a voice.
Polar medals with four bars
Were awarded to two 'stars'.
Frank Wild was one, the other Ernest Joyce.

Arctic Exploration

The Arctic proved a draw,
For those wishing to explore.
John Franklin went in 1845.
Two years elapsed. No word
From the party had been heard.
Though his wife had hopes of finding him alive.

'We must search for him,' she pleaded,
And this didn't go unheeded.
The quest became a very big crusade.
All had perished – that was plain –
In this icy cold terrain.
Unrewarded were the efforts that were made.

The North Pole still eluded.
No boot print there intruded –
The claims of two Americans disputed.
To that view, we must incline
For in 1969,
'Wally' Herbert reached it. That can't be refuted!

Aurora finally cleared the pack of ice after drifting for 312 days, and covering a distance of about 1,840 miles. On the rescue mission, Shackleton was aboard as a supernumerary officer.

Wild and Joyce were the only two British explorers to be awarded the Polar Medal with four bars.

Sir John Franklin (1786–1847) was a Royal Navy officer and former Lieutenant Governor of Tasmania. He disappeared during an expedition to the Northwest Passage. He was in command of HMS *Terror*, and the second ship was HMS *Erebus* (see verse 1278). Both became trapped in ice. *Erebus* was found, upright and intact on the ocean floor, in 2014. *Terror* was discovered in 2016. She was in pristine condition.

More ships and men were lost in the search than on the original expedition. Franklin and his party were presumed to still be alive for several years after the last contact, and he was promoted to Rear Admiral of the Blue in 1852.

Two Americans claimed to have walked to the North Pole – Robert Peary (1909) and Frederick Cook (a year earlier). It is unlikely that they succeeded. The first person confirmed to have reached it overland was British explorer Sir Walter William 'Wally' Herbert (1934–2007) on 6 April 1969, (the same year as the first moon landing).

In 1926, Roald Amundsen flew over the North Pole in an airship.

10 Into the twentieth century

10

Into the twentieth century

The Anglo-German naval arms race

The Kaiser has ambitions,
And new German ships commissions:
His stock of vessels starts to look impressive.
He is acting so imperiously,
The British take him seriously,
Suspecting that his motives are aggressive.

Any challenge to our might,
Is considered far from right,
For our navy is what keeps this country great.
As the High Seas Fleet's expanding,
The public are demanding
Eight dreadnoughts, and they aren't prepared to wait.

These battleships outclassed
All the others from the past,
Their big guns had the power to fire long distance.
They were what we seemed to need;
The government agreed,
In accordance with the barrage of insistence.

Thus begins a naval race.
Wilhelm can't keep up the pace,
And his army needs investment, what is more.
But his submarine production,
(Highly secret this construction),
Will accelerate, the year we go to war.

That these vessels pose a threat,
Britain won't believe just yet.
They're a menace only Fisher would distinguish.
In this he proves quite shrewd,
But by others subs are viewed
As 'underhand', and also 'damned un-English'.

With no evaluation,
We adopt one innovation.
Our 'dazzle painted' ships looked very strange.
The aim was to confuse.
Weird designs the Brits would use,
To make it hard to gauge a target's range.

Between 1898–1912, Grand Admiral von Tirpitz oversaw expansion of the German High Seas Fleet.

Reviews of the fleet became a cultural part of the arms race. They were used to demonstrate the strength of the navy to potential enemies, eg to the Kaiser in 1889.

Fleet reviews have also been used to celebrate victories (eg in 1693), mark coronations (1820) and jubilees (1887).

The public's mantra in demanding dreadnoughts was, 'We want eight and we won't wait'.

In 1906 Britain's first dreadnought was built. It was very advanced, although other ships were kept in service.

In 1912, Winston Churchill was appointed First Lord of the Admiralty. In the same year, Germany proposed a fleet of 33 battleships and battle-cruisers. Churchill's response was to accelerate the Royal Navy's building programme. Five *Queen Elizabeth* class battleships (super-dreadnoughts), and five *Revenge* class battle-cruisers were ordered (1912–13).

John 'Jacky' Fisher (1841–1920) was First Sea Lord (1904–11 and 1914).

Admiral Sir Arthur Wilson condemned submarines as 'underhand, under water and damned un-English'.

The aim of dazzle painting was also to make it more difficult for the enemy to judge speed and vessel type. The efficacy of this tactic is uncertain. See image/page 1414–1420.

RETROSPECTIVE SUMMARY OF THE DREADNOUGHT DEBATE

'The Admiralty demanded six, the Treasury said we could only have four, so we compromised on eight.'

Winston Churchill

HMS *Dreadnought*, 1906

The Birth of the Fleet Air Arm

The navy's taken flight!
It is testing Cody's kite,
Which this showman from America designed.
Could a man, up in the air,
Do signalling from there?
Or determine if the waters had been mined?

Could the sea be photographed?
On a Zeppelin type of craft
Made in Barrow were the navy's hopes next pinned.
But this airship never flew:
Poor *Mayfly* broke in two,
After lurching in a sudden gust of wind.

Winston Churchill, unimpressed,
Thought that 'heavy' planes were best
And of 'hydro' types was also a supporter.
Trials on England's largest lake,
Had shown what it would take
For both lift off, and a landing made on water.

Aviation was still new,
And the strange machines men flew
Were basic wood-and-fabric types of craft.
Though in stunts they could be agile,
One can only call them fragile;
Their potential use in war considered daft.

Into tiny cockpits cramped,
With their spirits quite undamped,
Squeeze the brave (or else the fearless 'what the heck').
Then dawns a milestone day:
From a ship that's under way,
A plane's launched from a platform on her deck.

Inching closer now to heaven,
From the year 1911,
Officers began to learn to fly.
To keep our land from harm,
Soon the navy grew an arm
And was master both of sea, and of the sky.

For, just one short month before
The whole world went to war,
The 'RNAS' branch came into being.
To which Murray Fraser Sueter,
(Pioneering aviator),
Was appointed, with the task of overseeing.

Samuel Franklin Cody (1867–1913) developed a manned 'war kite', which the Navy tested in 1903.

In 1909, £35,000 was allocated to the Admiralty for the building of a 'dirigible balloon'. This was designed and built by Vickers, and broke up in 1911 as it was being taken out of the hangar for its first trial flight. Churchill was unenthusiastic about airships, and favoured 'heavier than air' military planes.

The so-called 'hydro-aeroplanes' were the forerunners of seaplanes.

In November/December 1911, an adapted plane had taken off from water, and another had landed on water at Sheerness.

Captain Edward Wheatcroft had been conducting experiments on Lake Windemere since 1908.

In 1912, Lieutenant Wilfred Parke RN accidentally discovered how to recover from a spin. The manoeuvre was known as the 'Parke Dive'. The first 'loop de loop' was performed by a Russian in 1913.

In the earliest planes, there was no room for a parachute, so it was impossible to bail out.

The first take-off from a ship was in 1912. Piloted by Lt Charles Rumney Samson, the plane took off from a wooden platform that had been installed on the foredeck of HMS *Hibernia*.

The first naval flying training course was run at Eastchurch, a place later established (1912) as the naval flying school. At this time, the only qualification awarded was the Certificate of the Royal Aero Club.

The responsibilities of the Navy's new air arm included the protection of London from Zeppelin bombing attacks. Failure to prevent these resulted in much criticism.

The Royal Naval Air Service (RNAS) came into being on I July 1914. It was one of two branches of the Royal Flying Corps (RFC), which had been established in 1912. The other branch belonged to the British Army. More accurately, Sueter was a pioneer in aviation, rather than a pilot.

'The airplane is useless for the purposes of war' (quote by an unknown General).

It exists not quite four years,
Then the RAF appears;
The navy lost control and got frustrated.
But things improved once more
When, in 1924,
It was ordered the Fleet Air Arm be created.

The Dogger Bank Incident, 1904

The Russian Empire sought
A nice warm water port:
Control of one in China was the plan.
But the dream was not to be.
A surprise attack by sea,
Resulted in a war against Japan.

Russia surely must prevail:
From the Baltic ships set sail,
To Far Eastern waters ultimately heading.
From the outset, crews were scared…
For the worst must be prepared:
Torpedo boats were what these men were dreading.

Had these Russians lost the plot?
Were they paranoid or what?
'Everywhere,' they thought, 'lurk Japanese.'
Who'd laid minefields to be missed,
(These did not, of course, exist),
Having sneaked unseen from home to northern seas!

So real danger must be faced
When a fishing fleet (Hull based),
Was sighted in a place called Dogger Bank.
This the Russians start attacking,
Though their aiming skills were lacking.
Many shells were fired, but just one trawler sank.

Those Hull boats weren't alone –
Russians also shot their own!
Their ineptitude beyond all comprehension.
Colossal was this blunder,
And it isn't any wonder
That the consequence was diplomatic tension.

As their fleet went on its way
The 'foe' was kept at bay.
The neurosis clearly hadn't been assuaged.
They were thus inclined to shoot
Any suspect craft en route:
And three more harmless 'warships' were engaged.

The RAF was established 1 April 1918. By then, the RNAS had become a large organisation, with more than 55,000 officers and men, almost 3,000 aircraft and 126 naval air stations. The Fleet Air Arm (FAA) was a branch of the RAF. In 1937, the Admiralty regained administrative control and, in 1939, full control. It was re-named the 'Air Branch' and reverted to being the FAA in 1952.

The Russian port of Vladivostok was only operational during the summer months. Russia wanted a Pacific port that was open all year round, and Port Arthur on the Yellow Sea, which it had been leasing from China, met that requirement. Russia then found itself competing with the expansionist ambitions in this area of the emerging Empire of Japan.

Russia's Baltic Fleet was dispatched to the Pacific via the North Sea, where the Gamecock fishing fleet was attacked. Its 48 vessels were believed to be Japanese torpedo boats. They were sitting targets because their nets had been cast and they couldn't flee. The trawler *Crane* was sunk. Her captain and first mate were killed, and another injured sailor died some months later.

Three further vessels were subsequently attacked by the Russians: a Swedish merchantman, a German trawler and a French schooner.

When real fighting did get going,
Very poor was Russia's showing:
She was beaten comprehensively and fast.
A new star was emerging,
(In the end, this would need purging),
And the western powers observed events aghast.

Transition to oil-powered ships

When steam supplanted sails,
It was boom time for South Wales.
New docks were built and others were extended.
But a 'new' fuel's day is dawning.
We heed Jacky Fisher's warning:
A switch to oil was what he recommended.

(The demand for coal still soared:
Tons and tons were sent abroad
To places where their own reserves were few.
Though to oil our navy turned,
Elsewhere Welsh coal was burned,
And in consequence the port of Cardiff grew.)

Coal won't instantly combust,
But it makes a lot of dust...
It takes up space, and loading's a commotion.
Ships with motors go more quickly
Oil, through pipes, runs nice and slickly,
Which means vessels can refuel whilst on the ocean.

Much less smoke would be emitted,
From the turbines that are fitted,
The advantages are numerous and clear.
No stokers are required,
To keep the engines fired,
Though the downside is – we don't produce oil here!

But its age has come to pass:
Five new dreadnoughts (*QE* Class)
Run on liquid fuel, eclipsing all their peers.
With the coal-to-oil conversion,
We sign up with Anglo-Persian,
In a secret deal that runs for twenty years.

Moving oil in wooden casks
Ain't the easiest of tasks:
Barrels are so heavy and can leak.
They add greatly to expense,
So it really does make sense,
To look for an alternative technique.

The Russian Fleet was not allowed to go through the Suez Canal, or to stop at neutral ports to refuel. It eventually reached its destination via the Cape of Good Hope, having coaled at sea (see verse 652). The newly-formed Soviet Union would regain control of Port Arthur after the Second World War (until 1953).

The new Welsh docks included, for example, Swansea's new Prince of Wales dock on the River Tawe (completed 1909).

Fisher was a self-proclaimed 'oil maniac' from as early as 1886. During the Anglo-German naval arms race, he was convinced (wrongly) that the Germans were developing oil-fuelled ships.

The transition to oil was a slow and lengthy process, which helped sustain the demand for coal. Unlike oil, coal won't explode if hit by a torpedo – an advantage during wartime.

Refuelling underway obviated the need for lengthy stops at coaling stations (see verse 970). It is estimated that, at any one time, a quarter of British ships had stopped for refuelling. Fisher argued that oil-powered ships would be able to outpace German vessels, and that speed would be increased by dispensing with armour.

The 5 *Queen Elizabeth* battleships were commissioned between 1915 and 1916. Their immediate predecessors were the *Iron Duke* class ships, four of which were built.

The Dutch Shell Group was the alternative oil supplier. Anglo-Persian, the forerunner of which was Burmah Oil (see verse 886), was a smaller company.

Bulk container distribution
Is the obvious solution,
Though achieving this has certain complications.
The cargo and its fumes
Must be kept from engine rooms,
Or else there might be fearsome conflagrations.

Oil expands and it contracts.
It's combustible. These facts
Must be thought through when producing a design.
The first two ships with tanks,
Were built upon the banks
Of northern England's famous River Tyne.

With our government as bankers,
Anglo-Persian buys some tankers,
And a dedicated fleet soon roams the sea.
In 1954,
Its name is used no more,
For that was when it turned into BP.

These days, your average boater
Has a vessel powered by motor:
The first diesel one dates back to 1912.
But more use of LNG
In the future we shall see,
And other fuels we may decide to shelve.

Their emissions are quite high,
And that's the reason why
People favour all these 'cleaner burning' schemes.
(But it also is a fact,
Gas is costly to extract,
So nothing's as straightforward as it seems).

Panama Canal

One feat of engineering
Its conclusion has been nearing;
Long journeys need no longer now be borne.
This canal, so long projected,
Means two oceans are connected,
Which avoids the dodgy route around Cape Horn.

One in twenty freighter ships,
Through this handy shortcut slips.
It's a nine hour trip and saves a lot of fuss.
But the US had resolved
Britain shouldn't be involved:
In the end the scheme had nought to do with us.

Built in 1863, the first two vessels with tanks were sailing ships.

In 1873 the first oil tank steamers were built for Belgian owners by Palmers in Jarrow.

The British Tanker Company (BTC) was formed in 1915 and its initial fleet comprised 7 ships, which were built by Tyne based shipbuilders – Armstrong Whitworth and Swan Hunter (see verses 1088–1089). Every tanker's name was prefixed 'British'.

Before becoming British Petroleum, Anglo-Persian had been renamed Anglo-Iranian Oil Company in 1935.

Most ships, with the exceptions of warships and icebreakers, are powered by diesel motors. The Danish cargo ship *Selandia* was the first ocean-going diesel motor vessel.

LNG = Liquified Natural Gas. Obtaining natural gas produces a lot of methane, which is harmful to the environment.

The Panama Canal was opened in 1914. In 1513, Spanish explorer Vasco Nuñez de Balboa (who gave his name to the district at the Pacific end of the canal) discovered that Panama was a slim land bridge and, in 1534, the Emperor Charles V commissioned a survey to find out whether a waterway could be built.

About 3 per cent of the world's freight traffic goes through the canal every year, but this is expected to double following the completion of the expansion programme (2016), which enables it to accommodate vessels three times the size it previously could. The canal, through the narrowest part of the Panama isthmus, is 51 miles long, and is the biggest man-made structure in the world. The comparative traffic figure for the Suez Canal, (see verses 1193–1195), is 7.5 per cent.

Britain and the USA were both parties to the original plans for a canal through Nicaragua. This idea has recently been revived by China, the major user (after America) of the Panama Canal.

First World War, 1914–18

There was no one single cause,
Of this 'war to end all wars',
Long and complex were the roots of altercation.
Several million lives were blighted,
Once the keg had been ignited
By a spark – an Archduke's shock assassination.

We'd been building up a fleet
Which the German threat could meet,
By keeping almost all her ships confined.
Thanks to Britain's strong blockade.
These in harbour mainly stayed.
The resources of the 'central powers' declined.

The German East Asia Squadron, 1914

But some ships von Spee commanded
Were in China – and were stranded!
He was wary of the might that was Japan.
In Tsingtao he had been based,
Now a long trip home was faced,
And some of it was 'catch us if you can'.

Once the Chinese port she's flown,
Emden sets off on her own
On a commerce raiding spree that really hurts.
Her hits include, alas.
The bombardment of Madras,
But finally, she gets her just deserts.

The others, with von Spee,
All head off the other way,
Inflicting damage as the seas they comb.
On their cross-Pacific trip,
They give allied ships the slip...
The plan was the Atlantic, and then home.

Near a place called Coronel,
A small squadron they will quell.
The Falklands is the next place on the list.
This time, they are ill-fated,
The odds against them weighted.
And most are sunk, unable to resist.

The phrase 'war to end all wars' was used by President Wilson when he addressed Congress on 2 April 1917.

On 28 June 1914, Archduke Franz Ferdinand, heir to the Austrian throne, was assassinated in Sarajevo.

Central powers Germany and Austria-Hungary were, like Britain, dependent on imported food and goods.

Vice Admiral Maximilian von Spee was in command of the German East Asia Squadron, based in an area where the powerful Royal Australian Navy also maintained a presence.

Under the command of Karl von Müller, light cruiser SMS *Emden* was detached for independent raiding in the Indian Ocean, where she captured almost two dozen ships.

Coronel is off the coast of Chile. The British squadron commander was Sir Christopher Cradock (1862–1914). 1,570 lives were lost, including Cradock's. Von Spee and both his sons were killed in the Battle of the Falklands (December 1914).

Other early naval actions

Now John Jellicoe let's meet,
He's in charge of our Grand Fleet.
As a 'moderniser', Churchill's views he shares.
But his caution when it mattered,
Left his reputation battered,
And resulted in his being 'kicked upstairs'.

An early confrontation
Caused the Kaiser consternation.
(The name of this engagement will not scan!)
So he told his High Seas Fleet,
'Don't confront what you can't beat,
But cause a bit of bother where you can.'

Our public were outraged,
When a coastal raid was staged;
Civilians died, towns subject to assault.
The shock left people reeling.
It fuelled anti-German feeling,
And a sense that Britain's navy was at fault.

By what he has destroyed,
Hipper's spirits have been buoyed
And – emboldened by this very nasty prank –
At a fishing fleet he'll aim,
But we've figured out his game,
And do battle with his ships at Dogger Bank.

To this scheme we have put paid.
He will quickly be dismayed
And surprised to find the British near at hand.
Blücher's sunk. The *Lion*'s maimed.
Though our victory's proclaimed,
There are lessons here we fail to understand.

Their ships are tough, well-armed...
Cannot readily be harmed...
Worse still they can out-hit us three to one.
Our communication's poor,
Which is something we ignore.
This will all come back to haunt us later on.

In February '16
Dogger Bank's once more the scene
Of a battle, and a British ship is fated.
She is but a little sloop,
Stands no chance when Germans swoop.
Their triumph would be much exaggerated.

John Rushworth Jellicoe (1859–1935) had fought in both the Egyptian War and the Boxer Rebellion. A supporter of modernising the fleet, he replaced Admiral George Callaghan, whom Churchill had removed. Jellicoe was extremely pessimistic about Britain's chances of being able to weather the German U-boat campaign.

See verses 1394–1395 for Jellicoe's decision in the Battle of Jutland.

The first naval battle of the First World War was the Battle of Heligoland Bight (August 1914), when Commodore Tyrwhitt (1870–1951) supported by David Beatty, (who had been sent by Jellicoe at the last minute), led a raid on a German patrol, sinking 4 German ships and damaging 3 others.

This British victory prompted an instruction from the German government and the Kaiser that their fleet should remain in port, and avoid further engagements against superior forces.

In December 1914, there were German attacks on Hartlepool, Whitby and Scarborough. (An earlier attack on Yarmouth in the previous month had prompted little reaction because the shells only landed on the beach.) In particular, significant damage was inflicted on docks and factories in Hartlepool, where naval guns fired from land proved ineffectual. It has been suggested that Scarborough was regarded as 'defended', and that the main target was Scarborough Castle rather than the town.

These attacks were part of a plan to pick off British ships individually, and were led by Franz Ritter von Hipper. The Royal Navy was blamed for failing to prevent what happened.

German radio messages were being intercepted and decoded (see verses 1388–1390).

The Battle of Dogger Bank took place on 24 January 1915. The arrival of a German naval Zeppelin (rigid airship developed by the Germans in the early 20th century), and a seaplane (which attacked with small bombs), led to the abandonment of British efforts to rescue survivors from the stricken SMS *Blücher*.

Poor communication was exemplified by Flag Lieutenant Ralph Seymour's combining two signals (not meant to be read together) on one hoist. The misunderstanding this caused was not corrected until Rear Admiral Gordon Moore was too far away to read the revised instruction.

Although the Germans claimed to have sunk 2 cruisers, the sole casualty was HMS *Arabis*, part of a minesweeping flotilla (the rest of which managed to escape).

A minesweeper is a small warship equipped to counter the threat of naval mines and keep channels clear for other shipping.

Sir John Jellicoe, wearing the uniform of the Admiral of the Fleet, post 1919

The blockade of Germany's High Seas Fleet

It's not easy to sneak freight
Through the narrow Dover Strait,
But preventing this is not our whole campaign.
German shipping to encase,
We need another base:
In the North Sea, fleets are harder to contain.

It's a name that all will know.
We selected Scapa Flow.
Ideal this spot for holding Germans back.
Crews and ships to Orkney hurried,
Only one thing had us worried:
There's a chance that lethal U-boats will attack.

Our methods were assorted
To ensure that these were thwarted.
To catch them, submarine nets were in place.
Fences were constructed,
By which they'd be obstructed,
And blockships sunk nearby our naval base.

Only two attempts were made,
These precautions to evade.
A trawler rammed the first sub and it sank.
The second was ejected:
It had early been detected,
For which we have the hydrophone to thank.

This 'listening' machine,
Can pick up a submarine:
Using sonar the device can sort of 'hear'.
It proved worthy of the wait,
(In the war, this came quite late),
Ernest Rutherford, a major pioneer.

The Gallipoli Campaign, 1915–6

Russia's sea route was contested,
And the allies would be bested –
By the Ottomans the Dardanelles were claimed.
It was here the Turks prevailed,
Even though their empire ailed
And had been, as Europe's 'Sick Man', aptly named.

There are reasons to be thinking
That the nation fast was sinking,
That a once great power must slide into obscurity.
When the straits are first contested,
And our fleet is unmolested;
This gives the Brits a false sense of security.

The Straits of Dover were defended by British submarines and mines. Additionally, the Dover Patrol, plus a number of ships based at Portland Harbour, and the Harwich Force protected the approaches to the English Channel.

The decision that a northern naval base was needed had been taken in 1904. Two other sites (Rosyth and Invergordon) were considered before the Orkney location was chosen.

Sea level fences were built at the entrances to shallow ports. Minefields and artillery also reinforced the base.

A blockship is a vessel sunk deliberately either to stop an attacking enemy from getting in, or to prevent a defending enemy from getting out.

After being rammed by a trawler, *U-18* fled then sank (November 1914). *UB-116* was blown up by shore-triggered mines before it could enter the anchorage (October 1918).

Hydrophones enabled the convoys escorting merchant vessels to detect submarines. Conversely, they were the means by which submarines detected ships.

New Zealand born British physicist Ernest Rutherford (1871–1937) was known as 'the Father of nuclear physics'. The only patent he ever took out was for a hydrophone.

The German Fleet in Scapa Flow, November 1918

The Allies fighting the Turks were Britain, Russia and France.

The epithet 'The Sick Man of Europe' is usually attributed to Tsar Nicholas I of Russia.

The first British foray was by trawlers seeking mines. They were escorted by obsolete destroyers (considered unfit for use anywhere else). The Turks regarded these vessels as unworthy targets for their limited ammunition.

Allied access has been closed,
To which Churchill is opposed.
His belief – an easy win – will prove misguided.
He sends ships and submarines,
But our foe does not lack means,
(Including vessels Germany provided).

Winston's record has a stain:
The Gallipoli campaign.
It is ten months long, this battle of attrition.
Antipodean squads
Help this fight against the odds,
And ANZAC Day commemorates their mission.

The straits are full of mines,
All arranged in careful lines.
The trawlers sent to clear them aren't effective.
With the tactics Turks apply,
Our plan is all awry,
But then hindsight is a wonderful perspective.

Hospital ships

The whole world was involved,
In this war that little solved.
And far and wide is where troops have to be.
Their supplies and their equipment
Are, too, in need of shipment,
And all of it must go across the sea.

Wherever there is warring,
We have to be ensuring
That for sick and wounded men there is attention.
The ships, where care is meted,
Must respectfully be treated,
But Germany defies the Hague Convention.

As the rules are not respected
Torpedoes are ejected –
Aimed at causing these infirmaries to sink.
This mission is iniquitous,
And submarines ubiquitous.
There's no easy means of telling where they slink.

When a mine struck the *Britannic*,
(A sister of *Titanic*),
To lifeboats were some passengers transferred.
The captain hoped, meanwhile,
To reach a nearby isle.
With the engine at full power, propellers whirred...

The commander of the allied fleet was Vice Admiral (later Admiral) Sir Sackville Hamilton Carden (1857–1930).

Battleships, submarines, minesweepers, contingents of Royal Marines and an infantry division were sent by Britain. France sent a squadron, and Russia a light battle-cruiser. Germany had given Turkey two ships, including the battle-cruiser *Yavuz Sultan Salim* (formerly SMS *Goeben*), which was the most powerful operating in the Black Sea.

The Gallipoli landings took place in April 1915.

A battle of attrition is one in which an attempt is made to wear down the enemy.

The minesweeping trawlers had been hastily adapted, and were manned by North Sea fishermen (see verse 953).

The first hospital ship, *Goodwill*, was commissioned for the navy in 1608.

During the First World War, many passenger liners were converted for such use and, by the end of that war, 77 were operational.

The first Hague Convention was in 1899, and the second (to which the verse refers) in 1907. Rules governing hospital ships had also been formulated in the interim period. See verses 1396–1400 on unrestricted submarine warfare.

German submarines were operational in the Baltic, North Sea, Black Sea, Mediterranean and North Atlantic. In July 1915, the Admiralty set up the Board of Invention and Research to investigate ideas for dealing with submarines (Anti-Submarine Warfare or 'ASW'), and the RN established an Anti-Submarine Division in 1916.

German U-boat *UC-73* had laid the mine in the Aegean Sea which struck the *Britannic*. The Greek island of Kea was her intended destination, after she'd been damaged. The third sister ship was RMS *Olympic*, (all of the White Star Line).

Another hospital ship, HMHS *Braemar Castle*, struck a mine in the same area 2 days later, but did not sink, and returned to service after repair.

HMHS *Britannic* sinking

... Towards these, two boats headed...
Were sucked in, and quickly shredded.
To no worse a fate could anyone befall.
The *Britannic*'s seen no more.
She lies on the ocean floor –
Of the ships we lost, the biggest of them all.

Inadequate this verse:
Kate Beaufoy was a nurse,
Representing here all others of her kind.
To the wounded she once tended.
By a crime her life was ended,
But the diary that she kept was left behind.

The Battle of Jutland, 1916

The Kaiser's fleet's stagnating,
Which gets more and more frustrating.
The Germans thus devise another ploy.
For their naval strength to prove,
They would need to make a move,
And a portion of our naval strength destroy.

The scheme of trap, then shoot,
Was really quite astute:
Each battleship our enemy might hit,
Meant one fewer to confront.
They would then repeat this stunt,
And sink the British navy, bit by bit.

'Secret' messages were sent,
Which told of the intent
To sail out from their Saxony abode.
The Germans weren't aware
We'd been able to prepare,
That we had a useful copy of their code.

Those working in 'Room 40',
Had full knowledge of this sortie.
Our encryption team had got their whole plan sussed.
Our mission's the frustration
Of this covert operation,
As our fleet sets out to meet them as it must.

All had radios on board,
Though by some these were ignored.
The preference for flags was quite a joke.
Our warships, for a start,
Were much too far apart,
And the signalled message oft obscured by smoke.

Britannic sank 55 minutes after being struck. She has since been explored by divers. She was the largest British ship to be sunk during the First World War. Now that the Italian cruise ship *Costa Concordia* (that capsized in 2012) has been salvaged, *Britannic* is again the world's largest intact passenger ship wreck.

Kate Beaufoy was a member of the Queen Alexandra's Imperial Military Nursing Service. The Naval Nursing Service, introduced in 1883, had later been named after the queen (who was also its president). It remains the 'QARRNS'.

About 300 nurses serving on hospital ships were killed in WWI. Miss Beaufoy was lost presumed drowned in February 1918 when HMHS *Glenart Castle* was torpedoed by a U-boat and sunk – an act regarded as a war crime. She had previously served on HMHS *Dover Castle*, similarly sunk in June 1916. Her vividly written diary, along with her medals, were auctioned in August 2016 for £11,200.

The British Grand Fleet was supplemented by ships from the Royal Australian and Royal Canadian navies. It was too large for the Germans to hope to take on in one attempt.

The main German Fleet was based in Wilhelmshaven, Lower Saxony, in a bay known as Jade Bight (or Jade Bay).

The Germans knew that the appearance of a British squadron at Dogger Bank had not been a coincidence, but concluded that an enemy agent had betrayed their plan. They did not therefore realise that their wireless codes had been compromised.

The work of Room 40 was based on material captured from German vessels by the Russians, and by the Royal Australian Navy.

Radio was first used in the 1890s (see verse 1132).

British efforts had already been adversely affected by inter-ship communication problems and mishaps, following the German raid on east coast towns, and during the Battle of Dogger Bank.

Warships were now known as battleships or battle-cruisers. The latter were as big as battleships and carried the same guns, but they were faster because they were less heavily armoured.

Sir David Beatty, wearing the uniform of Vice Admiral, 1916

There were 'picket lines' in place,
U-boats detailed to erase
The British force, and have us running scared.
But these caused no hurly burly:
We had known to set off early.
They proved harmless, as they hadn't yet prepared.

Heavy losses we sustain,
In part one of this campaign
David Beatty's squadron's subject to attack.
When the Grand Fleet then engages,
A full-scale battle rages,
In which the British take a lot of flak.

Sad to tell you in this verse,
There's no doubt we came off worse,
But the outcome is described as 'inconclusive',
We can't resume next day,
For the foe have slipped away.
As ever, they have proved to be elusive.

They might have been pursued;
Erroneous or shrewd?
The fact we didn't chase them back to port?
But Jellicoe opines,
That we might encounter mines,
And he doesn't want to risk us getting caught.

Was he wrong or was he right,
Discontinuing the fight?
There have certainly been critics of the man.
Though he had his share of blame,
The result was just the same:
Supplies stayed blocked – exactly Britain's plan.

Unrestricted submarine warfare

Their fleet ventured little more,
But the next phase of the war,
Was the unrestricted use of submarines.
The prize rules are thus flaunted,
Though the Germans don't seem daunted,
Indiscriminately using these machines.

Whilst warships are fair game,
By decree it's not the same
For neutral craft and other miscellanea.
With merchant vessels, too,
First evacuate the crew.
But we'd seen what fate befell the *Lusitania*.

Four British battleships and two battle-cruisers were lost early on.

Vice Admiral Sir David Beatty (1871–1936) succeeded Jellicoe as Admiral of the Grand Fleet.

Aboard HMS *Chester*, 16-year-old John 'Jack' Travers Cornwell, although mortally wounded, continued to man his gun. He was posthumously awarded the Victoria Cross.

Mines were a real danger. By the end of 1915, they had resulted in the loss of ninety-four ships. Most were placed by German mine-laying *UC* class U-boats operating off Belgium.

Following the Battle of Jutland, German ships made a number of sorties, (including an attack by light surface ships on a British convoy in late 1917), but most proved futile, and two were abandoned altogether.

'U-boat' is the anglicised version of the German 'unterseeboot' (undersea boat). The terrible capability of U-boats had been demonstrated as early as 22 September 1914 with the sinking by a single submarine of three British cruisers – *Aboukir*, *Cressey* and *Hogue* – when 1,460 men were lost. The first U-boat sinking of a merchant ship, SS *Glitra*, took place on 20 October 1914 off the coast of Norway. This was handled in accordance with the prize rules, in that the crew were first let off the ship and into lifeboats.

UC-1 class German submarine, *c.*1915

RMS *Lusitania* at the end of her maiden trans-Atlantic voyage, New York City, September 1907

They didn't come much finer,
Than that famous ocean liner.
In luxury, the elegant could swank.
She was spacious. She was fast.
All her rivals were outclassed.
But then she was torpedoed and she sank.

O so fast this ship expired,
Just one missile was required,
Hitting starboard of the trans-Atlantic queen.
The USA deplored,
The loss of those on board,
But stayed neutral until 1917.

To keep his country out
Was what Wilson was about,
But with 'Zimmerman' his firm resolve had wilted.
The US troops he sent,
Would the allied force augment,
And the balance in our favour had now tilted.

It is in that very year,
Women sailors first appear,
Though their roles aren't as extensive as the men's.
They're allowed to cook and clean...
Work the telegraph machine...
These females soon are fondly known as wrens.

Their jobs were all on land
And, post-war, they would disband,
But were re-formed when again there was a need
For the second global war,
And again they stayed ashore.
Men for service out at sea were thereby freed.

RMS *Lusitania* sank in just 18 minutes on 7 May 1915, having been hit by a single torpedo, which caused a second explosion.

1,198 of the 1,959 passengers and crew died, mainly from drowning or hypothermia. Despite there being outrage at the loss of 128 Americans, the USA did not declare war on Germany until almost two years later.

Although President Woodrow Wilson had made substantial and favourable loans to both the British and the French, he was determined that the USA remain neutral.

By April 1917, US shipping in the North Atlantic had been hit. The Zimmerman Telegram (January 1917) contained a German proposal that Mexico should join an alliance with Germany, should the USA enter the war. It was intercepted and decoded by British Intelligence.

The WRNS (Women's Royal Naval Service) was first formed in 1917 and 7,000 women had joined up by the time it was disbanded in 1919. It was re-formed in 1939 and continued until 2003, when it was integrated into the Royal Navy. Its first president was Dame Katherine Furse (1875–1952), who also founded the VAD (Voluntary Aid Detachment).

The 'wrens' were sometimes known as 'jennies'.

Their motto in 1917 was 'Never at sea'. Dame Vera Laughton Mathews (1888–1959) headed up the service from 1939, and 36,000 women joined during the Second World War. Women didn't serve aboard ships until 1990.

As their sailors idly stewed,
Germans scavenged for their food,
And shortages caused civil agitation.
This in time forced our contender
Into ultimate surrender –
The other option's being mass starvation.

We too have mouths to feed,
And in consequence a need
To ensure that our supply routes keep on working.
The merchant ships and crew
Did their best to bring stuff through –
This is dangerous if submarines are lurking.

The U-boats were a scourge
Which was difficult to purge.
Their unrestricted use caused much destruction.
They weren't easy to avoid
And they couldn't be destroyed
If invisible. And so we try seduction.

The Q-boat is invented.
It is temptingly presented
As a target, all alone and unprotected.
On this helpless sitting duck,
A sub might try its luck,
Then face firepower which had never been suspected.

The *Baralong* incidents

The *Lusitania*'s fate,
Inspired a lot of hate
Towards those whose actions caused so much mortality.
Then the *Arabic* was downed.
No survivors could be found
By the *Baralong*, when searching the locality.

She next hurries to the scene
Where a German submarine
Had prompted *Nicosian*'s SOS.
Our Q-ship in disguise,
Takes the U-boat by surprise.
Shot, it's sinking, with survivors in distress.

'Take no prisoners' is the notion
Of men governed by emotion,
And the vengeful thoughts so recently engendered.
Our men shot the U-boat's crew
Which they weren't supposed to do,
As those hapless sailors clearly had surrendered.

By 1915, German imports had fallen from pre-war levels by 55 per cent. There was looting and rioting in some places, and German industries were also running short of materials.

U-boats were extremely effective against merchant ships, and there were really only two methods of attacking in return: shooting or ramming.

The *Baralong* was one such Q-boat. She flew the US ensign as a false flag to mislead enemy vessels.

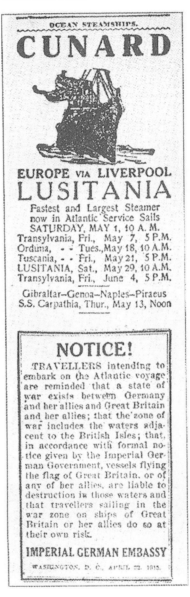

OCEAN STEAMSHIPS.
CUNARD

EUROPE VIA LIVERPOOL
LUSITANIA
Fastest and Largest Steamer
now in Atlantic Service Sails
SATURDAY, MAY 1, 10 A. M.
Transylvania, Fri., May 7, 5 P.M.
Orduna, - - Tues., May 18, 10 A.M.
Tuscania, - - Fri., May 21, 5 P.M.
LUSITANIA, Sat., May 29, 10 A.M.
Transylvania, Fri., June 4, 5 P.M.
Gibraltar—Genoa—Naples—Piraeus
S.S. Carpathia, Thur., May 13, Noon

NOTICE!
TRAVELLERS intending to embark on the Atlantic voyage are reminded that a state of war exists between Germany and her allies and Great Britain and her allies; that the zone of war includes the waters adjacent to the British Isles; that, in accordance with formal notice given by the Imperial German Government, vessels flying the flag of Great Britain, or of any of her allies, are liable to destruction in those waters and that travellers sailing in the war zone on ships of Great Britain or her allies do so at their own risk.
IMPERIAL GERMAN EMBASSY
WASHINGTON, D. C., APRIL 22, 1915.

White Star liner SS *Arabic* was sunk by *U-24* on 19 August 1915, with the loss of 44 lives. This attack, and their inability to find survivors, infuriated the *Baralong*'s crew.

British steamer *Nicosian*, apprehended by *U-27* when found to be carrying arms for the British Army, was being fired at.

After the U-boat had been mortally wounded, some of the crew were swimming, and others had made it to the *Nicosian*, where they were discovered and shot. This incident supposedly led to the Kaiserliche Marine's practising unrestricted submarine warfare. (Germany announced that its U-boats would engage in unrestricted submarine warfare on 31 January 1917.)

A second incident took place a month later when the *Baralong* sank *U-41*, and it was alleged that she had run down a German lifeboat.

Some viewed this as a crime.
It was not the only time
That our vessel for maltreatment would be blamed.
Linked twice with doing wrong,
What was once the *Baralong*,
As HMS *Wyandra* was renamed.

The creation of the Merchant Navy

What will prove the most effective,
Is the concept of collective.
In a convoy, merchant vessels group together.
By the navy they're escorted
And now goods can be imported.
The privations of the war the Brits thus weather.

Yet there's still a massive cost:
Many thousand lives were lost
And King George the Fifth this sacrifice rewarded.
For sustaining this great nation,
And for proving its salvation,
The title 'Merchant Navy' was accorded.

The armistice is signed;
The High Seas Fleet's confined
At Scapa Flow, and there it is destroyed.
There'd been thoughts that it be spared,
And between the Allies shared –
Something Germany was anxious to avoid.

There is no definitive information available on the exact numbers of British-flagged merchant and fishing vessels lost, but the Imperial War Museum's website states that more than 3,000 were sunk, and nearly 15,000 merchant seamen died. The Second World War figures given are 4,700 and 29,000 respectively. The Armistice of Compiègne was signed at 11.00 am (Paris time) on 11 November 1918.

The wrecks of the High Seas Fleet are protected by the Ancient Monuments and Archaeological Areas Act 1979. Some of the scuttled German ships have since been salvaged. Those that remain are popular with divers.

> 1914–1918
> TO THE GLORY OF GOD
> AND TO THE HONOUR OF
> TWELVE THOUSAND
> OF THE MERCHANT NAVY
> AND FISHING FLEETS
> WHO HAVE NO GRAVE BUT THE SEA

Inscription on the War Memorial

War Memorial, Trinity Square, Tower Hill, London

And those terrible machines,
The German submarines,
Can no longer use their awesome lethal power.
Their mission's been aborted.
At Harwich they're escorted,
Towards the mouth of Suffolk's River Stour.

The vessels have been parked,
And their crews are disembarked;
On a troopship all sail back to where they dwelled.
Once their secrets are unwrapped,
Some U-boats would be scrapped,
But the threat they pose is not yet fully quelled...

Many lives the war had claimed.
(Add the traumatized and maimed.)
In the Western Isles, they'd lost more men than most.
To greet those who'd been spared
At home folk were prepared;
There'd be kisses, hugs and perhaps a welcome toast.

The last leg was by sea.
There was bunting on the quay.
But, just yards from shore, the crowded boat was tossed.
That vessel was misguided,
And with cruel rocks collided:
So close to home, two hundred lives were lost.

For finding Mr. Right
The prospects weren't too bright.
On Lewis, of young men there was a dearth.
Mary Anne thus sailed away –
Destination USA –
There she married, and to Donald Trump gave birth.

Aircraft Carriers

Ambition would engender
The so-called seaplane tender:
For missions in the sky these vessels cater.
From the boat, each floating plane
Would be lowered off by crane,
And hauled on deck again – a sortie later.

From up high can now be seen,
The German submarine,
On which air attacks are seldom a success.
But the look-out role is working:
Ships are told where subs are lurking
So these ventures have their uses nonetheless.

The surrender of the German submarines was overseen by Admiral Reginald Tyrwhitt, (see verse 1364), who was in command of the Harwich Force. He ordered no fraternization with former enemy crews. The 120 or so U-boats, now manned by British crews, sailed one by one up the Stour, in a line stretching for 2 miles. After the submarines had been studied, some were scrapped, and others given to allied navies.

More than 1,000 men from the Islands of Lewis and Harris had been killed in the Great War. MHY *Iolaire* was carrying 284 men to Stornoway when disaster struck. Having failed to turn, it capsized on a rocky outcrop in the early hours of New Year's Day 1919. Two hundred and five men perished. Forty were led ashore by a brave man who dropped into the sea with a rope, and a further 39 survived the icy waters.

Mary Anne Macleod was born and brought up on the Isle of Lewis. She emigrated to New York in 1930, aged 18, and married property developer Frederick Trump.

The converted HMS *Hermes* (1913) was the first experimental seaplane carrier (or tender). In 1914, the *Engadine*, *Riviera* and *Empress* (cross channel steamers) were converted to accommodate seaplanes. From these, a largely successful attack on the Zeppelin base at Cuxhaven was conducted. Other conversions followed.

HMS *Ark Royal* (1914), which served in the Dardanelles and throughout the First World War, was the first vessel to be designed and built as a seaplane carrier. Seaplanes sometimes also flew ahead of the fleet to look for enemy ships: the principal roles for aircraft in the First World War were reconnaissance, inland sorties to Germany, and support for troops behind the lines.

The first 'moving ship' was HMS *Argus*, a converted ocean liner, which could accommodate 15 to 18 planes, and served from 1918–1944.

Aircraft carrier HMS *Argus* dazzle painted, 1918

Though the sceptics may well scoff,
Planes would soon be taking off
From moving ships, once full length decks were built.
The first landing was soon tried:
Sadly Edwin Dunning died,
When an up-draught caused his Sopwith Pup to tilt.

Landing gear was tested,
So that planes could be arrested,
For the decks of ships are really not that long.
Snagging tail hooks on a wire,
Takes a very skilful flyer:
In the early days, they often got it wrong.

Design would be improved,
Once control towers had been moved:
To the starboard side these islands would now shift.
Once jet fighters were in being,
We would later on be seeing,
The catapult – to generate a lift.

The day was soon to dawn,
When the CATOBAR was born,
Which gave acronym devisers so much joy.
An assisted launch from standing,
Plus the means to stop on landing,
Is the system that some carriers deploy.

In Britain, as time passes,
We'd see several different classes.
Some only reached the stage of being planned.
The fight deck's a terrain,
That depends upon the plane:
Thus the VTOL types don't need a 'rubber band'.

One *Ark Royal* was newfangled,
As its deck was upward angled.
This feature was progressive at the time.
And a ramp that slightly curves,
A useful purpose serves:
The 'ski jump' will assist the rate of climb.

If we leap bang up to date,
Poor old Lusty met her fate.
Sold for scrap, she left a gap, which some thought risky.
Then in 2017,
There was launched a brand new queen,
Not with bubbly, but with Isle of Islay whisky.

Edwin Harris Dunning (a Squadron Commander of the British Royal Naval Air Service) successfully landed his plane on a moving vessel (HMS *Furious*) at Scapa Flow in 1917, but was killed on a subsequent attempt.

After the First World War, HMS *Argus* was used for trialling arrest gear.

HMS *Hermes* (commissioned 1924) was the first purpose-built aircraft carrier to combine a full-length deck and classic starboard side control tower.

Whereas the wings of propeller planes could produce sufficient lift over short distances, jets rely on speed over longer distances to take off. Catapults were ultimately steam-powered (1954).

CATOBAR = Catapult-assisted takeoff and barrier/arrested recovery. There are 12 Catobar aircraft carriers in service today (the USA has 11 and France 1).

The *Malta* class, for example, never got beyond the design stage.

The *Audacious* class carrier HMS *Ark Royal* (R09), launched 1950, was the first to be equipped with an angled deck at its commissioning (1955), though sister ship HMS *Eagle* had such a deck as a post-commissioning modification. The angled flight deck was invented by Dennis Cambell (1907–2000), who became a rear admiral.

A 'ski jump' was developed for the *Invincible* class. HMS *Illustrious* (1978), known to her crew as 'Lusty', was the second of three in that class, and her completion had been rushed forward to enable her to participate in the Falklands Conflict (see verses 1648–1664). Initially it was hoped to preserve her for the nation. Her de-commissioning (2014) meant that Britain was without an in-service aircraft carrier for the first time in one hundred years.

The new *Queen Elizabeth* has a ski jump and is capable of operating STOVL (short take-off and vertical landing) aircraft.

The whisky used to launch her was from a long-established distillery now owned by a Japanese drinks company.

Dunning's plane about to land for the second fateful time

HMS *Hermes* and HMS *Dorsetshire*, June 1940

Naming ships

How are vessels' names selected?
Can a pattern be detected?
Does debate produce some loud dissenting voice?
How come HMS *Black Joke*?
Or the three that were called *Broke*?
Was *Quorn* supposed to be a veggie choice?

If your ship is the *Undaunted*,
Perhaps by worry you're not haunted,
And consider you're immune from being hurt.
If your vessel's called *Courageous*,
You might find this advantageous.
But what if you're on board the *Gnat* or *Flirt*?

Seven times a *Camel* features.
There've been sundry other creatures
Like *Elephant*, the *Badger*... *Beaver*... *Bat*...
Set up for feline quibbling,
*Tiger*s often had a sibling.
Though they bring good luck, there's never been a Cat.

Dianthus and *Gloxinia*,
Hollyhock and *Zinnia*...
This theme denotes the *Flower* class corvette.
And an *Insect* class existed:
Of gunboats this consisted.
Is *Cockchafer* the strangest ship name yet?

People of some note
Have found themselves 'afloat':
The royal brand bringing status and gentility.
A king or queen or prince,
Certain kudos will evince,
And the same applies to lesser-ranked nobility.

Two *Shakespeares* there have been
(One an *S* class submarine)
There are naval heroes, all from years gone by:
Boscowen, Raleigh, Drake,
Collingwood and *Blake,*
Anson, Nelson, Frobisher and *Bligh.*

And just who were the choosers
Of names for certain cruisers?
Why not make a pun of Crewe, or reuse *Cromer*?
It's for sure a thousand pities
They selected all those cities –
Making *Town* class an unfortunate misnomer.

Until the First World War, ships' names were chosen arbitrarily, although themes such as rivers and tribes had been used.

The name *Black Joke* was given to a tireless anti-slave trade vessel, which had been captured from Brazil.

Proud and inspirational names have always been popular. These include *Invincible, Victory, Glorious, Valiant, Indomitable, Inflexible* and *Obdurate*. *Gnat* and *Flirt* were both gunboats in the 1855–6 *Cheerful* class.

Many Royal Navy ships have been called *Tiger*, sometimes with a sister ship called *Lion*.

For 'lucky' cats see verse 37.

Modern corvettes were a class revived during the late 1930s by Winston Churchill. Serving during the Second World War as escort ships, HMS *Sunflower* (K41) and HMS *Hyacinth* (K84) were the most successful of their class against enemy submarines.

Most of the sixteen *Duke* class frigates (introduced in 1989) are still in active service with the RN.

HMS *Shakespeare* was ordered in 1940. The other *Shakespeare* was a destroyer, launched in 1917.

There were two groups (1909–12 and 1936–38) of cruisers named predominantly after cities, eg *Bristol, Glasgow, Liverpool, Gloucester, Manchester, Sheffield*. (These are not to be confused with the *Town* class destroyers, which Britain acquired from the USA under the 1940 'Destroyers for Bases' agreement (see verse 1502)).

The featured rhyme below refers to the first dozen *S* class submarines constructed from 1929 to 1935.

Twelve little S-boats 'go to it' like Bevin,
Starfish goes a bit too far – then there were eleven.

Eleven watchful S-boats doing fine and then,
Seahorse fails to answer – so there are ten.

Ten stocky S-boats in a ragged line,
Sterlet drops and stops out – leaving us nine.

Nine plucky S-boats, all pursuing Fate,
Shark is overtaken – now we are eight.

Eight sturdy S-boats, men from Hants and Devon,
Salmon now is overdue – and so the number's seven.

Seven gallant S-boats, trying all their tricks,
Spearfish tries a newer one – down we come to six.

Six tireless S-boats fighting to survive,
No reply from *Swordfish* – so we tally five.

Five scrubby S-boats, patrolling close inshore,
Snapper takes a short cut – now we are four.

Four fearless S-boats, too far out to sea,
Sunfish bombed and scrap-heaped – we are only three.

Three threadbare S-boats, patrolling o'er the blue...

Two ice-bound S-boats...

One lonely S-boat...

The fates of the remaining three were left unwritten. *Sealion* was scuttled, *Seawolf* was broken up and only *Sturgeon* made it to the end of the Second World War (lent to the Netherlands, returned and sold for scrap).

Based on a nursery rhyme and developed in submariners' circles

A different convention
Is worthy of a mention.
This accords names with the same initial letter.
Alphabetical selection,
After no doubt much reflection,
Has produced a few that maybe could be better.

Thus the 'D' some ships were sharing
Saw *Defender*, *Diamond*, *Daring* –
Each suggesting how our navy would deploy her.
Much strength these tags imply:
One might therefore wonder why
Dainty was bestowed on a destroyer.

They'd exhausted A to Z.
So what to use instead?
A themed approach was something that might work.
'Battles' were one such –
A patriotic touch –
And 'weapons' gave us *Howitzer* and *Dirk*.

Boaty McBoatface

Does democracy prevail?
Would a new ship due to sail
Be named by how the public chose to vote?
That process was made speedier
By using social media,
Which came up with the concept of 'McBoat'.

Intended to be droll,
The joke name won the poll,
Though *Attenborough* was in the end preferred.
But 'Boaty's' used to dub
The vessel's onboard sub –
So the people's voice has certainly been heard.

There was no *J* class.

The *C* class (eg *Crusader*, *Crescent*) and *D* class destroyers were 14 ships built in the early 1930s.

The name *Dainty* was used again with the immediate post-Second World War class. However, the most advanced *D* (or *Daring*) class guided missile destroyers (6 built between 2004 and 2007) do not include a *Dainty*.

Under the War Emergency Programme, fourteen flotillas (from 1939) used up letters O-Z, plus names beginning Ca, Ch, Co and Cr.

The names of *Battle* class destroyers (from 1942) were mainly maritime inspired (*Barfleur*, *Vigo*, *Sluys*, *Trafalgar*), although some land-based campaigns such as *Agincourt* and *Waterloo* also featured.

Counties (from 1959) and Cathedrals were among other themes used.

Britain's new £200 million polar research ship (launched July 2018) is named RRS *Sir David Attenborough*. The on-line poll to find a name was conducted by the Natural Environment Research Council (NERC). The new ship's remote controlled high-tech yellow submarine has been christened *Boaty McBoatface*.

Inter-War Naval Arms Agreements

In the States, there's discontent
About money being spent
On building ships. This surely can't be right?
What can Woodrow Wilson mean
By 'no wish to intervene',
If the countries of the world decide to fight?

There emerges an idea:
Major powers should all adhere
To a treaty setting naval limitations.
If everyone's disarmed,
Then no one can be harmed:
Thus agree the five participating nations.

Some in Britain are aghast.
They reflect upon the past,
And the peerless fleet no single other matches.
Seems the glory days have ended.
Can the empire be defended,
Without the ships to cover all its patches?

But we'd finally concur –
Short of money as we were.
Italy, Japan and France all signed.
The USA was pleased,
As Far Eastern tensions eased;
Thus the sizes of our navies were defined.

The reductions were still greater,
When we met up eight years later.
And five years on come further limits too.
But the parties who agree,
Are now down from five to three:
The Italians and the Japanese withdrew.

The Treaty of Versailles,
Means the Germans must comply,
With restraints upon the size of ships they build.
To the letter, they're adhering,
But with clever engineering,
The terms are merely technically fulfilled.

All those promises seem hollow,
In the war that soon would follow,
When no longer do the treaties' terms apply.
Naval strength was unrestricted.
The whole world was afflicted.
More than fifty million people were to die.

Woodrow Wilson (1856–1924) was President of the USA from 1913–21. The general feeling in that country favoured a resumption of the USA's anti-interventionist stance.

Negotiated from November 1921 – February 1922, the Washington Naval Treaty (or Five-Power Treaty) limited certain types of ships either by numbers, or by displacement tonnage.

The Treaty for the Limitation and Reduction of Naval Armament (1930), is more generally known as The First London Naval Treaty. The second London Conference was held 1935–6, but was only signed by Britain, France and the USA. The treaty ceased to have effect with the outbreak of the Second World War in 1939.

Britain and Germany also concluded the Anglo-German Naval Agreement in 1935, whereby the Kriegsmarine was restricted to about a third the size of the Royal Navy. This represented an easing of the restrictions imposed by the Treaty of Versailles (1919).

11 Second World War and its aftermath

11

Second World War and its aftermath

Second World War, 1939–45

The Battle of the River Plate, December 1939

The *Admiral Graf Spee*,
The restrictions did obey
Though, strictly, she was somewhat overweight.
She would run a short crusade,
And on allied shipping preyed,
Till the battle just beyond the River Plate.

She was damaged. Once in port,
Captain Langsdorff wrongly thought
There were many British ships his own must face.
'Scuttle her,' he said.
Shortly after, he was dead –
For suicide seemed better than disgrace.

The Battle of the Atlantic, 1939–45

From 1939,
When our freedom's on the line...
Through all the months when Britain stands alone...
Through our struggle to survive...
Till the year of '45,
Is fought the longest battle ever known.

Sugar, fats and cheese,
All come from overseas.
The Brits import a lot of what they eat.
The oceanic route,
Brings cereals and fruit,
Plus cattle feed, and half of all our meat.

Hitler's tactic – no surprise –
Is to interrupt supplies.
His U-boats are not easy to avoid.
Ever more are in production,
Each designed for the destruction
Of the merchant ships, against which they're deployed.

The *Admiral Graf Spee* was a 'pocket battleship'. German ships were limited to 10,000 displacement tons. She exceeded this by about 50 per cent. Deployed to the merchant shipping lanes of the South Atlantic before the outbreak of the Second World War, she sank 9 ships between September and December 1939. She sought refuge in Montevideo, in neutral Uruguay. Langsdorff was deceived by false intelligence reports suggesting that Force H, which included the carrier HMS *Ark Royal*, was on its way.

The Cunard passenger liner *Athenia*, carrying 1,103 evacuees from Liverpool to Canada, was the first civilian casualty of the war. She was sunk on 3 September 1939 by a U-boat to the west of Scotland.

Seventy per cent of the cheese, sugar, cereals and fats consumed by the British were imported, and the figure for fruit was 80 per cent. In addition to food, military supplies were being transported.

Among German U-boat commanders, the periods when their submarines had the upper hand were referred to as 'Happy Times'. The first was in 1940–1, and the second lasted from January–August 1942. In March 1942, 250 U-boats were deployed, and 15 were added each month. In that year, a total of 1081 Allied vessels (5,934,000 tons) were lost (see graph overleaf).

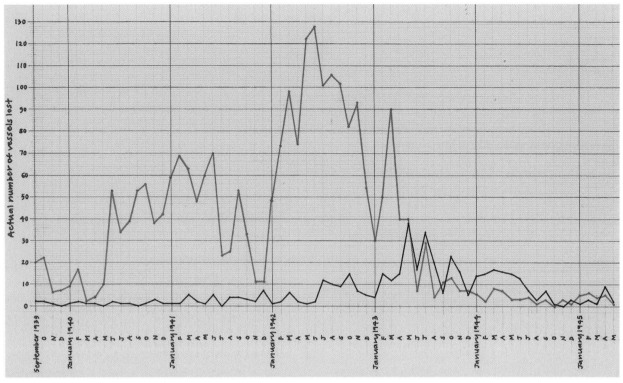

• Monthly summary of British, Allied and neutral ships lost in the Atlantic, including Russian convoys, from all causes
• **Number of German U-boat and Italian submarines sunk**

These menaces – submersed –
Look for prey whilst well dispersed,
Till a target's found that's worthy of attack.
Then others are alerted,
And the effort is concerted:
Soon these predators are hunting as a pack.

On the North Atlantic map,
In the middle, there's a gap,
Where cover from the air is unavailable.
Here, the convoys aren't protected,
And, as might well be expected,
It is also here they're at their most assailable.

The depth charge that we used
Was a kind of bomb that's fused.
When to launch these was a finely tuned decision.
To over/under shoot,
Would not destroy 'das Boot'.
As the war progressed, so too did our precision.

Contact between German submarines was by radio. At night, they attacked on the surface, where they could not be detected by Allied sonar, (or ASDIC).

The area that was out of range by air was referred to as the Black Hole. Allies increasingly used improvised aircraft carriers such as HMS *Audacity* for launching anti-submarine planes.

The British depth charges were originally filled with amatol; these had been deployed by the Royal Navy since 1918. An improved version, filled with Torpex, was introduced in 1941. Initially, only about one in sixty depth charges achieved a 'kill'.

For some time, things went as planned:
Hitler had the upper hand –
All was going very much the Germans' way.
But then radar helped detection,
There was better air protection,
And the 'hedgehogs' and the 'squids' came into play.

The former – spigot mortars,
Forward-thrown into the waters –
Look strange, but then appearance doesn't matter.
With the squids, which come in later,
The strike rate's even greater.
Their mortars have been angled, so they scatter.

Cracking the Germans' Naval Code

Enigma is a tease:
It's a gizmo that has keys.
By means of it, communications flowed.
Thanks to rotor wheels inside,
All access is denied
To anyone who doesn't have the code.

Every day, new combinations,
Of a zillion permutations,
Mean that enemy intelligence is scrambled.
No possible prescription
Solves the problem of decryption:
On the certainty of this, the Germans gambled.

But what they didn't know
Was that U-boat one-one-O
Had not sunk with all its secrets still intact.
Instead it had been boarded,
And the British were rewarded
With the means which helped Enigma to be cracked.

From a code book and machine,
Many secrets we would glean,
Thanks to geniuses based at Bletchley Park.
We began to understand,
What the kriegsmarine had planned –
Till the advent of their system known as 'Shark'.

This version was M4.
Wheel complement – one more.
Its introduction came as quite a shock.
For all Bletchley's expertise,
It wasn't sussed with ease:
It took nine long months of working round the clock.

Hedgehogs, which had 24 mortars arranged like spines, achieved a kill rate of slightly better than 1 in 6. With 3 mortars, squids had a 1:3 kill rate.

The Enigma machine had 159 million million million possible settings.

U-110, damaged by British fire, was boarded by a party – led by Sub-Lieutenant David Baume – from HMS *Bulldog*. The captured documents helped solve a German back-up code which, in turn, provided many 'cribs'. These were words, many obtained from weather reports, that were known to the code breakers.

Those at Bletchley Park used an early computer called a 'bombe', developed by Alan Turing. Information obtained by code-breaking was referred to as 'Ultra'.

(Coincidentally, another *U-110* had been sunk in July 1918, whilst attacking a merchant convoy near Hartlepool. Salvaged in November 1918, and dry-docked at Jarrow, work on her restoration as a British fighting unit, stopped with the November Armistice.)

'Shark' was the British name for the new system, which the Germans called 'Triton'. Its issue, early in 1942, for U-boat use resulted in a ten-month information blackout. The peak in Allied losses in the graph opposite coincides with this period, which also follows US entry into the war (see verse 1495), and the diversion of former escort ships to the Pacific.

U-534 Enigma machine at the *U-Boat Story* exhibition, Birkenhead

Information use (judicious
Lest the Germans get suspicious,
And realise just what the British knew),
Meant that convoys were alerted
And to other routes diverted:
Thus more supplies in consequence got through.

Operation Dynamo – the evacuation of Dunkirk

The Maginot's a line,
Defensive by design,
To protect the French against invading troops.
So they're taken quite aback,
To be subject to attack
When, through Belgium, Hitler's army quickly swoops.

Thence to sweep round in a curve...
'France has nothing in reserve,'
Gamelin declares, his manner candid,
'As a force, my country's spent.'
So the soldiers Britain sent
Are now vulnerable – and looking somewhat stranded.

Now that France has been defeated,
To Dunkirk they have retreated.
Rescue plans were drawn up straightaway.
Destroyers... little boats...
Almost anything that floats...
Every type of craft would have its part to play.

Small ones toed and froed,
And the bigger ships would load
As, shoulder-deep, men waded from the beaches.
For helping troops get back,
They earned the 'Dunkirk Jack'.
These events cued one of Churchill's best known speeches.

The Sinking of HMT *Lancastria*

There are further operations,
To effect repatriations
From the west coast. Many ships are heading there.
As France teeters on the brink,
The *Lancastria* will sink:
Overloaded, she has just left St Nazaire.

As she sets off to come back,
The Luftwaffe attack.
In the afternoon, three direct hits now blast her.
At the government's behest,
The bad news is suppressed:
Britain's biggest ever maritime disaster.

The Maginot line was a series of fortifications along France's border with Germany. Gamelin, Commander-in-Chief of the French Armed Forces, was dismissed on 18 May 1940.

The British Expeditionary Force (BEF) retreated under the orders of John Vereker, 6th Viscount Gort.

About 850 private boats, known as the 'Little Ships of Dunkirk', assisted with the evacuation (although only 700 or so were officially recorded). Most sailed from Ramsgate, and over 100 of them were lost. Vessels were requisitioned if they had enough capacity and speed. Larger ships could not sail in shallow waters. The RAF played a huge part in the success of Operation Dynamo by engaging the Luftwaffe. 338,228 British, French and Belgian troops were rescued. 40,000 left behind were either killed or captured. The rescue took place over 8 days between 26 May – 4 June 1940.

> It was the queerest, most nondescript flotilla that ever was, and it was manned by every kind of Englishman, never more than two, often only one, to each small boat. There were bankers and dentists, taxi drivers and yachtsmen, longshoremen, boys, engineers, fishermen and civil servants... It was dark before we were well clear of the English coast. It wasn't rough, but there was a little chop on, sufficient to make it very wet, and we soaked the *Admiral* to the skin. Soon, in the dark, the big boats began to overtake us. We were in a sort of dark traffic lane, full of strange ghosts and weird unaccountable waves from the wash of the larger vessels. When destroyers went by, full tilt, the wash was a serious matter to us little fellows. We could only spin the wheel to try to head into the waves, hang on, and hope for the best...
>
> **Arthur D. Devine, who manned a rescue boat, from *The Evacuation of Dunkirk, 1940***

> '... We must be very careful not to assign to this deliverance the attributes of a victory. Wars are not won by evacuations... we shall not flag. We shall go on to the end, we shall fight in France, we shall fight on the seas and oceans... we shall defend our Island, whatever the cost may be, we shall fight on the beaches... we shall never surrender...'
>
> **Winston Churchill, 4 June 1940**

British troops awaiting evacuation at Dunkirk

Two weeks after Operation Dynamo came Operations Cycle (the evacuation of Allied troops from Le Havre) and Aerial (the evacuation of civilians and troops from ports in western France).

During the latter, and five days before France signed an armistice with Germany, HMT *Lancastria* was sunk in the Loire estuary (17 June 1940). Her official capacity was 1,300. She was carrying an unknown number of soldiers and civilians. Estimates suggest up to 9,000. No one knows the exact, or even approximate, death toll. The number of fatalities is thought to have been between 3,000 and 5,800.

The Mediterranean – British attack on the French Fleet

France's army had been sacked,
But her fleet was still intact
And, above all else, was one thing Churchill feared.
Near Europe, it can't stay.
It needs to sail away –
Or by Germany, it might be commandeered.

The French prevaricated.
Things got very complicated.
Churchill, by his worries, still was driven...
Thought the risk too great to bear...
We attacked by sea and air.
By some, in France, we've never been forgiven.

The Mediterranean – Force H and Malta

With no French fleet in the Med,
We need something else instead;
Force H functioned from the British base, Gibraltar.
The main thing it must do,
Is ensure supplies get through,
To sustain the plucky island that is Malta.

Things were pretty much OK
Until planes came into play:
And the Luftwaffe's bombardment it must weather.
And worse still our trips would get:
Submarines, too, posed a threat,
And Italian flyers got their act together.

A quick look at the map
Will show just how small's the gap
Between Sicily and this – a British base.
To the isle, we still have title.
Her location's oh so vital,
Which explains the heavy pounding she must face.

From here operates Force K.
The part it has to play,
Is disrupting Axis shipping passing by.
To North Africa these head,
For to there the war's now spread,
And their armies' needs, the convoys must supply.

All this brought the little nation
To the threshold of starvation:
And an honour by her people would be earned.
The George Cross was bestowed
For the bravery they showed,
In hanging on until the tide had turned.

The Franco-German armistice was signed on 22 June 1940, and a collaborationist French government established at Vichy.

There were other French vessels elsewhere, including some, which had been captured, in British ports. In the British attack, (3 July 1940), one battleship was sunk and a further two damaged. Four destroyers were either damaged or grounded. Others fled. 1,297 French sailors were killed.

ULTIMATUM

His Majesty's Government have instructed me to demand that the French Fleet now at Mers-el-Kébir and Oran shall act in accordance with one of the following alternatives:

(a) Sail with us and continue the fight until victory against the Germans.

(b) Sail with reduced crews under our control to a British port. The reduced crews would be repatriated at the earliest moment...

(c) Alternatively if you feel bound to stipulate that your ships should not be used against the Germans lest they break the Armistice, then sail with us to some French port in the West Indies – Martinique for instance – where they can be demilitarised to our satisfaction, or perhaps be entrusted to the United states and remain safe until the end of the war, the crews being repatriated.

If you refuse these fair offers, I must with profound regret, require you to sink your ships within six hours.

Finally, failing the above, I have the orders from His Majesty's Government to use whatever force may be necessary to prevent your ships from falling into German hands.

Admiral James Somerville of Force H, based in Gibraltar

When, in November 1942, the Germans attempted to take control of French ships at Toulon, these were scuttled by the French.

Force H was formed in July 1940 under the command of Vice Admiral Sir James Somerville. Vice Admiral Sir Henry Harwood took over command in March 1942 until April 1945. There were relatively light losses in the Mediterranean theatre until 1941, when Britain suffered disastrously. The *Ark Royal* was sunk, and there was a damaging Italian raid on the eastern Mediterranean Fleet based in Alexandria (Egypt).

Germany's X. Fliegerkorps was based in Sicily, a little over 100 miles from Malta. In the space of 6 months, over 15,000 tons of bombs in 3,343 raids were dropped on the island – more than London suffered during the entire war. Despite the combined efforts of the German and Italian air forces, the beleaguered island managed to withstand attacks, claiming almost 1,500 Axis planes.

The main British Mediterranean base had been moved to Alexandria in October 1939 because of the vulnerability of Malta (see verse 689 for the acquisition of Malta).

• Allied   • Axis   • Under Axis control   • Neutral

The Mediterranean – The Battle of Taranto

Naval aviation
Had spent decades in gestation.
Now the 'useless' planes would show they'd come of age.
They set out to prove their worth,
In the sea called 'Middle Earth':
The harbour of Taranto was the stage.

There, Italian ships are tucked;
These our shipping could obstruct,
(Though they weren't exactly famed for their mobility).
From *Illustrious* planes flew;
This carrier was new,
And would demonstrate her awesome versatility.

Fairey Swordfish (now outmoded)
With torpedoes had been loaded –
Others carried bombs and flares as a diversion.
Braving barrage balloons and guns,
They set off on their runs,
And sunk or damaged ships on their excursion.

They caused carnage; even so,
It was not a 'knock-out blow':
It did not make safe our passage through the Med.
Right round Africa there loops,
Every convoy bearing troops,
As these had to go the Suez way instead.

The Mediterranean – The Battle of Cape Matapan

'The Regia Marina,'
Said an information gleaner,
'Will attack off Greece.' It can be interdicted.
The British are thus waiting,
For the fleet that comes predating:
At Cape Matapan, more damage is inflicted.

In command is 'ABC'.
There's no better man than he,
To take charge of such a very tricky patch.
And the *Warspite*, far from new,
Must take some credit, too:
Her pedigree is one few ships can match.

See also section/verses 1329–1336 **The Birth of the Fleet Air Arm**.

Mediterranean means 'middle earth' in Latin.

Taranto is located where the 'sole' joins the 'heel' of Italy's 'boot', and the attack on it (codename Operation Judgement) took place in November 1940.

HMS *Illustrious*, built on Tyneside by Vickers-Armstrongs, was commissioned in May 1940. She was the first aircraft carrier to have an armoured fight deck. Twenty-one planes were aboard *Illustrious*, two of which were lost during the attack. The 11 that were not playing a diversionary role carried modified torpedoes, and flew in at very low altitude. One battleship was sunk and two others, plus a heavy cruiser, were badly damaged. This halved the Italian battleship strength on one night.

The Italian Fleet was the Regia Marina. Force H suffered terrible losses, especially during 1941, although the Italians were reluctant to fight and risk damage to their irreplaceable capital ships.

As the reinforcement of Egypt and parts of the Far East (notably India) became an increasingly important British objective, the WS (Winston's Special) convoys were sent, travelling the long way round Africa via the Cape of Good Hope.

> Taranto, and the night of 11/12 November 1940, should be remembered for ever as having shown once and for all that in the Fleet Air Arm the Navy has its most devastating weapon.
>
> **Admiral Andrew Cunningham, Commander of the British Naval Forces at Taranto**

Hitler wanted to put a stop to the convoys which were supplying the British Expeditionary Force in Greece. Bletchley Park code breaker Mavis Batey had managed to read an Italian naval Enigma message about a planned attack off Greece. As it was imperative that the enemy didn't know their code had been cracked, the British arranged for a reconnaissance plane to be carefully directed to suggest that intelligence had come from a different source.

The Battle of Cape Matapan took place in March 1941.

'ABC' was the nickname for Admiral Sir Andrew Browne Cunningham (1883–1963), who was Commander-in-Chief, Mediterranean Fleet, from June 1939 to October 1943. He was responsible for defending supply lines, and oversaw the Anglo-American amphibious landings in Sicily and Italy.

Commissioned in 1915, Cunningham's flagship, HMS *Warspite*, had taken part in the Battle of Jutland (see verses 1386–1395). She had also played an important part in the second Battle of Narvik (off Norway), before heading to Alexandria in June 1940. 'The Old Lady' later served in the Indian Ocean, and in support of the Normandy landings.

HMS *Warspite* underway in the Indian Ocean, July 1942

The Sinking of the *Bismarck*, May 1941

Now the *Bismarck* will emerge,
With intent to prove a scourge
To the convoys, on which Britain so depends.
She reached the Denmark Strait,
There inflicted *Hood*'s sad fate,
Causing outrage at this sorriest of ends.

The *Bismarck*, in their 'duel',
Has been hit… is leaking fuel…
And this, in turn, affects the vessel's speed.
Captain Lütjens' only chance,
Is to try to head for France,
Where his damaged ship can get the help she'll need.

For our navy, giving chase,
There's a problem now to face:
Just what is the location of their prey?
In the midst of the Atlantic
The search becomes quite frantic,
But then radio will give the game away.

The pursuers – at some distance –
Are in real need of assistance.
Three vessels from Force H are duly sent.
From the *Ark Royal*, biplanes slipped –
With torpedoes well equipped –
And set about the *Bismarck* with intent.

One rudder has been caught.
Jammed at twelve degrees to port
The steering is kaput – no one can work it.
The ship's for nowhere bound,
She goes slowly round and round,
As her only course can be a giant circuit.

Now she's really out of luck,
And becomes a sitting duck,
Though she battled to the last and showed true spunk.
A debate continues still –
Was it suicide or kill?
Perhaps we'll never know, but either way she sunk.

The largest warship afloat at the time, the *Bismarck* was heavily armoured. Along with heavy cruiser *Prinz Eugen*, her commerce raiding mission was code-named Operation Rheinübung.

The Denmark Strait is between Iceland and Greenland.

Only three of the 1,421 men on board the battle-cruiser *Hood* survived. Her wreck was discovered in 2001 by shipwreck hunter David Mearns, and her bell was recovered in 2015. This is now on display at the National Museum of the Royal Navy in Portsmouth. It was actually the accompanying *Prince of Wales*, itself damaged, that delivered the crucial blow to the *Bismarck*, necessitating her bid to reach St Nazaire (see verse 1500) for repair.

Admiral John Tovey (1885–1971) called on all available ships to join the hunt for the damaged German vessel. In total, 6 battleships and battle-cruisers, 2 aircraft carriers, 13 cruisers and 21 destroyers were engaged in the chase.

When Lütjens radioed Paris, his call was intercepted. It was discovered after seven hours that his ship's position had been wrongly plotted. Decoded messages also revealed that the Luftwaffe was planning to provide air cover, once the *Bismarck* had got near enough.

The planes were the outdated but enduring Fairey Swordfish. Unaware that she was shadowing their target, their pilots first attacked HMS *Sheffield* using new magnetic torpedoes. These, thankfully, proved unreliable and caused no damage. Contact torpedoes were substituted.

HMS *Rodney* and HMS *King George V* disabled the *Bismarck*'s main battery early in the final battle, and HMS *Dorsetshire* scored two torpedo hits at fairly close range which would probably have been fatal, even if the Germans had not already activated scuttling charges. Recent sonar studies of the wreck seem to indicate that she was deliberately sunk.

The wreck of the *Bismarck* was discovered in 1989 by Robert D. Ballard.

The Arctic Convoys

Hitler's planning to besiege us:
From Ramsgate to Lyme Regis,
There'd be troops along two hundred miles of coast.
How could England be invaded?
'Not by sea,' he is persuaded.
'We'll beat them in the air,' is Göring's boast.

So the war takes to the skies,
To the brink of our demise,
And so many will owe much to a brave few.
The RAF thwarts 'Fritz' –
Though the price is London's Blitz –
And the Führer's armies head for somewhere new.

The invasion threat has ceased,
As he now looks to the East:
This second front becomes his fresh obsession.
Russia's brutally attacked,
Although there is a pact –
An odd way to interpret 'non-aggression'.

Now with Russia taking part,
The Arctic convoys start.
These take tanks and boots and foodstuffs and munitions.
Heavy losses would be seen,
As with *PQ17*.
These trips involve some truly dire conditions.

They assemble in Loch Ewe,
And in neutral Iceland too,
Or they sail from North America direct.
Though it's colder and more icy,
Winter sailings aren't so dicey:
In the darkness, they're less easy to detect.

German U-boats, German planes,
Patrol the shipping lanes.
They're responsible for many a fatality.
Though the States are not yet 'in',
They are helping us to win:
With the lend-lease scheme, it's nominal neutrality.

The original plan for Germany's 'Operation Sea Lion', which was postponed indefinitely in September 1940, was to establish beachheads from Ramsgate to just west of Portsmouth, and to send another invasion force from Cherbourg to Lyme Regis. Hitler did, at one time, consider the possibility of occupying Britain.

The German Luftwaffe was on the point of victory, when a stray bomb hit Croydon, south London. The British retaliated by bombing Berlin, and German attention was diverted to attacking London and other cities. This allowed the RAF to re-muster its depleted resources, and win The Battle of Britain.

Hitler attacked Russia on 22 June 1941, and 3 million German troops were sent to the Russian front. The Nazi-Soviet (or Molotov-Ribbentrop) Pact of Non-Aggression had been signed in August 1939.

The Arctic convoys started in September 1941. Their cargos also included fuel, raw materials and fighter planes.

PQ17 was attacked in June/July 1942. The ships were carrying $700 million worth of cargo. Only 11 out of 35 merchantmen made it to the Soviet Union. Other longer routes – via the Pacific and the Persian Corridor – were used, in addition to what became known as 'The Murmansk Run'. Churchill called these missions 'the worst journey in the world'.

From 2013, Royal and Merchant Navy veterans (and certain others) involved in the campaign have been able to apply for the 'Arctic Star' medal.

Part of the Kriegsmarine surface fleet, including the *Tirpitz* stationed off Norway, was also used to attack convoys.

In April 1940, Hitler had decided to invade neutral Norway. In a naval campaign of mixed fortunes, the British did at least manage to rescue the Norwegian royal family.

'An Act to Promote the Defense of the United States' (1941) was a programme which resulted in aid to Free France, the UK, the Republic of China and, later, the USSR and other allied nations.

Pearl Harbor and Force Z, December 1941

One attack the British wrought,
Some useful lessons taught:
It was studied by the watchful Japanese.
They were planning a surprise –
And to launch it from the skies –
Pearl Harbour a much larger-scale reprise.

Not just the USA,
Did they seek to strike this way:
We'd a battleship in place at Singapore.
But our Force Z's mission fails;
The *Repulse* and *Prince of Wales*,
Are attacked by air and sadly are no more.

Thus tragically began
Our war against Japan.
In this area, that country proved too strong.
Defenceless our position
V. expansionist ambition.
We lost Singapore, Malaya and Hong Kong.

Now the whole world is a stage,
For the fighting that would rage;
The 'War against Japan' would last a while.
Determined is the foe,
And reluctant to let go:
Strong resistance must be countered isle by isle.

When they plummet from on high,
Here the kamikaze die,
Their planes hit ships in missions quite fanatical.
(Flight deck armour is so thick,
That this suicidal trick,
For the British doesn't prove so problematical.)

Operation Chariot – The raid on St Nazaire

Though the *Bismarck* is no more,
There's another man of war:
The *Tirpitz* just off Norway has remained.
There she stays, a fleet in being –
Our navy stops her fleeing,
But must tie up ships to make sure she's contained.

If she ventures from her lair,
She'd be shot, and need repair:
In just one Atlantic place she might be mended.
She would certainly head there:
It's the port of St Nazaire,
With its huge dry dock, all heavily defended.

Like Taranto (see verses 1476–1479), Pearl Harbor is shallow water. Although it is highly likely that the Japanese were interested in British techniques, they had also developed their own.

Pearl Harbor was attacked on 7 December 1941, a date President Franklin Roosevelt stated would 'live in infamy'. Six aircarft carriers and 414 planes were deployed by the Japanese, in destroying or damaging 19 ships and over 300 aircraft.

The USA declared war on Japan on 8 December, and Germany declared war on the USA on 11 December 1941.

Force Z had been sent to intercept Japanese convoys taking troops to Malaya. *Repulse* was a veteran battle-cruiser built in 1916. HMS *Prince of Wales* was a new state-of-the-art battleship. They were attacked in open sea by land-based bombers and torpedo bombers.

There would be huge British losses in the Asian theatre.

In the latter stages of the war in the Pacific, suicide pilots targeted aircraft carriers. The latest British carriers had armoured flight decks that were 3 inches thick and the damage inflicted was often relatively light.

The British Pacific Force (BPF) was based in Sydney, Australia.

The last Japanese soldier to surrender did so in 1972.

> 'When a kamikaze hits a US carrier, it means 6 months of repair at Pearl [Harbor]. When a kamikaze hits a Limey carrier it's just a case of "Sweepers, man your brooms".'
>
> **United States Navy liaison officer aboard HMS *Indefatigable***

'Man of war' is a British Royal Navy term, (used from the 16th to 19th century), referring to a powerful warship.

Fast, heavily armoured and heavily armed, the revolutionary *Tirpitz* had the potential to cause extensive damage to Atlantic convoys. Britain had no equivalent warship. She was destroyed by the RAF in November 1944 using 'Tallboys' – special armour-piercing bombs devised by Sir Barnes Wallis.

The target of Operation Chariot was the Louis Joubert Lock (or Normandie dry dock).

Do the Brits have the ability
To strike this fine facility?
Soldiers manning massive guns are standing guard.
The entrance, closed and gated,
Cannot be penetrated...
Unless, maybe, it's hit by something hard?

This port must be attacked,
So the *Campbeltown* is packed
With explosives in a steel and concrete case.
By this heavy load encumbered,
This vessel's days are numbered:
It is hoped she will obliterate that base.

The Germans must not know
Of our plans to land a blow:
It's essential they are taken by surprise.
So the funnels she now bears
Make her look like one of theirs.
She will travel to her target in disguise.

Those who'll see this mission through,
Have a lot of work to do.
They practise laying charges in the dark.
Once they land, they will disperse,
But beforehand must rehearse,
Until, finally, they're ready to embark.

Those involved are highly skilled,
In their roles have been well drilled,
And courage isn't something that they lack.
Everyone could change his mind –
An offer all declined –
Although most of them would fail to make it back.

Five miles up the Loire...
All is going well so far
In what's shaping up to be a wartime thriller.
By a feat of navigation
They will reach their destination –
One big ship, and an eighteen craft flotilla.

The whole schedule has been timed.
And, with fuses duly primed,
The *Campbeltown* now slams into the gate.
Once the entrance has been rammed,
Our ship is firmly jammed –
According to the plan, four minutes late.

The gates, which were on rollers, weighed 1,500 tons.

Originally a US destroyer (USS *Buchanan*), HMS *Campbeltown* was an obsolescent ship, transferred to the Royal Navy in 1940 as part of the 'Destroyers for Bases' Agreement. Britain in return granted the USA land in various possessions for naval or air bases. Two of *Campbeltown*'s four funnels were removed, and the remaining two were angled to resemble those on German destroyers.

622 men of the Royal Navy and Commandos took part in the raid (March 1942), under the auspices of Combined Operations Headquarters. Lord Louis Mountbatten was the director at the time. Only 228 returned to England.

Those tasked with laying explosives in the port's facilities first practised in daylight, then blindfolded, and finally in complete darkness.

With a mile to go, the *Campbeltown* was detected by searchlights and fired upon, but was fast enough to reach her destination. There was only a narrow channel which was deep enough for large vessels.

Her captain was Stephen Beattie (1903–1975). The motor launches in the flotilla were intended to be the means by which men returned to Britain after the raid.

HMS *Campbeltown* prior to explosion

Things have not gone undetected.
There's resistance, as expected,
Under fire, there is a tragic human cost.
They're in something of a scrape,
For there's no means of escape.
Almost every single little boat is lost.

Those who make it onto land,
Lay their charges, as was planned.
Some are captured and are out for the duration.
But the job has been well done:
Adolf Hitler this will stun,
So complete was the resultant devastation.

Once our big ship had impacted,
Local interest was attracted,
And occupying soldiers came to view.
On her decks, these Germans strode,
Unaware she would explode –
A massive bang the last thing that they knew.

This tale's a shortened version
Of a dangerous excursion,
And the full account is certain to enthral.
So meticulously planned,
By the bravest it was manned
And, in short, was dubbed 'the greatest raid of all'.

Operation Frankton – 'The Cockleshell Heroes'

France was occupied and so,
The harbour of Bordeaux
For the Germans proved a valuable location.
Britain came up with a ruse:
Royal marines in small canoes,
Would plant limpet mines and thus cause devastation.

They would sneak up the Gironde,
To the port that lay beyond.
Five 'cockles' and ten crew – all highly trained.
Dropped off-shore by submarine,
In a bid to stay unseen,
They'll hide by day, so secrecy's maintained.

One pair drowned, (it is assumed).
Two other pairs were doomed.
They were captured by the enemy and shot.
Though they must have been afraid,
Their comrades weren't betrayed.
Four paddled on to carry out the plot.

The men who landed were mainly those who disembarked from the *Campbeltown*. Those in the motor launches fared less well. These craft were easy targets, and very few in them made it.

Of the ones who did land, the majority were either killed or captured. Only five managed to escape via Spain. Those who ventured onto the *Campbeltown's* decks included a party of 40 senior German officers, some accompanied by their French mistresses. An estimated 360 people in total were killed in the explosion.

The port was out of action throughout the remainder of the war, and was not fully restored until the early 1950s. The Germans never used it again. 89 decorations were awarded to those taking part, including five Victoria Crosses. Captain Beattie, who was taken prisoner and held captive until 1945, was one such recipient.

> For great gallantry and determination in the attack on St Nazaire in command of HMS *Campbeltown*. Under intense fire directed at the bridge from point blank range of about 100 yards, and in the face of the blinding glare of many searchlights, he steamed her into the lock gates and beached and scuttled her in the correct position.
>
> This Victoria Cross is awarded to Lieutenant-Commander Beattie in recognition not only of his own valour but also that of the unnamed officers and men of a very gallant ship's company, many of whom have not returned.
>
> **Stephen Beattie's Victoria Cross citation**

The port of Bordeaux was important to the Germans for landing supplies for troops in France, and for importing raw materials such as oils and natural rubber from the Far East. It was also used as a U-boat base. An outright bombing attack on the port had been ruled out because this would incur civilian casualties.

Operation Frankton was carried out by men from the Royal Marine Boom Patrol Detachment. Five miles off the coast, the cockles were disembarked on 7 December 1942. One of the 6 collapsible canvas canoes, *Cachalot*, was damaged as it was being taken from the submarine HMS *Tuna*, and could not be used.

Forced to swim ashore after their canoe, *Conger*, had been damaged by a rip-tide, one pair either drowned or (now the prevailing theory) died of hypothermia.

The crews of *Coalfish* and *Cuttlefish* were captured and, after interrogation, shot. They gave up details of their training, but did not divulge the fact that others were involved.

A total distance of some 90 miles, most of it upstream against a strong current, was travelled by the men in the remaining two canoes, *Crayfish* and *Catfish*. The latter was crewed by mission leader Major Hasler and Marine Sparks, who were the only two to make it back to England. With the help of the French Resistance, they travelled through Spain to Gibraltar.

In line with what was hatched,
The devices they attached –
(Each one of these had carefully been primed).
Then they slip off undetected.
The explosives they'd connected,
Later detonate at 9 pm, as timed.

The effect was as predicted,
Much damage was inflicted
On the half a dozen ships that had been mined.
The exploits of the four,
Helped abbreviate the war
By six months, as Churchill later on opined.

The *Scharnhorst*

To be lucky she purports –
A talisman of sorts –
Any hits the *Scharnhorst* takes are always mended.
And brazen, unabashed,
Up the Channel she'd once dashed –
Had progressed unseen, so wasn't apprehended.

As she leads a life so charmed,
Allied ships are sunk or harmed:
How she and Deutschland fare seem intertwined.
And BOTH are 'all at sea'
Late in 1943
When, to icy depths, she's finally consigned.

Operation Neptune (Part of Operation Overlord)

In time, there'd be a need,
For Europe to be freed
From the awful scourge of German occupation.
This requires strong Allied forces,
And the problem there of course is:
How to get them to our chosen destination?

A reversal of 'Dunkirk'
Quite simply wouldn't work:
Some men – but not their lorries – had returned.
On Dieppe we'd tried a raid;
Such a heavy price was paid,
But valuable lessons had been learned.

An army of huge size,
Needs plentiful supplies:
Clothing, ammunition, food and tanks.
All this can't be left to chance,
As British men advance,
Together with Canadians and 'Yanks'.

Operation Frankton was completed on the night of 11/12 December 1942. The men in the team undertaking it were harbingers of the Special Boat Service (SBS), a specially trained and equipped unit which is the naval special forces equivalent of the SAS.

Despite Churchill's pronouncement, views differ on the effectiveness of the raid.

A monument commemorating the operation is in Saint-Georges-de-Didonne, near Royen.

> 'Of the many brave and dashing raids carried out by the men of Combined Operations Command, none was more courageous or imaginative than Operation Frankton.'
>
> **Lord Louis Mountbatten**

The *Scharnhorst*, together with sister ship *Gneisenau*, had completed Operation Berlin (a commerce raid on Allied shipping) early in 1941. Both severely damaged, they underwent repairs in Brest and were then ordered home. In the 'Channel Dash' (Operation Cerberus), they were accompanied by *Prinz Eugen* and escorts. *Scharnhorst* (and the others) successfully reached Wilhelmshaven, albeit she was in need of further repair due to damage caused by a mine.

Subsequently deployed to Norway to interdict Arctic convoys, she was sunk by the Royal Navy during the Battle of North Cape (December 1943). *Gneisenau* was sunk as a blockship (see verse 1372) in March 1945.

For the evacuation of Dunkirk see verses 1463–1466.

Operation Jubilee (1942) was an ill-fated amphibious landing with an objective of taking the port of Dieppe. Many of the troops taking part were Canadian, and huge numbers were killed, maimed or taken prisoner. 555 Royal Navy personnel also died. Thirty-three landing craft and a destroyer were lost, along with 106 aircraft, (more planes than on any other single day of the war).

Operation Overlord was the name given to the Allied invasion of German-occupied western Europe. Operation Neptune refers to the D-Day landings (6 June 1944), the largest seaborne invasion in history.

Troops from Australia, Belgium, Czechoslovakia, Free France, Greece, The Netherlands, New Zealand, Norway and Poland were also part of the force that landed in Normandy.

Normandy, (selected
As somewhat less expected
Than Calais), was where troops would go ashore.
To avoid a large reception,
We had practised much subreption,
With secret service input to the fore.

As we plan the final push,
A 'Mulberry's no bush…
A 'spud' is not a foodstuff that one mashes;
The 'crocs' aren't fierce and scary,
The 'gooseberries' aren't hairy,
And a 'phoenix' doesn't rise up from the ashes…

A 'beetle's' not a bug…
Parts are towed to France by tug –
For the largest-scale invasion ever known.
Where the Allies hope to land,
No harbour is to hand,
And in consequence, we have to bring our own.

Throughout the British nation,
There is frenzied preparation,
At a time when, of skilled workers, there's a dearth.
Huge effort is invested…
Then the scheme needs to be tested,
At Garlieston, upon the Solway Firth.

The Mulberries so-called
Must be carefully installed;
The components are designed to fit together.
Even when they're all in place,
There are elements to face –
And one of them falls victim to the weather.

Mulberry B stays operational,
Achieving the sensational,
As allies fight to end the dreadful war.
Cross-channel shipping runs,
Brought supplies (four million tons),
Plus trucks and troops – two million men and more.

Most went straight onto the beach,
Which was easier to reach,
Now a special type of craft was in production.
The amazing LSTs
Could unload their tanks with ease,
For untreated shorelines offered no obstruction.

The elaborate deceptions were code-named Operation Fortitude. 'Fortitude South' involved an entirely fictitious invasion force, under US General George Patton, 'stationed' across from Calais. It included inflatable tanks and planes. MI5 and MI6, as well as SHAEF (Supreme Headquarters Allied Expeditionary Force), were involved.

Mulberry A (serving Omaha & Utah beaches where USA forces were landed) and Mulberry B (serving the British and Canadian beaches of Gold, Juno & Sword) were artificial harbours consisting of various components, many prefabricated and towed across the Channel. Both were the size of Dover.

Spuds were massive four-legged pier heads containing generators, winches, a maintenance shop and living space. Crocs were steel bridge-building roads. (Crocodile is also the name of a flame-throwing tank.)

Gooseberries were breakwaters created by Corncobs (scuttled blockships that formed a reef). 70 old merchant ships were amassed at Oban in Scotland.

The Phoenix was a sunken steel-reinforced concrete caisson used as a breakwater, and a Beetle was a steel or concrete pontoon.

Preparation, conducted in secrecy, involved 300 firms around the country, and 40–45,000 workers.

Prototypes were tested at Garlieston (south-west Scotland), which was chosen because beach conditions there were similar to those at Normandy.

Hugh Iorys Hughes, a Welsh engineer and keen amateur sailor, produced some of the key ideas. His prototypes were constructed at the Conwy Morfa (north Wales). He remained closely associated with the entire project.

On 19 June 1944 (D-Day + 13) a huge storm mortally damaged Mulberry A. Nicknamed 'Port Winston', Mulberry B was eventually decommissioned when the Port of Antwerp started bringing in Allied supplies (26 November 1944).

A total of half a million vehicles were landed. On D-Day itself, 156,000 troops were landed. Operation Neptune involved 6,939 vessels (1,213 naval combat ships, 2,136 landing craft, 736 ancillary craft and 864 merchant ships). About 15 per cent of vehicles used the floating roadways.

LST is an acronym for 'Landing Ship, Tank' – a British concept. The first, HMS *Boxer*, was built at Harland and Wolff (Belfast), but most of the 1,000 plus constructed during the Second World War were made in the USA at inland building yards.

Mulberry B Harbour 'Port Winston' at Arromanches, September 1944

Getting men from sea to ground –
Or the other way around –
Needed detailed plans and careful delegation.
Bertram Ramsay's expertise
In matters such as these,
Proved vital to each major operation.

The allies from the west
Through Europe now progressed.
And the Soviets pushed forward from the east.
All these troops would persevere,
For almost one more year,
Till they reached Berlin, and all the fighting ceased.

This completed the agenda,
Of Germany's surrender:
The event is the fulfilment of a dream.
But the Europe that's to be,
Is not entirely free,
With large parts of it a communist regime.

Meanwhile, half a world away
We're still waiting for 'VJ'.
At an awful price, hostilities are stopped.
The Empire cannot win,
But refuses to give in –
Though it must, when two atomic bombs are dropped.

Soldiers did lose their lives when their transport could not get sufficiently close to shore, and a number drowned under the weight of their backpacks.

Admiral Sir Bertram Ramsay (1883–1945) spearheaded the evacuation of Dunkirk, planned the amphibious landings in Sicily (1943) and was in charge of naval operations for the D-Day landings.

VE (Victory in Europe) Day was a public holiday celebrated on 8 May 1945.

Victory over Japan (VJ) day, which effectively ended the Second World War, was on 15 August 1945.

After consultation with Britain, on 6 August, the USA dropped an atomic bomb on Hiroshima, followed by a second on Nagasaki (9 August). These were the only two occasions on which nuclear weapons have ever been deployed in warfare, and the ethics of doing so are still being debated.

THE ENEMY'S PERSPECTIVE

'To construct our defences we had two years, used some 13 million cubic metres of concrete and 1.5 million tons of steel. A fortnight after the landings by the enemy, this costly effort was brought to nothing because of an idea of simple genius. As we know now, the invasion forces brought their own harbours and built, at Arromanches and Omaha, on unprotected coast, the necessary landing ramps.'

Albert Speer (speaking after the war at the Nuremburg trials)

Canadian LST discharging a tank during the Allied invasion of Sicily, 1943

Post-War Defence Context

The deaths and the despair,
Of the horrible affair,
In which we saw the Axis powers defeated,
Were odious, insane,
Destructive, inhumane...
And we must ensure that none of it's repeated.

The world's a different place:
(It will soon be viewed from space).
The atomic bomb has made things much less certain.
The 'Cold War' has begun,
It would last till '91,
With a Russian threat behind an 'Iron Curtain'.

After talking many hours,
Twelve North Atlantic powers
Made a pact, which major problems should forestall.
Their defence would be combined
And the principle's enshrined:
An attack on one is deemed a strike on all

NATO thus came into being,
And thereafter we'll be seeing
This alliance as our mainstay of defence.
Since it started, it has grown.
No member stands alone.
The scale of war today would be immense...

The Yangtze Incident, 1949

Civil wars are often fraught.
Sometimes foreigners get caught,
In another country's fierce internal wrangle.
And in 1949,
Certain factors now combine:
These a hapless British frigate would entangle.

She is going to Nanking:
It's a routine kind of thing
For the *Amethyst* to sail the Yangtze River.
She then comes under fire,
Her situation's dire:
No return shot is she able to deliver.

The state of tension between the Western Bloc and Russia (and its Warsaw Pact allies) is generally deemed to have lasted from 1947–1991. The term 'Iron Curtain' was popularised by Winston Churchill in a 1946 speech, and refers to the physical border barriers between East and West.

The debate leading to the establishment of the North Atlantic Treaty Organisation (April 1949), took two weeks. The founding members were the UK, USA, Canada, Belgium, Denmark, France, Iceland, Italy, Luxembourg, Netherlands, Norway and Portugal.

Article 5, the principle of collective defence, is at the heart of the Washington Treaty. It does not, however, necessarily involve military intervention in every conflict but, rather, whatever actions are deemed necessary to ensure the security of the North Atlantic.

There are now 29 members, some of which, (as parts of the former USSR), used to belong to the Warsaw Pact.

> The Parties to this Treaty reaffirm their faith in the purposes and principles of the Charter of the United Nations and their desire to live in peace with all peoples and all governments. They are determined to safeguard the freedom, common heritage and civilisation of their peoples, founded on the principles of democracy, individual liberty and the rule of law. They seek to promote stability and well-being in the North Atlantic area. They are resolved to unite their efforts for collective defence and for the preservation of peace and security.
>
> **Preamble to the North Atlantic Treaty, 4 April 1949**

HMS *Amethyst* was travelling to Nanking to provide overdue relief for HMS *Consort* there. The remnants of the 'unequal treaties' (see verse 890) still applied, though British rights had diminished during the Second World War.

Return fire was not possible, as the two front gun turrets were at the wrong angle to fire, and the stern turret was quickly disabled.

The ship by shells is pounded,
And can't move because she's grounded,
Helpless victim of the Chinese PLA.
In this unprovoked assault,
(Which they claimed was Britain's fault),
Many died – some as they tried to swim away.

To nowhere she is heading...
Her leaks are plugged with bedding,
When the holes beneath the waterline are noted...
Consort then comes to her aid
Bids to free our ship are made;
After several failed attempts she is re-floated.

She moves a bit up stream
(Not the good news this might seem).
A new captain has arrived and is on board.
John Kerans is his name.
He must play a waiting game,
And will later earn the DSO award.

Help turns up from other quarters,
In those troubled river waters,
But unfortunately all to no avail.
Going on or moving back,
Will incite a fresh attack.
So there'll be no speedy ending to this tale.

It's the Amethyst's bad luck
That she's now a sitting duck –
A hostage, a negotiating pawn.
For our vessel to be freed,
The price can't be agreed:
It's that forces from all China be withdrawn.

No real chance of freedom beckons,
So Captain Kerans reckons
That there's just one way to end this dreadful plight:
He'll slip anchor chain and run...
Try to dodge the hostile gun...
And will do so in the darkness of the night.

In order to confuse,
A civilian ship he'll use.
This is carrying a lot of refugees.
The vessel is well lit.
He decides to follow it:
Both are spotted by the Communist Chinese.

The seriously injured coxswain was unable to steer properly, thus getting the ship stuck. Under attack, 22 men were killed and 31 were wounded either on board, or in the later bid to evacuate the Amethyst in sampans or by swimming. Captain Bernard Skinner was one of the first to die. There were a further 10 deaths and 23 casualties before the destroyer HMS Consort was forced to withdraw.

Amethyst was eventually refloated after lightening the load.

Replacement captain, Lieutenant John Kerans (1915–1985), was Assistant British Naval Attaché.

HMSs London and Black Swan went to Amethyst's assistance but faced heavy fire. The hapless ship remained at anchor for 10 weeks, and was unable to take on supplies.

The PLA, the force of the Chinese communists under Mao Tse Tung, was demanding the withdrawal of all British, French and US armed forces. It was not until 1988 that a former PLA member admitted that the PLA fired first.

HMS *Amethyst* during Second World War

The first ship takes the blast.
The *Amethyst* slips past.
The first is sunk, with many killed or drowned.
There will be more risks to face,
In this 'bid for freedom' race,
Till she's safe, and re-supplied, and Hong Kong bound.

In charge of China now,
Is the famous Chairman Mao;
Our free access to his country is no more.
The incident showed tensions,
Which had very wide dimensions,
And could very well have caused a Third World War.

The Korean War, 1950–53

Korea had been split.
The 'North' wants all of it,
And marches south, with Russia's fullest blessing.
Fearing communism's spread,
The US shakes its head.
'The invaders,' it's decided, 'need repressing'.

As we're part of the UN,
Brits are fighting once again,
Which means, of course, the navy is involved.
There were stalemates, escalations,
Many bloody confrontations,
Then a peace, which left the tensions unresolved.

The Fleet Air Arm's contribution,
To this conflict's prosecution
Saw a 'coming straight towards me' airborne threat.
Carmichael got in first:
He said, 'I fired a burst.'
Propeller powered, he'd killed a fearsome jet!

This war marks the real start,
Of the helicopter's part
In actions, which will often be repeated.
Those rotor blades are whirring
For the purpose of transferring,
The wounded to a place where they are treated.

An unknown number of innocent victims aboard the civilian ship perished.

With eventual support from HMS *Consort*, the *Amethyst* had to sail past troops stationed on both banks of the river, but was fortunately not spotted.

In a surprise attack, the Korean capital Seoul fell after just three days. At one stage, Russia did actively, but covertly, participate with air strikes. To avoid outright war with Russia, the Americans chose to ignore this.

After America, the British were the second largest fighting force in the Korean conflict. In 1950, RN cruiser HMS *Jamaica* and frigate HMS *Black Swan* were involved in one skirmish which resulted in the sinking of 6 North Korean vessels, but there was otherwise little action at sea.

On 9 August 1952, Commander Peter Carmichael (1923–1997) was leading a formation of four Sea Furies on a mission to attack railway facilities when they were attacked by eight MiGs. At the time, the North Korean MiG-15 fighters were much more advanced than any planes the UN forces could field.

RN Westland Dragonflies had first served in Malaya (1950), undertaking casualty evacuations. The Germans had used small numbers of helicopters in the Second World War.

The Suez Crisis, 1956

The world is post-imperial,
But that seems immaterial,
When it's claimed that 'our' canal is now Egyptian.
A covert deal is made:
With two others, we'll invade!
A show of force must be the right prescription.

The crisis is acute,
For Suez is the route,
Along which passes most of Britain's oil.
Our Prime Minister, it seems,
Of the glory days still dreams,
And this dreadful plot to seize it he must foil.

So, with Israel and with France,
We proceed to take our chance:
Our destroyers and support ships now set sail.
We send frigates, subs and sloops,
Civilian craft (for troops),
And sundry others – all to no avail.

The navy, as so often,
Shore defences first would soften.
The Royal Marines from landing craft then poured.
As solid ground was gained,
Naval cover was maintained,
And continued till the beachhead was secured.

It will end in British shame,
Though our forces aren't to blame:
They're to all intents successfully engaged.
We could bank, we'd wrongly thought,
On American support,
But the whole affair has Eisenhower enraged.

There had been no consultation
About this operation;
The President wants peace instead of war.
Our plan he'd not endorsed,
And now we're being forced,
To bow to US pressure and withdraw.

So Nasser's not deposed.
And our thoroughfare is closed:
Scuttled ships mean passage through it is prevented.
Russia's Middle East ambitions
Have suffered no remissions,
And our prestige as a power's severely dented.

President Gamal Abdel Nasser nationalised (ie effectively seized) the Suez Canal after the withdrawal of Anglo-American funding for the Aswan Dam. France and Israel had their own agendas for joining Britain.

Plans for the operation included air attacks, and aircraft carriers were paramount. There were also two ships from which helicopters could take off.

Softening shore defences had become the navy's traditional role. The landings, at Port Said, were part of Operation Musketeer.

Although the military operation looked like being successful, it had taken Britain and France 3 months to assemble the necessary forces.

At the time, President Dwight D. Eisenhower was seeking a second term in office, and Britain was seeking to borrow a large amount of money from the USA. Eisenhower's succinct response was, 'No ceasefire. No loan.'

Nasser scuttled about 40 ships that were present in the Suez Canal, with the result that it was closed from October 1956 to March 1957.

The first United Nations Emergency Force (UNEF) was created to restore order.

NB Between 1922 and 1991, 'Russia' should more accurately be referred to as the Soviet Union or USSR.

> The Suez crisis of 1956 proved to be the next watershed in post war defence policy... The rearmament package announced by Attlee in 1951 had proven to be financially unsustainable and had failed to produce the forces required to deal with the Suez crisis. The Anglo-French response to Nasser's nationalisation of the Suez Canal took three months to organise, mainly because of the shortage of available forces.
>
> **Andrew Dorman, from *Crises and Reviews in British Defence Policy* (2001)**

Factory ships

Our country's 'fish deficient'.
Round our shores there's insufficient
Of this foodstuff that we bake, steam, grill and fry.
Some is chilled in Arctic ice,
But this method won't suffice
To keep for long an adequate supply.

So they found a way to freeze,
What was garnered from the seas:
Thus with better fish, their vessels could return.
The new commercial boat,
Is a factory afloat,
And men fished, not from the side, but from the stern.

The first one to be seen,
Was built in Aberdeen.
The *Fairtry* had facilities galore.
Her full complement of crew
Would total eighty-two,
She started work in 1954.

Washed and filleted and skinned,
Beheaded and de-finned,
Fish were frozen and then ultimately packed.
To the holds they were consigned,
(These were aluminium-lined).
Catches reached the shore, all perfectly intact.

Disputes over fishing grounds

The year of Agincourt,
Sees a less dramatic 'war',
When England's trade with Iceland is contested.
King Eric views this region
As exclusively Norwegian.
It ends when his officials are arrested.

In 1893,
At loggerheads were we
With the Danes, who were protective of their zone.
This included all the miles,
Round its coast, and round its isles.
Which, to some extent, we'd treated as our own.

Should anyone encroach,
A gunboat would approach:
No trespassing allowed on Denmark's patch!
British boats, their trips aborted,
Were into port escorted,
Where they faced a fine, and confiscated catch.

The use of ice to chill fish dated from the 1830s (see verse 1203). Refrigerated cargo ships (reefers) were developed in the last quarter of the 19th century, initially for meat and then fruit, especially bananas. The first purpose-built factory trawler, *Fairtry* featured many innovations, including sophisticated navigational equipment and sonar.

The crew included technicians and 19 officers. Their accommodation was well-appointed and even centrally heated. There were four 28 foot lifeboats aboard.

Processing was automated. The refrigerating plant was capable of maintaining a temperature of minus 5° Fahrenheit. The hold was heavily insulated. *Fairtry* also had fish meal and liver boiling plants.

In 1974, in a storm in the Barents Sea, the Hull-based factory ship FV (fishing vessel) *Gaul* sank without explanation. The loss, involving 36 lives, has been described as 'the worst ever single-trawler tragedy'.

Fairtry LH8

In 1410, the Hansa (see verses 109–111) closed their fishing grounds near Bergen (due to declining stocks and for tax evasion purposes).

Viewed by some as the very first 'Cod War', the dispute with Eric of Pomerania (1381/2–1442) lasted from 1415 to 1425. Eric was king of the Kalmar Union (a union of Norway, Denmark and Sweden under a single monarch). The English arrested his officials in Iceland.

With the advent of steam trawlers, the British were able to go further and catch more fish (see verse 1202).

At the 1882 Hague Conference on North Sea Fisheries, Norway and Sweden argued for a 4 nmi (nautical mile) limit, whereas the other parties, including the UK, were prepared to accept a 3 nmi exclusive rights limit.

However, in 1893, Denmark (which governed the Faroe Islands and Iceland) claimed a larger limit, (50 nmi), which the British refused to recognise. Gunboats were used to enforce the limit and, sometimes, all or part of British trawlers' fishing gear was also taken. The dispute was resolved in 1901 with the Anglo-Danish Territorial Waters Agreement, which stipulated a 3 mile limit.

> The fishermen of each country shall enjoy the exclusive right of fishery within a distance of 3 miles from low-water mark along the whole extent of the coasts of their respective countries, as well as of the dependent islands and banks.
>
> **Article II of the** *Decree of the Hague Convention for the Regulation of North Sea Fisheries* **(1882)**

When the *Caspian* transgressed,
The Danes were not impressed;
They opened fire. Its skipper was arrested.
To their mast, the man was lashed,
As away our vessel dashed,
Then limped back home, all bullet-hole infested.

Where we fished got more extreme,
Once boats were powered by steam,
(Instead of a reliance on the sail).
Now the industry's commercial,
And by stages controversial,
As we're doing this on quite a massive scale.

Once World War Two had ended,
Norway's limit, now extended,
Was subject to tough action and enforced.
'Not good,' the British thought,
So we took the case to court.
The Norwegian stance the ICJ endorsed.

The Anglo-Icelandic Cod Wars

As their fish stocks had declined,
Iceland also redefined
The exclusive belt around her chilly shores.
On this, we weren't too keen,
And the tensions set the scene
For the conflicts that were later dubbed 'cod wars'.

Once more, the Brits appealed
And, once more, were forced to yield
To restrictions – which the Icelanders would shelve –
As, unhappy with just four,
Soon they're seeking even more,
And the mileage round their coast is upped to twelve.

NATO members don't much like
This unilateral hike;
(And briefly by such friends we feel supported).
But a threat they can't ignore –
'From NATO we'll withdraw!' –
Means Great Britain's cause is ultimately thwarted.

Our fishing boats must heed,
The dozen miles agreed.
A zone of fifty miles was then declared.
We'll ignore this and be damned!
Nets were cut, and trawlers rammed –
But the 'NATO card' has others running scared...

The *Caspian* was a steam trawler from Grimsby fishing off the Faroe Islands in 1899. Skipper Charles Johnson ordered his brother to make a dash for it. Johnson allegedly threatened the Danish captain and was tied to the mast for 'safety reasons'. Found guilty of illegal fishing and attempted assault, he spent 30 days in prison on a bread and water diet.

See verses 999 & 1200–1206 for steam-powered ships.

In 1930, the League of Nations Hague Codification Conference of International Customary Law failed to produce conventions on the territorial sea, but did begin a complex debate about islands, and how far they needed to be from the mainland to have their own territorial waters. Norway's claim to 4 miles, made during the 1930s, was endorsed in 1951 by the International Court of Justice (ICJ).

Following independence from Denmark in 1944, Iceland annulled the 1901 agreement (which was due to expire 1951). In 1952, the country claimed a 4 mile limit.

The British trawling industry imposed a ban on landing Icelandic fish in British ports, which created a huge gap in Iceland's export market. The Russians stepped in to provide an alternative outlet, as did the USA, Spain and Italy.

In 1956, the British distant water catch peaked at 8.5 million tons. That same year, Britain was thwarted by a decision of the Organisation of European Economic Co-operation, which supported the 4 mile claim. The UK was forced to recognise this.

Iceland claimed an extended exclusive zone of 12 miles in 1958. Following the UN's inconclusive first International Conference on the Law of the Sea, the First Cod War began in 1958. It ended when the second UN Conference on the Law of the Sea (1960–1) confirmed the 12 mile limit.

The Second Cod War (1972–3), which ended with the signing of a temporary agreement, was prompted by a further increase in the limit to 50 miles. An Icelandic withdrawal from NATO would have entailed the expulsion of US forces from Iceland, and left open the door for Russian replacements.

To examine the law of the sea, taking into account not only of the legal but also of the technical, biological, economic and political aspects of the problem and to embody the results of its work in one or more international conventions or such other instruments as it may deem appropriate.

Task of the 1958 UN Geneva Conference on the Law of the Sea

It is therefore true to say,
Things could never go our way,
Though our boats, by naval power, were well defended.
With two hundred miles imposed,
Iceland's grounds were all but closed.
It's unlikely that they'll ever be contended.

By lost livelihoods affected,
Many folk were left dejected,
And got nothing in the way of compensation.
Schemes that later came along,
Were to get it very wrong,
And were criticised for maladministration.

Could our industry revive?
Once again be strong and thrive?
('It's the EU's fault!' has been a constant moan.)
Now that 'Brexit's' our decision,
Will some EEZ revision,
Mean reclaiming much more water as our own?

At the peak of the disputes, 37 Royal Navy warships were mobilised to protect British trawlers in contested waters.

Following the Third Cod War, 1975–6 (during which Iceland ended diplomatic relations with the UK), the limit was extended to 200 miles.

The fishing industries of Grimsby, Hull and Fleetwood went into terminal decline, and a number of Scottish ports were also badly hit.

Thousands of trawler men (regarded as self-employed), and even more on-shore workers, lost their jobs. Some payments were made between 1993 and 1995, and a compensation scheme ran from 2000 to 2002. A highly critical 2007 report by Ann Abraham (Parliamentary and Health Service Ombudsman) resulted in a new scheme (2008).

There is almost certainly no realistic prospect of a revival of Britain's fishing industry, given too many people seeking too few fish.

The Common Fisheries Policy was updated in 2002. Britain's future adherence will doubtless be on the agenda for negotiating our withdrawal from the EU.

EEZ = Exclusive Economic Zone.

The United Nations Convention on the Law of the Sea (UNCLOS) was adopted in 1982, and came into force in 1994. Under the agreement's terms, territorial sea was fixed at 12 miles, and there is provision that a 200 mile EEZ may be established for coastal states.

The Hovercraft, 1956

When this craft was first conceived,
Success was not achieved:
Early engines did not have sufficient power.
A clever man called Chris,
Ponders carefully on this,
And in time the buds of thought begin to flower.

Something simple, it appears,
Can help those Big Ideas:
And the concept needs much better formulation.
An experiment begins
With two modest empty tins,
A hairdryer and careful observation.

Once his tests have been conducted,
A model is constructed –
Out of balsa wood the prototype is made.
All that's obviously lacking
Is some sound financial backing,
But those who might invest cannot be swayed.

The government – approached –
Fear the notion might be poached,
For the many applications are not missed.
Though its import's been agreed,
Our inventor can't proceed:
For his project now is on the secret list!

'It's a plane and not a boat'
Sir Christopher would quote;
Thus the navy's needs cannot be satisfied.
'It's a boat, and not a plane',
Is the Air Force's refrain.
The result is that the scheme's declassified.

Now a useful corporation,
Ends the venture's sad stagnation,
And the funding that it needed is produced.
Version one is not quite right:
It has insufficient height,
Despite its engine's helpful added boost.

Prince Phillip, as you'll know,
Is the type to want a go
And takes control, on thrill and speed intent.
There's a real risk of disaster.
As the Duke goes ever faster.
The damage caused is called 'the Royal Dent'.

John I. Thornycroft & Sons (or simply Thornycroft), a British shipbuilding company based in Woolston, Southampton, developed the initial idea of the hovercraft, and also worked on early designs for hydrofoils.

Sir Christopher Cockerell (1910–1999) was a mechanical engineer from Cambridge. His first experiment was with one empty coffee tin and one empty cat food tin. He discovered that greater lift could be achieved if air were channelled around the perimeter from the front, to create a momentum cushion. His first working model was made from lightweight balsa wood. The private aircraft and shipbuilding sectors considered the concept to be outside their core interests.

'Hovercraft' was originally a trade name, so other terms such as AVC (Air Cushioned Vehicle) have been used. The appropriate funding for the project eventually came from the National Research Development Corporation, and they contracted Saunders-Roe, a British aero- and marine-engineering company based in East Cowes, Isle of Wight to build and demonstrate the first practical hovercraft to Cockerell's design. This was the *SR.N1*.

The top speed recorded by a hovercraft is 86mph, and it was HRH The Duke of Edinburgh who 'dished the bow' on a visit to Saunders-Roe in December 1959.

> 'The Navy said it was a plane, not a boat, the Air Force said it was a boat, not a plane; and the Army was "plain not interested".'
>
> **Sir Christopher Cockerel**

The *SR.N1*.

The height glitch was addressed,
And designers onwards pressed.
A number of refinements soon would figure.
What was once so controversial,
Has now become commercial,
For some hovercraft have grown, and got much bigger.

They are not sailed but flown,
For they float on air that's blown;
The lift's due to the pressure this exerts.
For stability's propounded,
A shape that's slightly rounded
And, to further help, these 'vessels' must wear skirts.

Be it land, or ice, or mud,
Or the waters of a flood,
Over most terrains, these craft won't come to grief.
They can carry tanks and troops,
Ferry pleasure-seeking groups,
And in crisis-stricken zones will bring relief.

Nuclear Submarines

1958's
When the UK and the States
Reach a mutual agreement on defence.
This concerns atomic power –
Should some enemy turn sour,
To help each other makes a lot of sense.

Two years on, we'll see the Queen
Launch a special submarine.
On Trafalgar Day the big event was held.
The *Dreadnought* this was called.
A reactor was installed,
For this British 'first' was nuclear propelled.

In the next breed is inherent,
A powerful deterrent –
The Polaris missile (1968).
Those in favour of disarming
Consider this alarming,
As their protests up in Faslane demonstrate.

CND's voice has been strident,
On renewing Britain's Trident:
It's 'illegal' and 'immoral', they have said.
Damage caused would be immense;
It's a very big expense.
Better spend more on the NHS instead.

Hovercrafts can self-lift and do not need forward thrust, unlike hydrofoils.

It was C.H. Latimer-Needham, a British aircraft designer, who developed the improvement with skirts, which means that hovercraft can travel over small obstructions without damage.

The RNLI (see verses 1038–1046) introduced four hovercraft in 2002 for use on mud flats and in river estuaries.

The US-UK Mutual Defence Agreement on the use of atomic energy is renewed every 10 years (currently due to run until 2024).

Dreadnought was launched on Trafalgar Day (21 October) 1960. With a USA-supplied reactor, this was the UK's first nuclear-powered submarine (built in Barrow by Vickers-Armstrongs). Now outdated, it is currently laid up afloat.

The USA had launched the world's first in 1954 (USS *Nautilus*).

The first of four in its class, HMS *Resolution* was Britain's first ballistic missile submarine.

The aim of the Campaign for Nuclear Disarmament is the UK's unilateral disarmament.

In July 2016, MPs voted by an overwhelming majority to renew the Trident weapons system.

It was announced in 2016 (again on Trafalgar Day) that the *Successor* class (to follow the 1990s *Vanguard* class) would be named the *Dreadnought* class. Work began on the first (which will also be equipped with Trident) late that same year. The new *Dreadnought* is being built by BAE Systems Maritime in Barrow-in-Furness, and is planned to be operational in 2028. She reflects the government's commitment to maintain a continuous at-sea deterrent (CASD).

Do they feel less pessimistic
When the weapons aren't ballistic?
Not nuclear the ones our *Artful* shoots.
This latest sub – and best –
Has certainly impressed...
In its class, it is the third of the *Astutes*.

Its energy supply,
Lasts for years and won't run dry.
Its water and its air can be renewed.
This all seems very clever:
It needn't surface – ever –
(Or, at least, not till the crew's run out of food.)

British Docks, Post-War

Docks, where cargo came and went,
Had seen growing discontent:
With the call-on system, work's not guaranteed.
A strike makes things chaotic,
(Though it's dubbed unpatriotic).
To a special scheme the government agreed.

This secures men 'jobs for life',
But it doesn't end the strife,
And the fifties and the sixties see unrest.
This has little part to play,
In the change that's on its way,
For the import/export system has progressed.

A balanced load is key,
To stability at sea,
And what went where the stevedore would choose.
Sixty years ago,
Handling freight was very slow.
On the waterfront were twenty-plus men crews.

Now ninety odd percent,
Of goods received or sent,
Will travel in a giant metal box.
It could not have been much plainer:
With the modern-type container,
It was curtains for our city centre docks.

(An English engineer
Once had had the same idea:
By Brindley was the concept first enshrined.
His 'box boat' had the goal,
Of conveying crates of coal,
On the network of canals he had designed.)

The missiles carried by *Artful* (commissioned 2016) can hit a target within a range of 1,240 miles (and to an accuracy of a few yards).

The *Astute* class submarines are successors to the *Trafalgar* and *Swiftsure* classes. A total of 7 are planned. They utilise the Common Combat System. *Astute* will not need refuelling during 25 years service, and can circumnavigate the globe without resurfacing. Its only limitation is a 3 months' food supply.

For the call-on system, see verse 1269.

The strike started in September 1945 and eventually fizzled out. The National Dock Labour Scheme (1947) was scrapped in 1989 by Norman Fowler, Secretary of State for Employment.

Bigger ships needed deeper water, which was also a factor in the relocation of docks.

In January 2015, the *Hoegh Osaka* car transporter was grounded off the Isle of Wight after listing more than 40° starboard. Loading computers have now replaced the stevedore.

The modern container was introduced in 1956. The first international voyage (Port Elizabeth, USA, to Rotterdam) was in 1966.

Teams of 20 to 22 longshoremen (dockers, stevedores, lumpers etc) were once needed to load and unload ships.

The percentage figure given relates to non-bulk (ie packaged) cargo. Bulk cargo is either liquid (eg oil) or granular (eg coal, grain, gravel or biomass). Dry bulk accounts for 25 per cent (and liquid bulk 38 per cent) of what goes through ports.

Britain is the fifth largest importer, and ninth largest exporter, in the world.

James Brindley (1716–1772) was a master canal engineer. He invented his 'box boat' in 1766. It was designed to carry 10 wooden containers. Brindley also standardised the size of narrow boats.

A container ship at DP World London Gateway

Fitting ship, plane, train and truck,
Could not be down to luck,
So everyone agreed to standardize.
Now it's all been simplified,
The system's used worldwide,
With the 'TEU' by far the favoured size.

Fast these units can be shifted,
As on or off they're lifted.
This is 'Lo-Lo' freight – how logical that feels!
When vehicles embark,
They roll on – and then they park.
They can 'Ro-Ro', as they come equipped with wheels.

We were once a coal exporter.
Now much comes from o'er the water.
On fossil fuels, the British still depend.
Many million tons are landed.
Ports like Immingham expanded...
And now biomass is yet another trend.

When this stuff once lived and grew.
It used up CO2.
If it's managed well, this biofuel is good.
The carbon is returned,
When these substances are burned.
The biggest source of all, of course, is wood.

At ports, there is equipment,
To unload each massive shipment,
And transfer it into silos, where it's stored.
Then trains roll along the tracks,
To power plants such as Drax,
With combustible material on board.

The capability to fit various types of transport is called intermodalism (see verses 1674–1675). Standardisation was agreed in 1961.

'TEU' is the acronym for 'Twenty foot Equivalent Unit'.

Lo-Lo accounts for about 12 per cent of what goes through British ports. Ro-Ro (roll on, roll off) represents 20 per cent.

Due to a combination of factors, in 2015 Britain also became a net importer of oil for the first time since 1984.

Biomass is a 'closed carbon cycle' fuel, and typically comes in the form of wood pellets. The term can equally refer to animal-derived material. There are some critics of biomass, and sources need to be carefully replenished if it is to be truly environmentally friendly. Its use cuts carbon emissions by 80 per cent (compared to coal).

The world's largest ever single shipment (60,000 tons from British Columbia) was landed at Immingham's renewable fuels terminal (IRFT) in 2015. Continuous unloaders transferred this cargo to a conveyor system.

A new £100 million biomass handling facility at Liverpool Docks (also destined to supply Drax) became fully operational in 2016, and there are similar proposals for Hull.

Permission was granted in 2012 for a new 150MW dedicated biomass power plant at Royal Portbury Dock, Bristol. This dock has the largest entrance lock into any UK port.

Comparative port statistics

1913

TOP 20 BUSIEST UK PORTS (BY MILLION TONNAGE) IN 1913

'Total net* tonnage of British and foreign vessels arriving and departing with cargoes'

1	London	8.58	
2	Liverpool (inc Birkenhead)	4.23	
3	Tyne	3.44	Newcastle, North and South Shields combined
4	Belfast	3.12	
5	Clyde	2.76	Glasgow, Port Glasgow & Greenock
6	Tees and Hartlepool	2.54	Hartlepool, Stockton & Middlesbrough
7	Cardiff	2.20	
8	Portsmouth	1.61	
9	Bristol	1.61	
10	Forth	1.59	Leith, Bo'ness, Methil, Burntisland & Graingemouth combined
11	Southampton	1.57	
12	Beaumaris (inc Holyhead)	1.52	
13	Sunderland	1.45	
14	Hull	1.44	
15	Manchester (inc Runcorn)	1.20	
16	Cowes (inc Isle of Wight)	1.02	
17	Newport	0.98	
18	Plymouth	0.92	
19	Aberdeen	0.92	
20	Isle of Man	0.86	

ANNUAL STATEMENT OF NAVIGATION, 1913: Table No. 36

*Tonnage figures are calculated slightly differently for the years shown, and are therefore not directly comparable

TOP 20 BUSIEST UK PORTS (BY MILLON TONNAGE) IN 2015

'Total gross* tonnage of cargo moved inwards and outwards'

	Port	Tonnage	Notes
1	Grimsby & Immingham	59.10	
2	London	45.43	
3	Milford Haven	37.68	
4	Southampton	37.66	
5	Tees and Hartlepool	35.84	
6	Liverpool	31.25	
7	Felixstowe	27.97	
8	Dover	27.29	
9	Forth	27.07	
10	Belfast	16.70	
11	Clyde	12.48	
12	Hull	10.02	
13	Medway	9.09	About 29 wharves on the Rivers Medway & Swale and their tributaries
14	Bristol	8.87	
15	Rivers Hull and Humber	8.26	New Holland, Tetney Terminal, Barton-on-Humber & Barrow-on-Humber
16	Port Talbot	8.11	
17	Manchester	6.52	
18	Sullom Voe, Shetland Islands	6.12	
19	Glensanda, Scottish Highlands	5.59	Port is a granite quarry, used only for exporting
20	Tyne	4.99	

DEPARTMENT FOR TRANSPORT: *UK Port Freight Statistics: 2015 Final figures report*

12 Modern times

12

Modern times

Marine Pollution

Humans make a contribution
To the problem of pollution:
Our activities on land affect the seas.
We can't cling to the hope
That 'they're big enough to cope',
And we now know we can't treat them as we please.

Vessels play a part –
Greenhouse gasses for a start,
Plus the noise they make, and all the stuff they 'leak'.
And cruise ships are contenders
As the very worst offenders:
Each dumps a million gallons' waste each week.

And, worst of all maybe,
Tons of plastic in the sea,
To marine life is now proving deleterious.
It takes eons to degrade,
So attention must be paid
To a problem which can only get more serious.

Of the life forms that abound,
(Like those *Challenger* had found),
Some feed themselves by acting as a filter.
The water they thus sweeten,
But if toxic stuff is eaten,
The eco-system might get out of kilter.

A design fault with the steering,
Had the *Torrey Canyon* veering
Onto Pollard's Rock. She couldn't be refloated.
Her break-up caused a slick,
Very large and very thick:
Huge areas of sea and coast were coated.

Attempts to set this burning
Didn't work: the waves were churning,
And the fires went out in much too stiff a breeze.
To disperse it was so urgent,
They resorted to detergent –
This cure, in part, was worse than the disease.

About 80 per cent of marine pollution originates on land.

In the 1950s, the United Nations recognized that there was a problem, and there were several conferences on the Law of the Sea.

Vessels leak oily bilge water for example. Sound travels faster through water than it does through air, and there is evidence that acoustic pollution is affecting wildlife.

The million gallons discharged by cruise liners is an average figure, which includes grey water waste, (from sinks, galleys, baths and showers), and human sewage.

It takes centuries for a plastic bottle to biodegrade, possibly as long as 1,000 years. Government action could prove effective. The 5p charge for plastic bags has reduced their single use by 85 per cent.

For *Challenger* see verses 1256–1262.

'Filter feeders' include certain types of fish, baleen whales (see verse 393), sponges, bivalves and crustaceans (see verses 1677–1691).

Human navigational error was also to blame for the *Torrey Canyon*'s running aground (1967). The supertanker was carrying about 31,000,000 gallons of crude oil, from Kuwait to Milford Haven, when she struck Pollard's Rock (between the Scilly Isles and Cornwall). The spillage is regarded as the world's first environmental disaster. Bombing by the Fleet Air Arm only made matters worse. Dispersants (a more accurate term than detergent) were used in 'Operation Mop Up'. These are toxic.

Those on board were rescued, although the captain and three of the crew initially stayed on the ship.

The Sea – challenge and recreation

Heroes and Heroines

Francis Chichester (from Devon),
In 1967,
Reached Plymouth, to acclaim and celebration.
He deserved all this idolatry:
His round-world trip was solitary,
A major feat of circumnavigation.

Of his ilk, we'd quite a crop.
Knox-Johnston raced non-stop,
In the 'Golden Globe' – his win was undiminished
By the fact that, though inspired,
All the others had retired,
Leaving Robin as the only man who finished.

One who gave that race a try,
Scottish yachtsman Charles 'Chay' Blyth,
Would make his solo trip by heading west.
Then a record-breaking Dame –
Miss MacArthur is her name –
Succeeded in her 'fastest ever' quest.

Although she's less well-known,
In the race 'Around Alone',
Emma Richards clocked two memorable firsts.
When the company's you only,
It must sometimes feel quite lonely,
Pursuing that for which your spirit thirsts.

Those who yearn for salty air,
Have some time and cash to spare,
But no desire to be both crew and skipper,
Those whose stamina won't fail,
Those who want to learn to sail,
Should think about enrolling for 'The Clipper'.

Folk who seek Olympic glory,
Should heed Ben Ainslie's story –
Then rue the fact they started way too late!
To medal, as did Ben,
Start competing when you're ten,
Having mastered all your skills at aged just eight.

Sir Francis Chichester (1901–1972) was born in Barnstaple. His achievement, aboard the yacht *Gypsy Moth IV*, is regarded as the first true single-handed circumnavigation (one stop in Sydney).

In the *Sunday Times* Golden Globe Race (1968–9), Robin Knox-Johnston (*b*.1939) achieved the first single-handed non-stop circumnavigation aboard *Suhaili*. He needed to take sufficient provisions for the 312 days it took him to complete the 30,000 mile round trip.

In the race, Nigel Tetley's trimaran sank and he was rescued. He later became the first person to circumnavigate the world solo in a trimaran. Donald Crowhurst, after radioing false positions, committed suicide. Naval Officer Bill King, the oldest participant, eventually achieved his solo circumnavigation dream in 1973 aboard *Galway Blazer II*.

A 50th anniversary race, with eighteen participants, started on 1 July 2018 following (like the original) an eastbound route.

Chay Blyth (*b*.1940) competed in the Golden Globe with no previous sailing experience – though he had rowed the Atlantic. In the yacht *British Steel*, he later became the first person to sail solo around the world westwards (1971).

In 2005, aboard the trimaran *B&Q/Castorama*, Ellen MacArthur beat the existing world record for a single-handed non-stop circumnavigation (in seventy-one days), though the previous holder regained it two years later.

In 2008, Samantha Davies came fourth in the Vendée Globe (single-handed non-stop circumnavigation).

Emma Richards was the first British woman, and the youngest person ever, to complete Around Alone (previously the Velux 5 Oceans Race) – a single-handed yacht race with stops (2002–3).

In 1989, Tracy Edwards skippered the first all-female crew in the professionals' Whitbread Round the World Race (now the Volvo Ocean Race).

Conceived by Robin Knox-Johnston, the Clipper Round the World Race is run every two years. Qualified skippers lead amateur crews, many of whom (about 40 per cent) have had no previous sailing experience. Crews can sign up either for the whole race, or for individual legs.

Ben Ainslie is the most successful sailor in Olympic history.

The sea has never been friendly to man. At most, it has been the accomplice of human restlessness.

Joseph Conrad, writer

Cowes Week

At Cowes (the Isle of Wight),
For two centuries (not quite),
Has been held the best-established of regattas.
In the double-tided Solent,
The yachting may be volant –
But sailing's not the only thing that matters.

Britain's posh elite,
Had their 'season' to complete.
But, for royalty, a bitter contest beckoned.
To begin, Prince Bertie won,
But not to be outdone,
The Kaiser built his *Meteor the Second*.

With great determination
To prove German domination,
His yachts were ever larger, ever faster.
Naval power was his obsession;
Its purpose was aggression,
And, globally, in time this spelt disaster.

The Fastnet Race

Every two years, there takes place,
An oceangoing race,
Regarded as a classic of its kind.
To take part, there's no credential –
Strangely, training's not essential,
Though the route must be as tricky as you'll find.

For six hundred miles, a test...
The Channel, heading west
From the Solent, where the yachts line up to start...
From Land's End, it's Ireland bound...
Fastnet Rock to sail around...
Then back again. The weather plays its part.

Tragedy – inflicted
By a storm (quite unpredicted) –
Meant those fragile craft by massive waves were tossed.
Out of nowhere, it appeared.
Sails were ripped and masts were sheared,
Boats capsized or overturned, and lives were lost.

The first Cowes event was held in 1826. George IV (then Prince Regent) was a keen yachtsman and an enthusiastic supporter. Cowes Week has been held every year since then, except during the World Wars.

Cowes Week marked the end of the London 'season'. It still features on the social calendar (in early August, between 'Glorious Goodwood' and the start of grouse shooting).

Prince Bertie was later King Edward VII.

Meteor II competed in 1896. The Kaiser's first *Meteor* was the British cutter *Thistle*, which had been an unsuccessful challenger in the 1887 America's Cup. There would be five *Meteors* in all.

Kaiser Wilhelm II was an avid reader of *The Influence of Sea Power upon History* by Admiral Alfred Thayer Mahan. In 1895, he established Kiel Week, the German equivalent of Cowes Week.

See section/verses 1323–1328 on **The Anglo-German naval arms race**.

The Fastnet Race began in 1925, and was the idea of British yachtsman Weston Martyr. Although training is not mandatory, RYA (Royal Yachting Association) 'competent crew' training is recommended. The route of the race, which ends in Plymouth, is roughly 605 miles, depending on the exact course taken.

The disastrous 1979 race resulted in 18 fatalities (15 yachtsmen and 3 rescuers).

> The sea showed that it can be a deadly enemy and that those who go to sea for pleasure must do so in the full knowledge that they may encounter dangers of the highest order.
>
> **Concluding paragraph, Fastnet inquiry report, 1979**

The Tall Ships' Races and Sail Training

When by steam power overtaken,
Sailing vessels were forsaken,
And declined into a state of obsolescence.
A man from London city
Considered this a pity.
A thought he shared got ready acquiescence.

Bernard Morgan had the notion
Of a contest on the ocean,
In which youngsters under training would take part.
The original intent,
Was a grand 'one off' event:
But of yearly 'tall ships' races proved the start.

The purported 'last farewell'
Manned by trainee personnel,
Was something that gained popular appeal.
Now a global competition,
It gives ample recognition
Of the 'friendship-without-barriers' ideal.

Coastal pursuits

Some enthusiasts will buy
Boards on which to stand (or lie),
Then seek big waves to ride – once they have caught 'em.
Thurso East/Freshwater West,
Offer surfing at its best,
And apparently the time to go is autumn.

On the fringes of the sea
People like to sail and ski,
Or ride powered craft which travel at some speed.
Recreation's much more fun,
In the rare event of sun,
(When a good book and a deck chair's all you need?)

Morgan, a retired solicitor, first discussed the concept of a tall ships' race with the Portuguese Ambassador to the UK, who became a strong supporter, and helped to develop the idea.

The first race (Torbay to Lisbon), involving 20 vessels from 10 countries, was held in July 1956. A British ship, *Moyana*, won the overall race. The races and other events are organised by Sail Training International. Ships are nowadays being constructed specifically for the purpose of sail training.

Thurso East is in the north of Scotland. Freshwater West is in Pembrokeshire. Windswept, these beaches are reckoned to be havens for experts, although England's south west also offers good surfing conditions.

Founded in 1875, the RYA governs yachting, windsurfing, motor cruising, power boating and personal water craft (water scooters). It also manages the British sailing team, one of the most successful Olympic teams in recent years.

Shipwrecks and Diving

The esteemed United Nations,
Has done some calculations,
On how many wrecks lie on the ocean floor.
Three million is the figure,
But that number might be bigger:
An 'at least' suggests there probably are more.

If you seek, then you may find
What the past has left behind.
Archaeologists do this. They're very clever.
So they must be quite frustrated
That they haven't yet located
The *Endurance*, and what's left of the *Endeavour*.

Both have featured in this book:
The latter, sailed by Cook,
V. America would have a part to play.
Of our troops, she was a carrier,
Then was sunk to form a barrier
To blockade the French at Narragansett Bay.

That most famous sunken ship,
Was on her maiden trip,
(Surely everyone has heard of the *Titanic*?).
An iceberg she had struck,
Which was really awful luck,
But the orchestra played on and didn't panic.

King Henry's *Mary Rose*
In The Solent did repose.
She was lost, then found, and lost then found again.
It was she – this they could tell
For inscribed upon her bell
Was the legend, 'I was made in 1510.'

This ship (now resurrected),
And those like her are protected –
Safely resting in their underwater berth.
Any damage is a crime,
As their preservation's prime
If, to history, they're deemed to have a worth.

UNESCO has decreed
That old wrecks are, indeed,
A heritage that no one should forget.
To make good this intention,
Now in force is a convention –
Although Britain hasn't ratified it yet.

More than 44,000 wrecks are located around the coast of Great Britain and Ireland. Discoveries are still being made. In August 2016, the Axe Boat (a late-/post-medieval coastal vessel) was scheduled under the Ancient Monuments and Archaeological Areas Act 1979.

Maritime (or marine) archaeology looks at the relationship of humans with the sea, through the study of the physical remains of vessels, seaside structures and cargoes. The approximate locations of the ships mentioned, and many others, are known.

2019 will see a major expedition in the Weddell Sea to locate Ernest Shackleton's ship (see verses 1307–1308).

As of May 2016, researchers believe they might finally have discovered the *Endeavour* (see verse 582), which was scuttled in 1778, during the American War of Independence.

The wreck of RMS *Titanic*, which sank in 1912 at the cost of more than 1,500 lives, was located in 1985. It is in two main parts. The doomed eight-man band had moved to the deck and continued to play 'cheery' music until the very end. It is probably untrue that the last song played, as recalled by Mrs Vera Dick, was 'Nearer my God to Thee'.

There were attempts to retrieve the *Mary Rose*'s guns after she first sank in 1545. She was rediscovered in 1836, when fishermen snagged their nets on her (recovery attempts followed until 1842). She was located again in 1971, and was finally raised in 1982.

The 1973 Protection of Wrecks Act includes vessels of historical, archaeological and artistic value. About 60 ships are currently protected. The act also covers dangerous sites (two wrecks currently designated as such). To qualify as 'old', wrecks must have been underwater for at least one hundred years, and have a known location.

There are (as at May 2018) 60 parties to the UNESCO 2001 Convention on the Protection of the Underwater Cultural Heritage. Although the UK has not ratified this Convention, the Government has adopted the best practice principles contained in its annex.

One UNESCO project, (off the coast of North Carolina), concerns *Queen Anne's Revenge* – flagship of the pirate Blackbeard (see verse 489), and one-time slave-trading vessel.

Ships that lie beneath the waves
Are very often graves:
Interfering with them might make some object.
And this isn't any wonder
If the greedy dive to plunder,
For this doesn't show the requisite respect.

Any ship that comes to grief
Makes an artificial reef,
Which life forms in the sea will soon bedeck.
How such colonies evolve,
We are seeking now to solve,
By studying what's happened to a wreck.

The *Scylla* was submerged,
(Once of oil she had been purged).
Queen oysters made their home upon her frame.
In a plague of starfish zoomed,
And the oysters were consumed,
When these predators to dinner laid their claim.

Diving, and Working Underwater

This reef settled and is thriving.
It attracts those who like diving,
For the underwater world has fascination.
Though it's not a risk-free sport,
(The unwary can get caught),
Many 'scuba' as a form of recreation.

Nitrogen's a gas,
And it builds up more, alas,
The longer and the deeper one descends.
It can fizz and kill, unless
Bodies slowly decompress:
A sickness that's referred to as 'the bends'.

Without air, the sea means death,
Unless you hold your breath,
As the ancients did each time they took the plunge.
On the whole, it would be girls
Who free-dived seeking pearls.
It was fishermen who targeted the sponge.

Aside from sea bed treasures,
Men once took disruptive measures:
In wartime many covert schemes were hatched.
This was sabotage and sneaky.
Holes in hulls would make ships leaky:
Or rodes were cut, and anchors thus detached.

Certain sites are protected as war graves (see verses 1661–1662 on the Falkands Conflict).

HMS *Scylla* is a frigate which had performed a variety of roles during her naval career. She was deliberately sunk off Whitsand Bay, Cornwall, in 2004. After a year, fifty species of plants and animals had been identified on or around her. After eating all the oysters, the starfish also died off.

The acronym SCUBA stands for self-contained underwater breathing apparatus.

Pain in the joints is the more common symptom of 'the bends'. The term was first used in 1878, during the construction of New York's Brooklyn Bridge. In 1907 English physiologist Dr J.S. Haldane, whilst conducting experiments with the Royal Navy, discovered that the gradual release of pressure prevents the formation of gas bubbles.

Pearl-diving has thrived in many civilizations since 3000 BC. In most, the divers were predominantly women.

Ancient Greeks Homer and Plato both mentioned the sponge as an object used for bathing.

Free divers, who sometimes put oil in their ears to counteract pressure, could stay under water for up to 5 minutes, and go to a depth of 100 feet.

Underwater acts of sabotage were commonplace throughout Europe up to, and throughout, the Middle Ages.

A rode is a rope, cable and/or chain that connects an anchor to a ship.

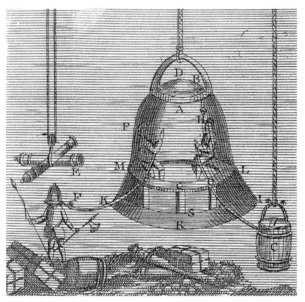

Halley's diving bell

The doubloons on Spanish ships,
Attracted William Phips:
A man who'd spent his childhood tending sheep.
He used, as his sustainer,
An upside down container,
When a fortune he was collecting from the deep.

Even if their lungs were strong,
Folk could not stay under long.
Buying time meant something functional and new.
Helmets had been tried,
But fresh air was not supplied –
And the wearer was soon breathing CO_2.

This leads men to conclude,
That the air must be renewed,
(Although *why* is something nobody yet knows).
Halley's diving bell appears –
A contraption used for years –
And then Smeaton would devise the pump and hose.

Two brothers, name of Deane,
Took to working sub-marine,
Using helmets John designed to cope with smoke.
This was modified en route,
With an added canvas suit
Which is waterproof, so can withstand a soak.

This apparel – all in one –
(Just how did they put it on?),
Soon would separate, and hence the 'diving dress'.
That was Pasley's bright idea,
And this clever engineer,
Had talents which are certain to impress.

Explosives were his 'thing',
And his expertise he'd bring
To their use – once he had made the correct deductions.
All his brainpower he would flex,
For the salvaging of wrecks,
Some of which were causing dire obstructions.

A caisson is a box,
(A component of some docks).
As it's watertight, with air it can be filled.
So workers who submerge
Can breathe, when they've the urge,
While they labour on the structures that they build.

Born in an American settlement in Maine (established 1639), Phips (1651–1695) was later apprenticed as a shipwright, then ran a successful shipyard. Under the patronage of English Rear Admiral Sir John Narborough, and a group of investors formed by the Duke of Albemarle, Phips plundered over 34 tons of treasure off Hispaniola. He was knighted by James II in 1687.

Aristotle wrote of divers using air-filled cauldrons. In 1531 an Italian used a workable bell to salvage a sunken Roman ship from a lake.

Devised (1691) by Edmond Halley (see also verse 509), and not much improved for almost a century, the diving bell allowed a team of divers to stay submerged for one and a half hours to a depth of 60 feet (18.3m).

John Smeaton (see verse 1064) devised his bell in 1788. Updated in 1790, it was used underwater during construction of the breakwater at Ramsgate harbour.

Charles (1796–1848) and John (1800–1884) Deane published the world's first diving manual – *Method of Using Deane's Patent Diving Apparatus* – in 1836. John's 'Smoke Helmet', patented 1823, was developed after he had rescued horses, trapped by fire, from stables. He wore a medieval knight's helmet, air-pumped by hose. Their diving suit was developed in conjunction with Augustus Siebe (1788–1872), a German born British engineer.

Sir Charles William Pasley (1780–1861) also devised the 'buddy' system of diving in pairs. He was the first director of the Royal Engineer training establishment at Chatham (founded 1812) where, among other things, he contributed to the development of telegraphy (see verses 652 & 1129–1141). A talented linguist, his interests were wide-ranging, and included Portland cement (see verse 1065). He cleared two wrecks from the Thames and, most famously (1836), the once magnificent *Royal George* (see images by verses 441 & 816). This ship had sunk at Spithead in 1782, with great loss of life.

The Deane brothers, whilst engaged on this same project, were alerted to the position of the *Mary Rose*. They were probably the first marine salvors of the modern era.

Caisson is the French word for big box. Decompression sickness ('the bends') was, (and occasionally still is), referred to as caisson sickness.

By the mid 19th century, hydraulic pumps were being used to maintain an air supply. Workers went in and out of the caisson by means of an airlock.

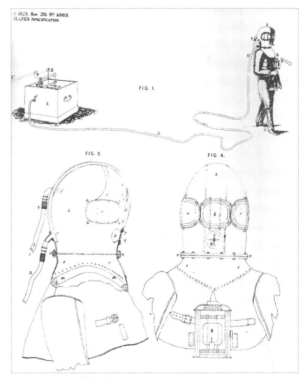

The Deane Patent Diving Apparatus

As always, things progress,
Now we have the DDS:
A work base used beneath the ocean's foam,
Eight hour shifts can be endured,
And some comfort is assured...
It has furniture and beds – quite 'home from home'.

Life can be maintained
With a tank that's self-contained,
The creator of the first deserves a mention.
Fleuss made his out of copper,
And he almost came a cropper,
Whilst testing out his cumbersome invention.

The Falklands War, 1982

We turn now to a place –
Once a useful British base –
Of the Falklands Islands we've already heard.
In 1982
Major trouble there would brew,
And this is an account of what occurred.

The future wasn't clear,
For those isles we once held dear.
They didn't pay their way, had no big dock.
But (and this was paramount),
We must take into account
Those who live there – almost all of British stock.

It was claimed that 'Las Malvinas'
By rights were Argentina's –
A thought which filled the islanders with dread.
Galtieri's harsh regime
Was abusive and extreme,
And word of its atrocities had spread.

When the islands first he seized –
His countrymen were pleased:
Such a joy to know they're back where they belong!
He thought Britain had forsaken
This possession he'd retaken,
But his supposition proved entirely wrong.

What he reasoned made some sense:
We had just reviewed defence
And, the year before, big cuts had been announced.
The *Endurance*'s patrol
Of those isles that we once 'stole',
Was about to end. Could this be why he pounced?

DDS = Deep Diving System. Such systems were used extensively in the 1970s and 1980s during the off-shore oil-rig boom.

Englishman Henry Fleuss, pronounced Flay-oose (1851–1933), patented the first self-contained apparatus in 1878. There is no truth in the account that claims he was killed by it. He died at home.

The Falkland Islands were useful to Britain, despite their lack of a dockyard and repair facilities. In 2014, a Houston based company opened a temporary dock facility to support oil exploration in the area. The Falklands had been a British Crown colony since 1841 (see verses 284 & 444) and a coaling station was once located there.

In 1965, the United Nations passed a resolution calling on Britain and Argentina to negotiate a settlement regarding the islands. Inconclusive negotiations had been conducted since then.

Leopoldo Galtieri led a three-man military junta which presided over the 'dirty war' in which many people became 'the disappeared'.

Argentina's invasion, inauspiciously termed Operation Rosario (see verse 295), began with an amphibious assault. The neighbouring island of South Georgia had already been occupied by Argentine marines posing as scrap metal dealers.

John Nott's 1981 Defence Review focused on supporting NATO, rather than on out of area operations. Drastic cutbacks affecting the Royal Navy included the decommissioning of the ice patrol vessel HMS *Endurance*.

Thatcher needed scant persuasion.
To rise to the occasion –
A rescue mission clearly the intent.
The islands' occupation
Caused a lot of consternation.
Every ship that was available was sent.

Submarines arrive there first.
Three are rapidly dispersed,
And a maritime exclusion zone's defined.
In five ships that deep-sea trawled
Apparatus is installed,
These will sweep the seas in case they have been mined.

Naval ships were in the Med.
These speed southwards now instead.
There's a hasty merchant vessel requisitioning.
Aircraft carriers (we've two),
Go to do what they must do.
(One's been sold. The other's down for decommissioning.)

Cruise ships find themselves committed,
And are rapidly refitted,
To accommodate the troops they must convey.
One such, 'The Great White Whale',
Is the first of these to sail –
Into the very thick of the affray.

The QE2 goes later.
Her facilities now cater
For three thousand troops. She's crewed by volunteers.
There are helipads installed.
The hull is part steel-walled.
Her departure's marked by bagpipes, bands and cheers.

Vessels prefixed 'RFA'
Have a vital part to play.
These 'auxiliaries' support the British fleet.
Though the task force is immense,
The situation's tense –
The challenge not an easy one to meet.

Seems the war zone doesn't count,
When our first attack we mount –
Controversy's since raged re: the legalities.
The Belgrano has been stalked,
And the British never balked.
She's torpedoed... sunk... with hundreds of fatalities.

Margaret Thatcher (1925–2013) was Prime Minister from 1979–1990. Under the command of Admiral Sir John Fieldhouse, the mission to recover the Falkland Islands was called 'Operation Corporate'. The main body of the Task Force arrived a month after the invasion.

Nuclear submarines HMSs *Spartan*, *Splendid* and *Conqueror* were the first to be deployed. Six British submarines in total were involved in the conflict. The first exclusion zone, with a 200 nautical mile radius, was later extended to within 12 miles of the Argentinean coast.

Five Hull trawlers, HMSs *Farnella*, *Cordella*, *Junelia*, *Northella* and *Pict* were requisitioned as minesweepers. They were crewed by RN personnel. Aircraft carrier HMS *Invincible* had been sold to Australia. Under the 1981 Review, HMS *Hermes*, which became the Task Force's flagship, had been due to be decommissioned. She was later sold to the Indian navy (1986) and is still operational.

'The Great White Whale' was the cruise ship SS *Canberra*. In the Mediterranean on the day of the invasion, she was ordered back to Southampton, and refitted within a week. Another cruise ship, the SS *Uganda*, was converted for use as a hospital ship. Like the *QE2*, she too was fitted with a helicopter landing area.

The Royal Fleet Auxiliary (RFA) was formed in 1905 to provide warships with coal. Today, the RFA continues to supply fuel in RAS (replenishment at sea) operations, and also increasingly works as part of NATO, and UN peacekeeping and humanitarian operations.

The task force comprised a total of 127 vessels.

Because the ARA *General Belgrano* was beyond the exclusion zone and heading away from it, there have been assertions that her sinking was a war crime. She was being tracked by look-out submarine HMS *Conqueror*, from which three torpedoes were fired. 321 crew and 2 civilians on board were killed. 772 were rescued.

ON THE SINKING OF THE *GENERAL BELGRANO*

'It was one of the easiest decisions of the whole war.'

Sir John Nott, Secretary of State for Defence

'It was absolutely not a war crime... It was an act of war, lamentably legal.'

Hector Bozo, Captain of the *General Belgrano*, speaking in 2007

'The location of the *Belgrano* outside the Exclusion Zone did not mean it was withdrawn from the war... The integrated naval force had been deployed to carry out an attack on the British Fleet in a co-ordinated operation with other naval groups... The heading away from the enemy fleet was only momentary, as the commander saw fit to wait for a more convenient time [to attack].'

Argentine Admiral Enrique Moilna Pico

ARA *General Belgrano* sinking

There's a big threat from the air.
Planes have missiles which can tear
Through a vessel, even though some don't explode.
Mortal damage is inflicted,
Once bombing's unrestricted,
And to this a lot of damage will be owed.

Causing *Sheffield*'s sad demise,
And delivered from the skies,
An Exocet would cause a fatal fire.
The ship is now the grave,
Of the men they couldn't save.
'Don't disturb' is what the legal rules require.

In four more protected places,
The chilly sea embraces,
The remains of those who didn't see it through.
Six ships in all are lost,
There is further human cost:
The *Glamorgan*'s spared, but not so fourteen crew.

As events move ever faster,
We see triumph match disaster.
Mixed emotions these events would all engender.
This nasty war was brief.
To the islanders' relief,
It resulted in an Argentine surrender.

Though this conflict's in the past,
We may not have heard the last
Of the Falklands. Britain's claim is still refuted.
Those whose home's there have clear views –
Staying British all would choose –
But, despite this, where they live remains disputed.

Argentine bombs had a particular, and generally fortunate, tendency not to explode, although this was not the case with HMS *Antelope* (1 technician was killed in an attempt to defuse one of two UXBs, and the ensuing explosions resulted in the ship's demise).

HMS *Sheffield* lies in a 'Protected Place', in accordance with the Military Remains Act 1986. The wrecks of SS *Atlantic Conveyor*, a 'Ro-Ro' container ship (see verse 1598) which was transporting helicopters, and RFA *Sir Galahad* (a landing craft) are both also in such places.

HMS *Coventry* (19 killed) is a Controlled Site under the 1986 Act. HMS *Ardent* (22 fatalities) is a protected site under the Falkland Islands' Protection of Wrecks Act, as is HMS *Antelope*. HMS *Glamorgan* was a further Exocet victim.

In 2012, the Argentine congress approved the Ushuaia Declaration claiming sovereignty over the Malvinas.

In a 2013 referendum, 99.9 per cent of Falkland islanders voted to remain a British Overseas Territory.

HMS *Dauntless*, (2007), Britain's most sophisticated nuclear warship, has been deployed to the South Atlantic.

HMS *Exeter* homeward bound after the Falklands War, 21 July 1982

HMS *Invincible* returning home, 17 September 1982

Ferries

If there's water to be crossed
But no bridge, all is not lost,
If a ferry serves your chosen destination.
Shore to not-so-distant shore,
Is what these boats are for,
Mostly running to a scheduled operation.

Perhaps the oldest route in Britain,
(About which a song's been written),
By Benedictine monks was first begun.
To the Pool (the only 'quay'),
For a very modest fee,
A 'ferry 'cross the Mersey' would be run.

That watery divider
Was, in bygone times, much wider;
To traverse it, not the easiest of missions.
At the priory some stayed,
When their journey was delayed:
They might wait some days for suitable conditions.

The *Herald of Free Enterprise* Disaster, 1987

Readers of the Sun,
Booked a bargain trip for fun:
On the *Herald of Free Enterprise* this jaunt.
They'll have thought it cash well spent,
For a memorable event.
What they got were recollections that would haunt.

As they left Zeebrugge port,
Surely no one had the thought,
That their ferry to much danger was exposed.
As she set off back to Dover,
She took moments to tilt over,
Swiftly flooded, as the bow doors were not closed.

To blame was human error
For the death toll, and the terror
Of the souls in icy water who were trapped.
For that vessel, part aground,
No buyer could be found.
She was taken to Taiwan, and there was scrapped.

A priory at Birkenhead (then a tiny hamlet) was established in 1150. In those days, the Mersey estuary had sand dunes, marshes and cliffs. Liverpool was a village, and the only suitable landing place was the Pool.

On 6 March 1987, 193 people perished aboard the *Herald of Free Enterprise*, many from hypothermia. Ensuring the doors were closed was the job of the assistant boatswain, Mark Stanley, who was asleep in his cabin. The first officer, Leslie Sabel, probably believed Stanley would arrive to secure the doors. Boatswain Terence Ayling did not close them, as it was not his duty. Captain David Lewry set off assuming the doors were closed. The disaster led to many improvements in ferry design, especially relating to vehicle decks.

The Thames Barrier

The encroachment of the sea
In 1953,
Prompted thoughts about how London might be spared.
Certain parts could be submerged
If the North Sea's waters surged,
And the capital would need to be prepared.

But what system could they try
For keeping London dry?
A kind of dam? Some clever flood conveyance?
Can't have anything that blocks
Ships from reaching all those docks:
For a while the notion fell into abeyance.

But a few years later on
Those big vessels all had gone.
Of their business now 'the Docklands' were deprived.
Trade had steadily been slowing,
Whilst Tilbury was growing,
For the standardized container had arrived.

The smaller drum or crate
Was once used to package freight.
All the handling this required made little sense.
It's much easier to deal
With huge boxes made of steel
And – in terms of labour needed – less intense.

There's no packing and unpacking,
They're designed for ease of stacking,
And will fit the ship, the lorry or the train.
Their use is international
And sensible and rational –
But they're heavy and need lifting with a crane.

Anti-flood schemes were rekindled,
Once that river traffic dwindled,
And did not include the massive cargo carrier.
The solution that was planned,
Across the water spanned:
Its cylinders rotate to form a barrier.

For coastal erosion see verse 27.

Fourteen people died in the Thames Flood of 1928.

A storm surge presents a tidal risk. There is also a fluvial risk, where high river levels combine with a normal high tide. The worst case scenario is when both extreme factors combine.

With the advent of containerisation (see verses 1595–1598), business in London's Docklands had dwindled to almost nothing by 1960.

Referred to as break bulk cargo, goods once had to be loaded individually. Boxes, sacks, bags and barrels were also used for packaging. Containerisation also reduced the risk of theft or damage – and the need for warehousing.

The Thames Barrier was officially opened by Her Majesty the Queen in 1984. The concept of rotating gates, based on the design of his gas cooker's taps, was devised in 1969 by Charles Draper. The gates are closed when a flood warning is issued.

The Thames Barrier

Shellfish

Bivalves

Either caught in nets or hooked,
At fin fish we have looked,
But other types of seafood can be found.
Some, regarded as delectable,
Are readily collectible,
And many are abundant all coast round.

Bivalves filter feed,
Which gives rise to the need
To ensure that, for consumption, they are fit.
So a process is applied
Whereby they're purified:
This gets rid of any toxins, germs and grit.

The Victorians of Britain,
With shellfish had been smitten:
It was relished in those urban conurbations.
It declined in popularity,
For causing much mortality
When, with typhoid, there were clear associations.

The mussel's unassuming.
Its numbers keep on booming.
It's been eaten for at least eight thousand years.
There has long been cultivation,
Which ensures its procreation:
To poles and ropes, it readily adheres.

Trowelled, or picked by hand,
Cockles burrow in wet sand.
They leave traces and can rarely truly hide.
On one tragic winter's day,
Pickers out in Morecambe Bay,
Fell victim to a fast incoming tide.

Catching oysters: there's no bar,
If the month contains an 'R':
If not, they're left alone and with good reason.
A bit of peace they need,
For when they choose to breed –
So the warmer months are very much 'closed season'.

They flourish in the south...
In the great Thames' river mouth...
Those from Essex and from Kent one can rely on.
From west Scotland, all can savour
The firmness and pure flavour,
Of the molluscs that folk harvest from Loch Ryan.

See verse 1605 for filter feeders.

Oysters, scallops, cockles, mussels, clams etc all need cleaning, which is done by a process known as depuration.

Consumption of shellfish slumped dramatically until about 1960. The link between illness, caused by *salmonella thyphi*, and shellfish was discovered in 1900. Tradition has it that Molly Malone, fictional Dublin purveyor of cockles and mussels ('alive, alive oh'), died as a result of sampling her own wares.

As with all species, there is a danger of overfishing mussels. This happened in the early 19th century when natural beds were over-exploited.

Blue mussel shells have been found in middens dating back to 6000 BC.

Like whelks and winkles, mussels live in the intertidal zone and stick to any substrate (including each other). From 1246, the French used poles called bouchots. Elsewhere in Europe, subtidal on-bottom culture plots were used.

Twenty-three migrant Chinese workers tragically drowned in February 2004, whilst cockle-picking.

The Romans are known to have farmed oysters, which are found all round the British coast. However, most fishing is in the south, (including Dorset, Devon and Cornwall), and in west Scotland. The Loch Ryan oyster bed was established in 1701 under royal charter. The company was winner of 'Scotland's Best Native Oyster Award' in 2016. Those from Pyefleet (near Colchester) are probably the most prized (and pricey).

Apart from any interference with reproduction, oysters aren't harvested in the summer because they don't taste good when they're spawning.

Seasonal fishing does not apply to Pacific rock oysters, introduced into British waters circa 1980.

Shrimp fishing in Morecambe Bay

Since the Normans first arrived,
One festival's survived.
It is held around the feast day of Saint James.
It's a yearly celebration
For the oyster's veneration,
And guarantees a week of fun and games.

Scallops, widely caught,
Are a product we export.
With its 'kings' and 'queens', the species sounds so regal.
The males are bigger sized,
And thus more highly prized –
And catches without limits are still legal.

Dredges don't discern,
Causing 'habitat concern':
Behind a boat this implement will drag.
Those bivalves that we take,
Are scraped up with a rake,
Then collected in a robust chainmail bag.

Crustaceans

Fish for prawns at night!
Scan the water with a light.
Their eyes glow red – the only clue one needs.
When the tide is going out
There are lots of them about.
They like to live amongst the rocks and weeds.

Shrimps – the prawn's small brownish cousin –
Can be captured by the dozen.
Round Britain, they are found in many parts.
The amateur's best bet,
Is a simple hand-held net;
Folk once used, for deeper water, horse-drawn carts.

Nine hundred years ago,
So the records seem to show,
The English first caught crabs, and these they ate.
To nab what they enjoyed:
Types of net were first employed:
Now we're using creels, or crab pots lined with bait.

A small float marks the spot,
Of each sunken luring pot:
But crabs are also sought for recreation.
In places where they lurk,
Any hook and line will work,
Especially if what's dangling is some bacon!

The modern Whitstable Festival is a revival of an ancient event which symbolically celebrates the 'Landing of the Oysters'. These receive a formal 'blessing'. The feast day of Saint James of Compostela (Galicia, Spain) is on 25 July. The games include the 'Mud Tug' competition.

The main scallop grounds are in the English Channel and Irish Sea but, since 2000, a moderate fishery has also been developed off the Yorkshire coast. In August 2018, French and British fishing boats clashed over scallops, which the British can lawfully gather all year round, whereas French law is more restrictive.

About 60 per cent are exported. Unlike fin fish, scallops are not subject to Total Allowable Catch limits (TACs). However, fishing for them is not allowed in an increasing number of Special Areas of Conservations (SACs).

The seabed-friendly dredge has yet to be invented. 98 per cent of British scallops are caught using the 'Newhaven' dredge, a 30 inch rake. The bags are sometimes made of netting. The 2004 Scallop Fishing Order does regulate the type, number and construction of permitted scallop dredges.

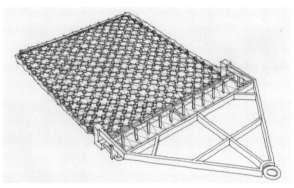

Scallop/oyster dredge

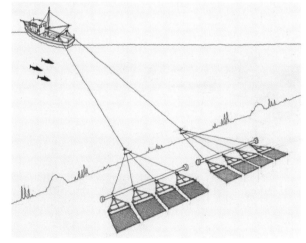

Scallop/oyster dredging

The majority of prawns (one of the 'Big Five' most popular fish consumed by the British) are imported.

Horse-drawn carts (now replaced by tractors) were used in Morecambe Bay to fish for shrimps. (See image on previous page.) Trawl fishing from small boats is prevalent in some parts eg off King's Lynn.

The English first started catching crabs in the 12th century (the Scots in the 13th), though it is thought that deepwater crabs were fished for in prehistoric times off Oronsay and Oban using plaited baskets. Scotland exports live crabs (now a declining industry).

According to contemporary art and literature, crabs were known to the ancient Greeks and Romans, but were not well liked as food.

Off shore, the Cornish inkwell pot tends to be used; the Scottish 'D' creel is favoured inshore. Commercial vessels may float 2,000 pots, and leave them for a few days.

Until 2010, an annual crab catching competition was run at Walberswick (Suffolk), but it became so popular that health and safety concerns led to its cancellation.

Lobsters, too, are caught in traps.
They prefer to live in gaps.
They're not scavengers: on live prey like to feed.
In their crevices they'll stay,
Not moving much by day.
Females are protected when they breed.

Sustainable fishing

There's a fish that's known as pollock,
A word which rhymes with a male body part.
One can buy it (and it's almost always frozen).
Folk were put off, Sainsbury's claimed,
So the species was renamed,
And 'Colin' was the new tag that was chosen!

Though this foodstuff is delicious,
Folk at one time were suspicious,
And thought it something only cats might savour.
Its promotion is explainable:
The species is sustainable,
And well deserves the upsurge in its favour.

Yet people would far sooner
Eat their salmon, cod and tuna,
And stick to what they're used to for their food.
The familiar persists,
But 'Seafish' now exists,
To encourage types more readily renewed.

It seems sensible to swap,
When we do our weekly shop –
Although what we switch to may not look that pretty.
The ugly can be tasty,
So we shouldn't be too hasty:
To reject on looks alone would be a pity.

It won't do to fill your plate
With the now endangered skate,
And plaice too is a breed that grows but slowly.
It's suggested that you nab,
A flounder, ray or dab
Or, for chunky fish, try gurnard, or try coley.

And we perhaps should give some thought
As to how our fish are caught,
For nets can snare unwanted things inside.
As too small some are regarded,
So the youngsters are discarded,
But not till the majority have died.

There is a closed season (October to December) for lobsters. Lobsters are not caught unless they have reached a minimum size. Berried (egg-bearing) females are avoided, as too are immature females, which sometimes have notches cut into their tails to denote this. Numbers are thereby maintained.

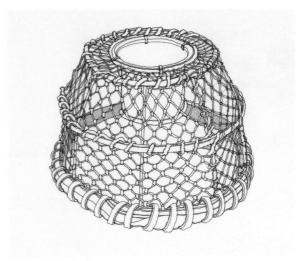

Top-entry inkwell crab pot

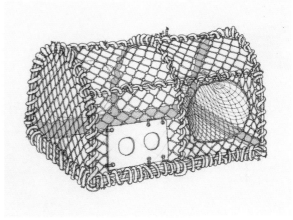

Lobster 'D' creel pot

North Pacific (Alaskan) pollock is one of the most important commercial fish in the world. Pollack, which is very similar, is found in British waters. This spelling distinction is often blurred. 'Pollack for puss, coley for cat,' was the saying. It is now Britain's eighth most popular fish.

Colin is the French word for hake. Pilchards have also been re-branded as 'the Cornish sardine'.

Salmon, cod and tuna are still the three most popular fish in Britain (by volume). Seafish is a government organisation that was established 'to support a profitable, sustainable and socially responsible future for the seafood industry'. It was formed in 1981 as an amalgamation of the Herring Industry Board and the White Fish Authority.

Once commonplace, skate are now critically endangered. Plaice reproduce and grow very slowly, and can live up to 50 years. Lemon sole is also a good alternative flat fish, although this species is one of several which may now be under threat from rising temperatures in the North Sea.

Getting caught in nets often fatally damages fishes' swim bladders.

Therefore stocks are often harmed,
But not so if fish are farmed,
Though this practice isn't always a solution.
Excessive feed, and faeces,
(If carnivorous the species),
Go straight into the sea, and cause pollution.

There is not so much abuse,
If a pole with line's in use;
This method goes back many thousand years.
Fish aren't captured by the ton,
But hooked singly, one by one:
The bycatch problem almost disappears.

This way's uncontroversial,
And increasingly commercial,
As discerning shoppers make clear their priority.
This is good news. Even so
There is still some way to go:
For tuna caught by line are a minority.

Fishing's long existence,
Was once mainly for subsistence,
Using methods that were simple and 'low tech'.
But factory ships and 'fleeting',
Mean that stocks are fast depleting…
Which explains the bids to keep all this in check.

Rhymes like this don't seek to bore…
There are reams and reams of law…
Under which the act of fishing's now constrained.
But feel free to take a look
At the MMO's Blue Book,
In which all the legislation is contained.

The Decline of British Shipbuilding

Post the Great Depression gloom,
In the war there'd been a boom,
But for shipbuilding this proved a brief remission.
One reason is quite clear:
Japan and South Korea
Start up industries in direct competition.

Britain used to be so strong,
So just what is going wrong?
A committee is convened in '65
To conduct a full review,
Into what the heck to do,
To ensure our once great companies survive.

The technical name for fish farming is aquaculture.

Salmon farming is not without its problems. Feed additives, and the toxic chemicals used on the net cages are damaging substances. Captive fish need wild fish for food; crowded conditions give rise to disease and parasites; and many escape, only to compete with wild salmon for habitat.

There is also a downside to large scale longline fishing. Lines, baited with thousands of hooks, can stretch up to 60 miles. These lines either hang near the surface (pelagic), or are sunk (demersal). Marine life, other than the target species, can become entangled – as can seabirds, especially when the line is being set. (See verse 1208).

Simple subsistence fishing is sometimes referred to as artisan fishing.

Popular with Hull and, to a lesser extent, Grimsby fishermen, fleeting involved a number of boats staying out at sea for as long as 8 weeks. The catches were transferred almost daily to fast cutters, and thence to market.

The UK's Marine Management Organisation (MMO), which enforces relevant laws, has consolidated all UK and EU legislation into *The Blue Book*.

> We have to fish less, waste less, use less destructive methods to catch what we take, and provide safe havens where fish can reach their full reproductive potential.
>
> **Professor Callum Roberts, Marine Conservation Biologist**

> 'The European Common Fisheries Policy is a laughing stock in many parts of the world. People… don't understand how Europe could get something that should be so simple so badly wrong. The extinction of its own – and the world's – fisheries is being presided over by people who ought to know better.'
>
> **Brendon May, former Chief Executive of the Marine Stewardship Council**

In addition to Japan and South Korea, China currently has more than 2,000 vessels on its books. Even before the Geddes Committee, (1965), had reported, Fairfield Shipyard (see verse 1113) got into financial difficulties and was bailed out.

UNCOMPETITIVE

'There was always that uncertainty. You were always trying to find out whether there was another job on the books… We could still build ships but we just couldn't compete, building them the way we did. Our standards were really high. I remember tacking bulkheads: if a weld was just a fraction out, he (the gaffer) would snap it so it had to be done again.'

Alan Adams, former welder at John Brown's during the construction of the *QEII*, speaking in 2007

'Efficiency is poor...
Production's slow... What's more
There are problems with industrial relations...
The recommended course is,
Firms should group to share resources...'
That's the outcome of the group's investigations.

So, accepting what's suggested,
The Government's invested.
There are grants and loans... economies of scale.
It's the industry's bad luck,
To be classed as a 'lame duck',
When, four years on, some yards appear to fail.

'I will not bail out this mess,'
Said Ted Heath, of 'UCS',
When the companies were facing liquidation.
'A work-in's what we need,'
Said the firebrand Jimmy Reid,
And this highlighted the workers' situation.

Short-lived was the reprieve
That this managed to achieve:
Public ownership was tried as a solution.
'Buy British' was ignored:
Owners purchased from abroad.
And old problems also made a contribution.

Europe doesn't share this plight,
So what's it getting right?
For to everyone strict EU rules apply.
To these the British stick,
Maybe others are more slick?
Is some subtle sleight of hand the reason why?

There's no doubt we've missed the boat
With those big hotels that float:
In the cruise ship market, Asia can't compete.
(Though that region clearly stars
Building tanker ships for MARS,
To replenish out at sea the British fleet.)

Though our industry is slimmer,
Of some hope there's just a glimmer.
BAE's announced its Govan yard's to stay.
Perhaps a niche we ought to find,
So we don't get left behind.
Could sea energy help Britain lead the way?

Even as recently as 1967, Britain still had the world's largest merchant fleet.

The Geddes Committee found that British prices for oil tankers and bulk carriers were uncompetitive. The industry was deemed inefficient, and consolidation into large groups was recommended to enable resources (especially research and development) to be shared, and to create the means to construct bigger vessels. Finance was provided and other measures were taken under the 1967 Shipbuilding Industry Act. The Shipbuilding Industry Board (SIB), to oversee the proposed reorganisation, was also set up.

'Lame duck' was Prime Minister Edward Heath's term for unprofitable industries.

Formed in 1967, the Upper Clyde Shipbuilders (UCS) was a consortium of five companies. Only one (Yarrow) made a profit, although the others had full order books.

James 'Jimmy' Reid (1932–2010) was a trade union activist, and one of the leaders who organised the UCS workers to continue production. In a classic U-turn, Heath provided belated financial assistance for UCS. This amounted to £101 million over a period of 3 years.

The industry was nationalised in 1977 under the Aircraft and Shipbuilding Industries Act. The British Shipbuilders Corporation (BS) was established and took over 27 major shipbuilding yards. By 1982, BS had closed half its yards, and a process of re-privatising its remaining assets took place from 1983.

The European Union has strict rules on subsidies. It has been suggested that other EU countries are 'less transparent' than the UK when it comes to abiding by the regulations. A likelier explanation is that, during the 1980s, the strong pound made British ships too expensive.

Germany, Italy and France have all made policy decisions to construct cruise liners (see verse 1017). France has built Cunard's new *Queen Mary 2*.

The Maritime Afloat Reach and Sustainability (MARS) programme is introducing new modern tankers for the Royal Fleet Auxiliary (RFA). The contract to design and build up to 6 of these has been awarded to Daewoo Shipbuilding and Marine Engineering, (a South Korean company).

Large defence company BAE Systems operates two yards in Glasgow – Govan and Scotstoun. Until very recently, the Govan yard appeared to be under threat, but an investment programme was recently announced.

Rescued from closure in 2014 by Jim McColl, Ferguson Marine Engineering Ltd in Port Glasgow plans to take on oil and gas and renewable energy fabrication contracts – as well as leading the way in innovative ferry design.

THE SENTIMENTS THAT EARNED A REPRIEVE

'A rat race is for rats. We're not rats. We're human beings... From the Olympian heights of an executive suite, in an atmosphere where your success is judged by the extent to which you can maximise profits, the overwhelming tendency must be to see people as units of production, as indices in your account books. To appreciate fully the inhumanity of this situation, you have to see the hurt and despair in the eyes of a man suddenly told he is redundant, without provision made for suitable alternative employment, with the prospect in the west of Scotland, if he is in his late forties or fifties, of spending the rest of his life in the Labour Exchange. Someone, somewhere has decided he is unwanted, unneeded, and is to be thrown on the industrial scrap heap. From the very depth of my being, I challenge the right of any man or any group of men, in business or in government, to tell a fellow human being that he or she is expendable...'

Jimmy Reid, Upper Clyde Shipbuilders trade union activist, from his inauguration speech as Rector of Glasgow University, 1972

The sea as a source of energy

North Sea Oil

By the 1960s, Britain
With the motor car was smitten,
And overall, our oil use was extensive.
We imported every drop,
But soon this was to stop,
Which was just as well; this substance was expensive.

We'll produce it for ourself,
From the continental shelf.
In '67 men began to bore.
Then AMOCO had some luck,
When a huge reserve was struck –
And now we had to get the stuff ashore.

What was there would be conveyed
Through the pipelines that were laid;
A golden button's pressed to get it going.
And once it reaches land,
There's a terminal at hand,
To process all the oil and gas that's flowing.

A new benchmark is in use.
It is named after a goose!
It's of relevance to one who buys or sells.
It will probably suffice
To say it sets the price:
Brent's a field of north-east Shetland wells.

Huge industry surrounds
All this new wealth that abounds,
As more rigs above the North Sea's waters rise.
Manufacturing sustains
All those platforms, pumps and cranes,
And workers in their thousands need supplies.

It's a perilous existence,
When dry land's at such a distance:
Massive waves make men feel vulnerable and small.
Perhaps unstable their abode...
What they deal with can explode...
Which explains the worst disaster of them all.

The whole country was aghast,
At the Piper Alpha blast,
Which caused shock waves, back in 1988.
Soon new rules were in position
To prevent a repetition,
But for those who died such measures came too late.

Following the 1964 Continental Shelf Act, UK exploration licences were issued for the North Sea. The first well was drilled in 1967.

The first major find was in the Montrose field, followed by BP's discoveries in the Forties field in 1970, and the Brent field off Shetland 1971. The Queen formally opened the first pipeline in 1975.

In 2010, there were about 8,000 miles of pipeline running from the North Sea platforms (source: Oil and Gas UK 2010 Economic Report).

Oil platforms may float, be fixed to the ocean floor on legs or take the form of an artificial island.

Regarded as the world's deadliest ever oil rig accident, 167 workers were killed in an explosion off the coast of Aberdeen. A lack of communication at a shift change meant that those coming on duty were not aware that they should not use a key piece of pipe work, which had been temporarily covered with no safety valve in place. It took American oil well fire fighter Red Adair almost three weeks to bring the fire under control.

Tidal Energy

All that oil… coal… gas… we've kindled,
Mean that fossil fuels have dwindled.
They've caused climate change, which worries politicians.
'Global warming', 'acid rain',
Mean we need to think again,
And regulate our greenhouse gas emissions.

It's our government's intent,
That at least fifteen percent ,
Of the energy we're using is renewable.
So some schemes are now in motion
To utilize the ocean:
These are challenging – but likely to be doable.

In some littoral locations,
Only tiny variations
Occur between a high tide and a low.
The moon has some effect,
Though not easy to detect,
But elsewhere, like round our coast, this isn't so.

The in/out choreography
Is down to seabed geography,
And the volume of the water that's in play.
Variations can be large,
Where huge oceans are in charge,
And the sea recedes to what seems far away.

Out of estuaries it peters;
Drops as much as fifteen metres,
So to quite a distance hence it can withdraw.
The ranges of a tide,
Into three are classified,
And, in metres, 'large' are those exceeding four.

All this nearness and this farness
Means there's energy to harness,
Which, of late, we have re-thought about recruiting.
Surely schemes can be made viable?
Tides are utterly reliable,
Predictable, and also non-polluting.

The French have played their part,
And at one time made a start,
But the project that they tried was overtaken.
By atomic power replaced,
Despite the toxic waste,
The use of tides to all intents forsaken.

Fossil fuels take millions of years to create and 'when they're gone, they're gone'.

The UK is committed to 15 per cent renewable energy use by 2020. The current figure is just 5 per cent. The EU's target is 20 per cent.

For tides see verses 24–30.

The largest tidal range is found at the Bay of Fundy in eastern Canada. Britain and France have the second and third largest tidal ranges in the world.

The greatest tidal range in Britain is in the Severn Estuary. The Severn Bore is a natural phenomenon which occurs when a rising tide funnels into the Severn. The surging waters cause a series of waves which travel upstream to Gloucester and sometimes beyond.

There are half a dozen places in Britain (eg Poole in Dorset) with little or no tidal range. These are called nodal points.

Macromareal (the largest) tidal ranges are those where the water level drops by more than four metres. The smallest (micromareal) are ranges of lower than two metres.

Solar and wind energy can be intermittent and require back-up generation. The Anglo-Saxons, and possibly the Romans, constructed mills run on tidal power (see verses 29–30).

The project called 'The Rance'
Was a major step by France:
On an estuary a barrage had been built.
Eels and plaice the river spurned,
(And they haven't since returned)
As their habitat was clogging up with silt.

Sadly now, not coming soon,
Is the Swansea Bay lagoon...
A six mile wall, with turbines placed inside.
Ecological effects,
Conservationists might vex,
But no carbon footprint's planted by the tide.

From Weston-super-mare
To Cardiff – that is where
Some believe a tidal barrage would be suited.
Where the flow is very strong.
It would be some ten miles long,
And proposals in some detail have been mooted.

It is claimed this would be bad
For the salmon... lamprey... shad...
(As they travel through this estuary to spawn).
Perhaps the underwater fence
Will be found to make more sense?
(It resembles what you'd use to mow your lawn)

Wave Energy

Wave power's also 'green'.
It's renewable and clean,
And the sites with most potential have been mapped.
We have started now to test,
Which technology works best,
To ensure this source of energy is tapped.

On experimental scale
Is a 'wave hub' just off Hayle.
There is testing near the Orkney Islands too.
An experimental site
Snares the North Atlantic's might.
It's located at a place called Billia Croo.

A converter, half submersed
Has scored a world-wide first:
It feeds the grid, to which it is connected.
Still commercially not viable,
As machines get more reliable
The methods used, in time, might be perfected.

The Rance Tidal Power Station, on the estuary of the River Rance in Brittany, was opened in 1966. It was the world's first tidal power station and, for 45 years, the largest. It supplies 0.12 per cent of France's power demand.

Six British tidal lagoons (including Colwyn Bay, Cardiff and Newport) have been proposed by Tidal Lagoon Power Limited. The first, in Swansea Bay (sitting between the Tawe and the Neath, across the Severn Estuary), had been subject to a promising DECC (Department for Energy and Climate Change) feasibility study.

Developed by Kepler Energy, a spin-out of Oxford University's Department of Engineering, it is claimed that the Severn Tidal Power scheme would have no adverse effects on marine life, although anglers in South Wales and the Bristol Channel expressed concerns about the possible impact on marine and migratory fish stocks. It would comprise horizontal turbines to harness low velocity currents.

In June 2018, it was announced that the government would not proceed with this scheme, favouring (mainly on cost effectiveness grounds) a mix of offshore wind and nuclear power instead. The decision does not rule out other options to enable the project to go ahead.

It is estimated that the whole world's energy requirements could be met five times over by harnessing just 0.1 per cent of the wave energy in the oceans. Carbon Trust have mapped suitable sites.

The wave hub is located ten miles off the north coast of Cornwall. EMEC (European Marine Energy Centre Ltd) are also testing tidal energy devices.

Great care is being taken,
Lest marine life be forsaken:
The environmental impact isn't known.
There are constant observations,
Both of sea birds and cetaceans.
Have their population numbers shrunk or grown?

Offshore Wind Farms

When off shore winds are blowing,
They keep many turbines going:
These clever things make use of every gust.
Their systems of detection,
Pick up wind strength and direction,
And the three large blades accordingly adjust.

They move slowly, it appears,
So they need the help of gears,
Which are able to produce much greater speeds.
Magnified one hundredfold,
These rotations are enrolled,
To generate the power that Britain needs.

Where our coast by nature's fanned,
More farms are being planned –
All are subject to the necessary rigour.
Off the Kent coast, an array
Had shown the world the way.
But off Cumbria there's now one even bigger.

But large rotor blades that turn
Have been causing some concern:
Since their possible effect on birds was noted.
Plans for more here have been scrapped,
In case divers can't adapt:
It's the winter home of those that are red-throated.

Which way forward is the best,
Must always be assessed.
To maintain a balanced eco-system's vital.
To the fen, the marsh, the pond,
To our sea shore and beyond.
Human beings aren't the only ones with title.

Eleven of the world's largest offshore wind farms, (size is determined by output capacity), are in UK waters. Wind turbines have vanes which identify prevailing winds. Their usual speed is 10–20 revolutions per minute (rpm).

An array is a systematic arrangement of similar objects, often in rows. The London Array consists of 175 turbines, and was completed in 2013. It was, for 5 years, the largest offshore wind farm in the world. Gwynt y Môr (off the north coast of Wales) was the second largest. Opened in September 2018, the Danish-built Walney Extension off Cumbria is now the world's biggest but will only remain so until 2020, when it will be supplanted by both Hornsea Project One, and East Anglia ONE.

Planning permission for Phase 2 (a further 166 turbines) of the London Array was refused in February 2014, after the Royal Society for the Protection of Birds raised concerns about its impact on red-throated divers – a migratory aquatic bird.

Wind farms are good for fish, as they create additional reefs and enclosed areas. The possibility of using the power generated by changes in water temperatures and salinity is also being investigated, although the technology is as yet only in the early stages of development.

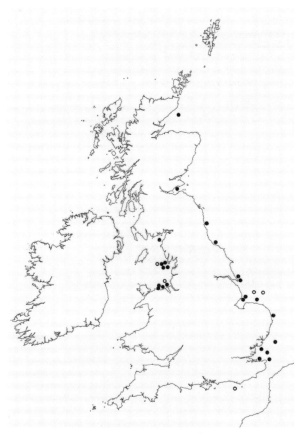

● Operational offshore wind farms, as at 2016 (24)
o Offshore wind farms under construction, 2016 (5)

The Commonwealth of Nations

We've a dwindling merchant fleet.
Shipwrights struggle to compete.
In the past is all that greatness, all that glory.
What the coming years may hold,
Is not easily foretold,
And unwritten is Britannia's future story...

Though our empire's all but gone,
A legacy lives on,
From the days of long ago, and British rule.
From the times of exploitation,
And of natives' subjugation –
Well meant at best, but sometimes downright cruel.

Now, a strangely fitting sequel,
Are the concepts 'fair and equal',
To which nations of the Commonwealth adhere.
Basic rights apply to all,
Be they large or be they small.
And no one's forced to join – they volunteer.

In 1975, 9.7 per cent of the global merchant fleet was British. It is now just 0.8 per cent (measured in deadweight tonnes).

Created in 1926, and then called the 'British Commonwealth of Nations', the Commonwealth has 53 member states. These are mainly, but not exclusively, former territories of the British Empire.

THE COMMONWEALTH CHARTER

We the people of the commonwealth:

... Recalling that the Commonwealth is a voluntary association of independent and equal sovereign states, each responsible for its own policies, consulting and co-operating in the common interests of our peoples and in the promotion of international understanding and world peace, and influencing international society to the benefit of all through the pursuit of common principles and values.

Affirming that the special strength of the Commonwealth lies in the combination of our diversity and our shared inheritance in language, culture and the rule of law; and bound together by shared history and tradition, by respect for all states and people; by shared values and principles and by concern for the vulnerable...

As agreed by all Commonwealth Heads of Government, 14 December 2012 and presented to Parliament (March 2013) by the Secretary of State for Foreign and Commonwealth Affairs

INDEX